HABITUS: A SENSE OF PLACE

Habitus: A Sense of Place

Second Edition

Edited by

JEAN HILLIER
University of Newcastle

and

EMMA ROOKSBY
Centre for Applied Philosophy and Public Ethics, Australia

ASHGATE

© Jean Hillier and Emma Rooksby 2005

All rights reserved. No part of this publication may be reproduced, stored in a retrieval system or transmitted in any form or by any means, electronic, mechanical, photocopying, recording or otherwise without the prior permission of the publisher.

Jean Hillier and Emma Rooksby have asserted their right under the Copyright, Designs and Patents Act, 1988, to be identified as the editors of this work.

Published by
Ashgate Publishing Limited
Gower House
Croft Road
Aldershot
Hants GU11 3HR
England

Ashgate Publishing Company
Suite 420
101 Cherry Street
Burlington, VT 05401-4405
USA

Ashgate website: http://www.ashgate.com

British Library Cataloguing in Publication Data
Habitus : a sense of place. - 2nd ed.
   1.Sociology, Urban - Congresses 2.Social ecology - Congresses 3.Human beings - Effect of environment on - Congresses
   I.Hillier, Jean II.Rooksby, Emma
   307

Library of Congress Control Number: 2001096521

ISBN 0 7546 4564 9

Printed and bound in Great Britain by TJ International Ltd, Padstow, Cornwall.

Contents

List of Contributors   *viii*
Acknowledgements   *xv*

INTRODUCTION

Introduction to Second Edition: Committed Scholarship   3
Jean Hillier and Emma Rooksby

1   Introduction to First Edition   19
     Jean Hillier and Emma Rooksby

2   Habitus   43
     Pierre Bourdieu

POLITICS OF SPACE AND PLACE

3   Democracy and the Question of Power   53
     Ernesto Laclau

4   Politics: Territorial or Non-Territorial?   68
     Paul Hirst

5   Toleration and the Art of International Governance: How is it Possible to 'Live Together' in a Fragmenting International System?   83
     Grahame F. Thompson

6   Which Kind of Public Space for a Democratic Habitus?   109
     Chantal Mouffe

7   Metropolitan Liberalism and Colonial Autocracy   117
     Barry Hindess

8   Governmentality and Regional Economic Strategies   131
     Joe Painter

PROCESSES OF PLACE-MAKING

9	Mind the Gap *Jean Hillier*	161
10	Place, Identity and Governance: Transforming Discourses and Practices *Patsy Healey*	189
11	Difference, Fear and Habitus: A Political Economy of Urban Fears *Leonie Sandercock*	219
12	Spectral Cities: Where the Repressed Returns and Other Short Stories *Steve Pile*	235
13	Crime and the Design of the Built Environment: Anglo-American Comparisons of Policy and Practice *Ted Kitchen and Richard H. Schneider*	258
14	The Silent Complicity of Architecture *Kim Dovey*	283
15	Belonging: Towards a Theory of Identification with Space *Neil Leach*	297

DECOLONISING SPATIAL HABITUS

16	Place-making as Project? Habitus and Migration in Transnational Cities *John Friedmann*	315
17	Enduring Landscape, Changing Habitus: The Sa'dan Toraja of Sulawesi, Indonesia *Roxana Waterson*	334
18	The Endurance of Aboriginal Women in Australia *Fay Gale*	356

| 19 | Belonging, Naming and Decolonisation
Val Plumwood | 371 |

CONCLUSIONS

| 20 | Conclusions
Jean Hillier and Emma Rooksby | 395 |

Index *409*

List of Contributors

Pierre Bourdieu

Pierre Bourdieu was elected to the Chair of Sociology at the Collège de France in Paris in 1981. He was also Director of Studies at the École des Hautes Études en Sciences Sociales and Founder and Director of the Centre de Sociologie Européenne. Pierre Bourdieu directed the sociological journal *Actes de la Récherche en Sciences Sociales* and his own collection, *Liber*, for the publishing house Éditions du Seuil. Pierre Bourdieu published over 40 books and some 400 articles during his lifetime. His later books (in English translation) include *Firing Back: against the tyranny of the market* (Verso, 2003), *The Social Structures of the Economy* (Polity, 2002), *Masculine Domination* (Polity, 2001), *Pascalian Meditations* (Stanford University Press, 2000), *The Weight of the World: social suffering in contemporary society* (Polity, 1999), *Acts of Resistance: against the tyranny of the market* (Polity, 1998) and *Practical Reason: on the theory of action* (Stanford University Press, 1998). Pierre Bourdieu passed away on 23 January 2002.

Kim Dovey

Dr Kim Dovey is Professor of Architecture and Urban Design at the University of Melbourne. He was educated in architecture at Curtin University, the University of Melbourne and UC Berkeley (PhD). He has published and broadcast widely on issues such as urban iconography, Aboriginality in architecture, the politics of urban space and the meanings of house and home. His most recent books are *Fluid City* (Routledge, 2005) and *Framing Places: Mediating Power in Built Form* (Routledge, 1999).

John Friedmann

John Friedmann is Professor Emeritus in the School of Social Policy and Research at the University of California at Los Angeles and an Honorary Professor in the School of Community and Regional Planning at the

University of British Columbia. His latest books are *China's Urban Transition* (University of Minnesota Press, 2005) and *The Prospect of Cities* (University of Minnesota Press, 2002). He currently lives in Vancouver.

Fay Gale

Fay Gale is Honorary Visiting Research Fellow at the University of Adelaide. She is the past President of the Association of Asian Social Science Research Councils and former President of the Academy of the Social Sciences in Australia. She was Vice Chancellor of the University of Western Australia from 1990 to 1997 and a President of the Australian Vice Chancellors Committee. Her publications pertaining to women and indigenous people and art include *Woman's Role in Aboriginal Society*, *We are Bosses Ourselves: the status and role of Aboriginal women*, *Urban Aborigines* and *Aboriginal Youth and the Criminal Justice System: the injustice of justice*.

Patsy Healey

Patsy Healey is Emeritus Professor at the University of Newcastle and a specialist in cities, urban policy, planning systems and planning theory. In recent years, she has been developing institutionalist approaches to policy analysis and exploring collaborative processes in urban planning. She is the author of *Collaborative Planning* (Macmillan, 1997), *Planning, Governance and Spatial Strategy in Britain* (with Vigar, Hull and Davoudi, Macmillan, 2000), and *Urban Governance, Institutional Capacity and Social Milieux* (with Cars, Madanipour and de Magalhaes, Ashgate, 2002).

Jean Hillier

Jean Hillier is Professor of Town and Country Planning at the University of Newcastle where she is Director of the Global Urban Research Unit. She is also adjunct professor at Curtin University of Technology, Perth. Her research interests lie in extending praxis-based planning theories and in discursive and relational analyses of participatory planning strategies. Books include *Shadows of Power*, (Routledge, 2002) and *Consent and Consensus* (with Cryle, D., University of Queensland Press, 2004). She is currently working on a volume of poststructuralist planning theory.

Barry Hindess

Barry Hindess is Professor of Political Science at the Australian National University. His most recent books are *Discourses of Power: from Hobbes to Foucault* (Blackwell, 1996) and *Governing Australia: studies in contemporary rationalities of government* (Cambridge University Press, 1998) and he is currently preparing books on democracy and on liberal government. He can be contacted at: b.hindess@anu.edu.au.

Paul Hirst

Paul Hirst was Professor of Social Theory at Birkbeck College University of London and Academic Director of the London Consortium Graduate Programme in Humanities and Cultural Studies. He was author of, among other works, *The Pluralist Theory of the State: Selected Writings of G.D.H. Cole, J.N. Figgis and H.J.Laski* (Routledge, 1989), *Associative Democracy* (Polity, 1994), *From Statism to Pluralism* (UCL Press, 1997) and *Globalisation in Question* (with Thompson, G., Polity, 1999). Paul Q. Hirst passed away on 17 June 2003.

Ted Kitchen

Ted Kitchen spent most of his career as a practitioner in British Central and Local Government, finishing as City Planning Officer of Manchester. These experiences provided the basis for his book, *People, Politics, Policies and Plans*, (Paul Chapman Publishing, 1997). He moved to Sheffield Hallam University in 1995 as Professor of Planning and Urban Regeneration, becoming Director of what was its School of Environment and Development in 1997, a position from which he stood down in 2001. His research collaboration with Richard Schneider of the University of Florida has resulted in a book, *Planning for Crime Prevention: a transatlantic perspective* (Routledge, 2002), plus several other papers, with a second book planned in this same field.

Ernesto Laclau

Ernesto Laclau is Professor of Political Theory at the University of Essex and Professor in the Department of Comparative Literature at SUNY,

Buffalo. He is the author of *Emancipation(s)* (Verso, 1996), *New Reflections on the Revolution of our Time* (Verso, 1990) and *The Making of Political Identities* (Verso, 1994). He has co-authored (with Chantal Mouffe) *Hegemony and Socialist Strategy* (Verso, 1985) and the recent volume with Judith Butler and Slavoj Zizek *Contingency, Hegemony, Universality* (Verso, 2000).

Neil Leach

Neil Leach is Professor of Architectural Theory at the University of Bath, and tutor at the Architectural Association, London. He has also been visiting Professor at Columbia University, New York, and Reader in Architecture and Critical Theory at the University of Nottingham. He is author of *The Anaesthetics of Architecture* (MIT Press, 1999) and *Millennium Culture* (Ellipsis, 1999); editor of *Rethinking Architecture* (Routledge, 1997), *Architecture and Revolution* (Routledge, 1999) and *The Hieroglyphics of Space* (Routledge, 2001); and co-translator (with Joseph Rykwert and Robert Tavernor) of *Leon Battista Alberti, On the Art of Building in Ten Books* (MIT Press, 1988).

Chantal Mouffe

Chantal Mouffe is Professor of Political Theory at the Centre for the Study of Democracy at the University of Westminster. She has taught at many universities in Europe, including the Centre National de la Recherche Scientifique in Paris, in North America and Latin America. She is a member of the Collège International de Philosophie in Paris. She is the editor of *Gramsci and Marxist Theory* (Routledge and Kegan Paul, 1979), *Dimensions of Radical Democracy* (Verso, 1992), *Deconstruction and Pragmatism* (Routledge, 1996) and *The Challenge of Carl Schmitt* (Verso, 1999); co-author (with Ernesto Laclau) of *Hegemony and Socialist Strategy: towards a radical democratic politics* (Verso, 1985); and author of *The Return of the Political* (Verso, 1993) and *The Democratic Paradox* (Verso, 2000). She is currently elaborating a non-rationalist approach to political theory; formulating an 'agonistic' model of democracy; and engaged in research projects on the rise of right-wing populism in Europe and the limits of the 'third way'.

Joe Painter

Joe Painter is Professor of Geography and Director of the Centre for the Study of Cities and Regions at the University of Durham. He has written widely on the geographies of the state and regulation, on urban and regional governance and politics, on local and regional development, and on regionalism and citizenship in Europe. He is the author of *Politics, Geography and Political Geography* (Arnold, 1995) and the co-author of *Practising Human Geography* (Sage, 2004). He is currently working on questions of urban citizenship and is preparing a book on the everyday political geographies of state power.

Steve Pile

Steve Pile is Reader in Cultural Geography in the Faculty of Social Sciences at The Open University. He has published on issues concerning place and the politics of identity. He is author of *Real Cities: modernity, space and the phantasmagorias of city life* (Sage, 2005). He has also worked on many collaborative projects, including *City A-Z* (co-edited with Nigel Thrift, Routledge, 2000) and *Patterned Ground: entanglements of nature and culture* (co-edited with Stephan Harrison and Nigel Thrift, Reaktion Books, 2004). He has been wondering whether there is redemption in the shape of angels.

Val Plumwood

Val Plumwood, Australian Research Council Fellow at the University of Sydney, with a project on decolonising nature, has published four books and over 100 papers. 'Shaking philosophy to its foundations', read one review of Val Plumwood's 1993 book *Feminism and the Mastery of Nature*. (Routledge). Her new book is *Environmental Culture: the ecological crisis of reason* (Routledge, 2002). Trained initially in logic and analytical philosophy (which she characterises as a good servant but a poor master), she draws on feminist philosophy especially in her work on ecological philosophy. Plumwood is an environmental activist, forest-dweller and bush-walker.

Emma Rooksby

Emma Rooksby is a Research Fellow at the ARC Special Research Centre for Applied Philosophy and Public Ethics (CAPPE), Australia. She is a Visiting Fellow at the Australian National University and the University of Melbourne. She has published in the areas of computer ethics, urban planning theory and feminist philosophy. Her research is focused around computer ethics, including Internet democracy, on-line relationships and the ethics of text-based communication. Publications include *E-Mail and Ethics* (Routledge, 2002) and 'Understanding Condemnation: A Plea for Appropriate Judgement', in Pedro Tabensky (ed.) *Judging and Understanding; Essays on Freedom, Justice, Forgiveness and Love* (forthcoming Ashgate, 2005).

Leonie Sandercock

Leonie Sandercock is Professor of Planning and Social Policy in the School of Community and Regional Planning at the University of British Columbia, Vancouver. Her most recent books include *Cosmopolis II, Mongrel Cities of the 21st Century* (Continuum, 2003), *Towards Cosmopolis: Planning for Multicultural Cities* (Wiley, 1998) and *Making the Invisible Visible* (University of California Press, 1998). She is guest editing a special issue of CITY on 'Alternatives and Resistances to Neo-liberal urban regimes in North America' (forthcoming early 2005).

Richard H. Schneider

Richard Schneider is Professor and Graduate Coordinator at the Department of Urban and Regional Planning at the University of Florida's College of Design, Construction and Planning. He has long been interested in relationships between human behaviour and design, and especially in comparative international work focusing on linkages among planning, crime and urban quality of life issues. Recent research in the US and the UK in this connection resulted in the publication of 'Planning for Crime Prevention: A Transatlantic Perspective' (Routledge, 2002) which he co-authored with Professor Ted Kitchen of Sheffield Hallam University. A planning consultant to communities and public agencies, Schneider is a member of the American Institute of Certified Planners.

Grahame F. Thompson

Grahame Thompson is Professor of Political Economy at the Open University, UK. Recent books include: *Economic Dynamism in the Asia-Pacific: the growth of integration and competitiveness* (ed., Routledge, 1998), *Globalization in Question* (with Paul Q. Hirst, Polity Press, 1999), *Governing the European Economy* (ed., Sage, 2001) and *Between Hierarchies and Markets: the history and significance of network organization* (Oxford University Press, Oxford, 2002).

Roxana Waterson

Roxana Waterson is an Associate Professor in the Department of Sociology, National University of Singapore, where she has been teaching since 1987. She took her PhD in Social Anthropology at New Hall, Cambridge (1981), and has done fieldwork with the Sa'dan Toraja people of Sulawesi (Indonesia) since 1978. She is the author of *The Living House: An Anthropology of Architecture in Southeast Asia* (3rd Edn, Thames and Hudson, 1997).

Acknowledgements

This paperback edition of *Habitus* represents the second edition of the volume, *Habitus: A Sense of Place*, published by Ashgate in 2002.

All the papers in this volume are based on papers which were originally presented at the conference, *Habitus 2000*, in Perth, Western Australia in September 2000. We should like to acknowledge the generous sponsorship of Curtin University of Technology and, in particular, the School of Architecture, Construction and Planning, in making this conference possible. As such we thank Lesley Parker, Tom Stannage and especially Laurie Hegvold for their support and encouragement.

We should also like to thank the *Habitus 2000* Conference Committee, which Jean Hillier chaired, for co-ordinating the several conference streams: Lynn Churchill, David Dolan, Xing Ruan, John Stephens, Reena Tiwari and David Wood and also Steve Basson and Denise Plowman for their considerable support.

Finally, we should like to thank those people who double-refereed the chapters in this volume and provided the authors with valuable comment.

INTRODUCTION

Introduction to Second Edition: Committed Scholarship

JEAN HILLIER AND EMMA ROOKSBY

Since the original conference, *Habitus 2000*, from which the chapters in the first edition of this volume were drawn, and since its publication in 2002, we have mourned the untimely deaths of Pierre Bourdieu and Paul Hirst. We dedicate this second edition to the memory of these two fine scholars and commence this Introduction with a tribute to their work.

We then provide a brief overview of Pierre Bourdieu's thoughts on habitus published since the first edition went to press, followed by a review of the wide-ranging research which Bourdieu's work has stimulated, again post-2000. As time has passed, several of the stories presented in the first edition have taken new turns and the authors have taken the opportunity to add postscripts to their chapters. We conclude the Introduction by outlining where such new material is to be found.

Pierre Bourdieu and Paul Q. Hirst: A Tribute

Pierre Bourdieu, who died from cancer, aged 71, on 23 January 2002, and Paul Q. Hirst, who passed away, aged 57, on 17 June 2003 following a stroke and brain haemorrhage, were two of the most inspiring social and political thinkers of their generations. Both were committed alienated (in the Marxist sense) activists, believing passionately that, far from being antinomic, intellectual autonomy and civic engagement should be linked synergistically (Bourdieu, 1989). Both were politically active and endeavoured, in Bourdieu's words, to reduce 'the gap between the official and the effective' and to 'create the conditions for the institution of civic virtue' (Bourdieu, 1998: 145). Bourdieu's engagement included, for example, his defence of the workers' strikes in France in 1995, the *sans papiers* immigrants and his support for José Bové, leader of the French small-farmers in 1999.[1] Hirst's engagement is exemplified through his work in the 1990s on associative democracy and his involvement in the constitutional pressure group, Charter 88 (which he chaired for some years).

Few academics take the effort to 'make heard the voices of those who cannot speak for themselves' (Bourdieu, 2002a: 68), whether because they lack the symbolic reputational capital to do so, or because they lack interest. Both Bourdieu and Hirst, however, lived their concepts. They both founded radical journals: Bourdieu's *Actes de la Recherche en Sciences Sociales* (1975 onwards) and *Liber* (1989-1999), which stood steadfastly against 'the undiscussed beliefs of academic orthodoxy' (Bourdieu, 1991: 1) as did Hirst's brief-lived journals, *Theoretical Practice* (which published eight issues from 1971-1973) and *Politics and Power* (1980-1982). Bourdieu also created a publishing house, Liber-raisons d'agir, to produce low-price works of 'engaged social science' which spoke to 'a broad educated public in an accessible form, as well as analyses censored or marginalised by the dominant media' (Poupeau and Discepolo, 2004: 89).

Both Bourdieu and Hirst were sociologists who held 'utopian' visions of a more democratically just society, proposing fundamental reforms of European political systems and union movements (eg Bourdieu, 2000, 2003; Hirst and Khilnani, 1996). In their own ways, they attempted to involve academics in a broad coalition or social movement to challenge the political and economic inequalities in French and British societies. They both linked economics and sociology, problematising globalisation and its so-called 'hollowing-out' of democracy (see, especially, Hirst and Thompson, 1996, and Hirst, this volume).

Bourdieu's and Hirst's bodies of work represent two sides of the same coin, namely critical analysis of socio-political reality, on one side, and direct contributions to its attempted transformation on the other. For both scholars effective and realistic politics comprised intervention in institutional structures 'such that political agents acquire an interest in pursuing vigorous strategies benefiting the citizenry at large' (Poupeau and Discepolo, 2004: 85). They both believed passionately in sociology as a tool for changing the world.

Paul Q. Hirst

Paul Hirst began his academic career as a Marxist, although he soon scandalised the sociological left by using an Althusserian framework to challenge orthodox Marxism in his book *Pre-Capitalist Modes of Production* (with Barry Hindess, 1975).[2] Gradually, Hirst tempered his Marxism, eventually finding his niche in associative democracy, located between pragmatic left-wing politics and communitarian ideals (*After Thatcher*, 1989; *Associative Democracy*, 1994). His pioneering work (especially in 1994 and 1995) on associative democracy argued for strong, voluntary, free communities providing a self-governing civil society that could deliver a decentralised welfare state and regenerate regional economies. He would have been heartened by the Labour administration's plans for direct elections to a North East Regional Assembly in 2004 and disappointed with the negative referendum result. Nevertheless, he was a strong critic of New Labour's record on decentralisation, which he saw as a thin veneer over a deeper strategy of ongoing bureaucratic centralisation.

Hirst's problematisation of globalisation, its ubiquitousness and contorted meaning (1996, 1999), demonstrates the continuing relevance of territorial states for the division of labour in governance, while also recognising that politics is no longer exclusively territorial. His associational approach to urban crime control is regarded as extremely radical. Hirst (2000) argues in favour of splitting urban societies into self-governing interest-based communities with publicly-funded services. Diverse social groups would coexist, yet retain their own values through a mix of micro-governance (special zones where different rules apply) and mutual extra-territoriality. Tolerance of otherness is key, as is the argument for self-regulatory strategies across all groups in the city. 'Citizens would have to accept that different rules applied to different communities with informal self-regulation and arbitration' (Hirst, 2000: 279). His book, *War and Power in the 21st Century* (2001) has been prophetic in its analysis of international conflict.

Pierre Bourdieu

During his lifetime Pierre Bourdieu published over 400 articles and 40 books. Since his death several new texts have appeared and more will surely follow. This is not the place to produce an evaluation of Pierre Bourdieu's life work. We direct interested readers to Fowler (1997), Shusterman (1999), Lane (2000), Dortier *et al.* (2002) and Wacquant (2004a).

The major theme underpinning Pierre Bourdieu's work is that of inequality. In Algeria (from 1958), his anti-institutional disposition was honed (Wacquant, 2004b: 4) by his experience of the horrors of French colonial policy in action. His championing of the downtrodden and marginalised is illustrated by his work on the Kabyle, Berber nomads (1962, 1964), whose lives reminded him of the peasant-farmers in his native Oc-speaking Béarn (2002).

By 1981, when he was appointed to the Chair of Sociology at the Collège de France, his politics were firmly to the left of the new President Mittérand. Bourdieu had already launched *Actes de la Recherche en*

Sciences Sociales and completed several books on what Giddens later termed 'structuration': *Outline of a Theory of Practice* (1972/1977), *Distinction* (1979/1982), *Sociology in Question* (1980/1993) and a cluster of papers on ruling-class ideology and the workings of politics (1976, 1977).

Bourdieu's conceptualisation of habitus also developed in the 1970s and 1980s (1970/1977; 1971/1985). Starting from a version of Panofsky's tool to explain Gothic architecture, Bourdieu arrived at the idea that people possess an inherited experiential concept of society which they then modify for themselves, thereby each generating new concepts appropriate for their respective circumstances (Robbins, 2000: 27).

In his last decade, Bourdieu became increasingly politically active. Proud of being on the radical left, *gauche de gauche*, Bourdieu embraced the politics of refusal (*'celui qui disait non'*) (Osborne, 2002), denouncing the French government's neo-liberal programmes and the political complicities of journalists and the media (1993/1999; 1996/1998; 2000). He argued that his theorising of habitus, field and symbolic power gave him greater understanding of the institutions he sought to influence. He came to regard multinational corporations, international institutions such as the IMF and World Bank, and the USA as together embodying 'the cunning of imperialist reason' (1999) in an international situation in which 'the global community has given carte blanche to the US to enforce a particular kind of order' in which 'relations of force overwhelmingly favour the dominant' and 'might alone makes right' (2001a).

Bourdieu believed that significant change would require a wholesale transformation in the politics of habitus, paying close attention to the social production and modalities of expression of political proclivities (Wacquant, 2004b: 10). To this end, Bourdieu was incessantly active in civic struggles, from his initiation of the International Parliament of Writers in 1993-1994,[3] the Association for Reflection on Higher Education and Research (ARESER) in 1992, the International Committee of Support for Algerian Intellectuals (CISIA) in 1993, to his many appeals and protests in *Le Monde Diplomatique* and appearances at rallies and demonstrations, where he spoke against the government's neoliberal strategies of welfare cuts, immigration policies and complicit journalism and in favour of establishing a European-wide social movement.[4]

In conclusion, both Pierre Bourdieu and Paul Hirst 'walked the talk'. They wrote and lived their own tireless efforts to make social relations less arbitrary, institutions less unjust, distributions of resources and opportunities less unbalanced and recognition less scarce (Wacquant, 2004b: 11).

Pierre Bourdieu's Twenty-first Century Published Oeuvre

Pierre Bourdieu's activism was motivated by his belief that 'those who have the good fortune to be able to devote their lives to the study of the social world cannot stand aside, neutral and indifferent, from the struggles in which the future of that world is at stake' (2003: 11). He railed, in particular, against the 'logical monstrosities' of accepted clichés such as 'normative observations' (the economy is becoming global; therefore we must globalise our economy), 'pre-emptory and fallacious "deductions"' (if capitalism is winning everywhere, this is because it reflects humanity's deepest nature), 'nonfalsifiable theses' (by creating wealth you create employment), unquestionable commonplaces (the welfare state is a thing of the past), 'terratological paralogisms' (more market means more rationality), 'technocratic euphemisms' ('restructuring companies' rather than 'firing workers') and 'a welter of semantically indeterminate ready-made notions or locutions, routinised by automatic usage, that function as magic formulas, endlessly repeated for their incantatory value (deregulation, voluntary redundancy, free trade, creativity, competitiveness, economic growth, technological revolution etc.)' (2003: 79-80). From an urban planning viewpoint we would add to this list concepts including 'sustainability', 'development', 'public good' and 'multiculturism', all of which are empty signifiers, but which have achieved an unquestionable status as absolute doxa.

On Habitus

In a 1990 interview (published in 2002), Bourdieu defined habitus as a generative machine engendering many seemingly unrelated responses to many situations, but which a sociologist can demonstrate to be interrelated (2002c: 16-17, our translation). The positive aspect of generation or improvisation is noticeable, as is Bourdieu's continuing emphasis on the interrelations between contextual structures and agents: 'structures cannot function without the complicity of agents which have internalised them' (2002c: 20, our translation).

Traces of Fouauldian ideas are increasingly apparent in Bourdieu's later work, from his genealogical approach to habitus in *Science de la science et réflexivité* (2001b) and *Si le monde ...* (2002c) to the declaration in *Esquisse pour une auto-analyse* (2004: 102-107) of Foucault's inspirational influence on his work.[5]

Bourdieu's genealogical study of the French single-home market since the 1970s (2000/2003) demonstrates an economic habitus to have a clear social genesis of public rational choice formed by long apprenticeship in the housing field. Residents' tenure choices are thus manipulated by implicit assumptions which became reified in policy decisions. In a wonderful passage, highly relevant to English local planning practice in 2005, Bourdieu (2000: 143-145) describes how those public officers who have established bureaucratic capital share similar characteristics of experience (of age, education, length of service, etc.) and techniques (i.e. similar habitus), and have tended to become obstinately resistant to change.

Throughout his life Bourdieu was interested in uncovering the mechanisms of power responsible for symbolic violence to the powerless (2002c) and the habituses which generated, legitimated and perpetuated such violence. Practice, for Bourdieu, is thus 'an effect of actions and interactions which are shaped, simultaneously and in equal measure, by the habitus and capital of agents, as well as the context and dynamism constituted by their shared participation in a common "game"' (Crossley, 2003: 44).

On Neo-liberalism, Globalisation and the Complicit Role of Science

Pierre Bourdieu has continued to declare his overt and strong opposition to the 'rhetorical smoke screens' of current European 'social charters' and 'British-style "social liberalism", that barely made-over Thatcherism that relies, to sell itself, on the opportunistic exploitation of the symbols of socialism recycled for mere media consumption' (2003: 54) and the dismantling of national frameworks of publicly-funded education, health and social protection. Yet, as Bourdieu (2002a: 66) explains, the fact that neoliberal policies are being implemented by people who call themselves 'socialist' renders critical analysis extremely difficult as it reverses all the terms of the debate.

In common with Paul Hirst, Bourdieu regards globalisation as being a 'pseudo-concept, at once descriptive and prescriptive' (2003: 85, emphasised in original) which manipulates science and scientific research to its own ends (2001b). Developing his earlier explorations (1992) of science as geared towards furthering the interests of the particular field and scientist/s involved rather than those of the outside world, Bourdieu's 2000-2001 lectures (published as *Science de la science*, 2001b) indicated how scientific research has become hostage to funding economics and to military and economic demands (such as those of biotechnology and genetics). In an analysis that is extremely pertinent to the UK RAE (Research Accreditation Exercise), Bourdieu reveals how researchers involved in 'purer' forms of research. and those working on less 'attractive' issues are increasingly marginalised in academic worlds where scientific excellence is measured by quantity of publication and value of funding received (2001b: 27). Bourdieu describes the scientific field, and scientific capital especially, as being hierarchically structured, with particular individuals and laboratories achieving capital or 'status' in a fiercely competitive field where exclusive 'rights of entry' are afforded to certain groups only. 'Objectivity' is a social construct specific to each scientific field, where each field has its own habitus, its own 'rules' to be followed, career trajectories and so on. The legitimacy or honorific credit (2001b: 105) of one's knowledge is dependent on it having undergone certain phases of production and having acquired recognised 'seals of approval' (such as peer-reviewed funding applications and publications). Track record is crucial. Success breeds success, making it difficult for new researchers to break into scientific cliques.

Bourdieu calls for more analysis, of the kind undertaken by Knorr-Cetina, Callon and Latour, into the inseparable character of the scientific and the social strategies of researchers in practical wisdom (habitus) whereby different paradigms (or 'turns') become accepted and draft papers become publications. Bourdieu stresses the importance of authorial self-reflexivity – perhaps through a position statement – to ensure that one's biases are transparent. In the final chapter of *Science de la science*, he presents his own lucid and sincere self-reflections, later to be more fully developed in his final work, completed just before his death, *Esquisse pour une auto-analyse* (2004).

On a New European Social Movement and an Intellectual Collective

While Pierre Bourdieu challenged neo-liberal neo-rational economic habituses, he also advocated the need for development of a new habitus embodied in a European-wide critical social movement. He believed that the role of intellectuals is to pool their complementary competences of scientific analysis and creative communication to bring 'the most rigorous products of research to bear on salient public debates in a continuous and organised manner' (Wacquant, 2004b: 10). As Bourdieu (2000: 99-107) explained, the intellectual collective has two urgent missions: to 'produce and disseminate instruments of defence against symbolic domination', and to contribute to 'the work of political intervention' in renewing critical thought so as to wed sociological realism and civic utopianism.

Bourdieu (2003) calls for academics to leave their ivory towers and engage in active politics rather than simply in 'paper revolutions' (2003: 19). He urges scientists and researchers to 'throw their grain of sand into

10 *Habitus: A Sense of Place*

the well-oiled machinery of resigned complicities' (2003: 65) to fuse scientific inquiry and political activism in 'a scholarship with commitment' (2003: 17) aimed at helping the victims of neo-liberal policies by giving 'a visible and sensible form to the invisible but scientifically predictable consequences of political measurement inspired by neoliberal ideology' (2003: 25).

Would that more scholars shared the commitment and energy of Pierre Bourdieu and Paul Hirst to work for the overturning of oppression and to speak out openly those unpalatable truths which nobody wants to know (from Bourdieu, 2004: 141).

Scholarly Work on Habitus in the Twenty-first Century

The Bourdieuian habitus has been deployed in wide-ranging historical, geographical, anthropological, sociological and political research across a broad range of disciplines in the last four years.[6] Amidst all the recent theorising around corporeality, 'Bourdieu's work on habitus stands out because of the sophistication it provides in dealing with complex processes of embodiment' (Noble and Watkins, 2003: 521). As such, Noble and Watkins claim that habitus is an invaluable tool for exploring the interdependence of human agency and social structure. Bourdieu's attempt to overcome the structure-agency divide is finally being given the credit it deserves. It not only avoids the pitfalls of mechanical determinism which often vitiate structuralist approaches; it also avoids presupposing a fully rational, calculating agent, as in rational action theory. In this manner, habitus has been recognised as a useful 'corrective to certain theories of reflexive transformation which overestimate the extent to which individuals living in post-traditional order are able to reshape identity' (McNay, 1999: 113) and offers a 'way of thinking of possible transformations within gender identity as uneven and non-synchronous phenomena' (McNay, 1999: 96).

As McNay (1999) demonstrates, Pierre Bourdieu's conception of habitus has important implications for feminist theories of gender identity, a point further developed by Ostermann's (2003) critical examination of different habituses at an all-women police station and a feminist non-governmental crisis intervention centre. Ostermann's analysis of interactions between staff from these institutions and victims of domestic violence reveals significant differences between the two groups' relationships between the way in which the female staff position themselves in their practice worlds (their habitus) and their treatment of the victim women.

Noble and Watkins' (2003) study of the sport of tennis examines the role of training or learning (habituation) in developing the practical intuition (habitus) necessary to play. A reasonable 'feel for the game' or prereflexive level of practical ability (Bourdieu, 1990) is essential if progress is to be made. Reay's (1995, 1996, 1998, 2001, 2002, 2004) continuing research on the importance of habitus in education, from primary to higher levels, provides excellent case material about students' perceptions of who they are, their opportunity structures, and what would be necessary to enable them to succeed. Using habitus in a similar analytical frame, Allen (2004) examines how the social class background of visually impaired children may predispose some from middleclass families to resist their disabilities and to challenge their exclusion from certain social spaces, such as white-collar professional employment. Those from working class backgrounds, however, were found to have more limited expectations of their future place-in-the-world. They tended passively to accept their visual disabilities and consequent limitations on future opportunities as 'the way things are' (Allen, 2004: 494).

Habitus has also been used as a critical tool in organisation studies. Mutch's (2003) study of public house managers and their communities of practice revealed that managers' social and educational origins, together with their tacit knowledge and ways of doing things developed through experience, explained management practices to a large degree. Mutch also notes that recent technical changes which have occurred in the industry, together with the increasing number of women managers, has led to people having to negotiate new habituses. Habitus is confirmed as a generative rather than a determining structure in most cases, which establishes an active and creative relation between people and their worlds. As we outline in the following section, researchers increasingly agree that habituses can and do transform.

In similar vein, Lau's (2004) work with trade unionists in China suggests the crucial importance of experience in developing practical sense or habitus. Habitus was found to affect unionists' taken-for-granted assumptions and understandings of their worlds and their sense of possibilities ('that's not for the likes of us' or 'that's the only thing to do') (Lau, 2004: 377). Contrary to the role for unions for which Pierre Bourdieu fought in Europe, unionists in China recognised their mission not as representing the workers, but as managing the workers to achieve the Party's objective of establishing a socialist market economy. Rather than resisting downsizing and redundancies, unionists 'spend a lot of time explaining to workers the demands of a market economy' (Lau, 2004: 380), attempting to remain in favour with the Party elite by accepting their lot in life and, in addition, reinforcing the sense of place of the workers.

Crossley's (2003) analysis of what he terms a 'radical habitus' presents a marked contrast to the passive habitus of Lau's unionists. Crossley suggests that Bourdieu's theory of practice and conceptualising of habitus provide a strong basis for analysing and understanding social movements. He agrees with Bourdieu (1982) that the educated middle-classes are more disposed towards and better resourced for engagement in the public sphere than are the working classes; something confirmed by many studies of NIMBYism, environmental protest and resistance to land use-related threats to property rights and values. As Hillier (2000) indicates, protesting often involves learned participatory know-how, whether it is environmental organisations' lobbying or trade unions' tactics. The worlds of protest have their own particular habituses.

The same is true of performance at job interviews, according to Scheuer (2003). Employing a linguistically-informed version of habitus, Scheuer analysed a male candidate being interviewed for a position in a Danish company. Presenting clear differences between the habituses of the interviewing panel and the candidate, the author demonstrates the role of experience in the way in which habitus generates strategies for coping with situations. During examination of the interview transcript it becomes apparent that the candidate's embodied habitus is ill-suited to the situation, although this is not realised by the unfortunate candidate.

Turning to issues of urban studies and land use planning theory and practice, geographers such as Thrift (2004) and Bridge (2001) continue to call on habitus as a fundamental concept in understanding what Thrift terms 'knowledges of position' and the concomitant spaces of anticipation as forms of social power. Various logics of sense, such as habitus, influence our perceptions of 'the way things properly are' (Lanzara and Patriotta, 2001: 965) and result in 'practical anticipations of how situations can be performed' (Thrift, 2004: 175). Flyvbjerg (2001) similarly highlights Bourdieu's emphasis on the decisive role of timing and tempo in human expertise and the importance of having a feel for the game for operating successfully.

Finally, Howe and Langdon (2002) argue that a new reflexive theory of planning, based on a Bourdieuian stance, will offer planning researchers improved tools for understanding the nature and outcomes of planning practices. The authors contend that actors' understandings of the world 'should be pivotal in understanding land use planning development and policy-making' (Howe and Langdon, 2002: 212). Comprehension of agents' habituses, influencing their tendencies to act in particular manners, their motivations, preferences, worldviews, aspirations and expectations, will, according to the authors, enable better improvisation and navigation around the complexities of the social practices which constitute planning processes.

Clarifying and Developing Bourdieu's Conceptualisation

One of the most persistent debates about Bourdieuian habitus, as several chapters in this volume indicate, is whether habitus is essentially static or whether its properties can change dynamically with different conditions and circumstances. Since 2000, two related strands of this debate have received much attention in the literature: the question posed by Weiss (2003), namely, 'can old dogs learn new tricks?'; and secondly the question of the role of psychoanalysis in Bourdieu's thinking about habitus and the prereflexive unconscious (e.g. Fourny, 2000; Frère, 2004).

Weiss argues that a habitus is continually expanding in response to new situations. It is a generative phenomenon, as Bourdieu repeatedly emphasised, capable of regulated improvisation, or the ability to transform to fit new circumstances and experiences on occasions when agents' habitual responses break down or clash and when agents consciously reflect on themselves and their changed contexts, and reconstruct their habitus accordingly.[7] Habitus does not, therefore, simply present agents with 'ready-made solutions or fixed ways of viewing a given problem' (Weiss, 2003: 7). It may be 'cleaved' or 'torn', bearing 'the mark of the contradictions which produced [it]' (Bourdieu, 1997: 78).

Sweetman (2003) argues persuasively that transformation of habitus is becoming increasingly commonplace due to the various geographical, economic, social and cultural shifts which people make or undergo during their lifetimes. He suggests that habitus should be regarded as an adaptive construct, rather than a determinate one, and that it is no more 'fixed' than the social terrain in which it finds itself. Entry into a new game or field will generate a different set of responses from those conditioned by the old habitus. As Bourdieu (1990: 63) wrote, 'a permanent capacity for invention [is] indispensable if one is to be able to adapt to infinitely varied and never completely identical situations'. Critical reflexivity concerning the adaptability of habitus (and cognate logics) may indeed accelerate the pace of transformation.

Mutch's (2003) and Noble and Watkins' (2003) case studies, mentioned above, identify empirical examples of habitus transformation. Mutch's public house managers have needed to adapt to the requirements of changing technology and increasing numbers of women in what were traditionally male roles, while Noble and Watkins' tennis players extend and transform their bodily capacities and mental habituses as they enter new situations and undergo new experiences. As the chapters by John Friedmann and Roxana Waterson in this volume demonstrate, habitus has a dynamic quality, so that when it enters an unfamiliar field or game, transformation is generated and the agent or actant develops new facets of the self.

Moreover, the notion of a social actant as a multiplicity is now widely accepted within the social sciences. Recognising the probability of plural sources of influence on habitus, authors such as Lahire (1998) advocate conceptualising individuals as having multiple habituses. For instance, a young woman may regard herself as a teenage daughter, a college friend, a rap fan, a tennis club member, a part-time work colleague in a public house and a lover, all identities embodying a different habitus, sense of place and feel for the game.

The treatment of habitus as multiple, interacting and evolving suggests a development of Bourdieuian theory that leaves substantial scope for individual agency, in the sense that individuals are not immersed inextricably in any single habitus, but can move from one to another, and can develop new adaptive behaviours within a habitus. A parallel recent development, the exploration of Bourdieu's use of the methods and tools of psychoanalysis, suggests that even when agents have multiple habituses and operate in multiple fields, similar fundamental psycho-social dispositions are at work. Jean-François Fourny, highlighting the similarities between psychoanalysis and Bourdieu's socioanalysis, locates the dispositions referred to by Bourdieu – 'denial, anamnesis, splitting of the ego, return of the repressed, etc.' – centrally within the discipline of psychoanalysis (2000: 110). Fourny construes Bourdieu's later work as heavily dependent on psychoanalysis, reflecting perhaps the influence of Foucault and Deleuze.

Other recent writers have stressed the differences between Bourdieu's socioanalysis and psychoanalysis. While many methods and techniques are similar, they are applied, in Bourdieu's work, to an irreducibly social subject, and take as their object social structures far larger, more flexible and historically embedded than those typically theorised by psychoanalysis. As Nick Crossley observes, for '[Bourdieu] agents act on the basis of deep seated and socially shaped sentiments, tastes, perceptions. Their egoism is necessarily filtered through a process of cultivation and socialization which, as Durkheim (1974) emphasized, is irreducibly collective in nature [...] They unconsciously censor and sublimate their expressions to conform to the requirements of the field, assuming its values and ideas, and their action is attuned to its structure to the degree that those structures feel natural, inevitable and correct.' (2004: 95,94) (See also Bourdieu 2002d.)

In other words, we might argue that the terms and techniques of psychoanalysis are useful to socioanalysis, but tend to be applied rather differently by socioanalysts, and to an agent whose psyche is structured by inhabitation of multiple social fields. Bourdieu (1998) himself also stresses the historical awareness of socioanalysis, vis-à-vis psychoanalysis. Taking the notion of transformation of habitus into account, the Bourdieuian 'unconscious' is highly adaptive, able to develop a feel for the game in new fields and liable to repression, sublimation and so on as a result of pressures within each of those fields. Moreover, a socioanalyst's concern with habitus is not limited to the specific techniques pioneered by psychoanalysis, as Neil Leach highlights (this volume), who draws on Walter Benjamin's notion of 'appropriation' and Judith Butler's work on 'performative identity', as well as on psychoanalytic theory.

Judging by the above, future debates around the nature of habitus in a postmodern or poststructural world are likely to be lively and productive.

Conclusions

The force of Pierre Bourdieu's legacy is such that the notion of habitus is very much alive. It is moving forward productively in the minds and words of academics such as those mentioned above and the authors in this volume who seek to clarify the meaning of habitus and to develop it in critical ways. In the spirit of both Pierre Bourdieu and Paul Hirst, the authors express true scientific respect towards habitus through rigorous discussion and evaluation. Many authors cite empirical material and several of the stories narrated in the chapters of the original version of this book remained ongoing at the time of publication. We have invited authors to update their stories for this second edition. Updated material is located in a Postscript at the end of each chapter as appropriate. An updated Conclusion is included at the end of the volume.

> One cannot grasp the most profound logic of the social world unless one becomes immersed in the specificity of an empirical reality (Bourdieu, 1993: 271).

Notes

1. See Poupeau and Discepolo (2004) for more detail of Bourdieu's political engagement.
2. Bourdieu also studied with Althusser at the École Normale Supérieure in Paris.
3. Among the achievements of the IPW is the creation of a network of 400 safe havens in 34 countries (Poupeau and Discepolo, 2004: 86-87).
4. See Poupeau and Discepolo (2002) for more detail.
5. Bourdieu had followed Foucault's lectures at the École Normale (Bourdieu, 2004: 103).
6. See, for example, Hefner (2000); Eyal (2003); Derluguian (2004).
7. Burkitt (2002) elaborates further on habitus and capacity in situations where a habitus falls out of alignment with the field in which it operates.

References

Allen, C. (2004) 'Bourdieu's habitus, social class and the spatial worlds of visually impaired children', *Urban Studies*, 41(3): 487-506.
Bourdieu, P. (1962) [1958] *The Algerians*, Boston, Beacon Press.
Bourdieu, P. (1971) 'Champ de pouvoir, champ intellectuel et habitus de class', *Sociologies*, 1: 7-26.
Bourdieu, P. (1977) 'Questions de politique', *Actes de la recherche en Sciences Sociales*, 16(June): 64.
Bourdieu, P. (1977) [1970] *Reproduction in Education, Society and Culture*, London, Sage.
Bourdieu, P. (1977) [1972] *Outline of a Theory of Practice*, Cambridge, Cambridge University Press.
Bourdieu, P. (1982) [1979] *Distinction*, Cambridge MA, Harvard University Press.
Bourdieu, P. (1985) 'The genesis of the concepts of habitus and of field', *Sociocriticism*, 2: 11.
Bourdieu, P. (1989) 'The corporatism of the universal: the role of intellectuals in the modern world', *Telos*, 81(Fall): 99-110.
Bourdieu, P. (1990) [1980] *The Logic of Practice*, Cambridge, Polity Press.
Bourdieu, P. (1990) [1982] *In Other Words*, Cambridge, Polity Press.
Bourdieu, P. (1991) 'Liber continue', *Liber*, 7(September): 1.
Bourdieu, P. (1993) 'Concluding remarks: for a sociogenetic understanding of intellectual works', in Calhoun, C., Lipuma, E. and Postone, M. (eds) *Bourdieu: critical perspectives*, Cambridge, Polity Press: 263-275.
Bourdieu, P. (1993) [1980] *Sociology in Question*, London, Sage.
Bourdieu, P. (1997) *Méditations pascaliennes*, Paris, Seuil.
Bourdieu, P. (1998) [1994] *Practical Reason: on the theory of action*, Cambridge, Polity Press.
Bourdieu, P. (1998) [1996] *On Television and Journalism*, London, Pluto.
Bourdieu, P. (1998) *La domination masculine*, Paris, Seuil.
Bourdieu, P. (2000) *Les structures sociales de l'économie*, Paris, Liber/Seuil.
Bourdieu, P. (2001a) 'Interview with Lino Polegato' (14 December 2001), *Flux News*, December 2001-January 2002: 7.
Bourdieu, P. (2001b) *Science de la science et réflexivité*, Paris, Raisons d'agir.
Bourdieu, P. (2002a) 'The "progressive" restoration: a Franco-German dialogue between Pierre Bourdieu and Günter Grass', *New Left Review*, 14: 63-77.
Bourdieu, P. (2002b) [2000] *The Social Structures of the Economy*, Cambridge, Polity Press.

Bourdieu, P. (2002c) *Le Bal des Célibataires: crise de la société paysanne en Béarn*, Paris, Seuil.
Bourdieu, P. (2002d) *Si le monde social m'est insupportable, c'est parce que je peux m'indigner*, Paris, Éditions de l'Aube.
Bourdieu, P. (2002e) 'L'inconscient d'école', *Actes de la Recherche en Sciences Sociales*, 35: 3-5.
Bourdieu, P. (2003) [2001] *Firing Back: against the tyranny of the market 2*, London, Verso.
Bourdieu, P. (2004) *Esquisse pour une auto-analyse*, Paris, Raisons d'agir.
Bourdieu, P. and Boltanski, L. (1976) 'La production de l'idéologie dominante', *Actes de la Recherche en Sciences Sociales*, 2/3(June): 4.
Bourdieu, P. and Sayad, A. (1964) *Le Déracinement, la crise de l'agricolture traditionnelle en Algérie*. Paris, Minuit.
Bourdieu, P. and Wacquant, L. (1992) [1992] *An Invitation to Reflexive Sociology*, Cambridge, Polity Press.
Bourdieu, P. and Wacqant, L. (1999) 'The cunning of imperialist reason', *Theory, Culture and Society*, 16(1): 41-57.
Bourdieu, P. *et al.* (1999) [1993] *The Weight of the World*, Cambridge, Polity Press.
Bridge, G. (2001) 'Bourdieu, rational action and the time-space strategy of gentrification', *Transactions of the Institute of British Geographers*, NS, 26: 205-224.
Burkitt, I. (2002) 'Technologies of the self: habitus and capacities', *Journal for the Theory of Social Behaviour*, 32(2): 219-237.
Crossley, N. (2003) 'From reproduction to transformation: social movement fields and the radical habitus', *Theory, Culture and Society*, 20(6): 43-68.
Crossley, N. (2004) 'On systematically distorted communication: Bourdieu and the socio-analysis of publics', in Crossley, N. and Roberts, J. (eds) *After Habermas*. Oxford, Blackwell.
Derluguian, G. (2004) *Bourdieu's Secret Admirer in the Caucasus*, London, Verso.
Dortier, J-F. (ed.) (2002) *Sciences Humaines*, numéro spécial Pierre Bourdieu.
Durkheim, E. (1974) *Sociology and Philosophy*, New York, Free Press.
Eyal, G. (2003) *The Origins of Postcommunist Elites: from the Prague Spring to the break-up of Czechoslovakia*, Minneapolis, University of Minnesota Press.
Flyvbjerg, B. (2001) *Making Social Science Matter*, Cambridge, Cambridge University Press.
Fourny, J-F. (2000) 'Bourdieu's uneasy psychoanalysis', *SubStance* 93: 103-112.
Fowler, B. (1997) *Pierre Bourdieu and Cultural Theory*, London, Sage.
Frère, B. (2004) 'Genetic structuralism, psychological sociology and pragmatic social actor theory: proposals for a convergence of French sociologies', *Theory, Culture and Society*, 21(3): 85-99.
Hefner, R. (2000) *Civil Islam: Muslims and democratisation in Indonesia*, Princeton, NJ, Princeton University Press.
Hillier, J. (2000) 'Going round the back? Complex networks, informal action in local planning processes', *Environment and Planning A*, 34: 33-54.
Hirst, P. (1989) *After Thatcher*, London, Collins.
Hirst, P. (1994) *Associative Democracy*, Cambridge, Polity Press.
Hirst, P. (1995) 'Can secondary associations enhance democratic governance?', in Cohen, J. and Rogers, J. (eds) *Associations and Democracy*, London, Verso: 101-113.
Hirst, P. (2000) 'Statism, pluralism and social control', *British Journal of Criminology*, 20: 279-295.
Hirst, P. (2001) *War and Power in the Twenty-first Century*, Cambridge, Polity Press.
Hirst, P. and Hindess, B. (1975) *Pre-Capitalist Modes of Production*, London, Routledge and Kegan Paul.

Hirst, P. and Khilnani S. (eds) (1996) *Reinventing Democracy*, Oxford, Blackwell.
Hirst, P. and Thompson, G. (1996) (second edition 1999) *Globalisation in Question*, Cambridge, Polity Press.
Howe, J. and Langdon, C. (2002) 'Towards a reflexive planning theory', *Planning Theory*, 1(3): 209-225.
Lahire, B. (1998) *L'Homme Pluriel*, Paris, Nathan.
Lane, J. (2000) *Pierre Bourdieu: a critical introduction*, London, Pluto Press.
Lanzara, G. and Patriotta, G. (2001) 'Technology and the courtroom: an inquiry into knowledge-making organisations', *Journal of Management Studies*, 16(3).
Lau, R.W.K. (2004) 'Habitus and the practical logic of practice: an interpretation', *Sociology*, 38(2): 369-387.
McNay, L. (1999) 'Gender, habitus and the field', *Theory, Culture and Society*, 16(1): 95-117.
Mutch, A. (2003) 'Communities of practice and habitus: a critique', *Organisation Studies*, 24(3): 383-401.
Noble, G. and Watkins, M. (2003) 'So, how did Bourdieu learn to play tennis? Habitus, consciousness and habituation', *Cultural Studies*, 17(3/4): 520-538.
Osborne, T. (2002) 'Pierre Bourdieu: celui qui disait non', *International Journal of Cultural Studies*, 5(3): 259-262.
Ostermann, A.C. (2003) 'Communities of practice at work: gender, facework and the power of habitus at an all-female police station and a feminist crisis intervention centre in Brazil', *Discourse and Society*, 14(4): 473-505.
Poupeau, F. and Discepolo, T. (2004) 'Scholarship with commitment: on the political engagement of Pierre Bourdieu', *Constellations*, 11(1): 76-96.
Poupeau, F. and Discepolo, T. (eds) (2002) *Pierre Bourdieu: Interventions 1961-2001, Science sociale et action politique*, Marseilles, Agone, Comeau et Nadeau.
Reay, D. (1995) 'They employ cleaners to do that: habitus in the primary classroom', *British Journal of Sociology of Education*, 16: 353-371.
Reay, D. (1998) '"Always knowing" and "never being sure": institutional and familial habituses and higher education choice', *Journal of Education Policy*, 13: 519-529.
Reay, D. (2002) 'Shaun's story: troubling discourses of white working class masculinities', *Gender and Education*, 14: 221-234.
Reay, D. (2004) 'It's all becoming a habitus: beyond the habitual use of habitus in educational research', *British Journal of Sociology of Education*, 25(4): 431-444.
Reay, D., Ball, S. and David, M. (2001) 'Making a difference: institutional habituses and higher education choice', *Sociological Research Online*, 5: U126-U142.
Robbins, D. (2000) *Bourdieu and Culture*, London, Sage.
Scheuer, J. (2003) 'Habitus as the principle for social practice: a proposal for critical discourse analysis', *Language in Society*, 32: 143-175.
Shusterman, R. (1999) *Bourdieu: a critical reader*, Oxford, Blackwell.
Sweetman, P. (2003) 'Twenty-first century dis-ease? Habitual reflexivity or the reflexive habitus', *The Sociological Review*, 528-549.
Thrift, N. (2004) 'Remembering the technological unconscious by foregrounding knowledges of position', *Environment and Planning D*, Society and Space, 22: 175-190.
Wacquant, L. (ed.) (2004a) *Constellations*, special issue, 11(1): 3-101.
Wacquant, L. (2004b) 'Pointers on Pierre Bourdieu and democratic politics', *Constellations*, 11(1): 3-15.
Weiss, G. (2003) *Can an old dog learn new tricks? Habitual horizons in James, Bourdieu and Merleau-Ponty*, Cultural Studies Program, George Mason University, Fairfax, VA. (Copy available from cultural@gmu.edu).

1 Introduction to First Edition

JEAN HILLIER AND EMMA ROOKSBY

Introduction

The chapters in this volume represent revised versions of papers originally presented at the *Habitus 2000: A Sense of Place* conference in Perth, Western Australia in 2000.

The book commences with a brief contextual overview of Pierre Bourdieu's notion of habitus followed by a keynote chapter by Pierre Bourdieu himself. This Introduction serves to identify the key components of habitus which are addressed by the various authors throughout the volume:

- habitus as social space: as a sense of one's place and a sense of the other's place
- fields and games
- the several forms of capital; economic, social and cultural
- the role of symbolic capital
- aesthetic reflexivity
- practical knowledge

It also seeks to identify particular areas of challenge for habitus: its durability and/or adaptability and the notion of habitus as oppression.

The chapters which follow include reflections on each of these aspects of habitus drawn together under the themes of:

- whose habitus?
- what habitus?
- how habitus is constructed
- oppressive habitus – resistance, toleration and beyond
- durable and/or mutable habitus

The main body of the work is divided into three parts, each guided by questions central to conceptions, operation of and challenges for habitus.

Does habitus exist at a macro-level? How does the notion of habitus help us to understand international and national political structures and activities?

Does habitus help explain processes of place-making in fields relating to practices of the built environment?

How durable is habitus or might it undergo some form of transformation in changing circumstances? Does some people's habitus actually *need* to change?

Each chapter, however, does not address itself singularly to the question/s guiding its sectional location. There are many links between the chapters as each draws on a range of aspects of habitus in constructing its argument. The chapters thus present a set of interrelated and overlapping conversations between various authors and their stories of people and habitus from a wide range of disciplinary backgrounds, including sociology, philosophy, politics, policy studies, urban and regional planning, architecture, geography and anthropology.

In this way, not only are key constructs of habitus demonstrated as enhancing our understanding of a variety of different temporal and geographical circumstances, but habitus is also subjected to challenge from various quarters. Can the notion of habitus account for social transformation? Can habitus actually break down completely? If people's habitus can change, in what types of circumstances could it change to make the world a better place in which to live?

The concluding chapter attempts to draw together the various authors' answers to these challenges and to suggest where the concept of habitus might usefully be located at the beginning of the twenty-first century.

Habitus

One of the questions with which Pierre Bourdieu's work has been concerned is 'what motivates human action?'. Do people act in response to external stimuli? To what extent is people's reasoning about how they act influenced or determined by structural factors?

Pierre Bourdieu proposes a structural theory of practice which connects structure and agency in a dialectical relationship between culture, structure and power. He recognises the social relations among actors as being structured by, and in turn contributing to the structuring of, the social relations of power among different positions (of class, gender etc.). It is this theory which forms the basis for Bourdieu's concept of habitus.

Bourdieu has described one of the central motivations behind his work as a determination to challenge misleading dichotomies (Calhoun, 2000: 705). One of these dichotomies is the traditional academic opposition of theory and practice which encourages the notion (especially in professional discourses, such as those of the built environment) that practice is the application of theory. In such a regard, theory becomes a totalising view-from-nowhere rather than being a dialectical relationship with practice – a praxis. This volume attempts to engage in such a dialectical relationship, building theory on practice and stories of everyday lifeworlds.

As such, it pays homage to another of Pierre Bourdieu's key contributions to our understanding of behaviour, the distinction between synoptic and participatory views of activity. Whereas synoptic views stand apart from the activity process, describing what is taking or has taken place, participatory views regard action from what is avowedly a participant's standpoint, emphasising the perspectival nature of behaviour. Habitus provides a link between these two views. It 'mediates between a synoptic view of activity formations characteristic of a community and a dynamic view of the processes by which these activities are actually enacted on specific occasions by human actors' (Lemke, 1995: 33).

So, what is habitus?

Habitus is defined as 'a system of durable, transposable dispositions, structured structures predisposed to function as structuring structures, that is, as principles which generate and organise practices and representations' (Bourdieu, 1990: 53). Habitus is thus a sense of one's (and others') place and role in the world of one's lived environment. As the papers in this volume clearly demonstrate, habitus is an embodied, as well as a cognitive, sense of place.

Painter (2000: 242) describes habitus as 'the mediating link between objective social structures and individual action and refers to the embodiment in individual actors of systems of social norms, understandings and patterns of behaviour, which, while not wholly determining action … do ensure that individuals are more disposed to act in some ways than others'. Bourdieu's concept thus leaves room both for individual reason-based action and for social determination.

Habitus is the product of history. As such, it is 'an open system of dispositions that is constantly subjected to experiences, and therefore constantly affected by them in a way that either reinforces or modifies its structures' (Bourdieu and Wacquant, 1992: 133). As the chapters in this volume will indicate, habitus may be reasonably durable, but it is not immutable.

The dispositions of habitus serve to predispose actors to choose behaviour which appears to them more likely to achieve a desired outcome with regard to their previous experiences, the resources available to them and the prevailing power relations: 'the relation to what is possible is a relation to power' (Bourdieu, 1980: 4). Actors undertake a practical evaluation of their potential behaviour. However, as will be demonstrated in this volume, such a practical evaluation is often not a conscious pattern of rational thought, but rather an intuitive practical reaction to a situation based on experience; an embodied sensibility which leads to structured improvisation (Calhoun, 2000: 712). This is not to say, of course, that structured improvisation is entirely determined by factors outside of the control of the individual, or that no reason has gone into the acquisition of particular sensibilities/dispositions. But it is to say that habitus is not deliberative.

Bourdieu believes that human action is interested. Unlike rational actor theorists (such as Habermas), however, he regards interestedness as being generally a prereflective level of awareness which develops over time. Schwartz (1997: 19) asks whether different types of conduct vary in their levels of interestedness. For example, might some forms of behaviour respond more directly to perceived needs of survival than others? It would appear that Bourdieu's answer to this question is affirmative. When faced with entirely new situations, strategic calculation may be fully conscious, becoming unconscious with time as the same or similar situations are repeatedly encountered.

Habitus is constituted in practice and 'always oriented to practical functions' (Bourdieu, 1980: 52). Bourdieu regards habitus as an open concept since actors' dispositions are constantly subjected to a range of different experiences. The dispositions that comprise habitus may be affected by these experiences in terms of being either reinforced or modified. Although Bourdieu anticipates that most experiences will serve to reinforce actors' habitus (as people are more likely to encounter situations and interpret them according to their pre-existing dispositions rather than to modify their feelings), he does accept that changes may occur. Habitus 'is durable but not eternal' (Bourdieu, 1992: 133).

Fields and Games

Bourdieu terms the socially structured space in which actors play out their engagements with each other, a field. A field is a 'relational configuration endowed with a specific gravity which it imposes on all the objects and agents which enter in it' (Wacquant, 1992: 17).

A field is also a space of conflict and competition as actors struggle to achieve their objectives. As Bourdieu writes, 'even in the universe par excellence of rules and regulations, playing with the rule is a part and parcel of the rule of the game' (1990: 89).

A field, then, is a space of play within a network of objective relations between positions. These positions are objectively defined in the determinations they impose on actors and institutions, by their situation in the structure in the distribution of power.

Bourdieu frequently employs the analogy of a game when conveying the sense of activity/ies within a field. To be successful in a game situation requires not just understanding and following the rules, but having a sense of the game. It requires constant awareness of and responsiveness to the play of all the actors involved. It requires assessment of one's own team-mate/s' resources, strengths and weaknesses and also those of the opponent/s. It requires improvisation and flexibility and above all, it requires use of anticipation as to what one's team-mate/s and one's opponent/s will do. Behaviours cannot be reduced simply to theoretical rules.

There are few talented newcomers to games who have the abilities described above. More often, insight and a sense of the game – a habitus – develop with experience. Players learn from experience about what is possible and what is not; about how to work effectively within existing practices in the field and about how the rules might be modified. Players' activities are constructed, therefore, both by the external limits of rules and regulations, and also by their own internalisations and placing of limits on what they think they can do or what they want to do in the circumstances.

Habitus, therefore, offers an insightful way of understanding social interactions. Actors' behaviours will be related to their position *in* the field (in legal terms, and also in terms of the sense of their place and those of other actors in the field). Their behaviours will also be related to the resources available to them, and to their view *of* the field, including their ideological viewpoint and their perception of which issues are worth fighting for, this last being constructed from their position in the field

As Bourdieu (1980) indicates, an actor's practical relation to the future, which defines their present behaviour, consists of the relationship between the habitus, 'constructed in the course of a particular relationship to a particular universe of probabilities' (p. 64) and the opportunities offered to them. The relation to what activity is possible is a matter of whether it is within the power of the individual; this in turn depends on what position an individual occupies within the field. The 'sense of the probable future is constituted in the prolonged relationship with a world structured according to the categories of the possible ... and the impossible' (p. 64). Habitus is thus the selective perception of a situation which generates a response according to the practical potential of satisfying the actor/s' desire/s.

Capital and Power

The concept of the field is closely linked to that of capital: 'capital does not exist and function except in relation to a field' (Bourdieu and Wacquant, 1992: 101). Capital is effectively the resources which actors take to the field.

Capital should be regarded not only as having its more usual, economic, connotation, but as also having applicability to resources such as status, power, personal contacts and formal and informal forms of knowledge. Bourdieu identifies three types of capital as follows:

- Economic capital or material wealth and concomitant power.
- Social capital, which may be defined as the resources and power which people obtain through their social networks and connections.[1]
- Cultural capital, which refers to knowledge and skills which actors acquire either through formally examined or through less formal means of education. Cultural capital often relates to prestige and status and includes resources such as articulateness, persuasiveness, aesthetic preferences and cultural awareness.

Bourdieu suggests that cultural capital exists in three different states. The first is an embodied state, since cultural goods can only be 'consumed' by understanding their meaning, unlike material goods. Cultural goods include music, works of art, scientific formulae, professional jargon, religion etc.

Secondly, cultural capital exists in an objectified form as objects, such as books, scientific instruments, works of art etc. which require specialised cultural abilities to use.

Thirdly, cultural capital exists in an institutionalised form, most often represented by educational, and/or professional, credentials.

Bourdieu recognises the importance of the symbolic dimensions of capital. His term, symbolic capital, incorporates the other three forms of capital as it represents 'the form that the various species of capital assume when they are perceived and recognised as legitimate' (Bourdieu, 1989:

17). Bourdieu thus recognises the links and potential conversions between the various forms of capital and their relationship to power. Symbolic capital is a form of power that is not necessarily perceived as power as such, but as legitimate demands for recognition, deference, obedience or the service of others (Schwartz, 1997: 90).[2] The exercise of power through symbolic exchange (often of communication) rests on a foundation of shared belief about the relative positions of the agents involved; for example, of the planning officer as technical expert compared with local authority elected representatives, or the Mayor or high priest or family head as 'natural' leader.

The key to symbolic power is thus that it is a legitimating form of power which involves the consent or active complicity of both dominant and dominated actors. Dominated actors are not passive bodies to whom power is applied, but rather people who believe in both the legitimacy of the power and the legitimacy of those who wield it. Bourdieu (1987) regards symbolic power as 'worldmaking power' due to its capacity to impose a legitimised vision of the social world.

Concluding Habitus

'Social life requires our active engagement in its games' (Calhoun, 2000: 710). It is impossible to live as an outside observer. Actively engaged, we obtain a huge amount of practical knowledge. This knowledge, however, is filtered by the embodied understanding of our habitus, which reflects and affects our understanding of what is taking place in various situations and shapes how we practically engage with those situations.

Determining a preferred course of action in any situation requires an actor to employ insight and understanding. In many instances, simply playing by the rules and putting formulae into effect will not suffice. There is a need for the practical wisdom of Aristotelian phronesis[3] or Platonic orthē doxa[4] too. As Taylor (1999: 41) suggests, 'the person of real practical wisdom is marked out less by the ability to formulate rules than by knowing how to act in each particular situation'. There is a vitally important 'phronetic gap' between the rule or formula and its enactment. Practice, therefore, may be regarded as a 'continual "interpretation" and reinterpretation of what the rule really means' (Taylor, 1999: 41).

This volume seeks to explore some of the ways in which habitus influences people's behaviour and actions.

Themes and Challenges

Whose Habitus? What Habitus?

The chapters illustrate a range of forms of habitus operating in a variety of fields. Habitus is depicted as being a sense of the social places of oneself and that of others.

Paul Hirst demonstrates the importance of exclusion to habitus and, in particular, to a sense of the other's place. He maps the history of development of modern nation states, illustrating how the rise of the modern state transformed not only territorial landscapes but also imaginative landscapes and people's habitus. Hirst shows us how states have encouraged the territorial loyalties of their populations and how they use wars to build forms of identification between ruler and ruled. Such actions, added to the institutionalisation of homogeneous languages and customs, build a habitus of political nationalism which overrides local regional identification and habitus which people may hold. In such a manner inhabitants' sense of place takes on a spatial dimension which is gradually transformed from a local to a national scale.

Fay Gale depicts a strong sense of place amongst Australian indigenous Aboriginal women. She also indicates that many non-indigenous white colonisers in Australia have had even stronger senses of Aboriginal people's place as the Other. Gale's chapter commences with an evocative folk song, *The Drover's Boy*, which poignantly depicts the interrelations between white farmers and farm workers and indigenous people in Australia in the early twentieth century. This was a habitus of massacre; of regarding indigenous peoples as inferior, almost as animals; of taking indigenous women as mistresses and guides. The Aboriginal woman of the song was 'broken in' as one might break in a wild horse or animal. She was to be a 'faithful wife, never a bride' as she would be beneath the dignity of the sanctity of marriage.

Small wonder, then, that Australian indigenous people have tended to possess a dominated habitus; a sense of their place in the world as less than non-indigenous wadjellas. A history of white wadjella oppression has substantially changed the traditional roles and habitus of both Aboriginal men and women as they were taken off their land, segregated onto missions and reserves and still form a far higher proportion of those in police custody than do non-indigenous people.

Gale's narratives clearly depict the habitus of indigenous Australians for the land which has 'such a deep and unifying meaning covering every aspect of life'. This issue is further developed in the chapter by Val Plumwood who contrasts the habitus of indigenous people, a non-abusive love of the land, with that of the white colonisers. Colonisation brought a habitus which regarded nature as irrelevant Other. Its place was to be domesticated and commodified, envisaged in terms of private property. This is a habitus of disbelonging; an active state of denying or rejecting certain kinds of ties to the earth. Australian nature was to be remade in the image of the old European homeland, exemplified by the colonial naming of places which served to assimilate Australian land into an imperial empire.

Barry Hindess also develops the notion of a Western habitus with regard to 'less civilised' parts of the world. He describes a habitus of colonial autocracy; a belief in Western superiority, linked to a liberalist political doctrine. Colonial rule, or government at a distance, was deemed necessary for many reasons. These ranged from a belief that 'because of cultural or innate characteristics, some people are so far from being able to acquire the relevant capacities (to govern themselves) that they should simply be displaced or, more humanely perhaps, absorbed into the lower reaches of more civilised populations' to a belief that the role of the colonial administration was to 'improve' the condition of its subjects through provision of adequate education and so on.

The chapter by Roxana Waterson makes direct reference to habitus as she describes the Sa'dan Toraja people of Sulawesi in Indonesia. Waterson shows how the Toraja indigenous religion, the *Aluk to Dolo*, a set of embodied dispositions, has generated its own distinctive habitus. She clearly illustrates the importance of habitus as history, passed on through generations as often poetic recitations of myth and memory. The *Aluk*-based habitus 'involved an ongoing interaction with deities and ancestors whose presence was so much *in nature* that it saturated the landscape itself with meaning'. This habitus incorporated a strong sense of place of everyone and everything.

Leonie Sandercock delves into the idea of habitus as sense of the other's place. She examines contemporary urban dwellers' habitus of fear of the Other. Asking the question, 'who is the Other?', Sandercock unpacks a fear of strangers, of disorder and dis/ease in urban environments. She recognises the role of anxiety in influencing individual's habitus, especially in what has become a far less certain world. Such anxieties are projected onto strangers as the Other who threaten 'all that is familiar and homely, all that we have grown up with and take for granted, including the socio-spatial knowledge of our neighbourhoods'.

Sandercock offers several international examples of the institutionalisation of fear as the defining principle of urbanism. In many cases, fear is symbolised by a spatial segregation, or even containment, of distinct population groups. Upper class residents need to feel 'safe' from an abject Other. Yet Sandercock incisively points out the ambiguous nature of the habitus: 'the upper classes fear contact and contamination, but they continue to depend on their servants'.

Ted Kitchen and Richard Schneider continue the theme of fear in the city as they outline a series of habituses. We discern a distinct police habitus which affords the police not only a sense of their own place, but also a sense of the place of criminals and of the 'general public' in dealing with urban crime. We also gather a feeling for the public's sense of place of the police in this regard.

Emphasising a field pertaining to the built environment, Kitchen and Schneider explore the habitus of planning practitioners in terms of a sense of place of themselves and other stakeholders in shaping policies to combat crime. Kitchen and Schneider ask whose views matter in shaping responses to crime. Resonating with the chapter by Leonie Sandercock, their answer is that 'the most strident "fear of crime" views are those in effect expressed by the "haves" against the "have nots"'.

Steve Pile develops the affective aspect of habitus, as he expands the role of anxiety as an active constituent in the habitus of city dwellers. He suggests that we cannot begin to understand social sense of space unless we find a place for feelings, emotion and affect. As such, he explores feelings including fear, trauma, dread and grief and their roles in production of cities as spaces and places.

Pile graphically depicts city dwellers as possessing habitus of studied indifference and cynicism as a means of dealing with trouble and grief, somewhat reminiscent of a British cultural 'stiff upper lip' attitude. He speculates that a sense of the other's place has no place in people's minds; place becomes out of mind. He attributes such a 'deathlike' living to a loss of caring, of recognition, of reparation of others in the indifference of city life. He explores ways in which citydwellers may be haunted by the Others to whom they give no place.

Patsy Healey also demonstrates how a sense of the other's place has no place in certain people's minds. In this instance it is the elected representatives and officers of Newcastle City Council in Britain who have little sense of the place of their inner city residents. Faced with a declining tax base of economic capital and increasing costs of welfare provision in depressed inner city localities, the city council is attempting to transform parts of these areas through a strategy of residential demolition and gentrification. This strategy should serve to both release considerable asset value locked away in public housing and land and to also increase the council's tax revenue.

Some forty years on, the council has 'reinvented' a classic 1960s comprehensive development area strategy 'clothed with the vocabulary of community and diversity current in national urban policy discourse of the late 1990s'. The council 'acts the past' as it tells residents they have to move out and 'clears untenable stock'.

Despite spouting the rhetoric of community participation, there has been little consultation undertaken during preparation of a strategy which pronounces *at* residents rather than to them. The city council and its officers have a clear sense of place of the inner area residents and of themselves as paternalist service deliverers who had little need to either listen or respond to citizens' views.

The council has a distinct sense of its place in the vertical hierarchy of British governance. Delivery of local services traditionally has been (and still is) dependent on receiving funding from national, and more recently, regional levels of governance for which political games must be played correctly.

Remaining in the city, Jean Hillier also explores the habitus of local authority elected representatives with regard to land use planning decision-making. Her aim is to illuminate a possible habitus of elected representatives in order that urban and regional planning officers may begin to understand apparent whims of decision-making, to anticipate them and to combat them with their own reflexive improvisations in a search for more effective planning practice.

The stories in Hillier's chapter demonstrate how planning decisions may be taken by elected representatives on an often impulsive feel for the game. Hillier shows that elected representatives possess a strong sense of their own place and that of the public. High levels of satisfaction are gained from 'feeling important'.

'Feeling important' seems to be something that also drives architects. Kim Dovey's exposition of the silent complicity of architecture with the practices of power demonstrates a clear alliance of architecture with authority, sustained and propagated by those in professional practice, education etc. with an interest in maintaining the status quo. Dovey shows, in a profession which takes a certain habitus for granted, how architecture reproduces an unquestioned framework of everyday life full of oppression, empowerment and privilege in its various forms.

The Construction of Habitus

Habitus is constructed through, and in turn constructs, capital. The chapters in this volume offer telling depictions of all the various forms of capital and of their conversion to symbolic capital.

Joe Painter illustrates the literal construction of an attempted new habitus, but which may, in time, become part of an accepted way of thinking. Painter demonstrates how UK Regional Development Agencies 'produce and constitute' not only the spatial boundaries of their regions, but also their regional economies. Through amassing certain knowledge of the regions and of selected aspects of their economies, and by publishing these data in glossy, easily accessible strategies, they attempt to construct new senses of social, geographical and economic space.

Painter demonstrates the dominance of economic capital in these strategies. Regional 'development' is portrayed in primarily economic terms, with little regard for environmental or social sustainability.

Grahame Thompson and Paul Hirst both refer to the international importance of economic capital. Thompson outlines the importance of economic resources in 'an era where "money" is both revered and demonised' and signifies its potential in constructing a regime of international toleration. He identifies a need for a 'massive redistribution of economic resources and finance from the rich nations, groups and individuals to the poor nations, groups and individuals – which can only sensibly be organised through some form of public authority or agreement'. Hirst indicates the role of supra-national agencies of capital such as the WTO, IMF and World Bank in sharing power and governance capacity with states, although one would suggest the proven ineffectiveness of such agencies in increasing international toleration.

Also on an international scale, John Friedmann and Roxana Waterson both indicate the importance of economic capital to migrants and their extended families. In his 'mental journey' of transporting Kabyle families from rural Algeria to urban Germany, John Friedmann demonstrates the role of capital. His Kabyle migrate initially in search of earning wages as *Gastarbeiter* in order to improve their own quality of life and, through remittances back to Algeria, that of their extended families.

Similarly, Roxana Waterson explains that migrant Toraja workers transmit large sums of money home to their families from other parts of Indonesia and also return to spend money themselves at times of important ceremonies. She indicates how this economic capital has not only made the Toraja economy more dynamic over the past two or three decades, but how it has also introduced flexibility into what had previously been a rather rigid status system as newly rich players have succeeded in bending the rules of the old ceremonial economy, which previously served to reinforce differences of rank.

The importance of economic capital for Newcastle City Council is explored in Patsy Healey's chapter. The economic capital base of the city council is in severe decline, rendering the city heavily dependent on receipt of economic capital from national government and from private investment. It is only by demonstrating commitment to such externally set agendas that the city council can expect to capture the resources it requires. There is a need for the council to have a strong feel for the funding game if it is to be successful.

John Friedmann indicates the importance of social capital when he describes the affinity environments of migrants in Germany: 'people like themselves, similarly disoriented, to whom they could pout their pain, recall familiar scenes from the old country, and who would help each other cope with their new life'. Social capital networks are vital to coping with the several shocks of a new environment.

Leonie Sandercock's examples of urban political economies of fear implicitly identify the value of upper and middle class social capital. As she, Kitchen and Schneider point out, it is the contacts and networks of these groups which disproportionately influence law and order, land use zoning and planning policies in our urban areas.

In these instances, possession of social capital is intrinsically linked with possession of cultural capital. It is generally the more educated who constitute the middle and upper classes of society and who, often empowered by prestige and status, are better able to understand the democratic and urban planning systems and to articulate their concerns.

Neil Leach demonstrates how architecture can be understood as a form of 'objectivated cultural capital' in that it has no or little value unless strategically activated. The cultural capital of architectural buildings lays dormant until its meanings are unlocked by the narratives of use in which they are inscribed.

Cultural capital is also regarded as important by Friedmann's Kabyle youth living in Germany. Seeking to adapt to a Western way of life which many of them prefer, young immigrant males tend to be powerfully attracted to the material youth culture of their new homeland. The young males learn the rules of the game both formally and informally in order to 'fit in' and assimilate, often resulting in conflict between themselves and their parents' more traditional views on life.

This same form of tension is described by Roxana Waterson when she tells of the traditional forms of Torajan cultural capital, as embodied in the *Aluk to Dolo* religion, coming under increasing pressure from new forms of cultural capital associated with Christianity, urban life, modernity and concomitant changes in lifestyle. For many Sa'dan Toraja identification with modernity is important. However, modernity has come at the expense of a fracturing of traditional forms of community with their emphasis on collaborative ways of working, especially at the point where some members of a community have converted whilst others have not. Ironically, Waterson observed how, in the village she studied, this breach could in a sense be healed once all members had converted to Christianity, in the mid-1990s. But at the same time, parents had given up transmitting to their children much of the practical knowledge that constituted the old habitus, with its intimate spiritual links to the landscape.

Joe Painter's chapter clearly depicts cultural capital in its objectified state. Development of a Regional Economic Strategy becomes 'a matter of documentation, or writing, rather than practice'. Regions and their economies are 'brought into being' through the production of maps and glossy strategies 'loaded with business school rhetorical devices' such as organigrams and vision statements. Moreover, the cultural capital of certain academic regional economic and management gurus permeates the habitus of the strategies' authors.

Fay Gale and Barry Hindess both indicate the symbolic capital and power of colonial autocracy. Colonisers throughout the world have attempted to employ symbolic capital to reinforce their authority, and to command deference and obedience from others.

Jean Hillier similarly demonstrates the symbolic capital of status and prestige which appears to accompany holding a local authority badge of office as an elected representative. The symbolic power to approve or refuse land use planning applications lends itself to manifestations of benevolence and sometimes of petulance on the part of local councillors. Displays of posturing and political impression management give the elected representatives 'a kind of continuous justification for existing' (Bourdieu, 2000: 240), especially nearing times of local elections.

Moving disciplines from urban planning to architecture and urban design, Patsy Healey and Kim Dovey emphasise the symbolic capital of both an architect's name and the buildings which they design. Dovey demonstrates that the prestige of an architect is important, not only to the architect themselves, but also to the owners of the architect-designed buildings. Economic wealth is thus fixed into the built form and transformed into symbolic capital through architecture.

It was perhaps the architectural symbolic capital of the MI6 headquarters in London which caused it to become a bomb target in Steve

Pile's account of the September 2000 events. Striking at the heart of a symbol of British imperialist government by successfully bombing the offices of an agency which does not 'officially' exist also gained much symbolic capital for the terrorists involved. The terrorists broke the rules of the game by improvising a move against 'legitimate', albeit clandestine, authority.

As Neil Leach explains, the Polish-Canadian public artist, Krzysztof Wodiczko, also struck at the heart of architectural symbolic capital with his projection of the image of a swastika onto the pediment of South Africa House in Trafalgar Square, London. Protesting against the trade negotiations then underway between the apartheid regime in South Africa and the Conservative British government, Wodiczko selected a particularly evocative symbol of evil. Through breaking the rules of the game in terms of the architectural perception of Trafalgar Square and the forms which political protest might take, the 'stain of evil' was transferred to British colonial rule (symbolised by the history of the building), the Conservative British government and the inhabitants of the building, the South African regime itself.

Whereas Roxana Waterson identifies the importance of converting spiritual capital into symbolic capital for the Indonesian Sa'dan Toraja, Val Plumwood warns that in Australia the symbolic capital of spirituality as awarded to the land by many authors is seriously flawed. Plumwood claims that 'a broad and unqualified concept of spirituality is too indiscriminate to be particularly useful' and the resulting superficial spirituality offers us too easy a way out of the complex ethical problems associated with developing place or nature-sensitivity. Spirituality becomes simply an empty signifier if it lacks 'a philosophy and a politics to go with it'.

Oppressive Habitus – Resistance, Toleration and Beyond

Pierre Bourdieu has recognised the potentially oppressive nature of habitus, writing that 'it would be wrong to underestimate the pressure or oppression, continuous and often unnoticed, of the ordinary order of things' (2000: 141). The particularly oppressive aspects of a colonial habitus with regard to 'less civilised' parts of the world are clearly demonstrated in the chapters by Barry Hindess and Fay Gale.

Gale's emotionally powerful stories of Australian Aboriginal children who were stolen from their mothers and often taken some thousands of kilometres away partly in order to 'breed out' the indigenous race are poignant beyond description. Her own narrative of being effectively silenced when attempting to advocate on behalf of Aboriginal women also tells of the strength and reach of colonial oppression.

Val Plumwood describes colonialist oppression in Australia as being meted out to nature as well (or as badly) as it was to humans. Colonialist attitudes of denial and backgrounding nature typified early non-indigenous relationships with the Australian land. The failure to develop a rich land culture and deep knowledge of the land has led to non-indigenous Australia experiencing some of the worst vegetation clearance, land degradation and biodiversity extinction rates in the world.

With regard to urban environments, Leonie Sandercock shows how an upper and middle class habitus fuelled by fear can lead to oppression of the poor through measures of law and order and instruments of spatial containment and segregation. Continuing this theme, Kim Dovey demonstrates the oppressive potential of architecture. The deep complicity of architecture with the prevailing social order renders it a powerful force in framing people's lives. Architecture enjoys the power of 'oppression and empowerment; privilege and resistance' as buildings both constrain and enable certain kinds of life and experience. As Dovey explains, buildings are 'inherently coercive in that they enforce limits to action and enable social practice to "take place"'. Architecture enforces social order.

There is a definite sense of optimism about this volume, nevertheless. In the introductory chapter to the section on 'Politics of Space and Place', Ernesto Laclau challenges arguments articulated against the viability of democracy in a 'postmodern' age, as painting 'too rosy a picture' of classical democratic experiences and discourses and ignoring the possibilities of deepening such experiences which the new cultures of particularity and difference are opening up. Laclau stresses the ambiguity of democracy (it requires unity (universality), but is only conceivable through diversity (particularity)) and goes on to demonstrate why and how democracy is only possible on a hegemonic terrain. Defining hegemony as 'the type of political relation by which a particularity assumes the representation of an (impossible) universality entirely incommensurable with it', he explains the democratic logic as constituted by an unevenness of power and an asymmetry between universality and particularity; i.e. politics, the institutionalisation of the space of renegotiation of universality and particularity.

Laclau's optimism lies in his belief in the potentiality of democracy to open new forms of construction of communitarian spaces. He believes in a democratic potential of globalisation and an inherent limit to domination: 'there is only domination if it opens the possibility of its being overthrown'.

As Pierre Bourdieu indicates in his Introductory chapter, those whom he terms 'misfits', possessing a subversive habitus, are sometimes able to challenge existing structures to the extent of remaking them. Many of the subsequent chapters in this volume tell such stories of the possibilities of resistance to an oppressive habitus.

The Australian Aboriginal women portrayed by Fay Gale epitomise qualities of resistance and endurance. Despite their lack of economic capital, they have managed to prise open margins of freedom through persistence and acts of improvisation. Through such 'heresies' (Bourdieu, 1980: 128) of persistent speaking out, the construction of a lake at Todd River, near Alice Springs, has been resisted. In similar heretical vein, when Aboriginal people were not allowed petrol during World War II, a group of women gained mobility and economic return by removing the engine from a then-useless truck, harnessing it to feral donkeys and going rabbiting.

Steve Pile's story of the bombing of the London headquarters of MI6 is also a tale of resistance to the habitus of the British government with regard to its colonial sense of place in the Irish struggle. This 'cry for freedom' was improvised through a gap in the British surveillance system which enabled the organisation responsible to make public their political demands.

Residents of inner city Newcastle are also making public their political demands through innovative acts of resistance. As Patsy Healey describes, residents released hundreds of 'red balloons of distress' outside the Civic Centre in protest against an agenda for planned gentrification and displacement, 'not just of particular people, but of a remembered way of life'. Local residents, who once passively looked to government to address their difficulties, are developing a more active feel for the game of gaining political attention.

Jean Hillier tells of possible resistance by 'misfit' local planning officers to the symbolic power of elected representatives and the influence of their habitus on land use planning decisions. She suggests that planners who demonstrate practical anticipation and reflexivity, by '"getting into the heads" of likely actors to understand their habitus and to anticipate their reactions' to policy proposals and development applications and who then engage in practical reflexivity and improvisation are potentially more able to channel political will in specific directions in the interests of good planning outcomes.

Kim Dovey also argues for architectural self-reflexivity. If 'misfit' architects are to become more than simply an avant garde who enliven their field without disturbing its foundations, Dovey suggests that they must beware the trap of appropriation in which their images, produced in resistance to dominant aesthetic codes, are framed and emptied of subversive power to become a source of new symbolic capital in their turn.

Dovey is adamant that real resistance entails opening up breaches in the symbolic order. As such, he maintains that architecture needs to become engaged as a social practice to give voice to broad rather than to elite interests.

The chapter by Ted Kitchen and Richard Schneider provides a clear and optimistic example of 'breaching' the symbolic orders of the worlds of town planning and of crime prevention. As Kitchen and Schneider indicate, the two worlds have scarcely touched, let alone engaged with each other either in theoretical literature or in practice in the UK and the USA, but there is a growing need for more effective connections to be made; a growing acceptance of that need and a desire to see it translated into workable practical propositions. The authors present a series of nine such propositions which begin to offer a path forward, to breach the symbolic orders of individual disciplines and to create stronger ways of thinking and working.

Kitchen and Schneider's paper thus raises the important questions of how habituses 'fit' together and how that might happen. Is co-ordination among habituses itself a game that is part of (some) habituses? Should differences in habitus be tolerated or do we need to go beyond toleration? Grahame Thompson poses this second question when he asks how is it possible to live together in a world full of different habituses? He recommends that a new habitus of 'relative social peace' is necessary at the level of the international system. A habitus of toleration would cultivate 'a style of behaviour that embodies a studied indifference towards difference'.

Thompson outlines a number of conditions and principles that might form the basis for such a relative social peace of toleration. He admits the speculative nature of his list which includes the search for truces rather than truths. Truces offer 'in-between' opportunities for reflection and trust building. 'They provide an occasion to seek compromise and consensus, an opportunity to build cooperation and reconciliation.'

Chantal Mouffe goes further. At a state level she argues the real threat to liberal democratic institutions to be the increasing marginalisation of entire groups who are unable to identify with its values; groups of people whose sense of place is that they do not have a place in society as it currently stands. Such groups then attempt to resist the dominant values of society by various non-democratic means. Mouffe posits that there is a need to halt such resistance, not simply by rationally justifying democracy as a procedure, but by reaffirming a democratic habitus which enables the construction of democratic forms of individuality.

Mouffe urges the valorisation of 'the diversity of ways in which the "democratic game" can be played'. Such valorisation would entail opening up new fields of application for traditional concepts of value pluralism, liberty and equality in an agonistic pluralism which recognises the importance of discord in democracy rather than emphasising creation of rational consensus. 'A well functioning democracy calls for a vibrant clash of democratic political positions. Too much emphasis on consensus, together with aversion towards confrontations, leads to apathy and to disaffection with political participation.'

Bearing in mind Grahame Thompson's caveat that whilst we should perhaps tolerate the intolerant, this does not necessarily mean tolerating the intolerable, both Leonie Sandercock and John Friedmann advocate moving beyond toleration towards a vision of the city as a coming together of strangers. For the city to become a vital public sphere, Sandercock argues that urban fears and common goals need to be communicated and negotiated, while Friedmann advocates a four-pronged approach to integrating transnational migrants both socially and politically at the level of local government. Going well beyond toleration, the aim of Friedmann's approach would be 'to create an environment in which local places, torn apart by migrant settlement, can be sutured and healed and begin to become proactive on their own behalf'.

Steve Pile too seeks more than toleration. He talks of appeasement, of redress of the injustices of the past, of the completion of unfinished business if we are to 'exorcise the city's ghosts ... without losing sight of their accusations of injustice, both past, present and future'.

Durable and/or Mutable Habitus?

The question of the durability of habitus is probably the greatest challenge facing the concept. Pierre Bourdieu writes in his Introduction that 'the habitus is a fate, not a destiny'. 'Being a product of history, it may be changed by history', by new experiences. He suggests that the model of a vicious circle of structure producing habitus which in turn reproduces structure is a misrecognition of his work.

In this volume, Bourdieu indicates that where dispositions encounter conditions different from those in which they were constructed, there is a dialectical confrontation between habitus and the confronted objective structures. He continues: 'In this confrontation, habitus operates as a structuring structure able to selectively perceive and to transform the objective structure according to its own structure while, at the same time, being restructured, transformed in its makeup by the pressure of the objective structure'. Bourdieu accepts that habitus may change, and in fact does so constantly, but within limits inherent in its originary structure. He suggests that wholesale conversions are 'very exceptional and, in most cases, provisional'.

Both Roxana Waterson and John Friedmann challenge Bourdieu's claim for the long-lasting durability of the habitus. Roxana Waterson criticises Bourdieu for having presented in his earlier work an 'overwhelmingly conservative' image of society which fails to examine in depth the potentials for incompetent performance, resistance or change. Quoting from Bourdieu's *The Logic of Practice* (1980), she questions a conception of history based in 'constancy' and 'permanence' and provides evidence from her work with the Sa'dan Toraja in Indonesia of the disintegration of a religion-based habitus. Waterson indicates the creation of a hybrid form of habitus, adapted to the needs of survival in a modern world. She suggests that with an increasing rate of change in the twenty-first century, individuals, especially those from previously relatively isolated societies, are 'likely to become ever more self-conscious about what elements of the habitual repertoire they choose to maintain or to reject, and may end up transiting across several habituses in the course of a single lifetime'.

This point is reinforced by John Friedmann who criticises Pierre Bourdieu's conception of habitus for not explicitly tying it to a theory of social change. He then goes beyond Bourdieu's notion of a 'second birth' to suggest that habitus can be altered fundamentally by activities such as migration. Friedmann hypothetically takes several Algerian Kabyle families on a 'mental journey' to a new life in urban Germany. He does this in order to answer the question of what happens to habitus in circumstances where people choose or are forced to enter another field than that in which they are 'at home'?

Friedmann suggests not only that individual and collective habituses may be adapted to new experiences and circumstances, but he also proposes that habitus may actually break down under conditions where the existing social order is disrupted. Citing examples from Rwanda, Liberia, Somalia, Kosovo, Chechnya and the reputedly 'stable' societies of Japan and the United States of America, Friedmann contends that 'the twinned concept of habitus/field is a great deal more malleable than Bourdieu suggests'.

Other authors stress the relative durability of habitus. Fay Gale demonstrates that in outback Australia, a colonial habitus which regards indigenous Aboriginal people as inferior to white Australians persists to this day. Whilst hundreds of thousands of Australians may walk for

Reconciliation, a colonial habitus is sufficiently enduring that the Prime Minister, John Howard, still refuses to say 'sorry' for past injustices to the stolen generation.

Barry Hindess' chapter also indicates the durability of a liberal colonial habitus. He questions the extent to which the 'end of empire' has really transformed the habitus of people and places once thought to require authoritarian rule and argues that the 'post-colonial liberal condition' retains much of the colonialist habitus. The 'great liberal project of improving the people' remains, albeit now marketed under the label of development, but 'its underlying aims have barely changed'.

More perturbing is Hindess' final paragraph, in which he refers to the persistence of this project amongst liberal minorities in the now independent states. The suggestion is that, like colonial administrators before them, liberals in these societies regard the people as not yet ready to govern themselves – a view which, combined with a positive commitment to non-Western values, provides a 'culturally specific liberal rationale for authoritarian rule'. The 'post-colonial' states now find themselves in a domesticated version of the earlier colonial habitus.

Finally, several authors address the issue of whether certain habituses need to change to meet the demands of the twenty-first century. Grahame Thompson somewhat optimistically advocates a new habitus of toleration and relative social peace if nations are to survive together in an increasingly fragmenting international system.

The chapter by Joe Painter illustrates what could be several instances of changes to habitus. In what was 'an unusually decentralising move' for a British Conservative government, Government Offices for the Regions were established and collaboration encouraged between different government departments. However, decentralisation did not penetrate as deeply as to include elected representation at a regional scale.

The incoming Labour administration, which theoretically possessed a regional habitus, created the Regional Development Agencies, again however, lacking elected representation and demonstrating a 'heavy hand of the centre' overshadowing their work. Strategies are based on a 'set of assumptions about regional development that can be traced back to ... the late 1980s'. Is this really a change of habitus or rather an old habitus in a glossy new package?

Patsy Healey demonstrates the durability of a local government's habitus of its place on the national stage and its paternalist attitude towards its citizens. Its new strategic vision for the inner city might talk of the future and aim to displace the past, yet it still incorporates its old habitus in terms of both its content and mode of articulation. Healey states that this old habitus needs to be transformed. There is a new game being played for which the city council needs to develop a feel if it is to be successful. 'Maybe it is only through the uncomfortable pressure of citizen mobilisation that councillors and officials can collectively accept and undertake the deep re-thinking which could transform practices as well as discourses in a profound way.'

Steve Pile refers to city dwellers' non-sense of place of the dead and the not-yet-born. He suggests that if there is to be justice for the dead and the possibility of redemption for those yet-to-come, urban dwellers must change their habitus. There is a need to change habitus in order to exorcise the ghosts of the dead without losing sight of their accusations of injustice. 'Transformation (as the future), then, requires an attuning and adjustment to the feelings and affects of the present and the past, in search of a way of appeasing and giving justice to the accusing dead, in search of a form of justice that does not put the not-yet-born through the same injustices.'

Val Plumwood's call for a changed habitus resonates with that of Steve Pile. Her plea is for an Australian habitus which does justice to nature via a non-abusive land ethic and culture. She identifies a need to challenge the existing colonial habitus and to engage with the land as an independent presence on its own terms. The decolonisation of Australian place names could, she argues, serve as a beginning.

Conclusion

All the authors who have contributed chapters to this volume envisage making the world a better place in which to live. In their own ways each author offers a vision of a habitus which, albeit often in small ways, could begin to change the world. Some contributions contain exciting new explorations of aspects of habitus not previously focal to Bourdieu's own elaboration; some contain criticisms of Bourdieu's elaboration of habitus, and several propose ways of expanding it. Whether relating to the macro-level of international political structures and activities or the micro-level of local built environment architectural and planning decisions, the dynamic contingencies of the twenty-first century are demanding adjustment and transformation. We hope that this volume provides some insights, through the lens of habitus, into transformations that are occurring in the world, and offers some indications of how adjustments may be made.

In the words of Pierre Bourdieu, 'habitus is a fate, not a destiny'.[5]

Notes

1   Putnam's (1993) well known account of social capital formation in Italy develops Bourdieu's notion of social capital and has subsequently spawned what might be termed a 'social capital industry' with government initiatives internationally aimed at provision of incentives for creation of social capital, regarded virtually universally as a 'good thing'. See for example, Gittell and Vidal (1998); Williams and Windebank (2000).
2   See Bourdieu, (1992, 1989).
3   'Phronesis' is variously translated as practical wisdom or prudence. It goes beyond both analytical and technical knowledges and involves an instinctive knowledge of how to behave in particular circumstances. See Flyvbjerg (1993; 2001) and Hillier (1995).
4   See Bourdieu and Wacquant (1992: 128) for explanation of how opinion 'falls right' without knowing how or why and actors do what they 'have to do' without conscious calculation.
5   'Fate' represents one's lot in life, i.e. that from which one has come (French, *le sort*). 'Destiny' represents one's future (French, *la destinée*).

References

Bourdieu, P. and Wacquant, L. (1992) 'The purpose of reflexive sociology (the Chicago workshop)', in Bourdieu, P. and Wacquant, L. *An Invitation to Reflexive Sociology*, Cambridge, Polity Press: 61-215.
Bourdieu, P. and Wacquant L. (1992) *An Invitation to Reflexive Sociology*, Cambridge, Polity Press.
Bourdieu, P. (1977) *Outline of a Theory of Practice*, Cambridge, Cambridge University Press.
Bourdieu, P. (1980) *The Logic of Practice*, Stanford, Stanford University Press.
Bourdieu, P. (1986) 'The forms of capital', in Richardson J. (ed.) *Handbook of Theory and Research in the Sociology of Education*, Connecticut, Greenwood: 241-258.
Bourdieu, P. (1987) 'What makes a social class? On the theoretical and practical existence of groups', *Berkeley Journal of Sociology*, 32: 1-18.
Bourdieu, P. (1989) 'Social space and symbolic power', *Sociological Theory*, 7(1): 14-25.
Bourdieu, P. (1990) 'Droit et passe-droit. Le champ des pouvoirs territoriaux et la mise en oeuvre des réglements', *Actes de la Recherche en Sciences Sociales*, 81/82: 86-96.
Bourdieu, P. *et al.* (1993) *The Weight of the World*, Cambridge, Polity Press.
Bourdieu, P. (1998) *Acts of Resistance*, Cambridge, Polity Press.
Bourdieu, P. (2000) *Pascalian Meditations*, Cambridge, Polity Press.
Calhoun, C. (2000) 'Pierre Bourdieu', in Ritzer, G. (ed.) *The Blackwell Companion to Major Social Theorists*, Oxford, Blackwell: 696-730.
Flyvbjerg, B. (1993) 'Aristotle, Foucault and Progressive Phronesis: outline of an applied ethics for sustainable development', in Winkler, E. and Coombs, J. (eds) *Applied Ethics: a Reader*, New York, Blackwell: 11-27.
Flyvbjerg, B. (2001) *Making Social Science Matter*. Cambridge, Cambridge University Press.
Giddens, A. (1976) *New Rules of Sociological Method*, London, Hutchinson.
Giddens, A. (1977) *Central Problems in Social Theory*, Hutchinson, London.

Gittell, R. and Vidal A. (1998) *Community Organising: building social capital as a development strategy*, Thousand Oaks, Sage.

Hillier, J. (1995) 'The Unwritten Law of Planning Theory: Common Sense', *Journal of Planning Education and Research*, 14(4): 292-296.

Lemke, J. (1995) *Textual Politics*, London, Taylor & Francis.

Painter, J. (2000) 'Pierre Bourdieu', in Crang, M. and Thrift, N. (eds) *Thinking Space*, London, Routledge: 239-259.

Putnam, R. (1993) *Making Democracy Work*, Princeton, Princeton University Press.

Schwartz, D. (1997) *Culture and Power*, Chicago, University of Chicago Press.

Taylor, C. (1999) 'To follow a rule. …', in Shusterman, R. (ed.) *Bourdieu: a critical reader*, Oxford, Blackwell: 29-44.

Wacquant, L. (1972) 'Toward a social praxeology: the structure and logic of Bourdieu's sociology', in Bourdieu P. and Wacquant, L. *An Invitation to Reflexive Sociology*, Cambridge, Polity Press: 1-59.

Williams, C. and Windebank J. (2000) 'Rebuilding social capital in deprived urban neighbourhoods', *Town & Country Planning*, December: 351-353.

2 Habitus

PIERRE BOURDIEU

I must confess that I have a very strong feeling of responsibility as I contribute to reviving and elaborating the concept of habitus which is at the centre of discussion in this volume. So I hope that I shall be able to justify in this Introduction the confidence which the authors have put in this notion, which is in my view very important and indispensable to understand truly and adequately human action.

I want to address first a set of questions which were sent to me and which relate to the use of the notion of habitus, particularly in contemporary Western cities: in our fast-changing world, demanding from all of us multiple 'roles' and quick adjustments, is habitus still a useful research tool? Is it possible to use it efficiently in spatial analysis or, more precisely, in relation to space, meaning both geographic space and social space? Is it possible to use architecture, and especially the symbolic power of architecture, in order to restructure habitus and to break up the supposed vicious cycle obtaining between structures and habitus? In a word, is habitus a definitely *static concept*, intrinsically doomed to express continuities and to repetition, suited to social analysis in relatively stable societies and stationary situations, and only that? Could we use this concept to understand and explain situations of rapid change and to account for social transformation and for the tremendous changes we observe in contemporary societies, including at the level of daily life?

It is difficult to attempt to answer in a completely satisfactory manner such questions about habitus in a semi-improvised and very short Introduction, so I take the liberty of inviting readers to look at the book I published with my colleague and friend Loïc Wacquant, *An Introduction to Reflexive Sociology*, in which you will find a very thorough and precise discussion of all the problems concerning this concept. Now, I must first recall the definition of habitus as a system of *dispositions*, that is of permanent manners of being, seeing, acting and thinking, or a system of *long-lasting* (rather than permanent) schemes or schemata or structures of perception, conception and action. The word disposition, being more familiar, less exotic, than habitus, is important to give a more concrete intuition of what habitus is, and to remind you what is at stake in the use of such a concept, namely a peculiar philosophy of action, or better, of practice, sometimes characterised as *dispositional*. This philosophy is opposed to the Cartesian philosophy of action which is revived today in the tradition of *homo oeconomicus* as a rational agent, who chooses the best means, the best strategies by a conscious calculation oriented towards the maximisation of profits and, more generally, in the sociological current called 'Methodological Individualism', which accepts the same presuppositions concerning the logic of human action.

Now, a brief comment on the other aspect of the definition, that is, on the word *system*. As I tried to show in my book *Distinction*, the habitus of a determinate person – or of a group of persons occupying a similar or neighbouring position in social space – is in a sense very systematic: all the elements of his or her behaviour have something in common, a kind of affinity of *style*, like the works of the same painter or, to take a example from Maurice Merleau-Ponty, like the handwriting of a person who keeps her style, immediately recognisable, when she writes with instruments as diverse as a pencil, a pen or a piece of chalk and on media as different as a sheet of paper and a blackboard. So this example gives a concrete intuition of this systematicity. It is not a logical systematicity; it is a practical systematicity. There are discrepancies, there are exceptions, but the word 'style' indicates very well this practical unity. When I conducted my survey about practices in the domain of art, whose results were published in the book *Distinction*, I had in mind to break with the tendency of most of the socio-psychologists to study human behaviour by slices. They have studied attitudes towards art, attitudes toward politics, attitudes towards sport, attitudes towards painting and so on, through specialised surveys, directed only at an aspect of the behaviour of the person/s studied. So using a questionnaire, which was difficult to elaborate, I tried to study the behaviour of people in very different domains from what they like in terms of food, to what they like in terms of music passing by what they like in terms of sport with the hypothesis that there was some unity. I had in mind the intention to demonstrate this unity of human behaviour on one side and on the other side to break down a division which is very important in our implicit vision of aesthetics. This is the division between noble, noble practices, music, painting and so on and common practices like things of sex, of food and so on. And by making visible this unity I wanted to destroy the dichotomy, which is the basis of a kind of aesthetic racism, which is very common amongst cultivated persons.

So the best example of the unity of human behaviour of a person, but also of a group, is the *lifestyle* – again the word style – of the 'petty bourgeoisie', which may be recognised in their manner (a synonym of style, or in German, *Art*) of speaking (characterised by hypercorrectness in their language), of saving (they are thrifty in their manner), of loving (they have very few children), and so on. For in these things which are apparently independent, and that common sociology does not study together, fertility, artistic tastes, political opinions and so on, there is some unity. By emphasising this unity I am conscious of the danger of being seen as promoting the idea that human behaviour is monolithic and this is something that is sometimes said against the notion of habitus. But human behaviour is not monolithic. It is very open, very diverse, but within limits, and the idea of lifestyle is suited to express this loose systematicity which characterises human behaviour.

In that respect, habitus is very similar to what was traditionally called character, but with a very important difference: the habitus, as the Latin indicates, is something *non natural*, a set of *acquired* characteristics which are the product of social conditions and which, for that reason, may be totally or partially common to people who have been the product of similar social conditions (such as individuals occupying petty bourgeois positions in different societies or at different epochs). There is another difference which follows from the fact that the habitus is not something natural, inborn: being a product of history, that is of social experience and education, it may be *changed by history*, that is by new experiences, education or training (which implies that aspects of what remains unconscious in habitus be made at least partially conscious and explicit). Dispositions are long-lasting: they tend to perpetuate, to reproduce themselves, but they are not eternal. They may be changed by historical action oriented by intention and consciousness and using pedagogic devices. (One has an example in the correction of an accent of pronunciation.) A linguistic habitus, for example, is a product of primary education and cannot be corrected completely despite all one's efforts. It is the same with any kind of ethical habit. Any dimension of habitus is very difficult to change but it may be changed through this process of awareness and of pedagogic effort.

The habitus is not a fate, not a destiny. I must insist on this, as I have done many times before, against the interpretation which was proposed and imposed by some of the first reviews of my work and then constantly repeated by most of the English-speaking commentators (as if they spent more time reading the previous exegeses – according to a scholastic tradition which dictates that every reviewer reviews all the previous reviews at the beginning of his or her review). The model of the circle, the vicious cycle of structure producing habitus which reproduces structure *ad infinitum* is a product of commentators.

First, this closed circle is a *particular case*, namely, the case in which the objective conditions in which the habitus operates are similar to the objective conditions of which it is the product. That is not very common, but it happens even in fast changing societies like ours. For example in my book *Masculine Domination*, I try to show that the main structures of masculine domination are maintained, and survive since the Neolithic time. The opposition we make between soft and hard, software and hardware, soft sciences and hard sciences and this opposition, which is a mythical opposition, according to which everything which is soft, which is flexible, and so on, is feminine and everything which is hard is masculine, this opposition is at once an objective opposition, which may be found in objective structures, like, in universities, the opposition between masculine and feminine disciplines, for instance physics and economics versus psychology or art history, and 'subjective' cognitive structures which are dimensions of habitus. When you look at the statistics of the distribution according to gender between the disciplines for example in medicine, you will find a systematic difference between male and female doctors according to the medical discipline they are studying or practising, surgery or dermatology for instance.

When you look at the statistics you can see that the old mythical opposition still works. All the natural sciences are more masculine in terms of students, in terms of professors and so on. Why does it work? Because it is incorporated in our minds, that is in our bodies, and we act in the world according to this structure and by so doing we tend to contribute to reproduce this structure.

Secondly, even in traditional societies or in specific sectors of modern societies, habitus is never a mere principle of repetition – that is the difference between habitus and habit. As a dynamic system of dispositions that interact with one another, it has, as such, a generative capacity; it is a structured principle of invention, similar to a generative grammar able to produce an infinite number of new sentences according to determinate patterns and within determinate limits. The habitus is a generative grammar *but it is not an inborn generative grammar* as in Chomsky's tradition which is related to the Cartesian tradition. It is a principle of invention, a principle of improvisation. The habitus generates inventions and improvisations but within limits.

Thirdly, in all the cases where dispositions encounter conditions (including fields) different from those in which they were constructed and assembled, there is a *dialectical confrontation* between habitus, as structured structure, and objective structures. In this confrontation, habitus operates as a structuring structure able to selectively perceive and to transform the objective structure according to its own structure while, at the same time, being re-structured, transformed in its makeup by the pressure of the objective structure. This means, that in rapidly changing societies, habitus changes constantly, continuously, but within the limits inherent in its originary structure, that is within certain bounds of continuity (wholesale conversions are very exceptional and, in most cases, provisional, as one can see with the example of the students of bourgeois origin who made, around 1968, radical conversions to radical politics which, for most of them, did not last long – many of these 'radicals' were among the inventors of neo-liberal conservatism). I could take as an example of such tensions between objective structures and habitus, the dialectical confrontation between habitus and the place that one inhabits in geographic space, and correlatively, through housing and living conditions, in social space (I take the liberty of inviting those of you who are interested in the dispositional bases and socio-economic conditions of housing in Algeria and in France to look at my books *Algeria 60* and *Social Structures of the Economy*).

In other words, habitus must not be considered in isolation. Rather, it must be used in relation to the notion of field which contains a principle of dynamics by itself as well as in relation to habitus. This would require a long demonstration. A few indications will suffice: first, as a space of *forces* or determinations, every field is inhabited by tensions and contradictions which are at the origin (basis) of conflicts; this means that it is simultaneously a field of struggles or competitions which generate change. In such fields, and in the *struggles* which take place in them, every agent acts according to his position (that is, according to the capital he or she possesses) and his habitus, related to his personal history. His actions, words, feelings, deeds, works, and so on, stem from the confrontation between dispositions and positions, which are more often than not mutually adjusted, but may be at odds, discrepant, divergent, even in some sense contradictory. In such cases, as one can observe in history, innovations may appear, when people *en porte-à-faux*, misfits, who are put into question by structures (operating through the positions) are able to challenge the structure, sometimes to the point of remaking it. It means that it is possible to understand and explain the most extraordinary intellectual or artistic revolutions on condition that one takes into account (and accounts for) both the *subversive habitus* of the revolutionary agent – as I tried to do with Beethoven in music, Flaubert in literature, Manet in painting or even Heidegger in philosophy – and the field to which they were confronted, and the relation, the tension, the dynamic friction, between them.

I should develop this at length, but I want to come back to what seems to me the main epistemic function of the concept of habitus. I want to analyse briefly the case of artistic practice, especially painting or poetry (leaving aside architecture which is in some respects a very intellectual or intellectualist art, but which can anyway be understood according to the schema I propose to describe literature). The tradition of aesthetics is interested in the work of art as such, as *opus operatum*, work already done, finished, that it comments to great lengths (observing how such artwork is constructed, its composition, the equilibrium of colours, etc.). It does not analyse as such the 'work in progress', as James Joyce said, and the mode of production of that work, that is the *modus operandi*, the manner of acting, the *art* in the etymological sense, that the artist brings into play, 'met en œuvre', as we say in French, that is literally, brings into work. This art, this manner of doing, this *modus operandi*, this style, is his habitus, his *métier*, his craftsmanship, that is, a practical mastery without theory, without theoretical mastery of practical mastery. The notion of habitus, and the idea of practical mastery, practical logic, and so on, necessitate and effect a radical break with the scholastic bias that threatens most of the analysts of art, as teachers, that is *lectores*, scholars (as analysed in my book *Pascalian Meditations*). The scholastic bias is the tendency, very common among scholars, to put a scholastic mind, a scholar's mind into everyone's head – for instance to treat an artist like Manet or Flaubert, or any common person, including the scholar himself when he or she acts in everyday life, as a rational agent, an *homo calculans*. The most accomplished example of this illusion is *homo oeconomicus*, an academic man (of academic situations only) put into the head of any economic agent.

If it is so difficult to impose this dispositional theory of action, it is in my view because we have incorporated (as a part of our habitus of cultivated persons) a scholastic principle of vision and division, a *scholastic unconscious* in which we find a prefabricated series of oppositions, mind vs. body, subject vs. object, ego vs. alter ego, reflection vs. action, reason vs. emotion, etc., which prevents us from understanding practice and the logic of practice, that is, for example, the practical reflection which is very practically, and invisibly, involved in the countless minute choices, perfectly improvised and perfectly necessary, that one is able to operate instantaneously at every moment of life and whose achieved product one discovers, at the end, almost like a spectator. This logic is in one sense very simple, but in another sense very difficult to express, because one has to be a professional of reflection (that is, a scholar socially inclined to scholastic bias as well as distanced from the practical experience of practice, such as artistic practice) to produce a reflection on the limits of the scholastic mode of thinking, of the scholastic habitus and to make explicit the practical reflexivity which is traditionally ignored (and despised) by theoretical reflection (in part, because, especially in artistic domain, there is a quasi-mystical and mystifying exaltation of 'creation' which obscures yet even more the logic of artistic practice). As I tried to show in my book *Pascalian Meditations*, a genuine reflection able to go beyond the limits of the scholastic illusion, the true Maïa veil of the ancient Buddhist tradition, will discover that most of the objects of the philosophical tradition exist as such only by an effect of scholastic reflection – e.g., the lived body (*Leib* or *corps propre*) is not, in ordinary experience, an object for us, but an integral part of the perceiving subject; likewise other humans are not objects but alter egos.

So, to answer the question sincerely, and in a manner that I hope will not appear too arrogant, I hold that the concept of habitus is a very useful tool, indeed an indispensable instrument for social analysis. But to realise this, one must first rid it of all the misinterpretations it has received, and use it carefully, with theoretical rigour or, better yet, with a practical mastery of its properties – for sociology, too, is an art ...

References

Bourdieu, P. (1979) *Algeria 1960*, Cambridge, Cambridge University Press, (*Algérie 60*, Paris, Minuit, 1977).

Bourdieu, P. (1984) *Distinction: a social critique of the judgement of time*, Cambridge, Mass, Harvard University Press. (*La Distinction*, Minuit, Paris, 1979).

Bourdieu, P. (2000) *Pascalian Meditations*, Cambridge, Polity Press, (*Méditation pascaliennes*, Paris, Éditions du Seuil, collection *Liber*, 1997).

Bourdieu, P. (2001) *Masculine Domination*, Cambridge, Polity Press, (*La Domination Masculine*, Paris, Éditions du Seuil, collection *Liber*, 1998).

Bourdieu, P. (2001) *Social Structures of the Economy*, forthcoming, (*Les Structures Sociales de l'Économie*, Paris, Éditions du Seuil, collection *Liber*, 2000).

Bourdieu, P. and Wacquant, L. (1992) *An Invitation to Reflexive Sociology*, Cambridge, Polity Press.

POLITICS OF
SPACE AND PLACE

3   Democracy and the Question of Power*

ERNESTO LACLAU

Discussion on the viability of democracy in what can be broadly conceived as a 'postmodern' age has mainly turned around two central issues: 1) does not the current dispersion and fragmentation of political actors conspire against the emergence of strong social identities which could operate as nodal points for the consolidation and expansion of democratic practices?; and 2) is not this very multiplicity the source of a particularism of social aims which could result in the dissolution of the wider emancipatory discourses considered as constitutive of the democratic imaginary?

The first issue is connected with the increasing awareness of the ambiguities of those very social movements about which so many sanguine hopes were conceived in the 1970s. There is no doubt that their emergence involved an expansion of the egalitarian imaginary to increasingly wider areas of social relations. However, it also became progressively clearer that such an expansion does not necessarily lead to the aggregation of the plurality of demands around a broader collective will (in the Gramscian sense). Some years ago, for instance, in San Francisco there was widespread belief in the potential for the formation of a powerful popular pole, given the proliferation of demands coming from blacks, Chicanos, and gay people. Nothing of the kind, however, happened, among other reasons because the demands of each of these groups clashed with those of the others. Even more: does not this fragmentation of social demands make it easier for the state apparatuses to deal with them in an administrative fashion – which results in the formation of all types of clientelistic networks, capable of neutralising any democratic opening? The horizontal expansion itself of those demands which the political system has to be sensitive to conspires against their vertical aggregation in a popular will capable of challenging the existing status quo. Political projects such as the 'third way' or the 'radical centre' clearly express this ideal of creating a state apparatus sensitive to some extent to social demands, but which operates as an instrument of demobilisation.

As for the second issue, its formulation runs along parallel lines. With the breaking up of the totalising discourses of modernity, we are running the risk of being confronted with a plurality of social spaces, governed by their own aims and rules of constitution, leaving any management of the community – conceived in a global sense – in the hands of a technobureaucracy located beyond any democratic control. With this, the notion of a public sphere, to which was always linked the *very possibility* of a democratic experience, is seriously put into question. One has only to think of Lyotard's image of the social space as consisting of a multiplicity of incommensurable language games, in which any mediation between them can only be conceived as *tort*, as an external interference which some exercise over the others.

These statements are, however, overdrawn and unilateral. For they present too rosy a picture of those features of the classical democratic experiences and discourses which the 'postmodern condition' is undermining, while ignoring the possibilities of deepening such experiences that the new cultures of particularity and difference are opening. We could, in some respects, present the ensemble of the democratic tradition as dominated by an essential ambiguity: on the one hand, democracy was the attempt to organise the political space around the *universality* of the community, without hierarchies and distinctions. Jacobinism was the name of the earliest and most extreme of these efforts to constitute *one* people. On the other hand, democracy has also been conceived as the expansion of the logic of equality to increasingly wider spheres of social relations – social and economic equality, racial equality, gender equality, etc. From this point of view, democracy constitutively involves respect for differences. It goes without saying that the unilateralisation of either of these tendencies leads to a perversion of democracy as a political regime. The first is confronted with the paradox of asserting an *unmediated* universality which, however, can only be obtained on the basis of *universalising* some particularities within the community. The implicit ethnocentrism permeating the discourses of many vociferous defenders of universal reason is well known. But democracy, unilaterally conceived as the respect of difference, equally very quickly confronts its own limits, which threaten to transform it into its very opposite – i.e., it can lead to an acceptance without challenge of the 'actually existing' cultural communities, ignoring the forces which, within them, fight to break their narrow and conservative cultural limits.

Thus, the ambiguity of democracy can be formulated in the following terms: it requires unity, but it is only thinkable through diversity. If either of these two incompatible dimensions prevails beyond a certain point, democracy becomes impossible. That several forms of this tension are making democracy fragile in Western Europe is only too evident – witness the difficult questions concerning the status of immigrants in European countries and the explosion of all kinds of particularisms.

How are we to deal, however, with these tensions and this ambiguity once it is recognised that its terms are unavoidable but that there is no way of finding any impeccable, square-circle, solution to the problem that they pose? Our first step should, certainly, be to accept that both tensions and ambiguity are here to stay and that our only alternative is not to attempt to suppress them but to find a practical way of coping with them. What, then, does 'coping' mean in this connection? One first and, apparently, obvious answer would be: 'to negotiate'. This is, however, too easy an answer, among other things because it is not at all clear what is involved in *a practical* negotiation. If it involves finding an ideal point of agreement between what initially appeared as incompatible trends – as in a dialogical situation conceived *à la* Habermas – it is clear that the solution is theoretical and not practical, and that the term 'negotiation' is actually excessive. If, however, the outcome of the negotiation is that each of the intervening forces maintains its own separate, incommensurable identity and obtains as much as it can – given its relative strength – we are simply in the terrain of Lyotard's 'tort'. It is difficult to see what can result from it as far as *democratic* politics is concerned.

Perhaps, however, the solution has to be found elsewhere, moving resolutely away from the logic of 'negotiation'. Perhaps the way of properly approaching the riddle of democracy is to ask oneself whether one does not have to question the silent assumption on which both the unilateralisation of incompatible trends and the negotiation between them is based: namely, the assumption that any language game that one can play within that incompatibility finds in the latter an absolute limit. Would it not be possible to engage, starting from that incompatibility of different practices, to tropologically contaminate, for instance, one incompatible trend with the other and to explore the political productivity which derives from this contamination? Perhaps the universal and the particular, the substantive and the procedural, are less impenetrable to each other *once* ambiguity (or undecidability) is accepted as the terrain from which any strategico-political move has to start.

Let us begin by considering some classical categories of political analysis and putting them under the pressure of the contradictory requirements dictated by the ambiguity of the democratic logic. We will see that this contradiction is not an absolute limit, but rather the condition of possibility of more complex language games which throw some light on the discursive spaces which make democracy possible. Let me say, to start with, that 'hegemony' is for me the central category of political analysis. I conceive it as a special way of articulating the universal and the particular which avoids the two extremes of a foundationalist universalism – Rawls, Habermas – and a particularism which denies the possibility of any kind of mediating logic between incompatible language games. I have defined 'hegemony' in my work as the type of political relation by which a particularity assumes the representation of an (impossible) universality entirely incommensurable with it.[1] It is, as a result, a relation of transient and contingent *incarnation*. To this I will add that I see democracy as a type of regime which makes fully visible the contingent character of the hegemonic link. I will organise my argument around four theses. Each will start by defining a dimension of the hegemonic link and will later derive some conclusions from each of these dimensions for the understanding of the democratic logic.

First Thesis: Asymmetry and Power

As we said, the hegemonic link presupposes a constitutive asymmetry between universality and particularity. This broadly corresponds to the distinction established by Gramsci between a corporative and a hegemonic class. All groups are particularities within the social, structured around specific interests. But they only become hegemonic when they take up the representation of the universality of the community conceived as a whole. The question is, of course, how such a representation is possible. To start elaborating an answer to this problem, it is worthwhile quoting two texts by Marx. The first can be seen as the zero degree of hegemony:

> The proletariat is coming into being in Germany as a result of the rising *industrial* development ... By proclaiming the *dissolution of the hitherto world order*, the proletariat merely states the *secret of its own existence*, for it *is in fact the* dissolution of that world order. By demanding the *negation of private property*, the proletariat simply raises to the rank of a principle of *society* what society has made the principle of the *proletariat*, what, without its own cooperation, is already incorporated in it as the negative result of society.[2]

That is, there is no dialectic between the corporative and the hegemonic dimensions: the *particular* body of the proletariat represents, by itself, unmediated universality. The difference between this road to emancipation and a hegemonic one can be seen by contrasting the above passage with the following one from the same essay, in which all the structural moments of the hegemonic operation are contained *in nuce:*

> On what is a partial, a merely political revolution based? On the fact that *part of civil society* emancipates itself and attains *general* domination; on the fact that a definite class, proceeding from its *particular situation*, undertakes the general emancipation of society ... For the *revolution of a nation and the emancipation of a particular class of civil society to coincide*, for *one* estate to be acknowledged as the state of the whole society, all the defects of society must conversely be concentrated in another class, a particular estate must be looked upon as the *notorious crime* of the whole of society, so that liberation from that sphere appears as general self-liberation.[3]

Unlike the first road, which consisted in a non-political emancipation (for civil society constructed the universality of the community without passing through a separate political sphere), the second road presupposes political mediation as a constitutive moment (the identification of the interests of a particular class with those of society as a whole). And if for Marx only the first road constitutes true and ultimate emancipation, it is enough that the prospect of the emergence of a 'universal class', grounded in the simplification of class structure under capitalism, is not verified for political hegemony to remain the only way towards social emancipation.

The important point for our argument is that the asymmetry between the universality of the task and the particularity of the social agent capable of taking it up is the very condition of politics, for it is only as a result of it that the dualism between civil society and a public sphere could emerge. While for Hegel the duality state/civil society was grounded in a reduction of civil society to the particularism of a system of needs, Marx's dialectic of *political* emancipation (our second passage) involves a process of mutual contamination between particularity and universality which gives emancipation its political character.

Now, if a certain particularity is able to lead the struggle against a regime perceived as a 'general' or 'notorious' crime, it is not so much because its differential, ontic particularity predetermines it to play such a hegemonic role, but because – given a certain constellation of forces – it is the only one which has the power to do so. Without this unevenness of power at the level of civil society there would be neither 'politics' nor 'hegemony' (at the limit, both terms are synonymous as both are alternative ways of naming the constitutive asymmetry between universality and particularity). Here we find a first defining dimension of the hegemonic relation: *unevenness of power is constitutive of it.*

This can be seen even more clearly if we compare the hegemonic (i.e., political) link with some non-political ways of reaching the universality of the community – Hobbes's Leviathan and Marx's notion of *human* emancipation (the one alluded to in our first quotation). Hobbes explicitly denies the existence of any unevenness of power in the 'state of nature'. For him, in the state of nature, all members of society have equal power. As a result, as each tends to its own aims, which clash with those of all the others, there is a constitutive stalemate. Society is radically unable to create, by itself, any social 'order'. The consequence is that the covenant which surrenders *total* power to the sovereign cannot be a *political* act, as it is just the rational decision of all members of society and does not presuppose any clash between antagonistic wills. For strictly the opposite reasons, the same elimination of politics takes place with the Marxian notion of a fully self-determined, emancipated society. As the proletariat as universal class realises the universality of the community at the level of civil society, no hegemonic articulation is needed to reach the latter. Power and universality are strictly incompatible with each other. The state is there only to start the slow process of its withering away. The Saint-Simonian motto that Marxism incorporated – 'from the government of men to the administration of things' – consummates this transition to a non-political conception of the management of the community.

If we now come back to the question of democracy, we can see that its precondition is the same as the precondition of hegemony: the constitutive asymmetry between universality and particularity. Democracy presupposes that the place of power remains empty (Lefort) and that it does not predetermine in its very structure the nature of the force which is going to occupy it. Unlike a hierarchical society – such as the *Anciens Regimes* – where there is a strict continuity between the universal *form* of the community and the *content* which fills it, democracy presupposes a drastic separation between the two. In order to have democracy we need particular forces that *occupy* the empty place of power but do not identify with it. This means that there is only democracy if the gap between universality and particularity is never filled but is, on the contrary, ever reproduced. Which also means that democracy is only possible on a *hegemonic* terrain. However, the latter implies, as we have seen, that relations of power are constitutive of it, from which we can deduce that power is also constitutive of democracy. While in Marx's notion of human emancipation the obsolescence of power was synonymous with the very substance of the emancipatory process, political emancipation can only mean the displacement of the existent relations of power – the construction of a new power but not its radical elimination. Perceiving this was the historical achievement of Gramsci, whose theory of hegemony subverted Marxist theorisation by introducing an arsenal of new concepts – historical bloc, war of position, integral state, intellectual and moral leadership – which reintroduced the political dimension into the very logic of the emancipatory process. This is highly relevant for contemporary societies, where the fragmentation of social identities gives democracy its specific fragility, but also its inherent political possibilities.

A main conclusion of this argument is that a certain visibility of its own contingency is inherent to democracy – that is, a posing and, at the same time, a withdrawal of its own contents. One has to advance certain concrete, substantial aims in the course of democratic political competition, but at the same time one has to assert *the contingency* of those aims; if one asserted their constitutive character, one would have to assert at the same time that the place of power is not empty, for there would be no democracy if it was not occupied in a certain way. In that case, democracy would be one more substantive blueprint of society. But this is not the case; if democratic visibility involves both the advancing of some aims and the assertion of their contingent character, one has to conclude that an ontological difference between the ontic contents of the aims advanced by the various political forces and a specific ontological dimension permeating those contents, which lies in the permanent assertion of their contingent nature, is constitutive of democracy.

One could present this argument in terms of the distinction between metaphor and metonymy. Metaphor grounds its work in analogical relations; in that sense it tends to essentialise the link between the terms of the analogy (in our case, it tends to suture the relation between the empty place of power and the force occupying it). Metonymy, on the contrary, is grounded in mere relations of contiguity; in that sense, the contingent character of the tropological displacement it initiates becomes fully visible. Democracy is suspended in an undecidable game between metaphor and metonymy: each of the competing forces in the democratic game tends to make as permanent as possible the occupation of the empty place of power; but if there was no simultaneous assertion of the contingent character of this occupation, there would be no democracy. Is this not the same as asserting that the terrain of democracy is that of hegemonic logics?

Second Thesis: Incompleteness and Renegotiation

That power is embedded in hegemony is, however, only a first dimension of the hegemonic link – one which we have explained in terms of the asymmetry between the particularity of the hegemonic force and the universality of the task. But if that was all there is in the hegemonic link, the popular support for the force overthrowing the regime – seen, in Marx's terms, as the 'notorious crime of the whole of society' – would be limited to that act of overthrowing and would not give place to a more permanent identification by which a coincidence arises between the 'revolution of the nation' and the 'emancipation' of a particular class of civil society. What is the source of this more prolonged coincidence without which 'hegemony' would be inconceivable? I think that the answer should be found in the fact that the regime that is a 'notorious crime' is constructed around an internal split of its own identity. It is, on the one hand, this *particular* regime but, on the other, if it is going to be the notorious crime *of the whole of society*, its own particularity has to be seen as the symbol of something different and incommensurable with it: the obstacle which prevents society from coinciding with itself, from reaching its own fullness. Let us just think what happens when society is confronted with generalised disorder: what is needed is *some kind* of order, and the particular content of the force which brings it about becomes a secondary matter. The same happens with oppression: if a regime is seen as incarnating evil or oppression *in general*, its name tendentially loses its concrete reference and becomes the name of the obstacle which prevents society from coinciding with itself. That is why the fall of a repressive regime always liberates forces larger than what that fall, as a concrete event, can master: as the regime was seen as a symbol of oppression in general, all oppressed groups in society live for a moment in the illusion that all unfulfilled demands – in any domain – are going to be met.

It is important to see that this duality of the 'notorious crime' involves the reference to an object to which, strictly speaking, no literal content corresponds. Order, in our example, is just the name for an absent fullness, the positive reverse of a situation negatively perceived as 'disorder'. And the same can be said of other political terms such as 'justice', 'revolution', etc. Being the name of something to which no content *necessarily* corresponds, it borrows such a content from the particular force capable of contingently incarnating that empty universality at any particular moment in time. This is the very definition of the hegemonic operation. We see why, in Marx's terms, the 'emancipation' of a particular sector in society and the 'revolution of the nation' can coincide: because the latter lacks a content of its own and only acquires one through its tropological displacement to the aims of the hegemonic force. If we want to persist in this rhetorical image, we could say that, *sensu stricto*, the hegemonic operation is not only tropological but also of the order of the *cathachresis*, as there is no literal content to name what the *tropoi* refer to.

We can say, in this sense, that the hegemonic operation is only possible insofar as it never fully succeeds in achieving what it attempts – i.e., the total fusion between the universality (fullness) of the communitarian space and the force incarnating such a universal moment. For if such a total suture was possible, it would involve the universal having found its own and undisputed body, and no hegemonic variation would any longer be possible. This incompletion of the hegemonic game is what we call *politics*. The very possibility of a political society depends on the assertion and reproduction of this undecidability in the relation between the universal and the particular. That is why all conceptions of a utopian society in which human essence would have found its ultimate reconciliation with itself have invariably been accompanied by one or another version of the end of politics.

But this also shows that *democracy is the only truly political society*, for it is the only one in which the gap between the (universal) place of power and the substantive forces contingently occupying it is required by the very logic of the regime. In other types of society the place of power is not seen as empty, but as essentially linked to a substantial conception of the common good. So the conditions of democracy, the conditions of hegemony, and the conditions of politics are ultimately the same.

We can summarise our second thesis in the following terms: there is only hegemony if the dichotomy universality/particularity is constantly renegotiated: universality only exists incarnating – and subverting – particularity, but, conversely, no particularity can become political without being the locus of universalising effects. Democracy, as a result, as the instutionalisation of this space of renegotiation, is the only truly political regime.

Third Thesis: Empty Signifiers and Undecidability

We have seen that the representation of a 'notorious crime' splits the identity of the regime embodying it between its concrete, ontic content and its function of signifying the obstacle preventing a society from reconciling with itself. Now, if there is a 'general crime', there should also be a 'general victim'. Society, however, is a plurality of particular groups and demands. So if there is going to be a subject of a certain global emancipation, a subject antagonised by the general crime, it can only be *politically constructed* through the *equivalence* of a plurality of demands.

As a result, these particularities are also split: through their equivalence they do not simply remain themselves, but constitute an area of universalising effects. The equivalence involves that demands cannot be dealt with in isolation from each other, in an administrative way. It is its presence within a chain of equivalences with other demands which gives each its political character: if depoliticising, administrative practices flourish in a realm of pure particularities, the hegemonic articulation of a plurality of demands can only be satisfied through changes in the relation of forces in society. This is what the Gramscian distinction between corporative and hegemonic classes means. A certain universalisation of social actors derives from this aggregation of particularities, which is, to a large extent, the exact opposite of the homogenisation of the emancipatory subject in the Marxian notion of a universal class.

Thus, we have a movement of mutual contamination between the universal and the particular. The universal (the fullness of the community) can only be represented through the aims of the hegemonic sector. It will be, in that sense, a tainted, particularised universality. But the same contamination operates in the opposite direction: as the aims of the hegemonic group come to represent, through their universalisation, a chain of equivalences more extended than those aims themselves, their links with the original demands of that group are weakened. We have, this time, a universalisation of the particular. We can say that, as a result of this double contamination: 1) the more extended the chain of equivalences that a particular hegemonic sector comes to represent and the more its aims become a *name* for global emancipation, the looser will be the links of that name with its original particular meaning and the more it will approach the status of an empty signifier;[4] 2) as this total coincidence of the universal and the particular is, however, impossible – given the constitutive inadequacy of the means of representation – a remainder of particularity cannot be eliminated. The process of naming itself, as it is not constrained by any a priori conceptual limits, is one that will retroactively determine – depending on contingent hegemonic articulations – what is actually named. This means that the transition from Marx's political emancipation to *total* emancipation can never arrive. This shows us a third dimension of the hegemonic relation: *it requires the production of tendentially empty signifiers which, while maintaining the incommensurability between universals and particulars, enable the latter to take up the representation of the former.*

As for democracy, it is precisely this unsolvable tension between the universal and the particular that makes it possible to approach some of its apparently most intractable aporias. A purely formalistic conception of democracy, devoid of any substantive content, leads to the paradox of an entirely procedural approach which makes it possible to abolish those procedures as a result of strictly following them. But an opposite paradox emerges if democracy is so closely linked to a substantive content that the possibility of any hegemonic rearticulation disappears. Both paradoxes actually result from grounding democracy in an absolute terrain – procedural or substantive – which is not shaped by any hegemonic game. If we remain, however, within the latter, we immediately see that the tension between the universal and the particular is constitutive of democracy, as all universal principles are tendentially empty and yet nevertheless retain remainders of particularity giving them their specific historical content. Democracy is simply the name of the terrain of that undecidability between content and procedures (is separating the two not, actually, an artificial intellectual operation?) which can never coalesce into any clear-cut blueprint of society. To give either procedures or content some sort of supra-historical priority is to locate them beyond power, forgetting that democratic relations *are* relations of power, as they presuppose that undecidable game between universality and particularity which gives them their specific hegemonic dimension. This means that democracy requires the social production of empty signifiers and equivalential relations which involve both the posing and the retreat of the particular.

Fourth Thesis: Representation

A corollary of our previous conclusions is that 'representation' is constitutive of the hegemonic relation. The elimination of all representation is the illusion accompanying the notion of a *total* emancipation. But, insofar as the universality of the community is only achievable through the mediation of a particularity, the relation of representation becomes constitutive. We find here the dialectic between name and concept. If representation could succeed to the point of eliminating itself as a meaningful moment – i.e., if the representative was entirely transparent to what it represents – what we would have is the 'concept' having an unchallenged primacy over the 'name' (in Saussurean terms: the signified would entirely subordinate to itself the order of the signifier). But in that case there would be no hegemony, for its very requisite, the production of tendentially empty signifiers, would not obtain. In order to have hegemony we need the sectorial aims of a group to operate as the name for a universality transcending them – this is the synecdoche constitutive of the hegemonic link. But if the name (the signifier) is so attached to the concept (signified) that no displacement in the relation between the two is possible, we cannot have any hegemonic rearticulation. The idea of a totally emancipated and transparent society, from which all tropological movement between its constitutive parts would have been eliminated, involves the end of all hegemonic relations (and also the end of democratic politics). Here we have a fourth dimension of 'hegemony': *the terrain in which it expands is that of the generalisation of the relations of representation as condition of constitution of the social order.* This explains why the hegemonic form of politics tends to become general in our contemporary, globalised world: as the centring of the structures of power tends to increase, any centrality requires that its agents are constitutively overdetermined – that is, that they always represent *something more than* their mere particularistic identity.

This is why Claude Lefort's argument, according to which in democracy the place of power is empty, should, I think, be supplemented by the following statement: democracy requires the constant and active production of that emptiness. We would simply have the end of democracy if the names through which the community reaches its symbolic, universal image were so attached to particular *signifieds* that the representative mediation would lose all autonomy. This can happen in a variety of ways: though the reemergence of a hierarchical society, through totalitarian closure, or simply through administrative practices which deal bureaucratically with social issues, preventing their becoming loci of political confrontation.

But to say that democracy requires the constant recreation of the gap between the universal and the particular, between the empty place of power and the transient forces occupying it – in other words, that democracy can only flourish in a hegemonically constructed space – is the same as saying: 1) that relations of representation are constitutive of democracy; and 2) that the function of the representative cannot be purely passive, transmitting a will constituted elsewhere, but that it has to play an active role in the constitution of that will. It is only through a hegemonic aggregation of demands – which do not tend spontaneously to coalesce around any a priori point of confluence – that a certain emancipatory universality can be constituted. And so the name *representing* that collective will is never the passive expression of any previously achieved unity; on the contrary, the name retroactively constitutes the very will that it claims to represent.

That is why *representative* democracy is not a second best, as Rousseau thought, but it is *the only possible* democracy. Its insufficiencies are actually its virtues, as it is only through those insufficiencies that the visibility of the gap between universality and particularity – without which democracy is unthinkable – can be recreated. That is also why the attempts at homogenising the *social* space within which democracy operates (the universal class in Marx, the dissolution of social diversity in a unified public sphere in Jacobinism) necessarily produce a democratic deficit. Democracy faces the challenge of having to unify collective wills in *political* spaces of universal representation, while making such universality compatible with a plurality of social spaces dominated by particularism and difference. That is why democracy and hegemony require each other.

Conclusions

Let us draw some conclusions to close our analysis. They should concentrate on three issues which we have broached in the previous pages and which are closely linked to the contemporary experience of democratic practices, of their limitations but also of the potentiality that they open to new forms of construction of communitarian spaces.

The first issue concerns the language games that it is possible to play with the basic dichotomies around which classical democratic theory was organised. For a classical outlook, the more democratic a society, the more absolute the opposition between power and the fullness of the community is going to be. We have seen, however, that power, as the medium through which the incommensurability between particularity and universality shows itself, is not the antipode but the condition of democracy. Power, no doubt, involves domination; but domination shows, through the contingency of its sources, its own limits: there is only domination if it opens the possibility of its being overthrown. Conversely, there is only emancipation if what is emancipated is not an ultimately retrieved essence, but instead a new instantiation in the undecidable game of domination/emancipation (i.e., hegemony). Or, to put it in other terms which mean the same: there is only emancipation if the ontic order to be emancipated never exhausts, in some sort of ultimate *Aufhebung*, what is involved in the emancipatory logic. Again: there is only emancipation if there is never ultimate self-determination, if the gap between necessity and freedom is never finally bridged. The name of this asymmetry can be called – depending on the dimension we are emphasising – either democracy, power, or hegemony.

The second issue – related to our present predicaments in postmodern societies – concerns the ensemble of problems that have been subsumed under the term 'globalisation'. The dominant attitude of the left vis-à-vis the latter has been mainly defensive and negative. A globalised order would be one in which there is total concentration of power on one pole, while on the other there is only a fragmentation of social forces. What I want to suggest is that the problem is far more complex than that: if there is certainly a crisis of the old frameworks within which centres of power, social actors, and strategies were constituted, there is no new clear-cut framework of power emerging; there is, instead, a more radically undecidable terrain as a condition of strategic thinking. A dangerous universe, certainly, but not one in which pessimism is the only thinkable response.

Finally, and for the same reasons, I do not think that the plurality and fragmentation of identities and social actors in the contemporary world should be a source of political pessimism. The traditional markers of certainty are no doubt disintegrating and the *social* limits of hegemonic logics are clearly retreating. But this shows not only the dangers but also the potentialities of contemporary democracy. '*Les jeux sont faits*', but precisely because of that, one should not claim to be a loser at the very beginning. Especially, one has always to remember that collective victories and defeats largely take place at the level of the political imaginary. To construct a political vision in the new conditions, in which keeping open the gap between universality and particularity becomes the very matrix of the political imaginary, is the real challenge confronting contemporary democracy. A dangerous adventure, no doubt, but one on which the future of our societies depends. In 1923, Ortega y Gasset started the publication of the *Revista de Occidente* with the following words: 'There are, in the Western air, dissolved emotions of travelling: the excitement of departing, the tremor of the unknown adventure, the illusion of arriving, and the fear of getting lost.'

Notes

*   This essay was previously published in *Constellations* Volume 8, No 1. 2001. © Blackwell Publishers Ltd., 108 Cowley Road, Oxford OX4 1JF, UK and 350 Main Street, Malden, MA 02148, USA.
1   See my book *Emancipation(s)* (London, Verso, 1996).
2   Karl Marx, 'Contribution to the critique of Hegel's philosophy of law: introduction', in Karl Marx and Frederick Engels, *Collected Works*, vol. 3 (London, Lawrence and Wishart, 1975), 187.
3   Marx, K. (1975), 185.
4   See my essay 'Why do empty signifiers matter to politics', in *Emancipation(s)*, 36-46.

References

Laclau, E. (1986) 'Why do empty signifiers matter to politics', in *Emancipation(s)*, London, Verso: 36-46.
Laclau, E. (1996) *Emancipation*(s), London, Verso.
Marx, K. (1975) 'Contribution to the critique of Hegel's philosophy of law: introduction', in Karl Marx and Frederick Engels, *Collected Works*, vol. 3, London, Lawrence and Wishart.

4 Politics: Territorial or Non-Territorial?

PAUL HIRST

We still tend to think of politics in terms of what I shall call the 'flags of all nations' model. Politics is of course a much contested concept, but in this model it is perceived as state-centric and every inch of the globe is the territory of some state or another. We know that states differ in size and form, from continental-scale states such as Russia or the USA to small Pacific island statelets like Fiji. Since the 1950s, when as a boy I began collecting the cigarette card set of Flags of All Nations, the number of formally sovereign entities has risen to some 190. Political science has tended to follow folk wisdom in this matter, concentrating on politics within relatively homogeneous state-societies, and leaving politics beyond the state to a related sub-discipline, International Relations.

The widely perceived phenomenon of 'globalisation' has led many commentators to question the continued salience and viability of the nation state. They see economic and social processes escaping from territorial limitations and becoming truly global. That is, they become supra-national or trans-spatial, taking place either without relevance to borders, or in cyberspace. The consequences for politics are twofold. In the first place, politics disappears as markets and electronic interchanges replace the need for more than basic local regulation. States become like local authorities in a global market system. Markets and the Internet absorb the co-ordinative function of states. In the second place, politics becomes redefined as a cosmopolitan planetary system based on supra-national entities, like the UN, and orchestrated by new global political forces, such as NGOs. In the first case, politics is an irrelevance: it just gets in the way of more efficient, non-territorial forms of social organisation and resource allocation. In the second case, it becomes a cosmopolis, a world political community, but one which must rely, if it is in fact possible at all, on political processes quite different from those of the nation state.

Globalisation is a highly contested concept and the scale and scope of the phenomena grouped under it can be strongly questioned, as we shall see later. Yet the concerns about the eclipse of the nation state stemming

Politics: Territorial or Non-Territorial?

from this currently fashionable concept do help to remind us that the nation state is a highly specific historical form. It developed between the sixteenth and seventeenth centuries in Europe. The rise of the modern state not only changed the territorial landscape of Europe: it also transformed our imaginative landscapes. Since the seventeenth century, we have come to see political power as inherently territorial. Politics takes place within the state as the exclusive governor of a definite territory. We also identify political territory with social space, perceiving countries as 'state-societies'. This is not, as some modern social theorists believe, a conceptual error: it is a fact of political transformation, as sovereign territorial states reinvented themselves as nation states. Rulers and ruled became alike, and together they shared a distinct culture and institutions defined at least in part in opposition to those of other nations. Such differences were shaped in and by the conflict of states that has been inherent in the states system since its formation.

Territory and Political Power Before the Sixteenth Century

Clearly, politics has not always been identified with a power that claims to be the exclusive ruler of a given territory. Rulers and ruled have often been ethnically, culturally and linguistically different. Part of our difficulty in thinking about politics, power and territory is that our political ideas have been shaped by what we might call a 'double territorialisation'. The construction of exclusive territorial rule has been reinforced by a reinterpretation of the past as if it too conformed to modern models of political rule. The Renaissance thinkers who tried to conceive of the modern state, like Niccolo Machiavelli or Jean Bodin, tended to return to Greek and Roman models. They thought of post-feudal politics as a single political community with a single source of legitimate government and in which those who participated in politics shared a common culture. Thinkers like Machiavelli tended to identify the contemporary Italian city-states with the republics of Antiquity or, like Bodin, to compare the power of the French monarchy with Roman *Imperium*. This identification was made unexceptional by the general Renaissance practice of recovery of classical cultural models.

But Antiquity was actually very different in the relationship of space and politics. The Greek *polis* created an enduring model of the self-governing political community, a group of people who govern and are governed in turn and who shape every aspect of their lives through common institutions. The Greek city-state was, indeed, territorial and it was defined by a common culture. Yet the city-state was the exclusive ruler of a *small* territory, defined by the ability of the members of the governing class to meet in common and, therefore, by the distance that could be walked in a day. The culture of the city-state was doubly exclusive, of those in other cities, and of the large proportion of the population of the city who were not political participants: women, slaves, and resident aliens.

City-states were limited by a definite and symbolically significant territory, which they neither could nor wanted to greatly extend. Their military power was restricted by their relatively small, free adult male population. States could either grow by founding sister cities in the form of colonies, as the Greek cities did in Sicily and Asia Minor, or they could subordinate others in the form of tribute empires, as Athens did the cities of the Aegean. The empire depended on the Athenian fleet, its maximum size of about 300 *triremes* determined by the number of rowers in the free population.

When protracted war stretched Athenian manpower and public financing by the gifts of its wealthy citizens and residents to the limit, as it did during the Peloponnesian War, then the limits of the Greek *polis* were revealed. Greece above the level of the city-state was a cultural entity, not a political one. Greece was doomed once it was confronted by a major power, Macedon, that had absorbed its culture. The common elements of Greek society, the games and the great religious sites, did not provide a lasting basis for political institutions above the level of the city-state. The relationship between politics and territory established in Greece was thus quite unlike that of the modern state. The latter absorbed different self-governing cities and local powers into a common system of rule. Thereby, the new unified states were able to expand outside the core political territory and create overseas empires.

Rome was able to do both of these things. It expanded by incorporating Latin cities within its own political system and then by extending the rights of Roman citizenship to all qualifying free men. The Empire was a network of self-governing subordinate cities, of tributary kingdoms, and of tribes living by their own customary laws. Rome's empire was, however, conceived as universal. It was without fixed boundaries and saw itself as expanding to include all humanity, as the surrounding kingdoms and tribes were conquered and civilised. Rome recognised no legal or cultural limits to its expansion – no political community had a right to exist except as subordinate to it. It was thus quite unlike the modern state, which recognises other states as part of a common states system governed by certain rules of interaction between sovereign powers. Rome's only partner in the ancient world was Persia. But Rome's relations with the Parthian and Sassanian Empires were complex and de facto. Persia was never accepted as a legitimate partner in a stable international system. Rome was thus a state without territorial limits.

Other types of regime had little place within modern political theory, except as that against which it defined itself. The Ottoman Empire was perceived as a form of essentially arbitrary power, against which Western sovereigns could be seen as rulers bound to respect both the laws that they had made and the fundamental constitutional laws of the state. Thus, for Bodin, the French king is not a tyrant because, although he may make and change ordinary laws, he may not tax without the agreement of the *Estates General* and must abide by the Salic Law, which prescribes succession by the first-born male. Like Rome, the Ottoman state was a universal empire. It was committed to imposing the rule of the Sublime Porte and Islam wherever the force of Turkish armies could carry. It was only in the eighteenth century that the Ottoman state began to make normal treaties with other states and only in the mid-nineteenth century that it was accepted by other European states as a full member of the international system.

Other pre-modern forms of rule have had an even less definite relationship between space and politics. Nomad confederacies, like the Mongol Empire, were non-territorial. Mongol rule recognised neither spatial limits nor the right to existence of subordinate powers, let alone legitimate independent rulers. Mongol rule relied on free movement over the steppes of Eurasia, on a military community fed by its own sheep and horses that moved with it. The Mongols incorporated other nomadic tribes within their confederacy, but their ruling elite was defined by clan membership and by a tribally exclusive shamanistic culture. Whether Mongol rulers were Muslim, Christian or Buddhist, the key nomadic clan rituals defined the exclusive culture of the core of those who controlled the state. Mongol rule was thus both culturally exclusive and non-territorial. The rulers lived in a facsimile of a nomad camp, even when it was a permanent city like Karakorum with thousands of imported artisans providing goods for the court, or, as in Beijing, where the nomads created a miniature steppe in the form of a park at the heart of the imperial city.

Feudal forms of government that had developed after the decline of Roman rule in the West were non-territorial. They were based on personal ties between lord and vassal. The fief was a gift of land in return for obligation and service. It was contingent where it was located; territorial rights derived from personal obligations and could be changed. The unfree population was tied to the land by labour service and had no part in governance. Feudal elites served with their lords as dynastic acquisitions, conquest, or crusade dictated. Norman nobles, for example, could be found ruling in England, in Sicily, in the Holy Land, and on the Baltic coast. Typical of medieval feudal states were borderlands where rule and title were ill defined. The frontier was not a fixed and determined line, but an area of disputed marchlands. Medieval Europe steadily expanded across such shifting frontiers – raiding, settling and conquering as the occasion arose. In the Baltic and in Spain Christian power steadily expanded after the year 1000 against pagan tribes and Muslim rulers respectively. In the Balkans, by contrast, the Ottomans expanded by similar processes against the Byzantine Empire and the various kingdoms of Serbia, Hungary etc. Such moving frontiers existed within Europe before they became typical of the neo-Europes of North America, Argentina or Australia.[1]

Medieval states lacked not only exclusive control of a given territory by a single ruler but also a clear and coherent division of labour in governance. Powers competed to control the same spaces, claiming forms of territorial or functional rule that were ill defined in their scope and rights. Different entities would rule in the same space, often making contradictory claims upon the ruled. The Church claimed not only functional rule over religious matters and over clergy, the right to raise revenue, to have its own law, but it also disputed temporal power. The Pope claimed universal dominion over Christendom, as did the Holy Roman Emperor. Popes claimed the right to invest secular rulers in office, with the threat of veto, and hence to exercise hierarchical control. Kings in turn demanded the right to appoint bishops, for example, the French and the English kings. Not only was the Pope a secular ruler in the Romagna, but Prince Bishops elsewhere ruled their dominions and had armed forces.

Cities enjoyed extensive powers of self-government, either granted as particular liberties or privileges by monarchs in return for money or military aid, or appropriated de facto, as with the Italian city-states in respect of the Empire. Cities raised taxes, possessed armed forces, their own system of justice, and made treaties with rulers. Leagues of cities, like the Hanseatic League of northern trading cities, acted as powers in their own right. The Hanseatic League's cities coined money, donated armed forces to the common purposes of the League, as defined by its ruling institutions, made commercial laws, enforced trading privileges, and dealt diplomatically with rulers. The cities were drawn from territories that would later be part of Germany, Poland, Sweden, etc. The Hanse obtained exclusive trading privileges from rulers and the right to establish its own trading factories, with extra-territorial rights for its members. The League was a quasi-polity with common decision-making institutions and rules, its members being the participating cities. Within the League certain cities like Lübeck were its vital sources of financial and naval power.

Within medieval cities the guilds enjoyed functionally specific governance of their particular trade and its practitioners. Guilds determined entry to the trade, training, the quality of work, and prices, thus regulating the production and sale of goods and the number and character of the labour force. The guilds were typically controlled by the leading guild masters. Cities were ruled by an urban patriarchate made up of guild masters and leading merchants. For the ordinary journeyman, such functional governance was more important in ruling their lives than any other form of governance.

Within the Ottoman Empire the *millets* system of self-regulating religious communities allowed the subordinate peoples of the Empire a measure of control of their own affairs, according to their own religious laws. Christians and Jews had to pay additional taxes and were subject to other liabilities, but as religions of the Bible they were legitimate communities and had some rights to self-government. Ottoman cities were typically divided into closed quarters where the different religious laws prevailed. Throughout the medieval world, Muslim and Christian alike, laws thus depended on status. Priests, serfs, guild members, and so on, had different rights and were subject to different laws. Rulers and the ruled might be unlike in culture and rights. Nobilities and peasantries often had little in common. These are examples of the parallel governance by different groups within the same territory, but also of the functional governance of people across spaces.

Bodin's various marks of sovereignty – to give orders but not to receive them, to make laws, to administer justice, to coin money, to tax, to raise armies, to deal with other rulers – were complexly distributed across territory before the sixteenth century. Various agencies could do these things – including raise armed forces and enter into relations with other rulers. The Hanseatic League, the monastic military orders like the Teutonic Knights or the Hospitallers, mercenary forces like the Catalan Company, city-states, bishoprics – all acted much as later 'sovereign' states would claim exclusively to do and often across the same territory. Late medieval society was complex and political power was distributed differentially across it, creating multifaceted relations between space and politics.

The Sovereign Territorial State

From the sixteenth century onwards – starting with the centralising late medieval monarchies of England, France and Spain – states across Europe

74 *Habitus: A Sense of Place*

struggled and eventually succeeded in becoming the dominant powers within a definite territory to which they laid claim.[2] This is not the place to rehearse the reasons for the rise of the modern state or to look too closely into the temporality of the process with its numerous challenges, crises and conflicts. Suffice it to say that it has two defining characteristics:

I. Exclusion: all entities that are not exclusively sovereign are de-legitimised and eventually expelled from the international system. Thus the Hanseatic League, the monastic military orders, the Church as a pan-European institution, and the city-state are all either eliminated or marginalised. Both the Papacy and the Hanseatic League, having previously been major powers in the politics of the Germanic lands, therefore have no effective part in the Treaty of Westphalia of 1648 which ends the Thirty Years War. Likewise, the Hospitallers, having played a vital role in resisting Ottoman advance in the Mediterranean at the siege of Malta in 1565, become an increasingly honorific irrelevance in the European system, until removed by Napoleon. The Holy Roman Empire, itself a ghost after Westphalia, lingers on ever more marginal in relation to the member states until abolished by Napoleon in 1806. Exclusion is thus a process that takes place at the international level, as well as in terms of redirecting the capacities of local and functional powers within centralising states.

II. Mutual Recognition: states acquire powers over their societies to a substantial degree because they recognise each other as exclusive rulers of a definite territory. A central aspect of such recognition is non-interference, states refraining from acting directly within the territory of another state. During the religious wars of the sixteenth and seventeenth centuries, such intervention had become normal practice, with states aiding religious dissidents in other countries either for reasons of ideological affinity and/or for reasons of balance of power. France and the German lands were torn apart by religious civil wars, fostered in part by external powers. The Treaty of Westphalia established the principle of non-interference in domestic religious conflicts, thus enabling states to begin to assert control over their societies. Until they did so, confessional loyalty tended to take priority over loyalty to monarch or state. Once a stable relationship between religion and territory was established, with states being recognised as either Reformed or Catholic, the process of building a form of political or territorial loyalty of population, incorporating religion as part of state identity, could begin. The control of internal violence allows states to turn the aggression of their peoples outward, towards other states. Hence the succession of wars from the late seventeenth century into the early nineteenth century, ending with the peace of Vienna in 1815. States use wars to build forms of identification between rulers and ruled. Where this is successful, as in Britain, state, regime and nation come to be defined together in one form of legitimacy. Where this is less successful, as in France, state and nation are built against the existing regime, as after 1789.

Without territorialisation and exclusivity, there could not be political nationalism. Why should rulers and ruled be alike if political institutions are distributed by function and status, and different institutions compete to rule the same territory? How can subjects or citizens identify with a territory if it does not have definite symbolic spatial features? Nationalism typically claims not just an ethnos/national group, but also a territory that this group should inhabit as its homeland as of right. Without the prior existence of the sovereign state claiming a definite territory it is difficult to see how nationalism might arise. Typically, nationalism begins as the project of rulers seeking to harness people to states. Then rival projects begin, demanding unification or secession.

Without territorial nationalism, it is difficult to see how there could be democracy. Representative government can exist in heterogeneous polities: feudal estates or the councils of the Hanseatic League are 'representative' in that delegates speak for statuses or cities. People expect such delegates to be different one from another – to speak for their estate or the interests of their city. Democracy – where the government is chosen by the majority vote of the people – is quite distinct from this traditional representation. People have to feel sufficiently like their neighbours for a simple majority decision to be acceptable. Nationalism provides a basic cultural-social homogeneity that enables people to trust majorities.

Where such homogeneity does not exist, the introduction of democratic procedures simply exposes the conflicts of the wider society, as in the former Yugoslavia. 'Nations' are seldom homogeneous enough to begin with to suffice for political purposes; they are made up of *ethnoi*, the local customs and *patois* of various *pays*. Only homogeneous languages, customs and institutions will suffice for real political homogeneity, imposed by national schools, the army and universal military service, 'national' cultural institutions, and patriotic organisations in civil society, like the Boy Scouts. Given such a network of 'nationalising' cultural and social institutions, state and society merge. The continuation of such politics of nationalisation and the wars that are its inevitable outcome, as nations define their differences and establish their territories in conflict with others, leads to the unity of politics, culture and territory.

Such a unity gives borders a special salience. Borders existed before the modern state. They were either marchlands or zones of control, such as the border regions of the Roman Empire – Hadrian's Wall, the Rhine frontier, and the *limes* on the Danube. Such systems controlled the movement of barbarian peoples on the frontiers of the Empire in much the same way as the Chinese frontier with the desert and steppe. Where borders mattered otherwise, this was mostly in terms of *property* rather than politics. The borders of manors were typically well defined, whereas those of feudal states were not. With the modern state, the frontier becomes not a disputed region or a zone of control, but a line. Then we expect things to be socially and culturally different on one side as against the other. The frontier is marked and policed; that is a secondary effect of exclusive governance of territory and of peoples being defined culturally. Within those EU states that are signatories of the Schengen Agreement, borders now matter less and less, in some cases less than borders between US states. Once such frontiers were closely guarded: now they are often imperceptible. The reason is not merely because the states in question are no longer in conflict, but because it is increasingly difficult to tell the peoples of adjacent states apart.

Applying the classic definition of Max Weber and amplifying it, we may define the characteristic features of the modern state as follows:

- Hierarchy: the state is a superior political agency that decides on the role and powers of all subsidiary governments. Its rules – laws – are the primary rules.
- It possesses or claims a definite territory with clear boundaries and defines who may or may not reside in it.
- It has *exclusive* control of territory – 'sovereignty' means that no other agency has a legitimate or viable claim to rule.
- It possesses a monopoly of the means of violence within the territory – the state alone controls and sanctions the political use of armed force.
- Exclusive control by the state of the use of *external* violence – only the state can make war on other states.
- Mutual recognition by states of each other and their territories.
- A system of uniform and continuous administration throughout the territory of the state.
- The separation of the affairs of state from the private affairs of both rulers and ruled.

As we have seen, the formation of exclusive control within the state's territory owed a great deal to the fact that states were members of an international system. The modern state evolved not merely *pari passu* with the states system, but to some considerable degree as an effect of it. War was also a central fact in producing identification with the state, creating the territorialisation of populations that served as the foundation of nationalism. From the beginning, however, states did not just compete; they also co-operated, and from the earliest times their interactions were governed by norms. This normatively governed system created a radical disjuncture between the space governed by the states system and its rulers, and that beyond, the civilised and the uncivilised. As Carl Schmitt realised, international law created the conditions for the control of the 'non-civilised': 'A nation that was not civilised ... could not be a member of the community of states. It would be regarded not as a subject but as an object of that community's civil laws. In other words, it was part of the possessions of one or another of the civilised nations, as a colony or colonial protectorate.' (Schmitt, 1997: 39). By the late nineteenth century, European states had extended the states system to the whole of the earth. They had converted most non-European territory into colonies and had reduced China to a series of spheres of influence. Colonial control created new spatial patterns in Africa, the Americas and Asia, divisions based on European conquest, and political entities that were artefacts of conquest. Most of the states created by de-colonisation are thus marked in their very territory by the effects of European conquest.

The modern states system created the principle of no territory without a state, and this principle was vigorously applied, squeezing out marginal areas and political entities that did not conform to the norms of modern statehood, like the pirate enclave of the Dey of Algiers. The sea, however, was another matter. States did try to claim the sea. The Treaty of Tordesillas, concluded by the Pope between Spain and Portugal in 1494, imagined that the globe, including the sea, could be divided like a land barrier. Neither country in fact could exclude the French, British and Dutch from raiding and trading. Control of the high seas depended not on borders, but on the effective capacity to trade and on the dominance of one fleet over others. As the American strategist A.T. Mahan noted in *The Influence of Sea Power up on History* (1965), naval conflict and wars on land followed a different logic – one could not hold positions in the sea. In the early seventeenth century, the Dutch theorist, Hugo Grotius, developed the notion of the seas as commons open to all to trade and use. Law was based on fact not *fiat*, the seas could not be monopolised, nor did the passage of one ship diminish the utility of the sea to another.

The principal political projects that emerged from modern territorial statehood – dynastic absolutism, nationalism and democracy – all depended on a certain spatial order, of a claim to a given form of rule over a place. Dynasticism by right of inheritance, nationalism by the established co-residence of a people with distinct attributes, democracy as the will of the nation, link power and place together. The inter-state order, however, was never limited in this way. From medieval times, states had sought to foster and control commerce; trade bringing money and thus the sinews of war in train. In the mercantilist period in the seventeenth and eighteenth centuries, states sought to annex and monopolise trade, in efforts to concentrate long-distance trade in their ports and in their ships. They sought to control access to trade through monopoly companies like the Dutch VOC or the English Hudson's Bay Company. During the eighteenth century, these projects of monopolisation faltered as private traders sought to enter these markets. Adam Smith provided a rationale for free trade in *The Wealth of Nations*, and the origin of a new political principle, commercial liberalism.

In the nineteenth century, under British hegemony, a new international order was erected, based on the freedom to trade and the right of citizens freely to engage in private actions across the borders of their states. Commercial liberalism was the only doctrine that could build a genuine international order. Liberal sovereignty was founded on the freedom of private individuals to trade and, therefore, on the redefinition of the role of the state in facilitating such commerce. The liberal state was thus committed to definite international norms and thus used its power to enforce freedom to trade. Hence the forced opening of China and Japan that refused such freedoms. Hence the stigmatisation of states like the Russian Empire that prevent the free movement of people and goods as backward countries. The 'long' nineteenth century (1815–1914) created a world free trading system based on growing levels of international trade, investment and migration. In 1914, Britain, France and Germany had attained trade to GDP ratios comparable to those of today, levels of capital export to GDP not exceeded today, and levels of mass migration that dwarf those of today. Between 1800 and 1930 40 million Europeans migrated permanently overseas. The world created by commercial liberalism was unlike the world of today, which is controlled by borders, passports and visas that in the nineteenth century were regarded as devices of barbarous regimes like the Tsars.

The nineteenth century was the period in which an open global economy was erected, one based on exchanges across the borders of sovereign states. These states, far from being threatened by such developments, saw it as their role to promote and protect free commerce. Liberal sovereignty implies a world of other states bound by rules of international civility and a system of free exchange by private individuals across the borders of states. The liberal state is thus inherently internationally oriented; its exclusive control of its territory is designed to promote an open commercial system within and without. Liberal sovereignty is state power applied to promote commerce, whether in the form of compelling reluctant 'partners' to trade, as in the Opium Wars the British fought in China, or in the domestic social policies designed to force workers to participate in the capitalist economy, as catalogued in Karl Polanyi's *The Great Transformation* (1957).

In the first half of the twentieth century, the system based on liberal sovereignty nearly foundered as the defeated and frustrated powers of World War I sought through neo-mercantilist economics and authoritarian nationalist politics to create an alternative order based on the state control of large economic areas (Haushofer's *Grossraumwirtschaft*). The liberal powers, Britain and the USA, proved more resilient – aided by the USSR. After 1945 the USA rebuilt the liberal international economy, much as Britain had built it in the first place after 1815. After World War II two projects for the international order competed: American hegemony based on commercial liberalism and Soviet hegemony based on administered trade and satellite states. As in the nineteenth century, commercial liberalism proved far more capable of creating an international order in which states had a measure of autonomy and citizens were free to trade. The Soviet order crumbled precisely because it was not international; it relied on domination and the forcible control of movement of citizens.

Globalisation

What most people mean by 'globalisation' is the continued development of the international system of commercial liberalism. This system remains *inter-national*, not truly global, because it involves high levels of trade and investment between distinct national economies centred on major states. As Grahame Thompson and I have shown in *Globalization in Question* (1999), a global economy based on supra-national market forces has not developed. Instead, most major companies continue to sell about two-thirds of their products and keep the bulk of their assets in their home country/region. Despite the integration of short-term financial dealing, capital markets remain stubbornly local, with about 90% of investment sourced locally in the advanced countries, and migration is more highly controlled than ever.

Borders function now not to exclude invading armies, but to keep economic migrants out of welfare states. Even the vaunted de-localisation of information flows must be set in perspective. The telegraph transformed the world in the nineteenth century; IT makes running that new industrial world a whole lot easier. The clicks of e-commerce depend crucially on the spatially localised and bricks and mortar-based necessities of fulfilment.

If we look at globalisation in historical perspective, we can argue that after the massive contraction of international trade in the 1929 Great Crash, and after the effects of two World Wars in the twentieth century, the international economy is returning to something like its late nineteenth century heyday. Liberal states in the nineteenth century were limited governments but they were not weak; rather, they used their power to promote commerce abroad and to clear the way for private industry at home. In some ways current policies in the USA, UK and Australia mirror this, promoting global free trade and domestic de-regulation in a 'sound money' economy.

It would be foolish to pursue this analogy too far. The modern world is not like that of the *Pax Britannica*. Equally, it would be foolish to judge the capacities of the modern state by the excesses of regulation and control prompted by the World Wars and their aftermath. The essential differences between the pre-1914 world and now are twofold. First, a complex division of labour in governance has emerged in which states share power and governance capacity with supra-national agencies like the WTO, IMF and World Bank, and also with functionally-specific public, quasi-public and private bodies that control a plethora of things from the global radio wave spectrum to the insurance classification of merchant ships. Second, states have chosen to associate into trading blocs, like NAFTA, the EU and MERCOSUR, in which they accept free movement of goods and – in the case of the latter two – people. States are increasingly embedded in larger entities to which they have ceded certain sovereign powers; for example, members of the WTO accept its adjudication over a wide range of trade-related matters that impinge on the scope of national policy, and the EU member states under the Single European Act accept EU legislation in matters facilitating the single market as superior to those of their national legislatures and enforceable as such in their courts.

States are not only sharing power 'upwards' within supra-national bodies, but also 'downwards', with bodies that, whatever the constitutional formalities, are no longer subordinate agencies that exist by the state's *fiat* alone.[3] Economic regulation has increasingly devolved to regional governments and to functional agencies that possess more effective local knowledge in a volatile, flexible and rapidly changing economic system.

Examples are the German Länder, the new Scottish Parliament, or the English Regional Development Agencies. States that fail to effectively participate in this division of labour, shunning international agencies and failing effectively to devolve power, are not, however, strong, but weak. They seek to preserve political control at the price of sacrificing effective governance. For the paradox is that by sharing power with other institutions and agencies, states can stabilise their external environment and maximise their domestic economic performance, thus creating a less volatile environment in which to govern and enhancing the resources that feed into governance capacity. It is a mistake to view sovereignty in zero-sum terms, as if the state must become a weaker and less effective governor if it shares the tasks of governance with others.

The territorial state will not disappear. Indeed, this new division of labour in governance makes it ever more necessary. It becomes the key locus that ties the different levels and forms of governance together. States, because they are territorial, and if they are liberal democracies, are able to speak legitimately for their populations and to make international commitments that successor governments accept as binding acts of sovereignty. As such they provide the legitimacy for supra-national bodies, a derived or indirect legitimacy stemming from the will of the people. Equally, territorial states remain our primary source of accountability and democracy in such a complex system. Their representatives remain, in theory at least, subject to domestic political pressure. Cosmopolitan forms of democratic governance are unlikely to develop because we still operate in a world shaped by nationalism. Citizens still identify with nation states. They are the largest bodies that can claim any sort of primary legitimacy. International bodies are the preserve of elites, and the international technocracy needs the check of politicians directly answerable to national politics. Accountability of international agencies through national publics is at best indirect and weak, but strong supra-national democracy is just impossible. Democracy implies homogeneity; the world is just too unequal economically and too different culturally for the rich to submit to the decisions of the poor, or for one established culture to accept the internationalisation of the norms of another. Hence the unwillingness of the G7 states to give a greater say to developing nations in the core institutions of supra-national governance. Hence also the widespread resistance by other major cultures to international human rights norms that come in a box marked 'made in the USA'.

We thus live in a world constituted out of apparently contradictory components: territorial sovereignty and commercial liberalism; nationalism and international accountability; supra-national institutions and the continued viability of nation states. The territorial states will remain a central component of the new division of labour in governance, even if it no longer has quite the salience it had when it appropriated political power from the complex division of labour in governance of the later Middle Ages. Politics is no longer exclusively territorial; on the other hand, it cannot hold together unless it is rooted in the democratic political will of territorial states that practise liberal policies, that are internationally oriented and that submit to supra-national norms.

Notes

1. On the structure of feudal society see Bloch (1965), on the frontier in medieval Europe, Bartlett and MacKay (1989), and on the nomads and the Chinese empire see Franks and Twitchett (1994).
2. On the rise of the modern state see Ertman (1997), Spruyt (1994) and Van Creveld (1999). On the formation of sovereignty see Krasner (1988), and on territoriality Ruggie (1993).
3. For a further discussion of this role of the state as the suture that binds different levels of governance together, see Hirst and Thompson (1999: ch.9).

References

Bartlett, R. and MacKay, A. (eds) (1989) *Medieval Frontier Societies*, Oxford, Clarendon Press.
Bloch, M. (1965) *Feudal Society* (2nd edition), London, Routledge and Kegan Paul.
Ertman, T. (1997) *Birth of the Leviathan*, Cambridge, Cambridge University Press.
Franks, H. and Twitchett, D. (eds) (1994) The Cambridge History of China, Vol.6, Alien regimes and border states 907-1368, Cambridge, Cambridge University Press.
Hirst, P. and Thompson, G. (1999) *Globalization in Question (2nd edition)*, Cambridge, Polity Press.
Krasner, S.D. (1988) 'Sovereignty: an institutional perspective', *Comparative Political Studies*, Vol.21, No.1: 66-94.
Mahan, A.T. (1965) *The Influence of Sea Power Upon History 1660-1783*, London, Methuen.
Polanyi, K. (1957) *The Great Transformation*, Boston MA, Beacon Press.
Ruggie, J.G. (1993) 'Territoriality and beyond: problematizing modernity in international relations', *International Organization*, Vol.47 No.1: 134-72.
Schmitt, C. (1997) *Land and Sea*, Washington DC, The Plutarch Press.
Smith, A. (1976 [1776]) *The Wealth of Nations*, Chicago IL, University of Chicago Press.
Spruyt, H. (1994) *The Sovereign State and its Competitors*, Princeton NJ, Princeton University Press.
Van Creveld, M. (1999) *The Rise and Decline of the State*, Cambridge, Cambridge University Press.

5 Toleration and the Art of International Governance: How is it Possible to 'Live Together' in a Fragmenting International System?

GRAHAME F. THOMPSON

Introduction

In this chapter I ask the question 'How is it possible to live together in what looks to be an increasingly fragmenting international system?' It is concerned to uncover what might establish and maintain a regime of 'relative social peace' at the level of the international system. I would suggest that the effectiveness of any serious politics of place and space is dependent upon the existence of a 'relative social peace' – which constitutes a kind of *habitus* for the operation of 'ordinary' calculative politics. In this regard I try to bring the notion of *toleration* more squarely back into the international sphere than has been done up to now.

To a large extent toleration in its traditional sense has been seen as a supreme liberal virtue. And as a liberal virtue it is connected – closely connected – to individual conscience and private reflection. As we will see, the history of the rise of toleration generally is closely associated with the rise of religious toleration in particular and the rights of individuals to profess, practise and maintain whichever confessional doctrine they wish. Their adherence to this confessional doctrine is a matter of their private opinions, ruminations and consciences. All the public realm does is to provide a framework of conditions that allows that individual liberty to thrive. In this chapter I trace the very interesting history of exactly how public religious strife became a matter of the *holding of a private opinion* in this manner, and of such opinions being *upheld* by a sort of 'neutral' public power that oversees the domestic tolerant regime so established.

Clearly, there are a number of problems with this story if we are thinking analogously of a specifically international space for the operation of toleration. This is not a space of individual conscience in quite the same way as it operates in the domestic realm. The players in the international space are not 'individuals' in the sense of citizens of a polity, for instance. There is no formally constituted international polity and there is unlikely to be one in the near future, or even distant future, I would argue. So this means we are dealing with a somewhat different beast in trying to think about toleration at the international level. We are dealing more with a 'regime' – a kind of security regime. But this is not a security regime built upon a military alliance. Most military alliances are security regimes predicated on the 'balance of terror' (rather crudely put). They try to maintain peace by threatening war, and this is not the best way to secure 'relative social peace' in the long-term political sense (Hirst,1987).

I argue below that the original political struggles to establish religious toleration within the context and boundaries of the nation state were not entirely divorced from 'international issues'. After all the Treaty of Westphalia – which began the moves towards ending the religious wars and intolerance in Europe – was an international treaty. And it was an international treaty that established probably the first ever human right – religious freedom of a sort (see below). So international treaties have been a potent source for the establishment of rights of individuals as exercised within their domestic environments and borders. Domestic human rights have been bolstered by international treaties. But I do not think we are likely to see a single event like an international treaty in the current context of thinking about international toleration. Much more likely is to see it in the form of a perhaps rather unstable regime: a sort of constitutional order but not one written into international law and supported by the full panoply of sovereign state powers. As will become clear below, the notion of a regime I have in mind here refers to a relatively stable/unstable system of rules, procedures and norms that constitutes and supports a domain of public powers and authorities but which are not state-like in character.

The second introductory point to make about the way toleration is used in this chapter is to try and differentiate it from a conception that sees toleration as an essentially *repressive* act (Marcuse, 1965). In this case, the extension of toleration to ones 'enemies' serves only to temporarily placate them in the interests of maintaining authority over them or to bolster an existing inequality in favour of the more powerful party. As against this approach, I would wish to define toleration as *the cultivation of a style of behaviour that embodies a studied indifference towards difference*. In this sense, toleration is a genuinely mutual act, one that does not necessarily favour either party. Rather, whilst explicitly recognising differences between groups, however defined, its objective is to accept these for what they are, share a mild interest in them, but to leave it at that and not to interfere. Now, this might seem to precisely license gross inequalities and deny the existence of fundamental disagreements. But as we shall see it does not necessarily lead to this. As argued below, *whilst it might provide a mechanism for tolerating the intolerant, it does not necessarily mean tolerating the intolerable*. I try to make these distinctions clear below.

A final point to make in connection to the preliminary discussion of the notion of toleration explored here is to ask exactly what it is that is to be tolerated in the international sphere? In the historical case of religious toleration it was, of course, confessional choice that was to be tolerated. In the contemporary period, I will suggest, toleration has mainly to do with some very difficult issues associated with the existence of disputed international borders that define distinct territorial jurisdictions.

Antagonistic-Pluralism and the Age of Absolutism

In this section I trace the contours of the constitution of the modern state from the Age of Absolutism. It stresses the relationship between the rise of Absolutism and the rise of liberal toleration. The point of this return to the past is to provide a history of the present; it is to help in the analysis of the present conjuncture with respect to liberalism and its possible demise. This issue is taken up in the next main section.

Prior to the age of Absolutism subjects were placed in a loose configurative structure of responsibilities; as members of churches, of guilds, or other political institutions, dependent vassals, or as members of the feudal order of estates. By the late sixteenth century the traditional plural order based upon these subject forming positions was in disarray, undermined by acute religious strife and antagonistic sectarian conflict which threatened the disintegration of the European political system. However, these European religious wars were progressively brought to an end during the seventeenth century as Absolutism spread through continental Europe (note that after 1688 Britain took a somewhat separate course, and Scottish thinking is distinctively noteworthy in terms of its Enlightenment credentials).

It was the inauguration of the Absolutist State, as a response to the religious civil wars, that secured a lasting social peace in which the seeds of the bourgeois enlightenment were sown. It is from this period of Absolutist rule and the Enlightenment that so many of our cherished political and intellectual values emerged. There is no need to rehearse all of these here. A key element in the progressive 'rationalisation' of the social order during the seventeenth century was Neostoicism, which provided a practical guide to the art of living that was not inspired by theological disputation (Oestreich, 1982). This secular 'philosophy of life' stressed the ethical virtues of frugality, dutifulness, obedience, self-inspection and discipline, toleration and moderation, as at the same time it recognised the need for a powerful and efficient state and the acceptance for the central role of force and the army in centralising control. Of particular importance from the point of view of the subsequent discussion, however, is the connected notion of sovereignty founded by Absolutism. The 'dispersed' sovereignties of the old feudal order were centralised under the power of the Monarchy or a Parliament, which became *the* sovereign ruler. *Raison d'état* formed the modality for this movement (nothing should harm the state, while conscience and morality should be subject to the dictates of politics), which was highly successful both politically and in terms of the intellectual reflection upon political sovereignty. From this time on what Foucault has called the 'juridico-discursive' notion of sovereignty was with us with a vengeance (Foucault, 1981).

However, Absolutism also sowed the seeds of its own destruction in that the relative social peace it secured gave rise to a political and intellectual movement which, whilst heavily if not entirely indebted to that social peace, developed a critique of its very own conditions of existence (Koselleck, 1988 – first published in German in 1959). In addition, and at the same time, it opened the space for the appearance of an individualised private self and a life that was somehow beyond the jurisdiction of the state.[1] This offered a fertile ground for the Enlightenment's own project to exploit this gap in the armour of Absolute power. Thus one of the most alluring paradoxes of the modern political era is that it was the Absolutist State that provided the main conditions for its own eclipse – on the one hand relative social peace in which calculative political programmes could emerge and survive and on the other the figure of 'man' with an inner moral self beyond the legitimate measure of that State.[2] The religious wars were ended (substantially after the Peace of Westphalia in 1648), a *rapprochement* between the main parties secured, and in its wake a social movement whose main rationale was to criticise that milieu evolved. That movement we know as the Enlightenment and the 'liberal' governmental programmes it inaugurated. Thus liberalism (in its many guises) was predicated upon the social peace and theoretical reflection that its main political and intellectual rival was responsible for securing. Liberalism's project was to ruthlessly criticise the Absolutist State, and it inaugurated a programme of governmental reform that recognised the autonomy of the civil sphere, secured rights and obligations of citizenship, introduced democratic politics, governed through laws, etc., in a list of well known features all too long to reiterate.

But note the paradox. For liberalism to function properly and with effect requires the condition of 'relative social peace'. The radical importance of this is often overlooked. It is not that liberalism *secured* this peace, only that it benefited enormously from it. The programmes of liberal governmentality analysed so perceptively by Foucault and his followers (see, for instance, Dean, 1999), are not 'universal' programmes. They are highly contingent upon a particular state of the world; one typified by relative social passivity. If and as that 'state of the world' changes, so the liberal programmes of governmentality will themselves be challenged, recast or undermined.

Thus liberalism is challenged by social unrest and disorder – and fundamentally so since these undermine the very condition of its own existence. The issues, then, are twofold; a) it is to ask why liberalism seems susceptible to this problem, and indeed whether this is a unique problem for liberalism alone among calculative political rationalities; and b) it is to ask how we can conceptualise the contemporary situation, to adequately capture its political register through a process of intervention in the present, and to see what might be an adequate response to this situation. Each of these issues invites a rather ambitious task. All that is done here is to hint at some responses.

It is Koselleck's contention that it was the 'utopianism' of the Enlightenment project that was responsible for its breakdown, particularly during the Nazi period in Germany. Enlightenment rationalism raised the prospect of unending progress and human emancipation. This vision was transformed into the quest and prospect of a future realisable utopia through its articulation into various calculative political ideologies and programmes; the foremost amongst these being 'Liberalism', 'Socialism', and 'Communism' (and possibly 'Conservatism' as well). Society was propelled at an accelerating rate along a route towards an unclear but potentially knowable and livable future. The utopias of Liberalism, Socialism, Communism and the like provided for the hopes and aspirations of a desired utopian fulfilment. These visions in turn became the potential guarantees of their own fulfilment. Their ideological embodiment in competing political programmes laid the basis for a potential conflict between them. Finally, 'modernity' became the actual embodiment of such conflicts which are themselves endemic, self-generating and endless. Thus the outcome of the Enlightenment project is one quite different to its anticipation, but one grounded all the same in the aspirations of an enlightened rationalism.[3] For Kosselleck, then, the Nazi period was just an extreme example of the conflictual consequence of the Enlightenment. From this perspective, beware all those who insist on unconditionally defending the Enlightenment!

Here emerges another great paradox. In terms of this analysis, we are almost back where we started. The anarchy of the religious wars gave rise to the peace of Absolutism. The peace of Absolutism gave rise to the Enlightenment and liberal toleration. The Enlightenment and its liberalism then undermined that relative social peace on which it was predicated, and with the full maturing of modernity, endemic civil war returns (now mainly in the form of a 'civil war' between nation states driven by ideological disputes). Here is a powerful indictment of the current condition.

But perhaps it is one that needs to be newly nuanced in the post-Cold War period with the reappearance of religious sectarianism ('extremism') and ethnically based 'nationalistic' conflicts? This I return to in a moment. First let us consider some other implications of this form of analysis.

The first is whether the possibility of liberalism destroying itself is peculiar to Liberalism alone as a governmental technique or political rationality (which for the moment I run together in this discussion). It is a problem for the post-Enlightenment period in general, and invades just as much the other calculative political programmes/ideologies mentioned above as it does Liberalism. These are as equally threatening of social peace and threatened by its demise, in Koselleck's terms. The effectivity of their programmatic utopianisms ('we will emancipate you if only you follow us') relies upon an ordered social peace for its attractiveness and appeal, and falls prey to the very disorder it unwittingly engenders (as appearing within the domain of its *effects*).

The second point is to stress the changes within, and development of, liberal thinking from its early post-Enlightenment days. Two sub-points are worth stressing here. The first is to recognise the contingent relationship between liberalism and democracy that has actually emerged in the *practice* of liberal states. Liberalism and authoritarianism have not always been totally at odds. And nor are liberalism and democracy *necessarily* aligned.[4] In addition we are forced to loosen the connection between liberalism and the discourse of liberty in general, since Conservatism as a post-Enlightenment political ideology and the specific doctrine of *laissez-faire* have also made claims on this connection, and with effect. In addition, liberal state power has often been appropriated by dictatorships which have maintained or developed the terrain of 'liberal' policies in various forms.

Secondly, the core of liberalism need not be exclusively organised around the autonomous person with a 'private' moral domain of conscience and all the baggage that goes with this. On the one hand we can stress the crucial role of pluralism and tolerance as key liberal virtues that have had lasting organisational significance within liberal states, and which are not a direct effect of the individual commitments and pursuits of an ethically privatised citizenry (Minson, 1993 – see also below). What is more, the analysis of Neostoicism mentioned above demonstrates that this was part of a developed 'art of living' well before the advent of fully fledged liberalism. On the other hand we need to draw a sharp distinction between liberalism as a philosophically charged political doctrine with a certain juridico-institutional view of the political system, and liberalism as a set of discrete 'mechanisms of governance'. This is a form of what Foucault has called 'governmentality', which has as its objective the governance of populations via the activities of scrutiny, categorisation, normalisation, securitisation, etc., which produce multiple but definite 'knowledges of government' (Burchell, Gordon and Miller, 1991; Dean 1999).

Thirdly, liberalism has traditionally been committed to the notions of discussion and dialogue as a way of both reconciling differences and of propelling social advance. But dialogue is 'idealised' here under a principle of free expression and open discussion. This idealisation of free expression takes three forms:

> first, by making the ultimate purpose of a free and open exchange of views the attainment of truth and justice, through a process of rational persuasion; second (the paradigmatically political-romantic option) by idealising political discourse itself as an 'endless conversation', a never-finalised process of problematisation and dialogical mutuality; and third, by indexing it to the virtue of democracy as the ideal way of running a society (Minson, 1993, p172).

With this emphasis on discussion, politics itself becomes idealised as a *perpetual conversation*. Indeed, as we shall see in a moment, this was the main basis for one of the most trenchant critiques of liberal democracy, Schmitt's attack on parliamentarianism as being an endless 'game' of talk without action or decision, akin to the seminar in the senior common room of a liberal arts college; the disinterested meeting of minds as an occasion for self-display.[5]

As an alternative to these 'romanticised' views of language and discussion Minson proposes the notion of an 'art of negotiation'. This is not an idealised truth-orientated dialogue but a process of *truce*-seeking, looking for common ground, culminating in a binding decision, that is attentive to the capacities of agents in the process to muster their arguments and to preserve their positions. It becomes promoted as a *modus vivendi* for a particular type of governmental activity committed to the negotiation of differences. It is a 'technique of intervention' or 'technology' (but also, perhaps, an instance of what has come to be known as 'empowered deliberative democracy' – see Feng and Wright, 1999). Below I develop these notions a little more as one of the possible 'principles' for the establishment of toleration in modern day international affairs.

A further important salient feature of liberalism is its presumption that there exists a political community that is homogeneous enough to be governed, regulated or managed (Hindess, 1991, 1992). In this case sovereignty is able to exercise its effective control because a generalised consent is in principle possible. But without this presumption the juridico-discursive notion of sovereignty is unhinged. A number of centres of political capacity can exist amongst which there is no necessary presumption of social passivity and consensual agreement. Any such agreement must be negotiated or struggled for, and will only ever be contingently established. This relates to the next and final point in this section.

The fifth point is to raise the issue of war and peace within the broadly liberal programme. The analysis of peace as a political condition is not well advanced within this tradition, despite what might be thought from the analysis described above. Paradoxically this arises because of its analysis of the opposite of peace, that is of war. For liberalism war is a futile waste of time, life and resources. It is the unanalysed 'other' of the social peace it presumes as the norm. 'War is an abnormal political condition and one destined to be historically transient with the march of intellectual, moral and economic progress' (Hirst, 1987, p. 204). As we move inexorably towards the emancipatory utopia, based upon the forward march of reason and education, war will simply disappear. We come back to this in a moment when dealing with the future of toleration in the international system.

The New Medievalism or a New Holy Roman Empire

It is in this context that the 'return to Medievalism' conception has taken hold (Cerny, 1998).[6] The thesis of 'neo-Medievalism' stresses the fragmentation and disruption of the political order. This not only typifies the domestic but also the international order, which is the one concentrated upon here. As a consequence, instability and turbulence become the *norms* of political activity, not the exceptions. Thus we see the emergence of a large number of different and antagonistically poised political forces and actors representing *competing* centres of power and influence. In particular sub-state actors and organisations become more important. As a consequence of these processes the nation state becomes progressively undermined as a coherent entity which can exercise effective political authority. In fact, any governance mechanisms – whether domestic or international – no longer function. There is no 'social order' to govern. Rather a radical disorder prevails. As a further consequence, life becomes rather uncomfortable – it may even be brutish and short. The rise of terrorism, fundamentalism, local militias, peasant armies, mercenaries, etc., begin to forcefully enter the political scene. These become the categories for a popular political discussion.

It has to be said that this is an interesting and forceful presentation of the world we live in. There is some truth in it and it needs to be taken seriously. But it is an exaggerated view of our present predicament and is ultimately an inadequate expression of the current international situation. I argue that this is the wrong 'model' by which to judge the possible character of the emerging contemporary international social milieu. Rather, I argue, the Ottoman Empire (OE) or the Holy Roman Empire (HRE) represents better analogies to the present situation, such that one can establish any connection here. In fact, of course, neither of these is a satisfactory 'model' because, as yet, we have not fully degenerated into a complete antagonistic pluralist position – this is only a tendential process. Nor is the issue one of a 'new OE' or 'new HRE'. These are simply presented as more adequate frameworks for thinking about the present situation, not as fully adequate ones. Indeed, we would expect the contemporary situation to be unique, with no historical counterpart.

The HRE is interesting and important because it was the first truly *international* governance system. It was an international order as well as a domestic or 'national' one. The HRE was a system in which a whole host of different political allegiances and organisational entities existed, all potentially in conflict with one another. But this plurality of organised political forces and institutions was held together in a certain configurative order (if not always a peaceful one) by the constitutional nature of the Empire. The complexity of those estates and domains that existed under the umbrella of the HRE is difficult for us to appreciate in the context of modern politics which assumes a homogeneous culture and community of citizens. A vast array of religious groupings, principalities, guilds, city-states, free cities, leagues, and so on, existed as definite political entities within the HRE, exercising their semi-autonomous political jurisdictions and conducting their own political business, as at the same time they owed some allegiance to the constitutional order of the Empire (Bryce, 1968 – first published in 1864). In the case of the OE we can point to the very many instances of different confessional groupings, for instance, existing cheek by jowl within the same city-state or political entity, but operating under different legal and administrative systems, and practising their different religious rituals undisturbed (Braude and Lewis, 1982).

The difference between the image of the new Medievalism and that of the OE or HRE is that these latter were definite social and constitutional orders, all be it rather unusual ones (though not unique – similar heterogeneities of political, social and religious groupings existed in many other city-states of the Ancient World and the Middle- and Far East). Nor is this to claim more for these pre-modern political configurations than is warranted. The Ottoman Empire, for instance, was by no means an egalitarian order; it was riddled by differences of power and authority establishing practices of domination and subordination, often in quite harsh ways. But whatever the 'tolerances' of the OE and HRE, these began to break up in the sixteenth and seventeenth centuries with the European religious wars and the gradual dissolution of the OE, aided by the emergent European states. In fact the ending of the religious wars within the framework of the HRE was a very significant event in the conduct and understanding of modern international relations, and it is this aspect that we turn to next.

The Westphalian System[7]

Almost every elementary introductory international relations textbook mentions the Treaty of Westphalia of 1648 as marking the inauguration of the 'modern' state system and of international relations between sovereign national communities (actually this comprised two treaties, that signed at Munster and at Osnabruck, both of which were in Westphalia). This Treaty established the principle of 'non-interference' by states in the domestic affairs of other states. However, the usual way this is conceived is to consider it in terms of a set of already constituted and settled national communities with 'sovereignty' who come together in terms of the Treaty to establish the principle of non-interference in each other's affairs. With this conception, 'sovereignty' exists prior to the entry of the 'nation states' into an international agreement to limit the powers of those national states.

In fact the Treaty of Westphalia at one and the same time did both more and less than this. The Treaty essentially consolidated the provisions of the Peace of Augsburg (1555). It allowed the confessional character of a state to be determined by its ruler with the agreement that other states should not interfere or intervene in the internal religious affairs of that state; they should respect its confessional character and refrain from inciting trouble or supporting domestic religious strife in other states. (In fact this religious 'toleration' was only extended to those of Catholic, Lutheran and Calvinist faiths.) But this was not a question of already sovereign states making such an agreement, since no such sovereignty had yet been established. What the Treaty did was to enable the parties, at least in large part, to precisely establish their sovereignty by allowing them to construct their internal political arrangements as suited their purpose. It enabled rulers to consolidate their power and authority within a definite territorial domain without interference from outside or over which there had previously been some dispute. Thus this Treaty was the *source* of the ruler's 'sovereignty' not the effective exercise of its already configurated existence. For the first time an international treaty was instrumental in establishing not only the 'rights' of the ruler over his or her territory, but also certain 'rights' of individual citizens within that territory. A key clause in the Treaty was one allowing emigration for those who did not wish to adhere to the confessional character of the state in which they lived. From then on pogroms were no longer an 'acceptable' way of dealing with religious strife. Thus, in effect, this clause also established the right of individual religious conscience – probably the first ever 'civil right' – which could legitimately exist alongside the different confessional character of the state in which such individuals lived. The Treaty of Westphalia thus established the principle of religious toleration (if not always its practice, of course). It also showed how an *international* treaty was of key importance in establishing the rights of individuals within their domestic territories who, potentially at least, could claim these rights against certain powers of the ruler him/herself. This function of international treaties as establishing the possibilities for legal disputation amongst an aggrieved domestic citizenry is one of the most important lessons to be learned from the whole Westphalian reflection. It is a feature of many an international treaty since, and one, it might be added, that has proved invaluable in generalising and universalising the values of a liberal social order.

However, at the same time as indicating to the key role of the Treaty of Westphalia in establishing certain early *principles* of a liberal international order, this should not divert us from recognising the limitation of the Treaty as the founding moment for modern international relations. These 'principles' have never prevented states from usurping them at will as suited their purpose and 'national interest', particularly the European states. The boundaries between the European states have been continually redrawn since the 1650s. These states were active in undermining the Ottoman Empire to the east, and they embarked upon the 'great adventure' of imperialism with little regard for the niceties of the Treaty of Westphalia. In a certain sense, it was only during the period of the Cold War that national territorial boundaries within Europe were stabilised for any length of time. And since the demise of the Cold War many of the old ways have returned. Even in the heartland of the Western European state system, boundaries have again been redrawn (German reunification, for instance), let alone to the south and the east of Europe.

What Are the Consequences for a Better Understanding of the Present?

What does all this amount to for an analysis of the present period? First, to sum up on the discussion so far we can point to three things:

A] Liberalism – both domestically and internationally – is at least under a threat which should be taken seriously by all those who have an interest in the preservation of an open and tolerant society. These threats need to be 'attended to' and not ignored or dismissed as an irrelevancy, something of concern only to a few disgruntled intellectuals.

B] The present period is not one best characterised as a return to a new kind of medieval disorder. Rather it is better thought of as more akin to the fragmented order of the OE or HRE. The international system still exists within certain social and constitutional orders. These continue to provide the contours for an effective political and economic governance at both the international and national levels.

C] These constitutional orders are increasingly taking the form of 'confederal public powers' at the international level. A confederal public power is just what it says. It is a public power – thus in some way ordered and minimally accountable – but it does not exist in the form of a government or a state. It is 'confederal' as distinguished from 'federal' or 'unitary' forms of power. The difference between confederal and federal systems needs further clarification, since there is widespread confusion and misinformation about these in present political discussion (particularly in the context of the debate about the possible future of European governmental arrangements). Broadly speaking, the difference between a federal system and a confederal one is twofold. First, power and authority are derived in a 'top down' fashion in a federation, from the federal level to the federees, whereas they are 'bottom up' in confederations, with the confederees establishing the limits to the powers of the confederal authority which it is not allowed to exceed. Secondly, federation members have no legal right to leave a federation once it is established. The federation takes on the form of a sovereign authority. In confederal arrangements, however, the confederees retain the legal entitlement to leave the confederation if they wish, so that it is the confederees that retain their formal sovereign authority.[8]

The argument here is that existent and emergent new international organisations of political and economic governance are increasingly taking the form of confederal public powers, and not of governments or states. These are organised through treaties and international laws, establishing a network of overlapping powers, jurisdictions and responsibilities for the conduct of international affairs that still represents a relatively robust international constitutional regime (however frayed and challenged this may seem to be). What is more, these international treaties, laws and organisations are continuing to confer powers on the citizens of national economies and polities that often challenge the power and authority of national governments (who often resent this and try to undermine it).

However, as already indicated, this still existent international social order is increasingly under threat by the powers of a newly emergent and invigorated 'antagonistic pluralism'. This poses a real threat, making the brokering of 'peaceful' resolutions to conflicts all the more difficult. The question this raises is how to buttress the existing system of orders and regimes that maintain arrangements for domestic and international governance in the face of these kinds of threats.

The Present Conjuncture

The central analytical categories that drove much of post-World War II Anglo-American political science were those of *liberal pluralism* and its 'other', *totalitarianism*. These twin categories neatly summed up the virtues of the Western market model of plural capitalism on the one hand, and the evil of either fascist or communist dictatorships on the other. No matter the actual way Anglo-American foreign policy might have actually behaved towards either of these 'other' political formations in practice, the dichotomy between liberal pluralism and totalitarianism served its purpose well in providing a simple, but rhetorically effective, register for the good and the evil.

In particular it worked well in the context of the Cold War, and the supposed and real threats posed by the 'Evil-Empire' to the east. As that Evil Empire has collapsed, however, these categories no longer seem to serve their purpose so well. To begin with 'liberal pluralism' now seems only too restrictive in its embrace as the advanced capitalist countries are seen to demonstrate a variety of political and economic configurations, with quite different modes of politico-economic governance. What use is this category as a neat summary when even large parts of the Chinese economy are now recognised to be 'capitalist' in all but name? Similarly, in the case of Eastern Europe and the ex-Soviet Union itself, where the newly emerging 'peripheral' post-communist nation states can hardly all be described as 'liberal pluralist' nor as simply totalitarian in a new guise (though some of then may be heading that way).

Thus the ending of the Cold War has fractured many of the often complacent analytical attitudes towards economic and political investigation, that far from confirming the Enlightenment's emancipatory vision of the 'end of history', now poses a real challenge to that vision and its attendant liberal governmental project and to the conditions for the continuation of a relative open intellectual culture. The Hobbesian vision of generalised social anarchy could be about to reappear as ethnic and religious strife returns with a vengeance, with no overriding 'ideological' battle to provide the conditions for either a domestic or international hegemonic stability. Not only have 'localised' international relations become more fraught, but also domestic fragmentation and strife seems to be on the increase. This is a period in which it could be said that liberal pluralism has been eclipsed by a new period of generalised *antagonistic pluralism*.[9]

Antagonistic pluralism is a system in which the pluralisation of interests and social forces multiplies, in which it becomes increasingly difficult to organise compromises and agreement between them, and in which the usual channels of democratic activity look increasingly suspect and lose their legitimacy (they literally become just 'talking-shops' in the manner of the romantic-idealist variant of the celebration of discussion mentioned above). The new period is accompanied by an increase in the extent of ungovernable *manic capitalism* in a good many of the newly emergent post-communist countries, and in some of the older liberal democracies that have embarked upon massive 'neo-liberal' deregulatory programmes. Manic capitalism is a frenetic economic system embodying an intense and uncontrollable dynamic of competitive activity driven as much by corruption, marketeering, speculation, profiteering and mismanagement as by genuine ordered economic exchange.

This is also a period in which that carefully crafted liberal 'art of separation' begins to falter (Walzer, 1984). This art of separation draws lines of demarcation between different realms; between Church and state;

between the universities and the government; between different tiers of government; between civil society and political community; between the domestic and the public spheres, etc. Once these separations are removed all social activity can quickly become subject to a single dictate; continual and uncontrollable administrative reform along an unstable combination of 'neo-liberal' and 'neo-conservative' doctrinal lines as in the UK; sectarian religious orthodoxy in a number of Islamic countries; nationalistic fervour in many of the ex-communist states.

Where does this analysis leave us? The problem is to return to 'order' without returning to a new form of 'Absolutism'. It is to avoid a return to the Hobbesian nightmare of a new generalised social anarchy. It is to recognise the legitimacy and efficacy of a continued pluralism, while at the same time seeking to minimise its degeneration into intolerance, extremism or sectarianism; to strengthen the virtue of moderation and to remain confessionally neutral. At the level of political theory this implies a recognition of the 'pluralisation of sovereignties' (Reinicke, 1998; Krasner, 1999); the *de facto* effective dispersal of sovereignty needs to be embodied in a new political settlement which recognises this *de jure*. This itself implies the development of federal and confederal political formations, existing in different overlapping combinations and levels, but which continue to constitute a definite 'constitutional order' (in the form of an 'entity' but not necessarily as a 'unity'). Thus what is attempted here is to provide an essentially non-liberal defence of certain key aspects of liberalism.

Containing the Threats from Without and Within

Thus peace as a *political condition* – as something that must be established by negotiation and political action, not simply presumed as the normal – is problematical for liberalism and other emancipatory calculative political ideologies and programmes. Such that peace is taken seriously here, it usually appears as the outcome of some supra-national organisation *imposing* peace. In the extreme this can involve the call for 'world government' and a 'world state', another fanciful branch of the emancipatory project, but one, this time, with a rather sinister twist. World peace would be the outcome of a war to establish it; the war to end all wars. Less extreme 'liberal' suggestions involve the 'collective security' of agents like the UN, NATO, the EC or other supra-national organisations 'establishing peace', but again usually through the use of terror. 'Collective security' is often a euphemism for the organisation for war in anticipation that this will secure peace, which can very rarely by itself ever offer stable, long-term conditions for peace.

Long-term peace can only be established and maintained by the continual application of political acumen and the interventionary technique of negotiation, entered into 'voluntarily' by those potentially engaged in armed struggle. This will inevitably breakdown at times, so war will never be entirely eliminated in the same way that other conflicts will remain. Unfortunately, we cannot expect the operation of 'conscience' or 'ethics' to have much impact on establishing lasting peace. To his credit Kant in *Perpetual Peace* (Kant, 1977) did recognise the need for a political *rapprochement* between states (and other parties), and the establishment of ongoing institutionalised mechanisms for the organisation of peace as a political condition ('republican' constitutions; 'universal association of states', i.e. a treaty of respect between the parties; 'commercial' interactions between them, i.e. universal conditions of hospitality) and he is one of the few liberal intellectuals to have done so (see Hirst, 1987; Pagden, 1998). He challenged the mentality of authoritarianism and offensive war.[10]

One other productive way that some have approached the analysis of war is to try to draw a distinction between different types of war in terms of its rationality. Thus, broadly speaking, wars over economic resources are more 'rational' than wars involving ideological disputes, which in turn have the rational edge over wars involving race, ethnic or 'nationalistic' conflicts (Thompson, 1996). Making these distinctions is not meant in any way to 'defend' wars, but it is to point to important differences between them. There is a certain logic to wars over economic resources, for instance, where a clear set of interests can usually be discerned. These kinds of wars are also much easier to bring to a conclusion and secure a peace since the object of the dispute is relatively transparent. On the other hand, inter-ethnic or inter-religious wars are particularly brutal and 'illogical', with cessation of hostilities very difficult to broker. This is because they are often driven by an intense animosity based upon emotion and passion, which in many respects is so obviously extra-calculative in form. These distinctions clearly have important implications for the present conjuncture as this latter type of dispute seems to be growing. It is towards a more thorough assessment of this present conjuncture that the next section is addressed.

Toleration as a Political Condition

It is at this juncture that we need to raise a general issue of toleration and investigate the condition under which it might operate to support an open and liberal international system. Traditionally toleration has been thought of in the context of domestic circumstances rather than international ones. The objective of this section is to develop the idea of toleration in an international context and to consider the idea of toleration as a definite 'regime' (Walzer, 1997). For Walzer 'international society' constitutes one of five 'regimes of toleration' (the others being 'multinational empires', 'consociations', 'nation-states' and 'immigrant societies'). Each of these regimes involves a certain configurative arrangement that establishes principles, protocols, forms of argument and justification, and practices of government that organise and secure 'peaceful coexistence of groups of people with different histories, cultures, and identities, which is what toleration makes possible'.[11] These regimes, whilst definite configurative orders for Walzer, are not organic wholes with an essence. Rather they are contingent forms of organisation, historically and contextually specific but not simply circumstantial nor procedurally ordered.[12] They display different modalities of regulation and norms of everyday existence in both an ideal version and as a practical arrangement of exemplification and distortion. For the purposes of the explication here I also concentrate upon the international regime of toleration as a political form of toleration, rather than as a cultural, ethical or social one. It parallels the idea of peace as a definite political condition, outlined above. What I try to demonstrate in a moment are the political conditions of possibility and the political conditions of existence of such an international regime of toleration. In many ways, particularly at the domestic level (or in terms of the other regimes that Walzer considers), it is the ethical, social and cultural aspects of toleration that tend to predominate in the discussion, and there has been some difficulty in establishing the particular modality and specificity of *political* arguments about toleration in distinction to these other (quite legitimate) dimensions. This is nowhere more clearly illustrated than in the terms of the narrow theory of liberal toleration that tend to arise from within political philosophy. Here *individual* rights and responsibilities are stressed as against those of *groups* (Galeotti, 1993). In the case of a 'liberal-pluralistic' international regime of political toleration considered here, we are talking mainly of 'groups' rather than of individuals. In addition, we are talking of groups that cannot simply be considered as aggregations of individuals, or that act as surrogate individuals in a rationalistic sense.

But given the previous historical reflections in this paper it might be best to begin with the issue of religious toleration as the formation of the nation state began in the sixteenth and seventeenth centuries. This has the advantage of raising the issue of the individual versus the group as the object of analysis in terms of toleration, and allows us to raise another key concern, that of the legitimate boundary between *public* toleration and *private* conscience as the twin elements in any discussion. The establishment of the distinction between a public sphere and a private one at the domestic level, so to speak, and the parallel distinction (if this is possible or relevant) at the international level, is one we return to in a moment.

In a masterly analysis of the advent of religious toleration in the seventeenth and eighteenth centuries, Pocock (1988) argues that this was a two step process. The first was to disengage the state from the Church, asserting the former's independence from any confessional appropriation by the latter. The second step was to turn religious experience into a matter of holding of opinions. It was in this way that radical spiritualism could be recast as a matter of private conscience. Thus – in terms of religious belief in this case – these two moves at one and the same time served to both 'de-politicise' the Church and create a 'public sphere' of state activity in distinction to a 'private sphere' of individual conscience or opinion. 'Domestic religious toleration' followed by being confined within the civil sphere, over which the state would reside and would guarantee by acting as the impartial arbitrator between any competing, but now private, interests.[13]

Clearly, an analogy between this process and a potential international regime of toleration is not directly available in terms of the distinction between a public sphere and a private one. There is no equivalent international public sphere akin to a state, and no international civil sphere to speak of which could act as the counter-party.[14] This 'problem' is well known and does not need justifying or documenting here. But it means that one must begin the discussion of internationalised toleration from a somewhat different starting point than the traditional 'liberal' one.

Constructing a Regime of International 'Toleration'

In this section I outline a number of conditions and principles that might form the basis for the development of an 'international regime of toleration'. I do not pretend that this is an exhaustive list. It simply represents a way of thinking about these matters. Such a list represents a set of terms under which it might be possible to think creatively about a relatively robust complex of mutually reinforcing principles guiding the establishment of peaceful coexistence in a fragmented and antagonistically poised international system. This list is also a speculative one. The concrete circumstances under which they might operate or how they might be deployed is not discussed here. We start with the most obvious of these conditions, the availability of financial resources and their deployment.

Money

We live in an era where 'money' is both revered and demonised. It is revered if it is privately motivated but denigrated if publicly deployed. How often do we hear the cry that money cannot solve the problem? You cannot solve this or that problem by 'throwing money at it' is the refrain of increasing numbers of politicians, pundits, journalists and commentators alike.

This is silly and needs combating. Money, publicly deployed money, can solve many problems and buttress a liberal international order, and it needs to be used explicitly to do this. One of the great lessons of history, for instance, is that threatened communities have often quite successfully 'bought off' their more powerful neighbours to prevent conflict between them. But more importantly, there is a need for a massive redistribution of economic resources and finance from the rich nations, groups and individuals to the poor nations, groups and individuals – which can only sensibly be organised through some form of public authority or agreement. If potential threats and the further slide into antagonistic conflicts that cannot be controlled are to be avoided then this is an obvious conclusion. Unfortunately, the international community has been unable to fully recognise this fact, let alone institute effective mechanisms to address it.

An interesting aside in connection to this issue is the way that even the UN is thinking of employing paid private foot soldiers – mercenaries in other words – to conduct its interventions. Both the difficulty of persuading its member governments to contribute their own armed forces, alongside the complete ineffectiveness of many of these when they are actually deployed, has raised the possibility of the use of private armed forces. If nothing else this is a poignant reminder of the distorted priorities and double standards that pervade the private versus public money debate as it impinges on the international peace-keeping sphere.

Truths and Truces

Secondly, one further way to revive the lost virtue of toleration in international affairs is to emphasise the principle of 'truce seeking' above that of 'truth seeking'. Our social order is one in which truth seeking is the deeply embedded and widely deployed one. It appears in the form of the discourse 'I am right and you are wrong' which animates so many aspects of our daily lives and intellectual culture. Finding who is to blame as things go wrong, and attributing guilt to those responsible are the supreme objectives of both our legal system and that of common justice. The finding of a true cause for things also lies behind the commitment to an interventionary political and economic culture.

But truces are interesting situations, perhaps more interesting than truth situations, if we have in mind the fostering of toleration. Truces are positions – often only temporary – in which no party is fully satisfied or which has secured all its objectives. They are neither situations of continued conflict nor of outright victory or resolution, so they avoid celebratory gloating or humiliating defeat. They are 'in between' and thus uncomfortable. Nevertheless, they are truces; what more can we ask for in a world where outbreaks of conflict of some kind seem inevitable? They offer periods for reflection and trust building. They provide an occasion to seek compromise and consensus, an opportunity to build co-operation and reconciliation. In this way truce-seeking behaviours and mechanisms represent an important way of defusing potential and actual antagonistic conflicts. They are a prime example of establishing a more tolerant framework for social order.

Sieges as Stalemates

If the conditions for truces cannot be found it might be possible to develop the mentality of sieges, or perhaps better expressed as 'stalemates'. Like truces, sieges/stalemates are interesting states of affairs. We are accustomed to think of the 'decisive battle' as the key moment in any war, and particularly in bringing about the conditions for the enemy's defeat. But historically most wars were ended 'peacefully' in the context of a siege/stalemate. In fact until relatively recently, most wars were pretty leisurely affairs. There were few actual battles, which were quickly over anyway. Most wars took the form of long marches – endless wandering about the countryside looking for the enemy – and long sieges of towns and fortifications. The (re-)development of a 'siege/stalemate mentality' amongst modern day antagonistically poised combatants provides another opportunity for the 'temporary' interruption of conflicts. If such sieges/stalemates could be turned into semi-permanent states of affairs, in effect the equivalent of 'toleration' would have been established.

Appeasement

Perhaps more controversially, there remains something to be said for resurrecting the heavily discredited concept of 'appeasement' as a principle for the strengthening of toleration. Appeasement is a tougher category than a truce or a siege/stalemate because it requires the stronger party to genuinely give up an advantage that it could exercise if it wished. It thus requires the stronger party to be magnanimous; to forego or suppress its own interest in the name of the common good of both interests. It can also be considered as a way of tolerating the intolerant (always a problem for more conventional conceptions of toleration). This category is a 'dangerous' one, because it requires suppression of an advantage which could backfire. But the taking of such risks is a necessary feature of any system that has as its ultimate objective the strengthening of the peace overall.

Separation

Finally, however, we may have to face afresh the fact that agreement on an 'integrated' toleration is not possible to achieve. The conventional liberal wisdom is that integration and multiculturalism are the ultimate virtues for a tolerant society. Indeed, Julia Kristeva has strongly argued for this to constitute the key approach to the establishment of a genuine tolerant national and international order: the abandonment of a commitment to national borders and the radical embrace of 'otherness' (Kristeva, 1991 and 1993). Whilst these clearly remain worthy sentiments, they will probably remain just that – pure sentiments. The idea that groups will quickly and quietly give up national aspirations seems unlikely. In addition, this approach suffers from the 'postmodernist' conceptual weaknesses mentioned above when discussing liberalism as an endless conversation.

Rather, it may be necessary to reinstate physical separatedness as a realistic criterion for toleration. This would echo the points made above about the nature of the HRE and the OE, where physical separation between confessional, cultural and ethnic groupings was common, even as they existed in close proximity to one another. *De facto* separation has tended to arise in cases of extreme antagonistic pluralism anyway, so now may be the time to embrace this more formally, and organise for it, rather than maintain the pretence of integration and multiculturalism. Properly organised and supervised, such an approach might actually enhance toleration rather than undermine it, as is often argued. It is not necessarily a 'failure' of toleration to recognise the desire of particular communities to live apart if they cannot live together. This involves a (reluctant) substitution of 'mutual extraterritoriality' for 'separate territoriality'.

And this brief discussion of separatedness of combatants enables us to raise again the issue of what all this toleration is about. The problem is that the legacy of nation state building and imperialism has left some uncomfortable, or grossly unfair, and often unsustainable 'territorial boundary problems', the inequities of which are understandably the objects of struggle for those disadvantaged by the arbitrariness of those processes. The 'hand of fate' involved in nation building and imperialism has left many with an outcome that does not at all suit their purpose. Existing nation states are nothing more than a 'community of fate'. Why should those disadvantaged groups not challenge the existing boundaries of the international system and upset any carefully crafted toleration built around them?

Well of course they will. The regime of toleration suggested here does not justify the intolerable. There will always be conflict. The conception of politics deployed in this analysis perceives it as constituted by, and constitutive of, 'disagreements' (Ranciere, 1999) and 'antagonisms' (Mouffe, this volume). These cannot be neatly 'negotiated' out of the system as a generalised 'tolerant' consensus and agreement emerges. But what the suggested regime of toleration requires as a minimum is that all sides accept to a certain extent the existing boundaries of the system as a legitimate aspect of its existence. This does require a certain compromise, a certain appreciation that the legacy it embodies carries its own legitimacy, that these boundaries cannot be destroyed at will since they have constituted their own 'new' sets of expectations and commitments, whether this is liked or not.

To reiterate, then, what has been presented here is a modest attempt to suggest a set of terms under which international political toleration could be considered. I remain as uneasy and as uncomfortable about much of this as anyone else, but some of it needs to be confronted if we are to strengthen the fragmented international constitutional order in which we still rather precariously exist.

Conclusion

The attempt in this paper has been to take a realistic view of the 'end of liberalism' by defending some of its core values, but by doing this within a different intellectual context and register. It has been an attempt to defend certain aspects of the liberal project in overtly non-liberal terms.[15] What features of the enlightened liberal project are defended here (e.g. toleration, democratic plural political organisation, appeasement, etc.) are done so from a position that sees these as part of an 'art of governance' that has its roots not just in some emancipatory project of a post-Enlightenment form.

It is to disengage these 'arts of governance' from that Enlightenment project that constitutes one of the main objectives and the rationale of this chapter. The international regime of toleration hinted at in the last part of the paper might be considered just such an instance of the 'art of governance'. Whether this remains a 'liberal' one or not in large part misses the point. The position adopted here is not a liberal one but nor is it one that celebrates a total pragmatism. Any 'art of governance' needs principles or criteria to guide its politics, and these I have concentrated upon in the closing sections.

Acknowledgements

I am grateful to my colleagues at the Open University, particularly Simon Bromley, Montserrat Guibernau and Mike Saward, for discussion and comments. During and after the conference, Paul Hirst and Barry Hindess made telling comments about the paper, for which I thank them both. I have tried to respond to their comments in this chapter.

Notes

1. As Koselleck amply demonstrates, the great theorist of the Absolute State, Thomas Hobbes, was instrumental in developing this notion of an individual with an inner self exclusive to its private ruminations (Koselleck, 1988, pp. 23-40).
2. As Kamen (1967: 194-5) comments: 'It would be true – and paradoxical – to say that absolutism was in the long run the friend of toleration, since by asserting its authority and control over the majority church it subordinated Church to State and prevented the former from exercising undue coercion against dissenting minorities' (p. 217). And '... absolutism required not the elimination of dissident religions but the annihilation of their political autonomy'.
3. These themes are explored in the essays in Koselleck (1985), as well as in Koselleck (1988).
4. Although it is rather difficult to directly concretise this distinction in terms of particular national political regimes, the case of Israel comes to mind as one where the political system is democratic in a constitutional sense but that system is not quite a liberal one. Perhaps another example would be the old Yugoslavia, where the 'socialist' regime was clearly not liberal but where the constitution displayed certain strong democratic elements. On the *philosophical* difficulty of separating 'democracy' and 'liberalism' in the context of post-Enlightenment thinking and modern, but conventional, conceptions of the nature of a 'liberal toleration', see the discussion in Rorty (1988). In this case, Rorty's suggestion – drawing heavily on a particular reading of Rawls – is to prioritise democracy over liberalism (where the latter is summed up under the heading of 'philosophy' is the discussion) in suturing the two together again.
5. In many ways this idealised notion of liberal politics as endless open discussion involves the idea of language as a system of signification that implicitly invokes the

106 Habitus: A Sense of Place

'other' as a constitutive moment in its operation. It is common to the 'post-structuralist' and 'post-modernist' imperative to always seek to involve 'the other' in a reciprocal, dialogically imaginative discourse, or to see knowledge as *just* the result of an effective rhetorical strategy to argue and persuade. (Later I discuss Julia Kristeva's approach to toleration, which relies explicitly on this theoretical architecture of 'otherness' – see Kristeva, 1991 and 1993).

6 Cerny (1998) is a representative example of this trend, but it also animates much of his other recent writings on the international system. Probably the modern originator on the debate about neo-Medievalism was Bull (1977).
7 This section relies heavily upon Hirst (1997), chapter 14. See, also, Gelber (1997).
8 See Hamilton, Madison and Jay (1987: 159) and Wilson (1967: 249-55) for a discussion and specification of the differences between confederations and federations.
9 This is a term originally coined by Carl Schmitt in the context of the degeneration of the Weimar constitutional period in Germany prior to the World War II (see Schmitt, 1985 and 1986 in particular).
10 Kant cannot, however, be excused from situating his discussion of the evolution of international society squarely within terms of an overall emancipatory project in a classic Enlightenment form (see Pagden, 1998).
11 Kamen (1967: 84) nicely defines toleration as a '… spirit of charitable dogmatic comprehension and compromise'.
12 They are not properly circumstantial because they are not differentiated by time and place, and they are not procedural in terms of a sequence nor in terms of a single set of constitutional principles that 'procedurally' unfold to constitute them.
13 The defining relationship between toleration and religion is summed up by Kamen (1967: 7): 'In its broadest sense, toleration can be understood to mean the concession of liberty to those who dissent in religion.'
14 Hindess (1999: 66) has argued that, in effect, there was an external equivalent to a 'public sphere' that operated at the inauguration of the state system. To distribute populations to territories requires a certain mode of governance external to the subsequent independent and competing states so created. 'The division of humanity into distinct national populations, many of them with their own national territories and states, operates as a dispersed regime of governance of the larger human population.' But it is not clear quite what form this 'agency' took from his analysis.
15 For an outstanding analysis of the difficulties that arise for the 'philosophical liberal' attempt to defend religious (in)toleration in the contemporary era, see Isaac *et al.* (1999). These authors use the term 'apolitical liberalism' to describe what is here called 'philosophical liberalism'.

References

Braude, Benjamin and Lewis, Bernard (1982) *Christians and Jews in the Ottoman Empire: the functioning of a plural society*, Vol. 1 The Central Lands, New York, Holmes and Meier Publishing Co.
Bryce, James (1968) *The Holy Roman Empire*, London, Macmillan.
Bull, Hedley (1977) *The Anarchical Society*, Basingstoke, Macmillan.
Burchell, Graham, Gordon, Colin and Miller, Peter (eds) (1991) *The Foucault Effect: studies in governmentality*, Hemel Hempstead, Harvester Wheatsheaf.
Cerny, Phillip (1998) 'Neomedievalism, civil war and the new security dilemma: globalization as durable disorder', *Civil Wars*, 1(1): 36-64.

Dean, Mitchell (1999) *Governmentality*, London, Sage.
Feng, Archon and Wright, Erik O. (1999) 'Experiments in empowered deliberative democracy: introduction', Mimeo, University of Wisconsin-Madison.
Foucault, Michel (1981) 'Omnes et singulatum: towards a criticism of "political reason"', in S. McMurrin (ed.) *Tanner Lectures on Human Values Volume II*, Salt Lake City, University of Utah Press.
Galeotti, Anna E. (1993) 'Citizenship and equality: the place of toleration', *Political Theory*, 21(4), November: 585-605.
Gelber, Harry (1997) *Sovereignty Through Interdependence*, London, Kluwer Law International.
Hamilton, A., Madison, J. and Jay, J. (1987) *The Federalist Papers*, Harmondsworth, Penguin Books.
Hindess, Barry (1991) 'The imaginary presuppositions of democracy', *Economy and Society*, 20(2): 173-95.
Hindess, Barry (1992) 'Power and rationality: the western concept of political community', *Governance*, 17: 149-63.
Hindess, Barry (1999) 'Divide and rule: the international character of modern citizenship', *European Journal of Social Theory*, Vol.1, No.1, pp. 57-70.
Hirst, Paul Q. (1987) 'Peace and political theory', *Economy and Society*, Vol 16, No. 2, May, pp. 204-219.
Hirst, Paul Q. (1997) *From Statism to Pluralism*, London, ULU Press.
Isaac, J.C., Filner, M.F. and Bivins, J.C. (1999) 'American democracy and the new Christian right: a critique of apolitical liberalism', in Shapiro, I. and Hacker-Cordon, C. (eds) *Democracy's Edges*, Cambridge, Cambridge University Press.
Kamen, H. (1967) *The Rise of Toleration*, London, Weidenfeld and Nicholson.
Kant, Emmanuel (1977) 'Perpetual peace', in H.S. Reiss (ed.), *Kant's Political Writings*, Cambridge, Cambridge University Press.
Koselleck, Reinhart (1985) *Futures Past: on the semantics of historical time*, Cambridge, Mass., MIT Press.
Koselleck, Reinhart (1988) *Critique and Crisis: enlightenment and the pathogenesis of modern society*, Oxford, Berg.
Krasner, Stephen. D. (1999) *Sovereignty: organized hypocrisy*, Princeton, NJ, Princeton University Press.
Kristeva, Julia (1991) *Strangers to Ourselves*, New York, Columbia University Press.
Kristeva, Julia (1993) *Nations Without Nationalism*, Columbia, New York, University Press.
Marcuse, H. (1965) 'Repressive tolerance', in Wolff, R.P., Barrington Moore, J. and Marcuse, H. (eds) *A Critique of Pure Tolerance*, Boston, Beacon Books.
Minson, Jeffrey (1993) *Questions of conduct: sexual harassment, citizenship*, government. Basingstoke, Macmillan Press.
Oestreich, Gerhard (1982) *Neostoicism and the early modern state*, Cambridge, Cambridge University Press.
Pagden, Anthony (1998) 'The genesis of "Governance" and Enlightenment conceptions of the cosmopolitan world order', *International Social Science Journal*, 155, March: 7-15.
Pocock, J.G.A. (1988) 'Religious freedom and the desacralization of politics: from English civil wars to the Virginia Statute', in Peterson, M.D. and Vaughan, R.C. (eds) *The Virginia Statute for Religious Freedom*, Cambridge, Cambridge University Press.
Ranciere, J. (1999) *Dis-agreement: politics and philosophy*, Minneapolis, University of Minnesota Press.
Reinicke, Wolfgang H. (1998) *Global Public Policy: governing without government*, Washington, DC, Brookings Institute.

Rorty, Richard (1988) 'The priority of democracy to philosophy', in Peterson, M.D. and Vaughan, R.C. (eds) *The Virginia Statute for Religious Freedom*, Cambridge, Cambridge University Press.

Schmitt, Carl (1985) *The Crisis of Parliamentary Democracy*, Cambridge, Mass., MIT Press.

Schmitt, Carl (1986) *Political Romanticism*, Cambridge, Mass., MIT Press.

Thompson, Grahame F. (1996) 'Modeling war', *Review of International Politics*, 358-64.

Walzer, Michael (1984) 'Liberalism and the art of separation', *Political Theory*, 12(3), August: 315-330.

Walzer, Michael (1997) *On Toleration*, New Haven, Yale University Press.

Wilson, James (1967) 'Lectures on law, VIII: of man as a member of a confederacy', in Robert Green McClosky, (ed.), *The Works of James Wilson*, Cambridge, Mass, Harvard University Press.

6 Which Kind of Public Space for a Democratic Habitus?

CHANTAL MOUFFE

I would like to present some reflections concerning the kind of public sphere required by a vibrant democratic society. My starting point is that it is in the context of the increasingly irrelevant role played by the 'political public sphere' in democratic societies that we should understand the growing dominance of the juridical and moral discourses, dominance which I see as being inimical to democracy.

There are many reasons for the decline of the political, but I intend to concentrate my attention on one dimension which I take to be particularly important, the lack of democratic forms of identifications offered to citizens in current liberal democratic societies. Such identifications are important in that through them passions could be mobilised towards democratic designs; they could provide the basis for a vibrant agonistic debate about the shape and the future of the common life.

Because of the lack of a democratic political public sphere where the agonistic confrontation could take place, it is increasingly the legal system which is seen as being responsible for organising human coexistence and for regulating social relations. Given the growing impossibility of envisaging the problems of society in a political way, there is a marked tendency to privilege the juridical terrain and to expect the law to provide solutions for all types of conflict.

There are many reasons for the weakening of the democratic political public sphere; some have to do with the predominance of a neo-liberal regime of globalisation, others with the type of individualistic consumer culture which now pervades most advanced industrial societies. From a more strictly political perspective, it is clear that the collapse of communism and the disappearance of the political frontiers which structured the political imaginary in the second half of this century have created a void which has led to the crisis of the political markers of democracy. The steady blurring of the frontiers between left and right that we have witnessed in Western societies and which is often presented as progress and a sign of maturity is, in my view, one of the clearest manifestations of the disintegration of the political dimension. Indeed, when a society lacks a dynamic democratic life with a diversity of democratic political identities, the ground is laid for other forms of identifications to take their place, identifications of an ethnic, religious or nationalist nature. When passions cannot be mobilised by democratic parties because they privilege a 'consensus at the centre' and where there is no alternative to the dominant order, those passions find other outlets, in various fundamentalist movements and around particularistic demands or non-negotiable moral issues or they are mobilised by right-wing populist parties.

However, in the present intellectual climate it is not easy to recognise this problem, let alone to begin searching for remedies. Our present Zeitgeist is characterised by a profound aversion to the political. What is fashionable today is ethics, morality, law but certainly not politics. No wonder that so many people are heralding the 'end of politics' and claiming the disappearance of antagonism. Among politicians the dominant discourse is about the 'radical centre beyond left and right', the 'third way' and calls for a general reconciliation of all in an inclusive idea of the 'people'.

What we are witnessing with the current infatuation with humanitarian crusades, ethically correct good causes and the hypertrophy of the judiciary is the triumph of a moralising liberalism which pretends that the political has been eradicated and that society can now be ruled through rational moral procedures and conflicts resolved by impartial tribunals.

As a political theorist I am particularly concerned with the pernicious influence that political theory is playing in this displacement of politics by morality. Indeed, in the approach which under the name of 'deliberative democracy' is fast imposing the terms of the discussion, one of the main tenets is that political questions are of a moral nature and therefore susceptible to a rational treatment. The objective of democracy is, according to such a view, the creation of a rational consensus reached through appropriate procedures whose aim is to produce decisions which represent an impartial standpoint equally in the interests of all. All those who put into question the very possibility of such a rational consensus and who affirm that the political is a domain where it is unavoidable that one should rationally expect discord are accused of undermining the very possibility of democracy.

This theoretical trend to conflate politics with morality, understood in rationalist and universalistic terms, has very negative consequences for democratic politics because it erases the dimension of antagonism which is ineradicable in politics. It has contributed to the current retreat of the political and to its replacement by the juridical and the moral which are perceived as particularly adequate terrains for reaching impartial decisions.

There is therefore a strong link between this kind of liberal discourse and the demise of the political. In fact the current situation can be seen as the culmination of a tendency inscribed at the very core of liberalism which, because of its constitutive incapacity to think in truly political terms, always has to replace it by another type of discourse, whether economic, moral or juridical.

This leads them to miss a crucial point, not only about the primary reality of strife in social life, and the impossibility of finding rational, impartial solutions to political issues, but also about the integrative role that conflict plays in modern democracy. Indeed, a well-functioning democracy calls for a vibrant clash of democratic political positions. Too much emphasis on consensus, together with aversion towards confrontations, leads to apathy and to disaffection with political participation.

Consensus is indeed needed on the institutions which are constitutive of democracy, but there will always be disagreement concerning the way social justice should be implemented in and through those institutions. In a pluralist democracy such disagreements should be considered as legitimate and indeed welcome. They provide different forms of citizenship identification and are the stuff of democratic politics. However it is precisely the kind of questions that the dominant rationalist approach prevents us from grasping adequately. Hence the need for an alternative approach that will allow us to envisage the democratic public sphere in a different way.

A Wittgensteinian Approach to Political Theory

My claim in this paper is that an approach influenced by Wittgenstein's conception of practices and languages games could be very fruitful for clarifying some of the issues at stake in the contemporary debates about the nature of modern democratic politics and to begin elaborating a non-rationalist perspective in political theory.

For a start Wittgenstein allows us to think of consensus in a very different way from the rationalist. For him, to have any agreement of opinions, there must first be agreement on the language used. And he also alerted us to the fact that those agreements of opinions are in fact agreements in forms of life. As he says: 'So you are saying that human agreement decides what is true and what is false. It is what human beings say that is true and false; and they agree in the language they use. That is not agreement in opinions but in form of life.'[1]

This points to the fact that a considerable number of 'agreements in judgements' must already exist in a society before a given set of procedures can work. For Wittgenstein, to agree on the definition of a term is not enough and we need agreement in the way we use it. He puts it in the following way: 'if language is to be a means of communication there must be agreement not only in definitions but also (queer as this may sound) in judgements'. (Wittgenstein, 1958: 242)

Procedures only exist as complex ensembles of practices. Those practices constitute specific forms of individuality and identity that make possible the allegiance to the procedures. It is because they are inscribed in shared forms of life and agreements in judgements that procedures can be accepted and followed. They cannot be seen as rules that are created on the basis of principles and then applied to specific cases. Rules, for Wittgenstein, are always abridgements of practices, inseparable from specific forms of life. This means that the distinction between procedural and substantial cannot therefore be as clear as some would have it. In the case of justice, for instance, I do not think that one can oppose, as so many liberals do, procedural and substantial justice without recognising that procedural justice already presupposes acceptance of certain values. It is the liberal conception of justice which posits the priority of the right over the good but this is also the expression of a specific good. Democracy is not only a matter of establishing the right procedures independently of the practices that make possible democratic forms of individuality. The question of the conditions of existence of democratic forms of individuality and of the practices and languages games in which they are constituted is a central one, even in a liberal democratic society where procedures play a central role. Procedures always involve substantial ethical commitments. For that reason they cannot work properly if they are not supported by a democratic ethos or a democratic habitus.

This last point is very important since it leads us to acknowledge that a liberal democratic conception of justice and liberal democratic institutions require a democratic habitus in order to function properly and maintain themselves. This is something that Habermas's discourse theory of procedural democracy is unable to grasp, because of the sharp distinction that Habermas wants to draw between moral-practical discourses and ethical-practical discourses. It is not enough to state, as Habermas does, criticising Apel, that a discourse theory of democracy cannot be based only on the formal pragmatic conditions of communication and that it must take account of legal, moral, ethical and pragmatic argumentation. What is missing in such an approach is the crucial importance of a democratic 'Sittlichkeit'.

Democracy as a 'Form of Life'

The thesis I want to put forward is that allegiance to democratic institutions can only rest on identification with the practices, the language games and the institutions which are constitutive of our form of life. It is mistaken to believe that it is by providing them with some kind of rational justification that such an allegiance could be secured. One must accept that there can never be any final guarantee in those matters and that the only thing that we can do to consolidate democracy is to multiply the institutions and discourses that create and reproduce democratic forms of individuality. Only when liberal democratic citizens recognise that their identity depends on the social relations that constitute the liberal democratic form of life will they be prepared to fight for the defence of those institutions.

It seems to me that what such an approach brings to the fore is that allegiance to liberal democratic institutions requires that the individuals living in those societies value the identity and the form of life that liberal democratic institutions make possible. It is for that reason that the new forms of exclusion that we are witnessing in advanced liberal democracies represent a great danger for their survival. Indeed, it creates conditions in which an increasing number of people cannot feel any more that they are participants in a valuable way of life. Why should they give allegiance to institutions that have marginalised them so completely? The real threat to liberal democratic institutions lies in the growing marginalisation of entire groups that cannot identify with any kind of values, whatever their origin.

In order to better grasp such a situation, it might be useful to see it as a case of what Nietzsche described as 'nihilism' and which for him was a symptom of an increasingly uneasy relation between basic tenets of Western culture and modern experience. Indeed, I would like to suggest that some of Nietzsche's insights are very relevant here and that an approach which emphasises the role of practices can learn a lot from him.

In his book *Nietzsche and Political Thought*, Mark Warren states that, for Nietzsche, nihilism refers to 'situations in which an individual's material and interpretive practices fail to provide ground for a reflexive interpretation of agency'.[2] It indicates a failure of meaning that draws into question the very possibility of a goal-directed, meaningful action. Individuals become nihilistic when they are unable to constitute their social relations and their identity in order to form a will to act. I think that there is a very important insight here for grasping many aspects of our current predicament.

Indeed, if we see nihilism as expressing at the individual level a dissolution of the dominant forms of consciousness, Nietzsche can help us to understand that, for individuals to feel that they have a place in society, it is necessary that the dominant forms of social consciousness allow a fit between self-identity and social experiences. This means that when the dominant values are perceived as illegitimate and cease to provide individuals with a sense of identity, those individuals lose their sense of direction and selfhood. Such a situation, if it were to become generalised, would either lead to the dissolution of what constitutes the cement of society and to anarchy, or to the creation of a terrain that could be used by demagogues trying to provide a new sense of direction, new goals for the will, that might jeopardise the liberal democratic form of life.

When nihilism is taken to signify the loss of capacity to will democratically, it is clear that resolving nihilism requires an understanding of the conditions of the democratic willing subject. Against all the liberal theorists who put emphasis on the need for universal, rational justifications for liberal democracy and believe that liberal institutions would be more secure if we could argue that these are the institutions that would be chosen by rational individuals under the 'veil of ignorance' or in a situation of 'undistorted communication', I propose that we listen to Wittgenstein and to Nietzsche who remind us of the limits of the claims of reason. They can help us to grasp how universalistic claims relate to historically specific and contextual interests and are always limited by context. Following their lead will make us realise that the defence of democracy is not a matter of *rational justification* but of the construction of democratic forms of individuality. What is at stake is the constitution of an ensemble of practices that makes possible specific forms of subjectivity and individuality of a democratic habitus.

The failure of current democratic theories to come to terms with the present situation is the consequence of their operating with a metaphysical conception of the subject which sees individuals as prior to society, bearers of natural rights and utility maximising agents, or rational subjects. In all cases, subjects are abstracted from social and power relations, language, culture and the whole set of practices that makes agency possible. What is precluded in these approaches is the very question of the conditions of existence of the liberal subject of rights. Since they assume the existence of what should be seen as a precarious achievement, they cannot see that the problem consists in the collapse of the very activities that they take for granted. They overlook the crucial question which concerns the conditions of possibility of a democratic subject, of a democratic form of willing.

A political philosophy developed under the Wittgensteinian lines that I have delineated here offers, I believe, a fruitful alternative to rationalist liberalism. Because of the central roles that it gives to practices, it can be developed in a way that highlights the historical and contingent character of the discourses that construe our identities and constitute the language of our politics, language that is constantly modified, that is entangled with power and needs to be apprehended in terms of hegemonic relations. It does not need to be conservative and limited to defend the status quo. It leaves room for understanding the many transformations that are possible within the language game of liberal democracy through the creation of new uses and new fields of application for the key notions of liberty, equality and pluralism. It would allow us to take 'value pluralism' seriously in its multiple dimensions. And it would make room for the pluralism of collective forms of life and therefore of regimes, as well as for the plurality of subjects, individual choices and conceptions of the good.

Following Wittgenstein's lead would allow us to acknowledge and valorise the diversity of ways in which the 'democratic game' can be played, instead of trying to reduce its diversity to a uniform model of citizenship. This would mean fostering a plurality of forms of being a democratic citizen and creating the institutions that would make it possible to follow the democratic rules in a plurality of ways. Democratic citizenship can take many forms and such a diversity, far from being a danger for democracy, is in fact its very condition of existence. This will of course create conflict but this struggle should not be one between enemies but among 'adversaries', since all the participants will recognise the positions of the others in the contest as legitimate ones. Such an understanding of democracy, which I have proposed to call 'agonistic pluralism',[3] requires the existence of a 'democratic habitus' which is unthinkable within a rationalistic problematic. It is the great merit of Wittgenstein's emphasis on practices and languages games to provide us with many insights for the creation of such a democratic habitus.

Notes

1   Wittgenstein, L. (1958) *Philosophical Investigations*, I. Oxford, Oxford University Press: 241.
2   Warren, M. (1988) *Nietzsche and Political Thought*, Cambridge, MA, MIT Press: 17.
3   For a development of this approach, see Mouffe, C. (2000) *The Democratic Paradox*, London, Verso: chapter 4.

References

Mouffe, C. (2000) *The Democratic Paradox*, London, Verso.
Warren, M. (1988) *Nietzsche and Political Thought*, Cambridge, MA, MIT Press.
Wittgenstein, L. (1958) *Philosophical Investigations, I*, Oxford, Oxford University Press.

7 Metropolitan Liberalism and Colonial Autocracy*

BARRY HINDESS

One of the less endearing features of Western political thought has been the ease with which it distinguishes between civilised parts of the world and others that are less civilised. The West's ranking of peoples and the places they inhabit in terms of their general level of civilisation has been complicated by the existence of non-Western civilisations, each with their own, rather different opinions about these matters. However, these have usually been seen, at least in the modern period, as having never seriously approached the achievements of the West and, in any case, as now being well below the level of their former glory. The Western ranking of peoples and places has been complicated also by the belief that, even in the West itself, there are many people whose condition is far from being entirely civilised. Among the inhabitants of Britain, for example, those who have sometimes been viewed in this way are the Irish, Highland Scots and Romani peoples and much of the poor and uncultivated English majority. These complications have not seriously damaged the West's belief in its own superiority, but they have left it with a somewhat untidy image of the world as made up of various more or less civilised regions and peoples, each of which is further divided into more or less civilised components.

Appeals to this image are now so familiar that they often pass without notice, but they are nevertheless of considerable practical importance. The idea of a standard of civilisation, against which the conduct of peoples and their rulers could be measured, played a fundamental role both in the development of the European system of states and in the incorporation by that system of political units from other parts of the world (Gong, 1984). Many of these units were incorporated under Western imperial rule while others remained at least nominally independent. However, until they were judged fit to be admitted to the community of civilised states, members of this second group – China, Russia, the Ottoman Empire, Japan, Thailand – were subjected to unequal treaties, extra-territorial jurisdictions and other impositions.

118 *Habitus: A Sense of Place*

This chapter addresses a second major domain in which the appeal to a standard of civilisation has played a fundamental political role, namely in the organisation of government within the territory of a state. It focuses especially on the significance for liberal reflections on government of distinctions between, on the one hand, the metropolitan population and territory and their overseas extensions and, on the other, the peoples and territories subjected to imperial rule. The two major sections of the chapter deal respectively with the two sides of the liberal political coin, metropolitan liberalism and colonial autocracy, and with the liberal understanding of conditions which promote, or fail to promote, the development of individual autonomy. It is this latter understanding that accounts for much of the difference between these contrasting sites in the practice of liberal government. A short concluding section considers how the end of empire has transformed liberal perceptions of peoples and places that were once thought to require authoritarian liberal rule.

The Principle of Liberty and the Practice of Authoritarian Rule

Liberalism has often been described as a normative political doctrine or political ideology concerned with promoting individual liberty and especially with defending it against the power of the state. While there is an important element of truth in this description, it gives no sense of the powerful authoritarian and elitist strains in liberal political thought.[1] In practice, liberal political reason has had little difficulty in finding justifications for authoritarian rule: for example, in the criminal justice system, in regulating the poor and various cultural and ethnic minorities, and also, of course, in the practice of colonial government. The point to be noted about these examples is not only that, as a matter of fact, many liberals have supported authoritarian practices of rule in such diverse contexts. Indeed, this fact alone does little to establish my claim that there are distinctly authoritarian tendencies in liberal political thought. A liberal theorist wishing to dispute this claim might argue, for example, that states committed to liberal principles will often be subject to imperatives, like those arising in times of war, that pull them in distinctly non-liberal directions. My second and more substantial point, then, is that liberal political thought, from its earliest beginnings, has clearly acknowledged that it may be necessary to employ authoritarian means in the government of those who, like the subjects of colonial rule, are not regarded as presently capable of conducting themselves in a suitably autonomous fashion. The liberal apologist might still demur at this point, insisting that, while liberals have sometimes supported imperial endeavours they have done so only at the cost of denying their liberal credentials. Indeed, the apologist might continue, most of the eighteenth- and early nineteenth-century figures that we now identify with the development of liberal political thought were strongly opposed to imperial expansion. It is equally clear, however, that Alexis de Tocqueville, John Stuart Mill and many other liberals in the nineteenth century and the first half of the twentieth took a more accommodating view of the imperial endeavour.[2] Some commentators have cited the intrusion of nationalist sentiment as a major reason for this difference, thereby absolving liberal principle of any responsibility for liberal imperialism.[3]

The importance of European nationalism in the imperial politics of the later period is undeniable. However, it is far from clear that the striking change in liberal responses to the imperial enterprise can be explained in terms of such a crowding out of liberal principle. Indeed, to account for the difference in such terms is to treat liberal principle as the source of the earlier hostility to empire. Another possibility is suggested by Anthony Pagden (1995), who describes the negative eighteenth-century reaction to imperialism as responding to the manner in which the earlier imperialism had been promoted. Supporters of the first wave of modern Western imperialism constantly invoked Imperial Rome as providing a positive model for their endeavours. Many of their liberal critics invoked the same model but offered a different interpretation of its significance, citing imperial expansion as a major reason for Rome's corruption and decline. It is in this spirit, for example, that David Hume describes imperial conquest as 'the ruin of every free government' (1987: 529). The liberals who opposed the earlier imperialism feared the damage it would do to the imperial state at least as much as they abhorred the destruction which it visited on subjugated populations. Advocates of the later imperialism drew on a radically different imagery, replacing the earlier 'providentialist languages of imperialism [with] a pretence to enlightened rationalism' (Pagden, 1995: 10), thereby suggesting that the later imperial endeavours were considerably more enlightened than their predecessors had been. The nineteenth-century liberal response to that imperial vision was correspondingly more positive. Moreover, whatever British liberals in the nineteenth century and the first half of the twentieth may have thought about the manner in which Britain's imperial possessions had been acquired, the question of how best to govern those possessions still had to be addressed. This question, in fact, became one of the central preoccupations of liberal political thought in the later period (Mehta, 1999) and here, as we shall see in a moment, liberal principle played a fundamental role.

More surprising perhaps than the appearance of post-imperial liberal protestations that liberal principle had nothing to do with imperialism is the fact that such a claim has also been advanced by many of liberalism's post-colonial critics. A recent paper by Ranajit Guha, for example, discussing the peculiar sense of anxiety experienced by many colonial administrators, insists on 'the absurdity of Britain's claim to have fitted the roundness of colonial autocracy to the squareness of metropolitan liberalism' (1997: 485) – thereby suggesting that the practice of the one could not be defended in terms of the principles enunciated by the other. Or again, Edward Said refers us to Aimé Césaire's *Discourse on Colonialism*, published in 1955, which argues that 'colonisation routinely covered unpleasant European practices against people of colour with a *facade* of appeals to the greater civilisational levels attained by the white race' (Said, 1992: 184, emphasis added). Said goes on to insist that 'governments (and especially very powerful imperial ones) babble on about how really moral they are as they do some particularly gangsterish thing. The question I am addressing, however, is how there is appeal for liberals in such rhetoric ...' (190). Here, too, the suggestion is that if only they were to hold true to their principles, liberals would have nothing to do with such practices.

The importance of dishonesty and hypocrisy in political life can hardly be denied, but it is impossible to understand liberal imperialism entirely in such terms, as if it were really nothing more than a distasteful, and particularly destructive, outbreak of bad faith. The fundamental differences between metropolitan liberalism and colonial autocracy have little to do with the realisation, however partial, of liberal principle in the one case and its brutal denial in the other. Rather, they reflect the fact that, like two sides of a single coin, the liberal frameworks of metropolitan and colonial rule are inextricably related yet condemned to face in opposite directions. One side of the coin presents the familiar liberal claim that government should rule over, and as far as possible rule through, the activities of free individuals. The obverse displays the equally liberal view that substantial portions of humanity consist of individuals who are not at present capable of acting in a suitably autonomous fashion.

In fact, a belief in the necessity of authoritarian rule in certain cases follows directly from the fundamental liberal proposition that, as far as possible, government should rule over and rule through the activities of free individuals. This proposition supposes that individuals possess, or are in principle capable of acquiring, the various capacities required if they are to be able to conduct themselves as autonomous agents. But, to make this claim is also to suggest that there may in fact be individuals who do not at present possess the relevant capacities and who therefore should not, at least for the moment, be trusted with too much freedom. The commitment to liberty, coupled with the belief that many people are unfortunately not ready for it, results in a perception of the world as divided into places in which individuals, left to their own devices, can normally be trusted to conduct themselves as autonomous rational agents and other places – ranging from imperial domains to areas of inner city poverty – in which they cannot be trusted to behave in this fashion. The experience of empire in fact provides liberal thought with significant examples of both types, of places where the liberal conscience will feel at home and others where it will not.

Liberals have attributed the apparent inability of certain groups of people to manage their own affairs to a range of different sources and there are correspondingly different liberal views about what, if anything, can be done to remedy this deficiency and about how the individuals concerned should be regarded as objects of government. At one extreme we find the view that, because of their culture or innate characteristics, some people are so far from being able to acquire the relevant capacities that they should simply be displaced or, more humanely perhaps, absorbed into the lower reaches of more civilised populations. This, in effect, is John Locke's view of what should be done about the peoples of America[4] and the view that, until recently, Western states have taken towards their own indigenous minorities. At the other extreme is the view that, among relatively civilised peoples, there are individuals whose deficiency results from inadequate education, poverty, injury or disease and whose condition could therefore be improved without too much difficulty. According to this view – which finds its clearest expression in J.S. Mill's (1977) case for allowing participation in government and T.H. Marshall's (1950) arguments for the importance of social policy in the full development of citizenship – the role of government is to facilitate the development of its citizens' capacities by establishing appropriate social arrangements. Standing between these extremes is a view that has been particularly important in the history of colonial administration and, although it is hardly the concern of this chapter, in the history of liberal and neo-liberal practices of welfare.[5] It is the view that there may be a substantial inner resistance to overcoming, or even acknowledging, the deficiency in question and that, in such cases, the capacities required for autonomous conduct can be developed only through compulsion, through the imposition of more or less extended periods of discipline.

This patronising view of the characteristics of subjugated peoples is a standard refrain in the writings of colonial administrators.[6] Its most familiar expression in the realm of political theory appears in the Introduction to John Stuart Mill's *On Liberty* and again his *Considerations on Representative Government*, both of which were initially conceived as responses to Macauley's 'Minute on Indian Education' (Mehta, 1999: 6). Civilisation, Mill tells us, is the product of 'continuous labour of an unexciting kind ... in that without such labour, neither can the mind be disciplined into the habits required by civilised society, nor the material world prepared to receive it' (1977: 394-5). Thus, writing of the peoples of India and other dependencies whose populations were not sufficiently advanced, in his view, 'to be fitted for representative government', Mill maintains that they must be governed by the dominant country or its agents:

> This mode of government is as legitimate as any other, if it is the one which, in the existing state of civilisation of the subject people, most facilitates their transition to a higher stage of improvement (567).

Mill's reference to 'improvement' reminds us, if reminder is needed, that the Western ranking of peoples and places in terms of their degree of civilisation commonly draws on an evolutionary view of history which places modern Western societies at, or very close to, the pinnacle of human development. Peoples whose conduct differs from the Western norm are accordingly seen as less civilised, less advanced.

Mill does not dwell on the costs inflicted on subject populations in the name of their improvement, but he is seriously concerned with the demoralising effects of imperial rule on colonial administrators themselves. He observes, for example, that they may be tempted to 'think the people of the country mere dirt under their feet' (571). While, according to Mill's account, the imperial government itself is unlikely to take this view, it will not be able 'to keep it down in the young and raw even of its own civil and military officers' (ibid.). He uses this point to introduce the more general theme that imperial rule 'is as likely to produce evil as good'. 'Real good government,' he tells us, 'is not compatible with the conditions of the case. There is but a choice of imperfections' (572-3). Civilised distaste for the practice of imperial government has always been a significant component of liberal thought: it complements the patronising belief that, if it fosters the improvement of the subject population, imperial rule will nevertheless be a cross that more civilised peoples may have to bear.

A Social Animal

There is one further aspect of liberal thought to be considered before we can grasp the nature of its division of the world into settings in which individuals can normally be trusted to conduct themselves as autonomous rational agents and other settings in which they cannot. This concerns the classical Western view that human individuals are capable of autonomous action, at least in principle, and are essentially social animals. In liberal thought this autonomy has been seen as involving roughly the capacities of rationality and moral responsibility that are commonly invoked by the rhetoric of citizenship in contemporary Western societies.[7] Consequently, human sociality is understood as a matter of relations between individuals capable of possessing those capacities. Peoples who conduct themselves in ways that promote and depend on a different range of human abilities are accordingly seen as lacking the capacities required for autonomous action. They are seen, in other words, either as less than fully human (a view that was especially influential in late nineteenth-century Australia) or as fully human but as having yet to properly develop the capacities of rationality and moral responsibility.

A particularly clear illustration of the governmental ramifications of this second view is presented in the first chapter of Edward Said's *Orientalism*. Said examines a speech in which Arthur Balfour[8] argues that 'the problems with which we have to deal in Egypt ... belong to a wholly different category' than those 'affecting the Isle of White or the West Riding of Yorkshire'. A fundamental reason for this difference, Balfour insists, is that there are no traces of self-government in the civilisations of the East.

> All their great centuries – and they have been very great – have been passed under despotisms, under absolute government. All their great contributions to civilisation – and they have been great – have been made under that form of government. ... That is the fact. It is not a question of superiority or inferiority (cited in Said, 1985, p. 33).

Balfour's protestations notwithstanding, however, the assumption of superiority on one side and inferiority on the other is only too apparent – as indeed it is in Balfour's view of much of the British population. Balfour's point is simply that while Orientals are not essentially inferior, they have yet to acquire the capacity for self-government: it is their history and their culture that is at fault, not their nature.[9] Balfour goes on to observe:

that the working government we have taken upon ourselves in Egypt and elsewhere is not a work worthy of a philosopher – that it is the dirty work, the inferior work, of carrying on the necessary labour (ibid.).

This, of course, is a theme that we have already observed in our discussion of Mill. The difference that Mill perceives in the respective attitudes of imperial governments and many administrators in the field is the difference between a more and a less cultivated view of the inferiority of subject peoples. The demoralising effect of imperial rule that so concerns him, then, is that colonial administrators may learn to think of their human subjects not only as less civilised but also as less than human.

A second consequence of the view that humans are social animals capable of autonomous action is a belief that the capacities required by individuals if they are to be able to conduct themselves as autonomous agents will not be developed in isolation. Rather, they will normally be acquired and sustained in the course of interaction with other individuals of a similar kind. In *An Essay Concerning Human Understanding* and various shorter pieces on education and reform of the poor law administration John Locke draws precisely this implication from the classical view of humanity. We are all of us, he maintains, subject to the 'Law of Opinion and Reputation'. Thus, what people count as virtue and vice do not reflect the character of the actions themselves, for what is considered vice in one community will often be regarded with approval or indifference in another. Rather, the use of these terms reflects what is generally recognised as worthy of praise or blame by members of the community in question. We learn what virtue and vice mean and how to behave according to the standards that the differences between them represent by responding to the signs of approval and disapproval that we observe in the course of our interactions with others. No man, Locke tells us:

> escapes the Punishment of their Censure and Dislike, who offends against the Fashion and Opinion of the Company he keeps, and would recommend himself to. Nor is there one of ten thousand, who is stiff and insensible enough, to bear up under the constant Dislike, and Condemnation of his own Club (Locke, 1957: 357).

Similar mechanisms, he maintains, operate in relation to other aspects of human conduct, affecting what we regard as true and false, attractive and unattractive.

Liberalism takes this analysis one step further, suggesting that the market and other spheres of social interaction have a self-regulating character. Adam Smith's *The Wealth of Nations*, for example, offers an account of economic activity in commercial societies as a system of interaction in which the conduct of participants is regulated at two rather different levels. It is regulated not only by the values, interests and the like which participants bring to their interactions but also by the signals they receive from other actors – and especially, of course, by the prices for goods and labour resulting from numerous individual decisions to buy or to sell, or to seek a better deal elsewhere. This view of the manner in which economic activity is regulated suggests that state interference in economic interaction – for example, by setting prices or minimum wages – will produce misleading signals, thereby distorting the system's own regulatory mechanisms. Smith uses this point to argue that police regulation of economic activity and the mercantile system substantially reduce the overall wealth of the nation.

Foucault has argued that the market plays the role in liberal thought 'of a "test", a locus of privileged experience where one can identify the effects of excessive governmentality' (1997: 76). Liberalism perceives the populations of modern societies as encompassing a variety of domains – the sphere of economic activity, the workings of civil society, the processes of population growth and so on – each of which is regulated largely by the free decisions of individuals in the course of their interactions with others. The suggestion is that, once such domains of free interaction have become established, they will function most effectively if external interference in their workings is reduced to a minimum. On this view, then, rather than subject them to detailed state regulation, liberal government should aim to secure conditions under which these domains can safely be left to regulate themselves – the assumption being that they will then do so in such a way as to promote the well-being of the population and of the state itself. Liberal government, in other words, should aim to rule over, and to work through, the activities of free individuals.

This much, of course, is reasonably familiar. It suggests that liberal political thought, from Adam Smith to J. S. Mill and on to Friedrich Hayek, can be seen as a set of governmental variations on an underlying Lockean theme. But there is considerably more to be said about this theme than might be suggested by the anodyne picture I have presented so far. If individuals are governed by habits of thought and behaviour that are themselves acquired in the course of interaction with others, what does this imply for the liberal project of ruling over the free activities of autonomous agents? Perhaps the most important implication is that such activities can be found only under conditions in which interaction with others can be expected to promote the relevant capacities in the people concerned – notably, of course, in the market and what has recently become known as civil society. Individuals who appear to be bound up in conditions of a different kind must then be seen as less than fully autonomous and therefore as having to be ruled in ways that leave them less than entirely free. In his *Lectures on Jurisprudence*, for example, Smith observes that nothing 'tends to corrupt and enervate and debase the mind as dependency' (1978: 333). It is for this reason, he argues, that the level of crime and disorder – and therefore the amount of police regulation exercised over the population – is far greater in Edinburgh and Paris, with their large numbers of servants and retainers, than it is in London, where such people make up a smaller proportion of the overall population. The best way to reduce crime and disorder, he argues, is to promote 'freedom and independency' by reducing the proportion of servants and retainers and increasing that of free wage-labourers.

In effect, liberalism supposes, first, that the population to be governed by the state will also be governed by a variety of what Hayek calls autonomous social orders, patterns of interaction that have developed independently of central control, and secondly, that only a limited number of such orders can actually be expected to promote the autonomy of the individuals caught up in them. Liberals have tended to treat the market and other orders which they see as promoting individual autonomy as arising, at least in the first instance, from a long process of historical development and 'improvement'. Once such orders exist, the role of government is to secure the conditions required for the free interactions within them to continue. Orders that are not of this kind, however, are seen as more or less undeveloped, and the individuals within them judged as being comparatively uncivilised, as likely to behave in a fashion that is irrational and unpredictable. The role of government in this latter case is less to secure the conditions of free interaction within the subject population than it is to maintain some reasonable degree of public security and to foster its 'improvement': that is, to foster, by force if necessary, the development of the market and other orders that can be expected to promote autonomous conduct.

This treatment of humans as social animals capable of acquiring the capacities involved in autonomous action enables liberalism to distinguish, not only between individuals who are autonomous and those who are not, but also between populations (and sub-populations within them) consisting largely of one or other type of individual. To the extent that these distinctions also draw on an image of progress or improvement, the world will appear to be divided both historically and geographically into modern and not so modern populations. As a result, many of the latter – in Africa, India and other non-Western regions – will in fact be seen as anachronistic contemporaries of the modern world, as coexisting with the moderns while belonging to an earlier time.

While, in the case of what it regards as modern populations, liberalism has insisted on the promotion of individual liberty and the defence of that liberty against the state, it has tended to view not so modern populations in a rather different light. The fate of colonial administrators is to be creatures of the one setting who have to live and work within the other. Like police and other officials in deprived areas of contemporary Western societies, they find themselves surrounded by people they have learned to look down upon, who cannot be trusted to behave as autonomous social agents. They also see themselves, and are seen by their superiors, as vulnerable to an insidious kind of corruption, responding, as Locke's Law of Opinion and Reputation would lead us to expect, to expressions of approval and disapproval arising in their interactions with those they are expected to rule.

Conclusion

I noted earlier that the end of empire has transformed the manner in which populations that are regarded as less than modern impinge on the liberal conscience. Let me conclude this paper, then, by reflecting briefly on the implications of my argument for our understanding of the post-colonial liberal condition.

Perhaps the most important point to make here is that the end of Western imperial rule has done little to undermine the characteristic liberal demarcations between settings inhabited largely by autonomous agents and settings that are not of this kind: many of the latter can still be found in what had once been imperial domains – as indeed they can in Western states themselves. Nor has it displaced the great liberal project of improving the people who inhabit these domains. The project is now marketed under the label of development, but its underlying aims have barely changed.

What this rebadging indicates, rather, is that the end of empire has transformed the conditions in which the project has to be pursued.[10] Indeed, since the populations of ex-imperial domains now have states of their own, the liberal project of improvement can hardly operate through what might once have been seen as the civilising effects of imperial rule. The perceived need for improvement, however, remains and it is made more complex by the belief that rulers and public officials in the successor states will, because of their local connections, be even more vulnerable to corruption than colonial administrators from the West were vulnerable before them.[11] The project of improvement is still pursued by Western states, but now they work through a more remote set of indirect means. Updated versions of the standard of civilisation, and of the sanctions that it served to legitimate, continue to play a major role in the conduct of Western states themselves and of the international agencies which they control.[12] In addition to diplomacy, national and international aid programmes that assist, advise and constrain the conduct of post-colonial states and international financial institutions, the liberal project of improvement also makes considerable use of the market. In fact, reliance on the market has become increasingly prominent as we move further away from the period of large-scale decolonisations in the middle years of the twentieth century. The market appears to liberal eyes as serving a variety of necessary functions in the ex-imperial domains, just as it does in the West: it reduces opportunities for corruption by constraining state conduct, provides an alternative to the state provision of services, and promotes civilised attitudes and patterns of conduct among the inhabitants and the rulers of these less fortunate settings.

But the project of improvement is also pursued by significant minorities in non-Western states themselves, who aim both to modernise their societies and to reaffirm (and sometimes even to invent) their own cultural heritage. The view that the people of these states are not yet ready to govern themselves and a positive commitment to non-Western values come together to provide a culturally specific liberal rationale for authoritarian rule. Such liberal minorities experience a domesticated version of the fate which once befell Western colonial administrators – the fate of believing that they belong to one kind of setting while actually inhabiting the other – and they display a correspondingly domesticated ambivalence: combining civilised distaste with reluctant acknowledgement of the need for authoritarian means in governing their less advanced compatriots.

Notes

*   I am grateful to the editors and to Ian Hunter, David Owen and, most especially, Christine Helliwell for their advice and comments on earlier drafts of this chapter.

1   These strains are well brought out in Maurice Cowling's fine polemic (1963) against the liberalism of J.S. Mill. In fact, although I can hardly develop the argument here, the view that liberal principles are unfailingly hostile to authoritarian rule is itself a comparatively recent development, resulting largely from the emergence of political theory as a distinctive area of academic specialisation. See Hindess (1997) for discussion of a closely related issue.

2   See, for example, Mehta (1999), Pitts (2000).
3   Pitts (2000: 315), Richter (1963: 364), Said (1992).
4   See the discussion in Tully (1993, 1995).
5   Locke (1969[1697]) is an influential early formulation of this authoritarian welfare perspective while Mead (1997) offers a contemporary version. King (1999) discusses several authoritarian British and American programmes that have been justified in the name of liberalism.
6   Cf. Philpott (2000), Conklin (1997).
7   For a discussion of various non-liberal perspectives on human autonomy, see Patterson (1991) and Skinner (1998).
8   Balfour was a leading member of the British Conservative Party but, like most Conservatives of his time and since, his political views reflected the broadly liberal understanding of government set out in this paper.
9   A similar point could be made about the insistence by John Howard, Liberal Prime Minister of Australia since 1996, that he is no racist.
10 Of course, as the contributions to Sachs (1992) make clear, the modern project of development also has a variety of other sources.
11 Rose-Ackerman (1999) offers a particularly clear example of this perspective.
12 In this respect, there are clear, if inconsistently applied, limits to a regime of inter-state toleration of the kind proposed by Grahame Thompson in this volume.

References

Conklin, A.L. (1997) *A Mission to Civilize, The republican idea of empire in France and West Africa, 1895-1930*, Stanford, Stanford University Press.
Cowling, M. (1963) *Mill and Liberalism*, Cambridge, Cambridge University Press.
Foucault, M. (1997) *Ethics: subjectivity and truth* (edited by Paul Rabinow), New York, The New Press.
Gong, G.W. (1984) *The Standard of 'Civilization' in International Society*, Oxford, Clarendon Press.
Grey, J. (2000) *Two Faces of Liberalism*, London, Routledge.
Guha, R. (1997) Not at Home in Empire, *Critical Inquiry*, 23 (Spring), 482-493.
Hindess, B. (1997) 'The object of political theory', in A. Vincent (ed.) *Political Theory: tradition and diversity*, Cambridge and Melbourne, Cambridge University Press: 254-271.
Hume, D. (1987[1777]) *'Idea of a perfect commonwealth, in his Essays: moral, political and literary'*, Indianapolis, Liberty Fund.
Hunter, I. (1998) 'Uncivil Society: historical and methodological comments on liberal government', in M. Dean and B. Hindess (eds) *Governing Australia*, Melbourne, Cambridge University Press.
Hunter, I. (2001) *Rival Enlightenments: civil and metaphysical philosophy in early modern Germany*, Cambridge, Cambridge University Press.
Kant, I. (1970) *Political Writings* (edited by Hans Reiss), Cambridge, Cambridge University Press.
King, D. (1999) *In the Name of Liberalism: illiberal social policy in the USA and Britain*, Oxford, Oxford University Press.
Lindqvist, S. (1997) *Exterminate all the Brutes*, London, Granta.
Locke, J. (1957) *An Essay Concerning Human Understanding*, Oxford, Clarendon Press.

Locke, J. (1969) 'A Report of the Board of Trade to the Lords Justices Respecting the Relief and Employment of the Poor' (1697), in H.R. Fox Bourne (ed.) *The Life and Times of John Locke*, Darmstadt, Scientia Verlag Aalen: 377-91.

Marshall, T. (1950) *Citizenship and Social Class*, Cambridge, Cambridge University Press.

Mead, L.M. (1997) *The New Paternalism*, Washington, Brookings.

Mehta, U.S. (1999) *Liberalism and Empire: a study in nineteenth-century British liberal thought, Chicago*, University of Chicago Press.

Mill, J.S. (1977[1865]) 'Considerations on Representative Government', in J.M. Robson (ed.), *Collected Works of John Stuart Mill*, (vol. XIX). Toronto, University of Toronto Press: 371-577.

Pagden, A. (1995) *Lords of all the World: ideologies of empire in Spain, Britain and France c.1500-c.1800*, New Haven, Yale University Press.

Patterson, O. (1991) *Freedom in the Making of Western Culture*, (vol. 1), New York, Basic Books.

Philpott, S. (2000) *Rethinking Indonesia: postcolonial theory, authoritarianism, identity*, Basingstoke, Macmillan.

Pitts, J. (2000) 'Empire and democracy: Tocqueville and the Algeria Question', *Journal of Political Philosophy*, 8(3): 295-318.

Richter, M. (1963) 'Tocqueville on Algeria', *Review of Politics*, 25: 362-398.

Rose-Ackerman, S. (1999) *Corruption and Government: causes, consequences and reform*, Cambridge and New York, Cambridge University Press.

Sachs, W. (1992) *The Development Dictionary: a guide to knowledge and power*, London, Zed Books

Said, E.W. (1985) *Orientalism*, London, Penguin.

Said, E.W. (1992) *Nationalism, Human Rights, and Interpretation, Freedom and Interpretation, The Oxford Amnesty Lectures, 1992*, New York, Basic Books.

Skinner, Q. (1998) *Liberty Before Liberalism, Cambridge*, Cambridge University Press

Smith, Adam (1976) *An Inquiry into the Nature and Causes of the Wealth of Nations*, Oxford, Clarendon.

Smith, Adam (1978) *Lectures on Jurisprudence*, Oxford: Clarendon.

Tully, J. (1993) *An Approach to Political Philosophy: Locke in contexts*, Cambridge: Cambridge University Press.

Tully, J. (1995) *Strange Multiplicity, Constitutionalism in an Age of Diversity*, Cambridge: Cambridge University Press.

8 Governmentality and Regional Economic Strategies

JOE PAINTER

Introduction

Unlike many of the other contributions to this collection, this chapter draws its immediate inspiration not from Pierre Bourdieu and the concept of habitus, but from the notion of 'governmentality' proposed originally by Michel Foucault, but developed more broadly by subsequent writers. Given the theme of the book, some explanation of my decision to focus on governmentality rather than habitus seems in order. My substantive focus here is on the output of the state policy process, exemplified by the production of 'regional economic strategies' in the United Kingdom. The idea of habitus, with its concern for the dispositions of human agents, draws attention to, among other things, the social character of the state bureaucracy; for example the ways in which the characteristic outlook of the state's personnel is shaped by the acquisition of cultural and symbolic capital through schooling and professional training. These issues are of course vitally important. However, my principal focus here is on the forms of knowledge written into state policy and the ways in which those knowledges constitute particular kinds of objects of governance (such as 'regions'), in particular ways. There are some obvious connections here with Bourdieu's ideas – the concept of field, for example – and as I have shown elsewhere, (Painter 1997) Bourdieu's work has much to offer this kind of study. However, for my specific concerns in this piece I have found the idea of governmentality more immediately relevant. This should not be taken to mean that the approaches of Bourdieu and Foucault are somehow neatly complementary, or can be unproblematically combined. The tensions between them are as clear as they are fascinating. A full comparative analysis, though, is beyond the scope of this chapter, and in what follows I shall develop my argument principally in relation to the notion of governmentality.

The concept of 'governmentality' is becoming quite widely used across the social sciences (Barry *et al,*. 1996; Burchell *et al.,* 1991; Dean,

1999). Approximately the term denotes 'the art of government' and, by combining the ideas of 'government' and 'mentality', refers in particular to the relationship between the practices of government and knowledge of the objects of government. In line with Foucault's insistence on the intimate connections between power and knowledge, the idea of 'governmentality' suggests that knowledge is not simply a tool or resource for government, but is a condition of the very possibility of government itself. Knowledge affects government, but it also effects it.

Governmentality focuses attention on the diverse political rationalities of government, on its 'technologies', and on the considerable intellectual labour involved in bringing into being the things, people and processes to be governed. The idea has been applied in a number of fields including the welfare state and the realm of 'the social' (Donzelot, 1984, 1988), risk and insurance (Ewald, 1991; O'Malley, 1996), economic life (Miller and Rose, 1990), the concept of empowerment (Cruikshank, 1999) and many others. Indeed the methodology with which the concept of governmentality operates is one that shies away from grand generalisations about the nature of government in favour of more limited excavations of the operation of governmental power in specific contexts. It is in that sense more a methodological *approach to* the analysis of government (a kind of 'analytics of government' (Dean, 1999: 27-39)) than a substantive *theory of* government.

While territoriality has been identified by many writers as central to the governmentalities of the modern state, relatively little attention has been devoted to the importance of the state's *internal* territorial structure[1] and it is this issue that will form the main focus of this paper. In keeping with the emphasis in the governmentality literature on empirical analysis, I want to outline a preliminary interpretation of the governmentalities embodied in the Regional Development Agencies (RDAs) in the UK. In what follows, therefore, I shall first describe the genesis and functions of the eight RDAs, and consider one of the primary purposes of each RDA: to devise, publish and implement a 'regional economic strategy' for its region. I shall then outline the governmentality approach in a little more detail before applying it to the RDA phenomenon through a preliminary analysis of the eight strategies. In doing so I shall focus on the forms of knowledge, particularly geographical knowledge, embodied in the documents. The chapter concludes with a brief reflection on the value of the governmentality approach.

Governing Territorially: England's Regional Development Agencies

In one sense almost all the government undertaken by the state is territorial. States are themselves territorial phenomena and they expend much energy on policing, integrating, developing, regulating and monitoring their territories. Many, perhaps most, state policies are implemented in spatially sensitive ways. Public administration, policing, welfare provision, economic development, defence and many other activities commonly depend on a particular set of central-local relations and are undertaken at and through particular sites and locales. Indeed the constitutive role of space and place in social life is now so widely recognised that it has ceased to be the specialist preserve of geographers and increasingly commands attention from scholars across the social sciences and humanities.

However, my concern here is with governmental activity that addresses territory directly by treating it as its primary object of concern and intervention. The nature of such intervention varies markedly from state to state. In one case cities may be the prime focus, in another rural areas; in some countries interventions are highly selective and spatially targeted, in others policies apply uniformly across the territory and so on. Such variety cautions against sweeping generalisations about the nature of spatial restructuring: the 'inexorable' rise of regionalism, for example, or the 'universal' importance of global cities, or the 'inevitable' emergence of a borderless world. Foucault's approach emphasises specificity, detail and uniqueness.

The case of the UK is a complex one simultaneously hinted at and glossed over in the state's full name: The United Kingdom of Great Britain and Northern Ireland. In his recent magisterial survey of the history of 'The Isles', Norman Davies notes that over the last 2000 years, at least fifteen distinct territorial states have existed in the territories that today make up the UK and the Republic of Ireland (Davies, 1999: xl-xli). Moreover, the nomenclature relating to those territories is confusing, ambiguous and contested (xxvii-xl). Discounting for the moment its overseas colonies and imperial possessions, the UK has existed within its present territorial boundaries only since 1922 when the Irish Free State was established in what is now the Republic of Ireland. The state today consists of two 'countries' (England and Scotland), a 'principality' (Wales), and a 'province' (Northern Ireland). All of these labels are ambiguous and contested.

The UK is commonly regarded as a highly centralised state:

> The United Kingdom is [...] unusual for a large Western unitary state in that it has no comprehensive and uniform level of decentralised territorial administration between local and central government. It could be argued

that because of this high degree of centralisation, government is fundamentally concerned with a national public and policy agenda rather than with regional and local publics and policies, and public accountability tends to focus on national rather than local political institutions (Mawson, 1998: 228).

On the other hand this situation is now changing significantly. There has long been a degree of administrative decentralisation in the UK, as Mawson recognises. Noting the 'emphasis in Whitehall upon functional division at the expense of territorial integration and coordination', he adds that 'the exception to this situation arises in the case of the three Offices for State for Scotland, Wales, and Northern Ireland which have emerged over the past 100 years for various pragmatic political reasons associated with their historic national identities and political pressures for decentralisation' (Mawson, 1998: 228-9). Thus territorial government in the UK has long been asymmetrical; today it is becoming markedly more so.

Devolved government was introduced in Scotland, Wales and Northern Ireland in 1999 and in London in 2000. Although the precise nature of devolution varies between these four territories, the process has produced a distinctive break with the pattern of centralised government that was previously the norm, to the extent that some commentators identity an emerging '*de facto*' or 'quasi-' federalism within the UK, albeit one that involves a 'variable geometry'. As Neil MacCormick, legal philosopher and Member of the European Parliament for the Scottish National Party, puts it:

It is tempting to see the new pattern of devolved governments in the UK as yet a further instance of quasi-federalism inside a state which itself is confederated with the other member states of the [European] Union. [...] There remains, however, an acute problem – how to deal with England? If the UK is becoming a kind of federation, is England to be within it one federal state, or a patchwork of federal regions? Each solution has its own problems, and both are bedevilled by the absence of any widespread popular wish to create new units of government and new assemblies, though this may be changing in some parts of the country. There are now to be Regional Development Agencies and 'Regional Chambers' in the regions of England. In particular, there seems to have been some growth of opinion in Yorkshire, and in Tyneside and the North East of England in favour of emulating the Scots and the Welsh in seeking directly elected assemblies or parliaments, and of securing a similar budgetary settlement. Yet if developments along these lines do take off, and subsequently spread to other regions of England there will remain important differences with Scotland. [...] This means that there is inevitably a strangely uneven and unequal quality built into the kind of quasi-federalism the UK can have [...] It is not inconceivable that the right way to resolve the difficulties inherent in the emerging constitutional settlement is to put up with imbalance. [...] Variable geometry may be the very thing for the United Kingdom in the long run (MacCormick, 1999: 193-5).

This helps to explain a remarkable reversal in the tenor of dominant political discourse on territorial and constitutional issues in the UK in the last five years. Previously, England was the norm, with Scotland, Wales and Northern Ireland viewed as peculiar, aberrant or anomalous. Today the position is exactly the opposite, with the 'anomalous' post-devolution constitutional and cultural position of England currently the focus of obsessive media and academic attention.

In fact the genealogy (in Foucault's sense) of the concept of the English 'Regional Development Agencies' is to be found less in the development of the idea of devolution than in the history of the discourses and practices of 'public administration', 'regional economic planning' and 'regional economic development'. RDAs are more accurately seen as examples of regionalisation (a relatively top-down process of region-making) than of regionalism (a more bottom-up movement for decentralisation). It is only very recently that the institutional structures involved in regional administrative decentralisation in England have been viewed by campaigners for regional devolution as regional governments in waiting.

Some of the most comprehensive recent research on the regionalisation of the British state is that by Brian Hogwood (Hogwood, 1996a, 1996b, 1997). Hogwood (1996b) traces the history of England's 'standard', 'planning' or 'statistical' regions over the last 60 years. Their origins lie in the ten 'regional commissioners' appointed during World War II to provide the 'eyes and ears of central government' (1996b: 11). Other government departments appointed 'divisional officers' in each region, who kept in close touch with their respective commissioners. In the event of an invasion or other wartime crisis, the regional commissioners would have taken over direct control of government in their regions (Hogwood, 1996b: 11).

After the war, and until about 1956, the Treasury (finance ministry) tried to ensure that the regional organisation of all government departments conformed to standard regions. Thereafter, Hogwood notes, and until the mid-1960s there was a proliferation of different regional structures and a decline in the use of regional offices by central government. In 1964, the election of the modernising Labour government under Harold Wilson saw a revival of regional thinking. Regional Economic Planning Boards and

136 *Habitus: A Sense of Place*

Regional Economic Planning Councils were established in each region and the number of regions was reduced to the current eight. However, central government departments not directly concerned with regional planning did little to bring their boundaries into line with the new standard regions and even in the planning field co-ordination was limited (Hogwood, 1996b: 12). The present regional boundaries were established in 1974, the time of major local government reorganisation. The eight English regions are:

- Northern
- North West
- Yorkshire and Humberside
- East Midlands
- West Midlands
- East Anglia
- South West
- South East

Ironically, as Hogwood notes, no central government department uses the exact boundaries of these regions for its own regional structures and in many cases there is 'substantial deviation'. Their only remaining functions today are to form the standard regions for statistical purposes and to provide a framework within which central government issues strategic planning guidance to local authorities (Hogwood, 1996b: 13).

This, then, was the picture until the early 1990s. As Hogwood describes it:

> The picture up to mid-1993 [...] therefore appeared to be one of acceptance of the need for regional administrative arrangements for some infrastructure and regional industrial policy purposes, and a recognition of some need for administrative coordination, but antagonism to regional government or regional councils reflecting regional interests and to regions as a focus for economic planning (1996b: 16).

However, in an unusually decentralising move for a Conservative government, from April 1994 'Government Offices for the Regions' (GOs) were established. These brought together the regional offices of the Department of Trade and Industry, the Department of Employment (Training, Enterprise and Education Directorate), the Department of Transport, and the Department of the Environment (in 1997 the incoming Labour government merged the latter two to form the Department of Environment, Transport and the Regions and merged the Departments of Employment and Education to form the Department for Education and

Employment). The aim of the GOs was 'to work in partnership with local authorities and private firms to maximise the competitiveness, prosperity, and quality of life of their region' (Dynes and Walker, 1995: 257). This formulation contains several of the key discursive terms that will appear as particularly important in the subsequent analysis of the Regional Development Agencies. While part of the declared purpose behind the establishment of the GOs was to make policy more sensitive to the regional voice, it was central to the Conservative tactic that no political mechanism was established for this and in particular that no elected representation was proposed.

Ten government offices were established with somewhat different boundaries from the 'standard regions' described above. In apparent recognition of the severity of its socio-economic problems Merseyside got its own GO subtracting territory from the North West standard region. The GO for the North West gained Cumbria from the North standard region. An Eastern GO was established covering the standard region of East Anglia plus Hertfordshire, Bedfordshire and Essex from the South East standard region. London also gained its own GO from territory within the South East standard region. The regional boundaries of the Government Offices for Yorkshire and Humberside, the East Midlands, the West Midlands and the South West coincided with the standard regions of the same names. As Hogwood graphically illustrates, several major government functions have regional boundaries that vary, sometimes markedly, from those of the Government Offices. This is even true for several functions of the departments included in the Government Office scheme where those functions are delivered by the semi-autonomous 'Next Steps' agencies. For example, the regional structure of the Employment Service (an agency of the then Department of Employment that delivers job search and related services) differs from that of the GOs.

In May 1997 the Labour Party formed a new government under Tony Blair that came to power committed to an enhanced role for regional bodies in economic development, and possibly to devolved regional government in England, though this objective seems now to be firmly on the back burner. In April 1999 eight Regional Development Agencies (RDAs) were established by central government to cover the whole of England except London (which was to have its own devolved government and associated development agency from 2000). Their boundaries coincided with those of the Government Offices except that Merseyside was absorbed into the North West region again. The Government Offices continue to exist and are required to work with the RDAs.

The full list of RDAs is as shown in Table 8.1:

138 *Habitus: A Sense of Place*

Table 8.1   English Regional Development Agencies (RDAs)

Region	Agency	Budget (£M)
North East	One North East	121
North West	North West Development Agency	176
Yorkshire and Humberside	Yorkshire Forward	137
West Midlands	Advantage West Midlands	114
East Midlands	East Midlands Development Agency	59
East	East of England Development Agency	32
South West	South West of England Development Agency	60
South East	South East of England Development Agency	73

Source: (Robson *et al.*, 2000: 2).

The Agencies were established by the Regional Development Agencies Act 1998, which states:

> 4.1 A regional development agency shall have the following purposes:
>
> a. to further the economic development and the regeneration of its area,
> b. to promote business efficiency, investment and competitiveness in its area,
> c. to promote employment in its area,
> d. to enhance the development and application of skills relevant to employment in its area, and
> e. to contribute to the achievement of sustainable development in the United Kingdom where it is relevant to its area to do so.
>
> 4.2 A regional development agency's purposes apply as much in relation to the rural parts of its area as in relation to the non-rural parts of its area.

7.1 A regional development agency shall:

a. formulate, and keep under review, a strategy in relation to its purposes, and
b. have regard to the strategy in exercising its functions.

7.2 The Secretary of State may give a regional development agency guidance and directions in relation to the exercise of its functions under subsection (1), in particular, with respect to:

a. the matters to be covered by the strategy,
b. the issues to be taken into account in formulating the strategy,
c. the strategy to be adopted in relation to any matter, and
d. the updating of the strategy.

Thus the Secretary of State is able to issue both statutory and non-statutory guidance to the RDAs, and this he chose to do in some detail (Department of Environment, Transport and the Regions, 1999b; Department of Environment, Transport and the Regions, 1999c). The non-statutory guidance runs to seven fairly lengthy chapters covering respectively: regeneration, competitiveness, skills, sustainable development, rural policy, equal opportunities, and the voluntary and community sector (Department of Environment Transport and the Regions, 1999c).

Although RDAs are not elected and there is currently no elected regional level of government in England outside London to which they might be held accountable, they are required to undertake consultation within their regions. For this purpose eight 'regional chambers' have been designated. These 'are voluntary groupings of councillors from local authorities in the region and representatives of the various sectors with a stake in the region's economic, social and environmental well-being. They generally include representatives from business; education and training; the voluntary, cultural and environmental protection sectors; and the trade unions' (Department of Environment, Transport and the Regions, 1999a).

The Regional Economic Strategies

One of the most important initial tasks for the new RDAs was to develop a regional economic strategy (RES) for each region. The completed strategies were presented to the Secretary of State in October 1999. Each strategy consists of one or more A4 booklets, usually well illustrated in full colour.

They vary in length from 48 pages (West Midlands) to 128 pages (North East) and, as if to convey their seriousness, usually contain a lot of fairly closely-spaced text in a small font size. The production and design quality is variable, but fairly high, though there is clearly some tension between glossy publicity and place marketing functions on the one hand and the official reporting function in relation to central government on the other. The strategies are loaded with business school rhetorical devices such as bullet points, Venn diagrams, organigrams, flow charts and mission and vision statements. There are also copious supporting quotations from the 'great and the good' (and 'ordinary people'), as well as numerous case studies and vignettes of successful regeneration schemes, inward investors, innovative business start-ups, training programmes, community development initiatives and so on. All the strategies are available electronically, usually in 'pdf' format, on the World Wide Web.

The influence of the extensive statutory and non-statutory guidance from the Secretary of State is clear to see in all the RESs, most of which have chapter or section headings that reflect the issues set out in the *Supplementary Guidance* document (Department of Environment Transport and the Regions 1999c). References to competitiveness, the environment, skills, sustainability, rural areas and so on abound. The similarities between the eight strategies are so strong that it is tempting to suggest that they represent a single central blueprint for regional development, with limited adaptation to regional specificities. This view concurs with an early study of the RDAs, conducted by Robson, Peck and Holden:

> The similarity of the RESs does not suggest that the specific weaknesses and potentials of different regions have figured strongly in the formulation of strategies of the various RDAs. The hand of the centre seems to have lain heavy on the process. This may be inevitable, a consequence of the fact that the RESs have a common generic quality that reflects a process of synthesising existing policies and rationalising them within the context of an all-embracing and commonly shared vision. But the dilemma of bodies attempting to be *of* their regions while the centre may see them as agencies *in* the regions lies at the heart of an as-yet unresolved tension (Robson *et al*. 2000: 2).

This tension can be seen as an expression of the UK's enduringly fraught pattern of central-local relations and this is undoubtedly part of the picture. However, while this perspective points to the likelihood that the centre will attempt to inscribe some generic approach, it does not address the issue of why the approach that *is* so inscribed has taken the particular form that it has at this particular time. In my view, it is here that the concept of governmentality proves particularly useful.

Governmentality

The concept of 'governmentality' was first used by Michel Foucault in a lecture at the Collège de France in 1978. A transcription of the lecture by Pasquale Pasquino was published in Italian in 1978, with translations into English and French appearing in 1979 and 1986 respectively. A revised version of the English translation by Colin Gordon appeared in 1991 (Foucault 1991) in a collection of essays on governmentality under the title *The Foucault Effect: Studies in Governmentality* (Burchell *et al.* 1991). In Anglophone social science, very little attention was paid to Foucault's innovation until the appearance of *The Foucault Effect*. Since then, however, there has been an accelerating growth in the use of the concept, and evidence of its application across a diverse range of domains, including pedagogy, colonial studies, geography, citizenship theory, rural studies, welfare policy, risk and insurance, agricultural policy and political economy. The concept came of age in 1999 with the publication of a dedicated textbook (Dean, 1999).

Since there are now several useful guides to the concept of governmentality (e.g. Barry *et al.*, 1996, Burchell *et al.*, 1991, Dean, 1999), I shall confine myself here to a brief outline only. As noted in the introduction above, governmentality can be defined approximately as 'the art of government' and combines the ideas of 'government' and 'mentality'. The term denotes an approach to the understanding of governmental power that focuses on the intersection of governmental practices, ways of seeing, knowledges, political rationalities and the formation of subjects. 'Government' here is understood to include not only state practices, but also other kinds of activities that seek to co-ordinate or 'steer' processes, people and things. Thus we have the government of the self, corporate government, the government of children, the government of households and so on. Foucault's original essay is highly suggestive, but also relatively short and specific. In elaborating on the field of governmentality, therefore, Dean (1999) draws not only on Foucault's own formulations but also on a range of subsequent research to define an approach to the issue of governmentality that he terms an 'analytics of government'. In the following preliminary analysis of the RDAs' regional economic strategies I have drawn (rather loosely) on Dean's arguments, and it may be useful to highlight some key elements here.

First, there is a focus on the *constitution of objects of government*. Those engaged in government face an almost limitless array of possible targets for governmental action (people, things and processes). For government to occur some sub-set or aspect of these must be identified, made visible, and brought into being as something requiring and amenable to government. Foucault identified 'population' as perhaps the most significant object of government. National populations only exist today because they were constituted as an object of governmental attention from the second half of the eighteenth century.

The second element is *knowledge* of the objects of government (and increasingly of the process of government itself). Knowledge makes the objects of government visible, constitutes them in certain ways and enables certain kinds of governmental techniques to be applied to them. In the population example, statistics were (and remain) central to the discovery of 'population' as something with which government should be concerned. Such knowledges typically draw heavily on (certain branches of) the social and human sciences, such as economics, demography and psychology. Part of the analytics of government thus involves an excavation of the genealogy of the knowledges embedded in governmental practices.

Third, there is an irreducibly *technical* element to government. 'Here the literature on governmentality asks: by what means, mechanisms, procedures, instruments, tactics, techniques, technologies and vocabularies is authority constituted and rule accomplished?' (Dean, 1999: 31). For example, the government of populations involves technologies such as census taking, birth control, fiscal policy, public health measures and so on.

The fourth aspect concerns the *rational and reflective* element of government. Government involves not only the collation of knowledge in the sense of data and intelligence gathering, but also the formulation of strategies, plans and policies on the basis of that data and intelligence. These political rationalities include reflection on the process of government, itself a recognition of the chronic failure of government – compare Bob Jessop's concept of 'governance failure' (Jessop, 2000). In the field of population these rationalities appear in the form of policies for the growth, health and welfare of the population, or for its control, as in the case of the 'one child policy' in the People's Republic of China.

Fifth, governmentality involves organisations and practices that extend well beyond the institutions of the state. Drawing an analogy from the work of Bruno Latour, Miller and Rose (1990) refer to this as *'action at a distance'*. To continue with the example of population, the exercise of governmentality depends in good measure on the practices of the governed including the adoption of contraception, the work of families in raising children, co-operation or acquiescence in the exigencies of changing welfare regimes and so on. It thus has some similarities with the recently popular idea of 'governance', which denotes co-ordination through networks of state and non-state institutions (Rhodes, 1997), or, more abstractly, the 'self-organisation of inter-organisational relationships' (Jessop 1997: 59). However, governmentality should not be confused with governance. From the perspective of governmentality, the development of inter-organisational networks are one among a number of possible 'technologies of government' and these are failure-prone; thus it is possible to conceive of governmentality without governance.

Sixth, governmentality involves the production of particular kinds of *identities and subjectivities*. Indeed as with the constitution of objects of government more generally, particular aspects of subjects are made visible, knowable and governable through governmental practices. Thus identities such as 'family man' or 'housewife' that form part of a broader subject of the modern come into being through the invention of the idea of 'population' from the eighteenth century onwards, with 'families' being constructed as one of the building blocks of the national population.

The seventh element is the governmentality approach's resolute *anti-naturalism*. By this, I mean that entities (such as 'family', 'population', 'economy', 'nation', 'state' and even 'person' and 'individual') that are treated by much of the conventional social and human sciences as natural or quasi-natural and transhistorical phenomena are revealed as irreducibly historical and produced through, among other things, the process of government itself. So before the eighteenth century the aggregation of people residing in the territory of a state was not understood governmentally as 'the population' and 'populations' thus did not exist. 'Populations' are not naturally occurring aspects of a reality that exist prior to and outside government that governmental practice then seeks to control or develop. Rather, they are produced through the process of governing itself.

Finally, over time the art of government comes to be turned in on itself. Thus we see first the *governmentalisation of the state*, as the state becomes preoccupied with 'the art of government' in addition to its longer-standing concern with the exercise of 'sovereignty', and then the *governmentalisation of government* as the processes of government themselves become objects of government. In the field of population this can be seen when agencies involved in the government of population, such as healthcare organisations, themselves become the target of governmental action, perhaps through auditing, evaluation and the development of strategies for the future of the organisation, as well as for the future of the population.

There are several other elements to the governmentality approach that could be highlighted, but the ones I have mentioned are those most directly relevant to the situation of the Regional Development Agencies and their Regional Economic Strategies.

Governmentality and the Regional Economic Strategies

The governmentality approach is not an exercise in policy evaluation. Not only are such evaluations of the RDAs and the RESs available elsewhere, but more importantly 'evaluation' is itself a technology of government and thus internal to governmentality. Nor is the application of a critical analytics of government intended to belittle or undermine the important work being undertaken by RDAs (Robson *et al.* 2000). However, it is intended to disrupt some of the taken-for-granted assumptions on which the very idea of a 'regional economic strategy' depends.

A good starting place, albeit one easily overlooked, is to consider the implications of the very term 'regional economic development strategy'. 'Development' implies that regional economic change is not, or at least need not be, a process without coherence or lacking in 'direction' in the sense of 'heading'. 'Development', a term that has been subject to wide debate and more recently critique in the 'development studies' literature, implies progress from a less ordered, less prosperous, simpler economy to a more organised, more prosperous and more complex one. It is now so taken for granted by governments and society more generally that development is an unequivocal good that the use of the term in this context seems entirely unremarkable. Yet the idea that an economy (regional or otherwise) can undergo development, let alone be actively developed, should not be taken for granted. The possibility and process of 'development' are not natural features of economic life, but rather reflect ways of discursively ordering otherwise disparate and chaotic social processes and to describe differing forms of economic order in value-laden ways. This value-driven aspect of government is central to governmentality.

The term strategy also deserves to be problematised. To produce a strategy is self-consciously *not* to produce a plan, nor is it entirely to leave matters to 'market forces'. There has been over time a shift in governmentality away from planning and its discourses and towards strategy. Erstwhile planners have had to learn to be strategists, even if the degree of central government influence on the RESs suggests there is some way to go before *local* strategic thinking is the main influence on the content of the documents. To 'strategise' or to 'act strategically' are not neutral activities (Painter, 1997), but are themselves freighted with assumptions about the nature of government and the governability of regions and economies. It is no coincidence that the origins of the term lie in warfare, nor that there is a strong tradition of formal analysis of strategy in game theory. Whereas some of the dominant connotations of planning (though not necessarily the practices of planners) seem to depend on the assumptions that external environments are, if not completely controllable, at least predictable and knowable, and that direct control of development processes is possible, the concept of strategy accepts unpredictability, incomplete knowledge, and the impossibility of direct control. Thus developing a strategy is more about process, while traditional models of planning are more focussed on outcome. A good strategy accepts that change will occur that cannot be foreseen or entirely controlled and is likely to focus on developing robust procedures and organisational cultures to respond to an unpredictable environment. The shift from 'plan' to 'strategy' can thus be seen in part as an element of the rise of neo-liberalism, and in part as a governmental response to the neo-liberal critique of previous regimes of government. It is also worth pointing out that in RDA-speak no distinction is made between the strategy and the paper or electronic document in which the strategy is described. Thus developing a strategy becomes a matter of documentation, or writing, rather than of practice, and the document thereby forms one of the key technologies of governmentality.

The possibility of a *Regional Economic Strategy* depends on the assumption that there exists an entity called the 'regional economy'. A Regional Economic Strategy can thus be seen as a governmental technology through which an RDA seeks to bring into being, and make visible and governable 'its' regional economy. From a realist perspective (Sayer, 1992), the concept of the regional economy is largely spurious, if what is meant by the term is a relatively integrated, interacting economic whole, more or less bounded by the territory of the region. In practice, economic actors in regions (especially in the regions of England) have as many economic linkages beyond the boundaries of the region as they do within them, if not more. Most regions are highly heterogeneous and incoherent, unevenly developed and internally fragmented and certainly cannot be considered to be the subjects of economic and political action, nor the objects of effective governance. David Harvey, for example, notes that the 'tendency to the structured coherence of urban regions' (Harvey, 1985: 140) is just that, a tendency, and one that is continually undermined by the disrupted effects of counter-tendencies. In any case, the boundaries of the 'urban regions' discussed by Harvey are defined by the operation of substantive socio-economic processes, and have little or nothing in common with the bureaucratically defined and largely arbitrary boundaries of the RDAs.

In such circumstances, from the perspective of governmentality, the task of the RDAs, through their RESs, is quite literally to produce and constitute regional economies. This takes a huge effort of intellectual labour, much of which is hidden, but some of which can be excavated from the strategy documents. Much of this labour involves the construction of geographical knowledges:

> The state apparatus, with its interests in governmentality, administration, taxation, planning, and social control, has steadily been built up from the eighteenth century onwards as a primary site for the collection and analysis of geographical information. The process of state formation was and still is dependent upon the creation of certain kinds of geographical understandings [...]. For the last two centuries, the state has been perhaps *the* site for the production of geographical knowledges necessary for the creation, maintenance and enhancement of its powers. [...] Insofar as the state is itself organized hierarchically, it will typically produce knowledges at different spatial scales (local, regional, national). [...] The state, through planning mechanisms, likewise institutes normative programs for the production of space, the definition of territoriality, the geographical distribution of population, economic activity, social services, wealth and well-being (Harvey, 2000: 3).

Harvey argues that there are four generic elements of geographical knowledge associated with governmentality. These are:

- cartographic identifications, or knowledge of position in geographic space;
- understanding of spatio-temporal dynamics;
- knowledge of the qualities of locale, place and region;
- knowledge of environment, or the relations between the cultural and natural.

The map is fundamental to the first kind of knowledge, and most of the Regional Economic Strategies contain one or more maps sometime used mainly rhetorically. Thus the RES for Yorkshire and Humberside includes an outline of the region superimposed on a map of the world with Europe highlighted; a fairly obvious attempt to link the region symbolically with both Europe and the global economy. Intriguingly the UK has no special significance in this representation. The understanding of spatio-temporal dynamics is present in a number of ways. A good example is the reliance of the RESs implicitly or otherwise on particular theories of regional development, a point that will be discussed in more detail below. Each of the strategies attempts to construct a knowledge of the distinctive qualities of its regions, based on, among other things, its particular economic mix, social make-up, environmental qualities, and urban and rural contrasts. Finally, the strategies express particular understandings of society-environment relations, most obviously in their generic concern with 'sustainable development', but also in a variety of other ways such as a concern with technological innovation to reduce activities thought harmful to the environment and to promote new forms of technological mastery over nature.

In developing the Regional Economic Strategies, the RDAs have both drawn on existing geographical knowledge and developed their own. In the background of most of the strategies is a set of assumptions about regional development that can be traced back to theories of regional development current in academic geography in the late 1980s. Among many others, the work of Michael Storper and Allan Scott was particularly influential in refocusing attention on the importance of the regional scale in the process of capitalist production (Scott and Storper, 1986; Scott, 1996; Storper, 1995, 1997; Storper and Scott, 1992). They identified 'territorial production complexes' at the regional scale as providing the basis of a nation's position within the world economy. Regional milieux were seen as the key sources of competitiveness, providing networks of untraded interdependencies, social capital and innovative cultures. The region was 'rediscovered' as a central concept in economic development, and the 'new regionalism' quickly became the received wisdom in business schools, textbooks and monographs (see, for example, Keating, 1998: 136ff) and policy formation. Since Scott and Storper's early work their ideas have been subject to much criticism and further refinement. However, for my purposes here, and from the perspective of governmentality, the accuracy of their analysis is less important than the impact it has had on the government of regions as a kind of received wisdom in regional development theory (not least as a result of the publication of many over-simplified or even vulgarised accounts of their approach).

According to the 'new regionalism', economically successful regions are those that gain a competitive advantage in the world economy by exploiting the distinctive characteristics of their regional and local milieux. The two most famous, and most frequently cited, examples are the Italian region of Emilia-Romagna and the Silicon Valley district of California. In these regions, so the argument goes, economic prosperity and dynamism derives from the growth of 'new industrial districts', which consist of clusters of firms with strong economic, intellectual and cultural linkages between them. Much of the 'new regionalism' literature has been criticised for depending too heavily on these and a handful of other examples, for assuming that their model of development can be replicated, and for assuming that such replication can be generated through government action. Nevertheless such assumptions are written into the RESs. One of the clearest examples is provided by the RES for the North East region, produced by the Regional Development Agency 'One North East'. The strategy includes a description of the characteristics of economically successful regions to provide 'lessons' for the North East (Figure 8.1).

In preparing this Strategy, the characteristics of successful regions were identified:

- a pool of entrepreneurs who can access readily available sources of venture capital;
- a sound, diverse base of knowledge driven companies, competing in global markets, with a commitment to continuous innovation in process and product technologies;
- strong collaborative company and university research and development projects;
- a versatile healthy workforce which offers a wide range of advanced skills with all young people staying in education or work-based training;
- very high quality schools, colleges, and universities;
- a clear commitment to building socially inclusive urban and rural communities by providing routes back into the labour market;
- advanced telecommunications and transport links to the rest of the world;
- attractive urban and rural villages in the hinterland of a large metropolis with a thriving cultural and commercial life;
- an exceptionally beautiful natural environment; and
- effective public-private sector partnerships.

Figure 8.1   **Lessons from Successful Regions**

While not all the other strategies spell out these characteristic so clearly, they all implicitly adopt a broadly similar definition of regional economic success, and no doubt few people would object to their region acquiring these desirable features. What is interesting about the One North East case, however, is the reference to *lessons* from successful regions. This is an explicit recognition of the use of knowledge in the construction of the regional strategy, and on the importance of knowledge acquisition. Indeed the taskforce that drafted the strategy included two senior academics from the University of Durham; one from the Business School and one from the Department of Geography. An even more direct reference to the new industrial districts/new regionalism literature is provided by another aspect of the One North East strategy, namely its emphasis on 'clusters' and the establishment of a 'regional service for clustering' to assist their development. This latter feature is based clearly on the assumption that clusters can be developed through strategic governmental action.

This concern with clusters stems directly from the embedding in the strategy of knowledge derived from practitioners, management gurus and theoretical and empirical academic research. Such knowledge is, however, adapted by the RES. Thus the strategy contains two lists of actual and potential clusters in the North East of England. These lists include clusters such as 'low volume manufacturing' that are typical of the kinds of clusters emphasised in the academic and management literature, but they also include 'tourism', 'public authorities' and 'the voluntary sector' that appear to stretch conventional definitions of the term 'cluster' to breaking point or beyond. This all-inclusiveness is fairly typical of all the RESs and applies across a range of fields besides cluster development. It stems in part from a political requirement that the RESs should offer something for every locality, social group and economic sector. The danger where clusters are concerned is that the original concept may be so watered down by applying it too broadly that any benefits may be difficult to discern, or lost altogether.

This example of cluster policy in North East England is a clear instance of attempts to generate the 'action at a distance' that defines governmentality (Miller and Rose, 1990). Cluster development (and regional economic success more generally) cannot occur through state action alone, but depends crucially on the actions of companies and partnership bodies such as the Regional Service for Clustering. Governmentality thus involves attempts to co-ordinate actions by disparate institutions, most of which are not amenable to direct state control.

In addition to seeking to promote regional economic integration (whether through cluster development, or in other ways, such as infrastructure development), the RESs work to constitute regional economies by providing knowledge of the region and by aiming to develop improvements in regional data collection. This task is assisted to some extent by the coincidence (for the most part) between the boundaries of the RDAs and those of the standard regions that are used for statistical purposes. Nevertheless, it remains the case (and a number of the RESs make this point) that there is a distinct lack of broadly based, high quality social and economic statistics at the regional scale in England. In some regions this knowledge acquisition element is being taken further in proposals for 'regional observatories' to collate data about the region and promote improvements in regional statistics.

This emphasis on 'knowing the region' is a key aspect of governmentality. To know is to be better able to govern. However, the collection of data and information and the development of knowledge are far from innocent exercises. The methods of data collection and the types of data collected are shaped by, but also shape, governmental understanding of the process of regional economic development. The governmentality of the central state is an issue here, as the RDAs are required to measure their performance against certain centrally determined benchmarks. These are shown in Figure 8.2.

- GDP per head and GDP per head relative to the EU average;
- ILO unemployment rate;
- proportion of the population with above average living conditions – life expectancy measure drawn from the Standard Mortality Ratios;
- per cent new homes built on previously developed land;
- labour productivity – manufacturing gross value added and all sector GDP per worker;
- skills – per cent of 19 year olds with level 2 qualifications and per cent of adults with level 3 qualifications; and
- business formations and survival rates.

Figure 8.2   State of the Region: Core Indicators Proposed by Government

Source: South East England Development Agency,1999: 40.

One of the consequences of requiring all RDAs to measure themselves against a common metric is that it will be possible to evaluate their relative performances, and even to construct a league table of RDAs. Whether this kind of competitive evaluation is undertaken or not, the use of these kinds of statistical indicators remains a core feature of the governmentality evident in the RDA initiative.

The similarity between the eight RESs has already been mentioned, and this extends to the kinds of regional economic development knowledges to be found in the eight documents. Thus all the RDAs want to build to be 'world class', 'excellent' or 'globally competitive' regions, and there is a common view that this can be achieved by developing 'learning regions' (despite recent academic criticism of that idea), focusing on 'e-commerce' and promoting 'sustainable development'. These similarities could be dismissed as the product dependence on a litany of 'New Labour' shibboleths, but that would be to miss the ways in which many of the common themes feed directly into governmentalities which extend well beyond the phenomenon of New Labour.

To illustrate this, I will focus briefly on one of these themes, 'equal opportunities'. RDAs are required by central government guidance to address the issue of equal opportunities in their work, and to show how equal opportunities issues are incorporated into their strategies. Typically this can involve a separate section dealing with equal opportunities in the strategy document, though in some of the documents the treatment is much more gestural. For the most part the discussion of equal opportunities is highly conventional. From radical beginnings in the women's, black, disabled and gay and lesbian movements, a concern with equal opportunities has today become largely routinised and incorporated into standard public sector and business practice, partly to ensure compliance with the law, but also because 'equal treatment' has become, in public discourse at least, part of the common sense of everyday life. This is not to deny the importance of equality legislation and practice for groups suffering discrimination, but it is to point to the ways in which attempts to disrupt the status quo can come, not least via governmentality, to form part of the status quo.

A typical example (albeit from the more gestural end of the spectrum) can be found in the RES for the South East. Equal opportunities is mentioned explicitly in the strategy only twice, in the section on 'World class workforce':

> The priorities set out for world class business and learning need to be priorities for organisations, individuals and trade union and other employee representatives alike. Equally, the priorities for inclusiveness

152 *Habitus: A Sense of Place*

> and equal opportunities within the workforce must be mirrored throughout all areas of the region's economic strategy (South East England Development Agency, 1999: 23).

and:

> *Objectives*: Develop discussion across the region at workplace level, particularly on a cross-organisation basis, to share, develop and promote best practice in employee participation, equal opportunities/flexible working and strategies for achieving work/life balance, job enrichment and growth (South East England Development Agency, 1999: 23).

The increasingly 'taken-for-granted' character of equality concerns has arguably seen a diminution in the profile of active efforts to combat racism, sexism and other forms of discrimination. What seems to happen is that the RDAs (in common no doubt with other public agencies) can say that they have discharged their duty by including a section or a statement on equal opportunities, while leaving much of the rest of the strategy unchanged. There is thus the *performance* of equality, rather than the active *production* of equality. Indeed the priority of performance over production is evident throughout the RES documents, and is a further example of the reflective nature of governance in the sense that there is an awareness of the need to be seen to be engaging in certain kinds of practices. This is a clear example of the operation of a particular governmentality and produces particular kinds of effects in terms of the constitutions of subjects and identities. In the RESs, members of minority ethnic groups, for example, appear largely as members of the labour force, and frequently as 'socially excluded', that is as *unemployed* members of the labour force. They are thus implicitly cast as *victims* of a double exclusion: economic exclusion (unemployed) and discrimination (ethnic minority). Note that the term racism is never used. Without wishing to downplay the very real problems faced in the labour market by many people, the dominant application of the idea of 'equal opportunities' (at least in the regional economic strategies) leads to the construction of Black and Asian people principally as victims, or, more rarely, as community activists and voluntary workers. There are, for example, few references to Black or Asian entrepreneurs or to the enormous importance of minority-owned businesses to the economies of many British cities. To summarise more simply, ethnic minorities appear rarely in the strategy documents, and when they do they tend to be ghettoised in the 'equal opportunities' chapter or section. The featuring of the black businessman Arthur Blackwood is an honourable, if limited, exception to this pattern in the strategy for the East Midlands. The unfortunate consequence of the way in which equal opportunities is understood in the strategies is thus to perpetuate the perception that ethnic minorities are an economic cost to regions, rather than an economic resource, and that they act as a brake on, rather than as a motor of, economic growth.

Conclusion

Equal opportunity is by no means the only aspect of the regional economic strategies that exemplifies the operation of governmentality. Similar arguments could be made concerning the concepts such as 'community', 'learning', 'sustainability' and so on. On the other hand, it might be objected that the RDAs and the RES documents are rather too mundane to carry the weight of theory involved in the application of the concept of governmentality. However, as Foucault emphasised, it is often in the most taken-for-granted and commonplace areas of social life that the exercise of power is most significant, in part because it is most hidden. The operation of power/knowledge is most successful where it is embodied in routine.

Following from this, though, it should not be thought that the exercise of power is inherently negative. As Foucault argued and as Dean forcefully stresses in his development of the concept of governmentality, there can be no place of freedom beyond the reach of power relations. Power is productive and can generate all kinds of social outcomes, both positive and negative. The kind of analysis presented here, therefore, is not a substitute for programmes of policy evaluation that seek to assess whether RDAs have been successful on their own terms. Many of the aims of the RDAs are admirable and we need to know whether they have been achieved.

That said, there is also scope to step outside the framework of regional development within which the RDAs work and seek to analyse it in terms of the 'art of government'. The governmentality approach disrupts our taken-for-granted understandings of things and helps to reveal how the government of regional development is made possible, through the use of particular means and technologies and through the production of particular forms of knowledge, including geographical knowledge in the terms suggested by David Harvey.

A concern with geographical knowledge also draws attention to the relationship between governmentality and space. In one sense space is just another object of governance, constructed as such through particular kinds of spatial understandings and governed through particular kinds of spatial technologies. At the same time, space also lies at the heart of governmentality more generally. Like population, territory is fundamental to the constitution of modern governmentalities, and knowledge of space and spatial relations is central to the very possibility of government of any kind. From this perspective, the governmentalities embodied in RDAs may be seen not only as another example of the art of government, but also as the latest stage in a long struggle of states and other governmental institutions to manage the tension between central control and regional voice and between territorial integration and the pressures generated by uneven development.

Postscript

My chapter on 'governmentality and regional economic strategies' argues that economic regions and regional economies are not pre-existing natural entities but are brought into being through the practices of government. This may occur through the production of regional statistics, the elaboration of regional economic strategies, the formation of institutions of regional economic governance and in other ways. My original analysis used concepts of governmentality; how does it relate to habitus? First, although the phrase is suggestive, I am doubtful whether it makes sense today to speak of a 'regional habitus', if by that we mean a relatively enduring set of behavioural dispositions that is shared by a majority of inhabitants of a region and that arises somehow from the supposedly unitary character of that region. For one thing, such a 'regional habitus' would be disrupted by class, gender and ethnic differences (each of which, in Bourdieu's terms, function to structure habitus very strongly). More importantly, though, the idea of 'regional habitus' posits the existence of distinct integrated regions, that have a persistent enough internal unity and external differentiation to provide the basis for the enduring set of dispositions that (for Bourdieu) defines habitus. To be sure, some such territories can be distinguished within existing nation states: Catalonia, Scotland, Quebec and so on. But these cases acquire such distinctiveness because they are widely understood (from within and without) not as regions but as nations, albeit stateless ones. Regions that do not enjoy the cachet of nationhood are much more weakly differentiated from one another, and in many (I suspect most) such cases it is difficult to identify much spatial congruence between social, economic, cultural and political boundaries.

Second, and in consequence, the concept of region can be related quite clearly to Bourdieu's notion of field – a dynamic space of forces, contradictions and determinations (Bourdieu, this volume). A region does not 'have' a habitus of its own, but it is both the product and the object of practices (economic, cultural and political) that are themselves generated through the workings of (numerous) habitus(es). The development of regional economic strategies (to take the example discussed in my chapter) can be understood as the effect of a certain habitus (that of public policy professionals and economic planners) in relation to a certain field (the management of the regional differentiation of economic processes). Such strategies are not purely technical or instrumental documents (techniques and instruments are in any case never pure), but express and embody particular ways of seeing, of circumscribing problems, and of imagining the 'regional', the 'economic' and the 'strategic'.

In the five years since the English regional economic strategies discussed in my original essay were published they have been developed, updated and elaborated, and have to some extent become more regionally specific and less generic. At the same time they remain, of course, governmental technologies through which each region and 'its' economy is defined, described and diagnosed, and thereby, in many ways, created. Conflict is concealed (though 'diversity' is celebrated), visions are always bold, and renaissance is everywhere imminent. Bourdieu always insisted on the generative and productive potential of habitus; the evidence of official regional development policy in England suggests that the habitus of contemporary economic development professionals is certainly productive, but within necessarily circumscribed limits.

Note

1   Exceptions include Danny MacKinnon's recent work on local economic governance: MacKinnon, D. (2000). 'Managerialism, governmentality and the state: a neo-Foucauldian approach to local economic governance', *Political Geography* 19: 293-314.

References

Barry, A., Osborne, T. and Rose, N. (1996) *Foucault and Political Reason: liberalism, neo-liberalism and rationalities of government*, London, UCL Press.

Burchell, G., Gordon, C. and Miller, P. (1991) *The Foucault Effect: studies in governmentality*, Hemel Hempstead, Harvester Wheatsheaf.

Cruikshank, B. (1999) *The Will to Empower: democratic citizens and other subjects*, Ithaca, NY, Cornell University Press.

Davies, N. (1999) *The Isles: a history*, London, Macmillan.

Dean, M. (1999) *Governmentality: power and rule in modern society*, London, Sage.

Department of Environment, T.a.t.R. (1999a) *Regional Development Agencies Regional Chambers*, London, DETR.

Department of Environment, T.a.t.R. (1999b) *Regional Development Agencies' Regional Strategies*, London, DETR.

Department of Environment, T.a.t.R. (1999c). *Supplementary Guidance to Regional Development Agencies*, London, DETR.

Donzelot, J. (1984) *L'invention du social*, Paris, Fayard.

Donzelot, J. (1988) 'The promotion of the social', *Economy and Society*, 17: 395-427.

Dynes, M. and Walker, D. (1995) *The Times Guide to the New British State*, London, Times Books.

Ewald, F. (1991) 'Insurance and risk', in G. Burchell, C. Gordon and P. Miller (eds), *The Foucault effect: studies in governmentality*, Hemel Hempstead, Harvester Wheatsheaf: 197-210.

Foucault, M. (1991) 'Governmentality', in G. Burchell, C. Gordon and P. Miller (eds), The *Foucault Effect: studies in governmentality*, Hemel Hempstead, Harvester Wheatsheaf: 87-104.

Harvey, D. (1985) *The Urbanization of Capital*, Oxford, Blackwell.

Harvey, D. (2000) 'Cartographic Identities: geographical knowledges under globalization', 29th International Geographical Congress, Seoul, South Korea.

Hogwood, B. (1996a) 'Devolution: the English dimension. Public Money and Management', October-December, 29-34.

Hogwood, B. (1996b) *Mapping the Regions: boundaries, coordination and government*, Bristol, The Policy Press.

Hogwood, B. (1997) 'The machinery of government', 1979-97, *Political Studies*, 45: 704-715.

Jessop, B. (1997) 'A neo-Gramscian approach to the regulation of urban regimes: accumulation strategies, hegemonic projects, and governance', in M. Lauria (ed.), *Reconstructing Urban Regime Theory: regulating urban politics in a global economy*, Thousand Oaks, Sage: 51-73.

Jessop, B. (2000) 'Governance failure', In G. Stoker (ed.), *The New Politics of British Local Governance*, London, Macmillan: 11-32.

Keating, M. (1998) *The New Regionalism in Western Europe: territorial restructuring and political change*, Cheltenham, Edward Elgar.

MacCormick, N. (1999) *Questioning Sovereignty: law, state and nation in the European commonwealth*, Oxford, Oxford University Press.

MacKinnon, D. (2000) 'Managerialism, governmentality and the state: a neo-Foucauldian approach to local economic governance', *Political Geography*, 19: 293-314.

Mawson, J. (1998). 'Britain. The rise of the regional agenda to combat increased fragmentation', in P. Le Galès and C. Lequesne (eds), *Regions in Europe*, London, Routledge: 219-238.

Miller, P. and Rose, N. (1990) 'Governing economic life', *Economy and Society*, 19: 1-31.

O'Malley, P. (1996) 'Risk and responsibility', in A. Barry, T. Osborne and N. Rose (eds), *Foucault and Political Reason: liberalism, neo-liberalism and rationalities of government*, London, UCL Press.

Painter, J. (1997) 'Regulation, regime and practice in urban politics', in M. Lauria (ed.), *Reconstructing Regime Theory: regulating urban politics in a global economy*, Thousand Oaks, Sage: 122-143.

Rhodes, R. (1997) *Understanding Governance*, Buckingham, Open University Press.

Robson, B., Peck, J. and Holden, A. (2000) *Findings: Regional Development Agencies and local regeneration*, York, Joseph Rowntree Foundation.

Sayer, A. (1992) *Method in Social Science: a realist approach*, London, Routledge.

Scott, A. and Storper, M. (1986) *Production, Work and Territory: the geographical anatomy of industrial capitalism*, London, Allen and Unwin.

Scott, A. J. (1996) 'Regional motors of the global economy', *Futures*, 28: 391-411.

South East England Development Agency (1999) *Building a World Class Region: an economic strategy for the south east of England*, SEEDA.

Storper, M. (1995) 'The resurgence of regional economies, ten years later: the region as a nexus of untraded interdependencies', *European Urban and Regional Studies*, 2: 191-221.

Storper, M. (1997) *The Regional World: territorial development in a global economy*, New York, NY, Guildford.

Storper, M. and Scott, A. (1992) 'Industrialization and regional development', in A. Scott and M. Storper (eds), *Pathways to Industrialization and Regional Development*, London, Routledge: 3-17.

PROCESSES OF PLACE-MAKING

9 Mind the Gap

JEAN HILLIER

> 'It is what lies behind and in between actions ... that is important'
> (Murdoch, 1970: 67)

Preamble

More years ago than I readily admit, I came fresh out of University to my first job serving as a Planning Officer with a County Council planning authority in a then de-industrialising South Wales in the UK. The person who would now be known as the Executive Manager (Planning), then simply the Deputy Chief Planner, amused the Department with his constant use of the terms 'Political Will' and 'Prudence'.

    Political Will and Prudence were always together, so much so that the Departmental cartoonist depicted them as an old, somewhat argumentative couple. This pair was the Departmental joke, regularly signing memos and being responsible for all the mistakes or oversights we made. Yet I have to admit that I never really understood the meaning of this old couple until I embarked on this current research and realised just how important is planners' use of Prudence[1] in dealing with the vagaries of Political Will.

    I hereby dedicate this paper to Political Will and Prudence.

Introduction

Whilst attempting to pay attention to the important theory-practice gap, most recent theories of collaborative planning lack fine-grained analysis of what actually takes place and how arguments become convincing in deliberative dialogue. Moreover, collaborative planning theories tend to focus on the co-ordinating role of planning officers in attempting to achieve some form of con-sensus[2] eliding the vital gap between officers' recommendations and elected members' decisions; the gap between the authority of professional planners and the politics of public authorities. It is this gap on which I concentrate.

If planning theory is to be of real use to practitioners it needs to address practice as it is actually encountered in the worlds, not only of planning officers, but also of elected representatives. Analysis of instances where officer recommendations are ignored, or where representatives change their minds, suggests that actual decision-making may be exercised in ways which are contingent, complex and organised with little distinct or overt logic. I seek to uncover the communicative behaviours which precede and are construed in the ritualised formal process of political decision-making and which form a face of power that may remain invisible to practitioners and theorists. Such instances of communication form the hidden transcripts of decision-making; they constitute the functioning of habitus and the logic of democratic practice.

I seek to interrogate such logic; to bring into hearing various dialogical techniques and devices of communication, modes of authority and subjectifications and the telos of strategies and ambitions. I go beyond simplistic statements that planning is political and attempt to uncover 'the real principle behind strategies' (Bourdieu, 1987: 76), or as Bourdieu terms it, 'a feel for the game (*le sens du jeu*)'.

My aim in this paper is to add some sense of the political to planning theory. I seek to uncover the how and why of those seemingly errant decisions when increasingly assertive[3] elected representatives (ER) ignore officer recommendations or change their minds. I focus on the mechanisms through which politics influences what ERs want, 'what they regard as possible and even who they are' (Edelman, 1964: 20). I do not pretend to offer an exhaustive range of possible reasons. However, I believe that if planning practitioners are to act effectively they cannot afford to ignore or to misconstrue the contingent and dynamic nature of political habitus. They may then also be able to gain a feel for the game, to anticipate reactions to their recommendations and to take steps accordingly.

The State of the Debate: From Habermas to Habitus

Habermasian communicative action normatively calls for the creation of political institutions in which discursive processes have a central role in decision-making. In his recent work, Habermas (1998) has specified the basic shape which such political institutions should take for his concept of deliberative democracy to be practical. The cornerstone is public reason, which Habermas demonstrates in his model of the circulation of power. I am interested here only in the arc in which information generated in the public sphere is transformed through democratic procedures of governmental will-formation into communicative power. The rationality of decision outcomes should ideally be a function of the reasons proposed (the force of the better argument), assured through legally prescribed procedures of deliberation and decision-making designed to ensure sufficient approximation to ideal conditions of discursive openness under limitations of time and information. 'The state's raison d'être ... (lies) in the guarantee of an inclusive process of opinion- and will-formation in which free and equal citizens reach an understanding on which goals and norms lie in the equal interest of all' (Habermas, 1998: 241).

Habermasian communicative action has influenced the approaches to planning theory developed by Patsy Healey (e.g. 1992, 1996, 1997), Judith Innes (e.g. 1995, 1996, 1998) and others. These authors have emphasised that good planning policy decision-making should be a collaborative, deliberative process, in which actors reciprocally share knowledges and meanings. Knowledge claims are validated through inclusionary argumentation in institutional consensus-building processes.

Leonie Sandercock's (1998) implicitly Habermasian-grounded work stresses inclusion and the recognition of difference in her 'epistemology of multiplicity for planning practice'. The goal of her radical model of planning practice is to collectively empower the systematically disempowered whilst working towards structural transformation of systematic inequalities (1998: 97) in a more democratised process.

John Forester's (e.g. 1989, 1993, 1999a, b) theorising explicitly acknowledges how the counterfactual ideas of Habermasian critical theory help us unpack 'practical and institutional contingencies, ... political vulnerabilities' (Forester, 1993: x) as we listen to the actors' interpretations and representations of self and other. Habermas' ideas remind us that decision-making is shaped through arguments, by claims which may be rational or irrational. Forester's work is strongly grounded in empirical practice stories. He reads Habermas 'sociologically as a critical pragmatist' rather than as a 'Kantian moral theorist' (1999a: 204) to probe the production of meaning and its interpretation '*in the political and ethical work* of ... developing practical judgement' (1999a: 6, my emphasis).

Forester's emphasis on the politics of planning work is particularly important. Whilst Healey, Innes and Sandercock and others (e.g. Richardson, 1996; Tewdr-Jones and Allmendinger, 1998; Phelps and Tewdr-Jones, 2000; Flyvbjerg, 1998; and Hillier, 2000) stress the need to probe beneath a Habermasian surface rationality to explore the deeper dynamics of power beneath; whilst theorists such as Mouffe (1996), and, in relation to planning theory, Hillier (1998, 2000) challenge the possibility of consensus and propose that persistent agonism be made central to any epistemic improvement in deliberative democratic theory, it is John Forester who makes the crucial link between practical reasoning and political motivation.[4]

Forester acknowledges that the role of politicians/ERs and their tendency to strategic posturing can 'regularly undermine (planners') collaborative problem solving' (1999a: 2); that 'the distance between rational public policy and political will can be substantial' (1999a: 87). Forester indicates how planning practitioners must be able 'to search not just for what is good in some abstract sense but to find what is good in the political sense' (1999: 47). In order to do this successfully, planners must be able to understand politics and how it works. We may know this intuitively, but what Forester offers is an analysis of what it implies for effective practice.

In the 'game' of planning decision-making, a certain number of regular patterns of behaviour result from conformation to codified, recognised rules. However, other, generally political, patterns of decision behaviour do not appear explicable either by the invocation of codified rules or in terms of brute causality. It is here that Pierre Bourdieu's concept of the habitus intervenes.

The habitus is a way of framing the world or 'field' of social practice. It is a way of knowing social practice which both structures and is structured by it. Bourdieu (1991, 1993) defines a field as a social space which structures strategic action for control over resources. He likens it to a game board whereon people are positioned with varying resources available to them. The habitus is a set of dispositions to act in the game; a 'feel for the game' or 'practical sense'. The field in which I am interested here is that of local government land use planning decision-making.

Bourdieu defines habitus as 'systems of durable, transposable dispositions, structured structures predisposed to function as structuring structures' (1990: 53); a set of values internalised by actors in processes of socialisation. Choices for action are often made spontaneously; a reflex responding to some cue, perhaps semi- or un-consciously, of an opportunity to accumulate 'symbolic capital' of status and influence; 'a fascinated pursuit of the approval of others' (Bourdieu, 2000: 166).[5] Whilst several authors [6] suggest that this denial of analytical agency is an oversimplification, I nevertheless ask whether we can perceive a collective phenomenon (or political culture) in ER decision-making with regard to land use planning issues at local government level.

This paper is grounded in the practice stories of ERs. By reading such stories planners can learn about the habitus of local political culture; about what may be important to politicians, to what practitioners could pay attention and what may be really at stake behind the fictions of rational decision-making.

Where are the Gaps?

A concentration on traditional planning policy-making and decision-making ideas of survey-analysis-plan or officer recommendation – council decision – implementation obscures the complexity of the process. Such theories assume that policy- and decision-making proceed in a relatively orderly, unidirectional, step-wise, instrumental process towards a finite end point. They are too deterministic, however, to serve as adequate theories of reality and leave huge gaps.

Firstly, there is what Hindess (1997: 80) terms the 'democratic deficit', an absence of consideration of the role of democracy in, for example, public participation prior to the officer recommendation, public influence in the council decision, Ministerial ratification and so on.

Secondly, as Yanow (1996) and the debate (1999) on the planning theory email network indicated, there is a huge gap between decision and implementation. Thirdly, the work and recommendations of planning officers are traditionally perceived to be technocratic and value neutral. As I will indicate, this is not the case in practice.

I attempt below to represent what I believe to be some of the possible gaps in current planning theorising, applicable at a local authority scale.[7]

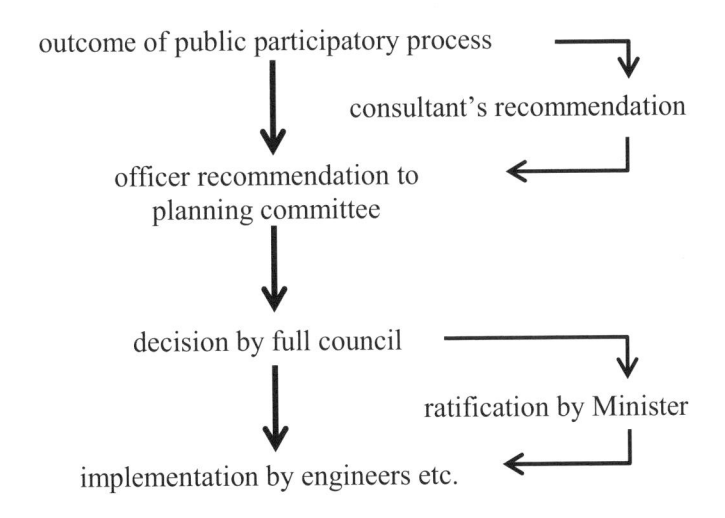

```
outcome of public participatory process ─────┐
         │                                    ↓
         │          consultant's recommendation
         ↓                                    │
  officer recommendation to  ←────────────────┘
     planning committee
         │
         ↓
  decision by full council ──────────────────┐
         │                                    ↓
         │              ratification by Minister
         ↓                                    │
  implementation by engineers etc. ←──────────┘
```

Figure 9.1   **Potential Gaps in Theorising Local Planning Processes**

I deal here only with the 'gap' between officer recommendation to the local authority planning committee and the council decision, what Bohman and Rehg might term 'the relation between reason and politics' (1997: xviii).[8]

John Forester (1999a: 253) terms the committee stage/s of decision-making 'enacted political drama'. Indeed, watching ERs in action, or listening to tapes of meetings, one can easily recognise the validity of dramatic or even sporting metaphors. Committee and council meetings are like games in which actors/players often reject any stance of objectivism and/or the rules. Meetings become a performance and practices are seen as no more than the acting-out of roles; the habitus.

Methodological Context

I seek to theorise practice; to step down from an objectivist viewpoint to situate myself in 'real activity', in practical relation to the world of local planning decision-making. In order to do this I have 'returned' to practice, and though unable to tell stories through participatory observation as an ER in the tradition of Altshuler (1965), Blowers (1980) and Throgmorton (1990, 1996), I have conducted conversational interviews ('looking inwards' (Kitchen, 1997)) with several currently serving and ex-politicians at local government level in Western Australia (WA) from metropolitan and country town authorities, in capacities ranging from member or Chair of the Planning Committee to Mayor[9] of their jurisdictions.[10] I attempt to hold together what Bourdieu calls a twofold truth; both the points of view of the agents caught up in local decision-making and my own inevitable agency in relating the ERs' 'position-takings to the positions from which they are taken' (Bourdieu, 2000: 189). I hope, that, in this way, the stories which ERs tell can reveal 'political judgements about opportunities and constraints, about more and less responsible efforts, about more and less supposedly legitimate mandates, about relevant history to be respected and learned, relevant concerns, interests, and commitments to be honoured' (Forester, 1999a: 47).

I have also interviewed several current and former public planning officers in senior positions from metropolitan authorities ('looking outwards'), who are widely regarded as exemplars of astute practitioners with integrity and participatory track records, and who are motivated by concerns for social justice.[11] My analysis also includes reference to published stories by ex-planners including Clavel (1980), Krumholz (1990) and Kitchen (1997).

For a contextual understanding of local planning practice in WA, I include key information in point-form:

- The Town Planning and Development Act 1928 (amended) requires local municipal authorities to produce/review Town Planning Schemes every 5 years.
- Town Planning Schemes (TPS) regulate land use zones and set the development standards which are the basic tool of Development Control within a municipality. They contain information on the physical form of developments, such as setbacks, plot ratios, parking bays etc. The TPS must be approved by the State West Australian Planning Commission (WAPC) and the Minister.
- Councils are able to delegate power to planning officers to approve/refuse development proposals which do/do not comply with selected aspects of the TPS. The extent of delegated authority varies according to the amount of control the ERs wish to retain. For example in WA, East Fremantle has delegated 0% of its authority to the planners, Stirling and Albany have delegated c90%, the City of Fremantle 50%. The WA average is about 60%.
- Local authority planning decisions must be taken on sound planning principles. Aspects of market competition, impact on property values, morality, compassion etc. are not deemed planning principles.
- Applications to subdivide land are decided at State level by the government-appointed WAPC, not at municipality level.
- Appeals against planning decisions may be made either directly to the Minister for Planning or the Town Planning Appeal Tribunal. Ministers are not compelled to give reasons for their judgements. Ministerial Appeals information is not available through Freedom of Information legislation.
- Conduct of planning officers and ERs is bound by the Local Government Act 1995 which includes provisions for:
- the roles of the council, councillors, the mayor etc. in representing the interests of the whole district and all its electors, ratepayers and residents;
- disclosure of financial interests in matters affording local government decisions and extent of subsequent participation and voting in decision-making meetings.
- Most, but not all, local authorities in WA have open planning committee and full council meetings at which the public is given opportunity to speak.

168 *Habitus: A Sense of Place*

- Mayors may be either directly elected by the public or from the ranks of ERs by the council itself.
- Voting in local government elections is non-compulsory and non-politically aligned.

As stated before, I am concerned here only with those decisions of planning committees and full council which are taken contrary to planning officers' recommendations and those which represent an endogenous change of mind between the decision of the planning committee and its 'ratification' by full council. Given the percentage of decisions taken under delegated authority and the norm of agreement between officer recommendation and ERs, we are concerned, therefore, with a very small amount of planning decisions; a figure Kitchen (1997: 86) estimates at about 3% of total strategic, policy and development control decisions.

I seek to uncover the 'hidden transcripts' (Scott, 1990) which influence ERs behind the scenes and those less hidden acts of communication which take place in public committee meetings; the transcripts which result in what would appear on the surface to be largely irrational decision-making. In what follows I am not going to be judgemental. I tell the stories as I heard them, at face value. I do this so that, in John Forester's (1999a: 34) words, 'these stories might nurture a critical understanding by illuminating not only the dance of the rational and the idiosyncratic, but also the particular values being suppressed through the euphemisms, the rationalisations, the political theories and "truths" of the powerful'.

I attempt to uncover the various types of frames through which ERs might view issues, but make no claims as to its being anywhere near an exhaustive list.

Filling the Gap? 'Decision first, rationalisation after' (Flyvbjerg, 1998: 20)

Planning is the art of persuasion. Whether it is officers persuading ERs of a technical recommendation or constituents persuading their representatives of a particular opinion, the constructive use of persuasion is important. Persuasion involves 'the proper framing of arguments, the presentation of vivid supporting evidence, and the effort to find the correct emotional match with your audience' (Conger, 1998: 86).

I am not interested in instances of large scale lobbying by interest groups[12] nor in exposing corruption.[13] I acknowledge that corruption in political decision-making may be widespread and probably accepted to a certain extent throughout the democratic world.[14] In Australia, it almost appears that ERs are expected to be corrupt. Their depiction in the popular media (e.g. the movie *Muriel's Wedding*, the soap opera *Sea Change* and in novels such as Thea Astley's *Reaching Tin River*) almost universally underscores that Australia 'from its very beginnings, has been built and thrives on scam and corruption' (Astley, 1990: 186). Indeed, Astley talks about political crooks having 'a respectability this country has learned to tolerate' (1990: 130), while Perry (1997: 61-65) states that some degree of corruption in state and local government can almost be taken for granted and is endemic. It has given rise to the distinctly Australian term 'rort' and to a well-known parody of a line in the National Anthem 'our land is rort by sea'.

Perry argues that opportunities for local government corruption with regard to land use planning 'stand out' (1997: 32). He cites a Miami lawyer as describing land use zoning as 'the biggest single corruptor of the nation's local governments' (1997: 99). In WA there have been recent inquiries into activities at the Cities of Wanneroo and Cockburn respectively.

In what follows I distinguish between what I term public and private actions. Public actions take place in open committee and council meetings which set the stage for performances and drama. Private actions take place backstage, often informally via meetings, telephone or email conversations. The public transcript of the committee or council decision, then, tells not the whole story. It ignores the hidden transcripts of backstage communication. It is to these which I turn as I outline possible reasons for ERs' behaviour.

Private: Personal Gain

I term as personal gain those decisions in which an ER directly stands to gain financially or has other interests in the outcome. I emphasise that my research suggests that such behaviour by late 1999 had become limited in WA: 'it's not pecuniary interest on the whole. Few come on Council specifically for that' (Mayor, rural Local Authority (LA)).

However, the Inquiry into the City of Cockburn (1999-2000) has been particularly concerned that 'the council has allowed itself to be manipulated by (the mayor), a dominant personality who had been pursuing his own interests' (Hunter, 1999a: 33) over development of a parcel of land owned by his family company, of which he is a Director. Evidence was also given to the Inquiry that a motion had been adopted by the council to delete certain items from its Code of Conduct. The deleted items included:

> Councillors will ensure that there is no actual (or perceived) conflict of interest in the impartial and independent fulfilment of their civic duties.
>
> Councillors (staff) will not take advantage of their position to improperly influence (other) Councillors or (other) staff in the performance of their duties or functions, in order to gain undue or improper (direct or indirect) advantage or gain for themselves or for any other person or body (City of Cockburn, Code of Conduct 1997, cited in Department of Local Government, 2000: 892-893).

Whilst the final outcome of the Cockburn Inquiry is not yet known, the Report (DLG, 2000) has concluded that the mayor and another Councillor have acted in their own interests for personal gain and recommended that the Council be sacked.

However, since the Cockburn and earlier 'Wanneroo Inc.' inquiries in WA, it would appear that instances of ER direct manipulation of decisions for personal gain have declined significantly:

> People are far more cautious (Mayor, metropolitan LA).
>
> I had X into my office, showed him the Cockburn summary and told him to substitute his name for that of Councillor G. He went absolutely white and withdrew the development application (Mayor, rural LA).

Clearly some ERs do put pressure on planning officers to make recommendations in their interests or persuade their council colleagues to overturn officer recommendations accordingly, but these are in a small minority. More difficult to discern is the receipt of gifts.

Private: Gifts

The issue of gifts is complex. It is linked with the sections below on favours and on culture. There is no simple 'black and white' manner in which to regard ERs' receipt of gifts from local residents and ratepayers or developers. Bourdieu (1990: 100) suggests that receipt of a gift implies 'the possibility of a continuation, a reply, a riposte, a return gift' as part of the very functioning of some forms of habitus 'and the logic of practice that proceeds through a series of irreversible choices, made under pressure and often involving heavy stakes'.

The notion of reciprocity is important. Reciprocity denotes gratitude for the gift received and often acknowledgement of its cultural meaning and implications. Gifts assign symbolic meaning to fundamental dimensions of personal relationships. Iris Marion Young (1997: 355) points out, however, that the equality and mutual recognition of gift giving is 'of a different order from the equality of contracts and exchange'. A true gift should not expect something in return or any consideration of the recipient 'owing' the donor. It is an altruistic transfer with no expectation of a material reward (Rose-Ackerman, 1999: 93).

This latter would seem to be the way in which most of the ERs interviewed regard gifts. They prefer not to receive gifts, or, if they cannot refuse, the gifts (such as artworks) are taken as donations to the local authority in general and put on display, given to charity, but 'certainly not touched' by the individual or their family (Mayor, metropolitan LA). Whether this type of sentiment is true or either an individual or part of some collective self-deception, it is open to interpretation as a twofold truth. If, as Bourdieu (2000: 192) suggests, 'a gratuitous gift is impossible', gift-giving to ERs may be regarded as an 'anti-economic economy ... based on the denial of interest and calculation' in which no one is really unaware of the logic of exchange, but no one fails to comply with the rule of the game, which is to act as if one does not know the rule. Bourdieu (2000:192) uses the term 'common miscognition' 'to designate this game in which everyone knows – and does not want to know – that everyone knows – and does not want to know – the true nature of the exchange'.

It is, then, as Bourdieu (1990) comments, all a matter of style. The choice of occasion, timing, cultural circumstances etc. of the gift and the personal relations between the giver and receiver, can have different implications and meanings, which the ERs themselves need to understand.

Private: Favours

Doing favours for another may be related to gift-giving in that there may be some expectation of reciprocity. Favours are often deemed to be part of an exchange. It seems in WA that ERs might occasionally perform favours of permitting/refusing a particular development application, for example, for people in the community who have supported them in some manner in the past or who might be called upon some time in the future:

> a standing in good stead – in case – you know. Future favours (Mayor, rural LA).

There would appear to be almost a logging or 'clocking up' (metropolitan LA planning officer) of favours in certain instances.

Favours might take the form of votes traded between council colleagues:

you scratch my back and I'll scratch yours (ex-ER, metropolitan LA).

part of the pervading business culture of exchange of favours and corporate dealings (ex-ER, metropolitan LA).

Or favours performed for the wider community:

the Freemasonry connection etc. (Mayor, metropolitan LA).

Pressure for favours is even greater in small, close-knit rural communities where everyone knows and may even be related to almost everyone else. In such circumstances the need for decisions to be made on valid planning reasons increases:

there is constituent pressure, neighbour pressure, especially when they're personal friends, but I remind people of the Acts and the sections on valid planning reasons and impartiality (Mayor, rural LA).

With applications from friends, however,

You obviously try to help, you know. You might give them quiet advice on how to improve their application or to withdraw it (Mayor, rural LA).

Whether 'doing future favours' is reciprocated or not is difficult to determine. Entrepreneur Alistair MacAlpine (2000: 55) warns against performing such favours and cites Machiavelli as advising that 'friendships that are obtained by payments and not by greatness or nobility of mind, may indeed be earned, but they are not secured and in time cannot be relied upon'.

Careful ERs seem to know how to act in each situation. They actively engage with the habitus.

Private: Factions

There are factions, alliances or caucuses in many groups and institutions. As Flyvbjerg (1998: 138) writes, 'alliances are an important part of the rationality of power', and Roelofs (1967: 252-253) defines a caucus as being 'usually private, certainly informal, and often marked by that somewhat stylised bonhomie typical of relations between men who, even if not friends, know that they need each other'. Bourdieu (2000: 145-146) writes of an implicit collusion, or *esprit de corps*, between agents, an agreement which does not presuppose a contractual decision, but which is the basis of a 'practical mutual understanding'. Such a *'collusio'* is based on habitus, 'spontaneously produc(ing) behaviours adapted to the objective conditions and tending to satisfy the shared individual interests, thus enables one ... to account for the appearance of teleology which is often observed at the level of collectives and which is ordinarily ascribed to the "collective will"' (Bourdieu, 2000: 146). Factions cross partisan lines of political party, ethnicity and gender. Communication is private, often by untraceable meeting or telephone call. Its aim is 'a deal, not an appeal' (Edelman, 1964: 146).

In WA, 'Purple circles' (ex-planning officer, metropolitan LA) exist in most local authorities, in which there are 'tacit agreements' to vote similarly, even to the extent that 'people go against their own ideals to vote with the faction' (ex-planning officer, metropolitan LA).

> It's their 'duty' to go along (ex-ER, metropolitan LA).

> There's logrolling. Any particular development is automatically good if it's supported by one of the inner sanctum (ex-ER, metropolitan LA).

What matters in co-ordinating 'beliefs' and votes is not what those beliefs are, but rather who holds them. The issue is exacerbated if the faction leader is also the local mayor. Several Department of Local Government investigations in WA have revealed this to be the case. Mayors have been found to dominate proceedings rather than being impartial Chairs, which thus 'denies the community fair, proper and open debate' (DLG, 1999: 20). In this manner 'power easily becomes an end in itself, to be sought by any means that can be rationalised or concealed, a perversion of Machiavellian strategy' (Edelman, 1988: 58), resonating with the advice in MacAlpine's best-selling book *The New Machiavelli: the art of politics in business* (1988).

Private: Culture

Australia is a multicultural country and WA is no exception. Apart from a large Angloethnic population, there are significant communities of Italian, Serbian, Croatian, Chinese and increasingly Vietnamese, Iraqi and Afghani people living in WA. Each community may have different cultural personal values and ways of working. In some Asian cultures, for instance, the significance of gift-giving as a mark of respect is important. Such gifts are definitely not intended as bribes, but are a cultural aspect of business relationships.

People's life experiences can also shape the ways they interact with ERs and officers of governance. Many migrants have arrived in WA from countries which do not have democratic systems in the Western sense. Ballot-boxes and ERs are unfamiliar, if not alien concepts, as are open committee and council meetings for people who have never had opportunities to publicly voice their concerns. Other migrants have arrived from countries which did not have a planning system. Such people tend to hold certain expectations that they can do whatever they like with their land. Having to submit planning applications which are then refused can be confusing and bewildering.

Local residents may thus find themselves in 'liminal limbo' (Meerwald, 1999), caught in an interstitial position between two or even more cultural ways of working. It should not be surprising, therefore, that people from particular cultural groups should seek out any ERs on council from that group, irrespective of whether that person is the relevant ward councillor or not; that some people give ERs gifts as a token of respect for those in authority; and that ERs from different cultural groups tend to 'look after their own' (ER, metropolitan LA).

It was also suggested that migrants (especially second generation and later) are keen to be involved in either development:

> development equals progress in a new life (ex-ER, metropolitan LA).

> and/or as ERs themselves as a means of affirming their Australianness as equal citizens and displaying loyalty to both Australia and their own culture through helping to protect the interests of their kin (Lee, 1999).

My argument is that ERs from such cultural groups may not believe that they are acting unethically in receiving gifts, helping kinspeople and so on. The Mayor of Cockburn, a Croatian, 'did not believe that he was doing anything wrong' (Hunter, 1999b: 37) in using his position to influence council decisions. The British-based planning system in WA is 'culturally insensitive to various ethnic needs' (Mayor, metropolitan LA).

At the same time, however, members of frustrated cultural minority groups see apparent favours and privileges given to 'the old school tie, Western suburbs private school "mates"' (Mayor, metropolitan LA) who seem to work covertly in similar fashions.

> That's the *real* Mafia (Italian constituent, metropolitan LA).

The WA planning system is 'a template which doesn't fit local needs' (Mayor, metropolitan LA). ERs are often not deliberately acting wrongfully but are resisting an inappropriate system. Whether the way forward is to change the system or to 'educate' ERs and the public as to what constitutes correct and incorrect conduct is a matter for debate. As Philp (1997: 25-26) argues, recent attempts to avoid imposing the cultural referents of Western society to the exercise of public office often fall into an unhelpful conceptual and moral relativism.

Public: Posturing, Grandstanding, Benevolence and Vote-Winning

In public arenas such as planning committees and full council meetings, ERs often use hortatory language, appealing for public support for their positions. Political debate is overtly rhetorical and emotional on all sides, including ERs and members of the public gallery. Symbols and stories are frequently used in the framing of issues.

ERs tend to be guilty of political impression management; posturing and 'grandstanding in front of the public' (Mayor, rural LA), especially in the lead-up to local elections, when they are eager to create a good image as concerned, involved representatives worthy of being voted back into office. One ex-metropolitan planning officer commented that 'committees are like circuses' as ERs 'bend to the whims of the most vocal element', to 'whoever turns up or who they happened to hear from' last (planning officer, metropolitan LA).

Politics is performance wherein participants perform roles through which they enact their positions, as humble petitioner, as oppressed victim (members of the public) or as all-powerful and/or benevolent provider (ERs). Meetings come to resemble Bakhtinian carnivalesque or Debordian spectacles. Yet, as Debord (1994) points out, the spectacle is also 'the locus of illusion' (p. 12) where, 'in a world that really has been turned on its head, truth is a moment of falsehood' (p. 14).

ERs generally like to be seen supporting their ward constituents. In particular, they seem keen to appease the local Ratepayers' Association, which is often their powerbase in the constituency:

> If the Ratepayers' Society says jump, they jump (planning officer, metropolitan LA).

This may involve, as Kitchen (1997: 41) indicates, speaking out against something or voting against an application, even when they know that in terms of council policies, which they themselves approved, it should be accepted.

Public perceptions of benevolence lead to the accumulation of Bourdieu's symbolic capital, including making the ER/s involved feel good about themselves; 'a kind of continuous justification for existing' (Bourdieu, 2000: 240). Politicians would appear to be 'suckers for hearts and flowers arguments' (Mayor, metropolitan LA) and virtually every interviewee recalled stories of people in the public gallery winning over ERs on decisions contrary to officer recommendation. Whether it is the small child with a ventilator in a wheelchair, the elderly grandmother silently weeping or the attractive young blonde woman bursting into tears, ERs seem to change their minds about issues, often to the frustration of planning officers whose reasoned, technical arguments get discarded. As one officer grumbled 'grovelling is good, tears are good, but tight jeans are better'.

Members of the public who play emotional strategies are often successful. They may use potent symbols of helplessness, such as wheelchairs and tears, to achieve their own goals. These goals may well be contrary to the good of the majority of the local population or of more marginalised groups in society.

Sometimes, however, people's strategies may misfire and serve to antagonise ERs rather than inveigle them. Behaviour such as making force-based threats and name-calling is counter-productive, as is dogmatically telling ERs that they are wrong:

> grovelling is good, begging for mercy is good, telling them they're wrong is not good (planning officer, metropolitan LA).

Such activities may generate 'planning by petulance' (Mayor, metropolitan LA) or Machiavellian-style revenge, against the people concerned. This may also result in decisions taken against officer recommendation and serve to reinforce ERs' feelings of omnipotence.

It could appear from the above that 'parochialism and populism rule OK' (ex-planning officer, metropolitan LA) in WA, but I emphasise that it is only a small proportion of predominantly development application related planning decisions which are influenced in these ways. Kitchen (1997) estimated that in his British local authority, it was in only 20% of cases where public speaking rights had been exercised that the planning committee decision was different from that of the officer recommendation.

Summing Up – Political Will: 'There goes the mob! I am their leader, I must follow them'

Are ERs simply puppets of populism or can we begin to discern more about the exercise of political will? Is there a political culture in the field of local government decision-making in which ERs' interests and options are shaped by the prevailing values, beliefs and practices of the society: the habitus?

ERs may be swayed by rhetoric rather than argument. The presence of an audience in the public gallery may lead to posturing and acts of benevolence or petulance. The spectacle of the committee meeting becomes a self-portrait of power.

Local politicians like the symbolic capital, the status and social prestige their position invokes, but as Baxter (1972: 106) suggests, 'possibly more important is the prestige it brings to a councillor in his (sic) own eyes – the satisfaction of feeling important'. This may be through helping family, friends, constituents or cultural kin. Decisions are taken according to an often impulsive 'feel for the game' which is being played out in public and/or in private. ERs tend to 'conduct themselves according to imagination and not prudence' (Ivison, 1997: 58).

We need to consider new theoretical conceptions of planning decision-making, those which account for the gap between officer recommendation and council decision. Political decision-making involves far more than rationality, far more than simple marketplace trading. I offer the narrative examples above to begin the work of recreating theory, turning the gap of 'in-between space' of ER decision-making into something more tangible. Unless planning practitioners begin to understand the complexities which take place on- and off-stage, they will continue to be frustrated and confused by seemingly irrational decisions which ignore their hard-worked recommendations.

What Can Planning Officers Do?

How might planning practitioners dilute the 'rogue' voices which occasionally dominate planning decision-making? How might they take 'practical action in a messy political world'? (Forester, 1999b: 184).[15]

We need to know how thinking, active practitioners attempt to counteract ERs use and abuse of power. We need to learn from their stories of effective responses and, in particular, how they *anticipate* and pre-empt the vagaries of political will. As Forester (1999b: 185) states, 'we should illuminate not only where progressive efforts get stuck, but how clever practitioners can get unstuck'.

Albrechts' (1999) valuable work in Belgium clearly indicates that planners have to explore political feasibility, to build alliances, to negotiate, to mobilise support, to lobby and to bargain if they are to push through controversial decisions. Albrechts' focus on the highly political role of planning officers helps to debunk the mythology of rational planning and its so-called technocratic neutrality.

In WA, interviews with several 'clever practitioners' revealed some strategies which it is useful to consider.

Veiled Threats and Warnings

When committee deliberations wander into territories of non-planning decision rationales, officers may remind ERs of the consequences of not following 'due process' or they may make reference to the Cockburn or Wanneroo Inquiries into the conduct of ERs. Officer reminders of 'due process' tend to be couched in legalese, by reference to the appropriate statutes. On the other hand, plain mention of Cockburn or 'Wanneroo Inc.' in WA at present is seemingly sufficient to remind ERs of their digressions. With such warnings, planners pragmatically attempt to get ERs to think through for themselves the possible consequences of their potential actions and decisions.

Planners may thus introduce an element of uncertainty into ERs minds (Forester, 1999, pers. comm.). As a planning officer explains, 'councillors have a simplified view of the situation and the legislation and tend to have and to want too much certainty. The role of the planner is to introduce uncertainty by making councillors aware of what they might lose, of the possibility, for example, of losing credibility' (and, by implication, votes).

In telling a story of an application to turn an area of undeveloped land into urban residential accommodation, this planning officer recalled how he managed to reduce his degree of uncertainty and to push the uncertainty onto the councillors 'by making them think twice about what they thought would be a black and white situation ... in terms of the ramifications of the decision in general, for the flora, and for them in terms of opposition and votes'. In this way, the planner shaped attention (shaped a tension?) round the issues involved and was able to facilitate a less environmentally harmful outcome whereby the council pushed the uncertainty onto the proponent/developer via imposing conditions on development and a required increase in provision of public open space.

'Heading Them Off at the Pass'

One metropolitan planner revealed that when he writes his officer reports and recommendations for the planning committee, especially on issues concerning facilities for marginalised groups, such as Aboriginal people, he attempts to anticipate the reaction from the ERs. One possible strategy is to 'head them off at the pass' by 'making my proposal more left wing so that the right wing elected members can nibble at it and you end up with something that's centre left'. He refers to this as a strategy of 'damage limitation'.

Delegated Authority: Skeletons in Whose Cupboards?

Planning practitioners require personal credibility to be effective when giving information to the public and to ERs. Several respondents stated that if planners appear reasonable and pragmatic and confident about their knowledge, then ERs are more likely to act on their advice and to delegate decision-making authority to officers.

As mentioned earlier, ERs may delegate officers authority to approve/refuse applications concerned with certain aspects of the local authority's Planning Scheme. Several authorities have delegated up to 90% of the decisions to officers. Planning committees simply receive a list of the applications and the officer decisions to 'rubber stamp'.

Officers are understandably keen to receive delegated authority over as many applications as possible, as this decreases the potential for 'the gap' to open and political will to intervene. However, as several ERs pointed out, an increase in officer powers means a decrease in democratic governance. This then 'begs the question as to what is democracy about' (ex-planning officer, metropolitan LA) and where does officer accountability lie, to the council or to the public?

Some ERs are wary of 'being squeezed out of our rightful place as decision-makers' (ER, rural LA) by 'giving too much power away' to the officers. Allmendinger (1996: 231) reminds us, moreover, that 'planners are people like everyone else; they have their own agendas, grudges, desires and idiosyncrasies and these are reflected in day-to-day practice'. Planners can make irrational decisions too!

It is also possible that although delegated authority 'minimises opportunities for ERs to get sucked in (to gifts, rhetorical persuasion etc.), it can relocate the pressure onto officers' (Mayor, metropolitan LA). This ER is worried about what to him are 'hidden parts of the process' and prefers as many decisions as possible to be made in public, at open meetings 'a public process, where who says what is identified'.

The ER's sentiment is supported by an ex-metropolitan planning officer who listed the benefits of open committee meetings as including: 'they render the decision-making process transparent. Thus justice or injustice is publicly seen to be done. Or, put another way, having sold the cupboards there is little room to store the skeletons.' Or is there? Other respondents suggested that open meetings simply drive factional and other deals offstage.

Distortion/Disclosure of Information

One of the planning officers interviewed asked the question 'sometimes is it not "better" to not do the "right democratic thing" by process to get an outcome for the marginalised?' He suggested that in instances such as the location of a remand hostel or Aboriginal drop-in centre, where one could anticipate resistance by neighbouring residents and a fairly right-wing council, that strategies such as minimal publicity and writing reports 'blinding the ERs with science' might be useful. Not, he was at pains to stress, that he had personally done so.

This planner also wondered whether 'if by making an area "nicer" ends in its gentrification and pushing out of poor people by the middle class, is this what we should be doing?' A hard question, which I subsequently raised with other practitioners. An ex-planning officer felt that 'bending the rules for social justice is democratically unethical. The suggestion argues that a coherent technical interpretation of planning should override planning decisions, but there's no rational basis to this argument as it overturns democracy. If you get caught doing it then the council won't trust you and they'll want to deal with everything and take away your delegated authority.'

Despite describing a strategy of 'bending the rules' as democratically unethical, this planner continued by saying that a more successful strategy would be to lobby ERs 'through the back door'. 'Planners need connections too. You try to get tacit agreement of the key faction councillors for what you want.' These narratives suggest ways in which planners may be able to counteract anticipated decisions which they believe could operate to the disadvantage of the already disadvantaged.

John Forester discusses issues of 'distorted communication' or 'misinformation' at length in *Planning in the Face of Power* (1989). He argues that 'planners themselves sometimes participate in distorting, and, in special cases, may be justified in doing so' (1989: 29). The crucial questions are 'when can misinformation be ethically justified?' (1989: 42) When should one tell freedom's necessary lies? My answer is that planners should anticipate the outcomes which might follow in circumstances with and without their 'mis' information (e.g. in the Aboriginal drop-in case) and make their own judgements.

Summing Up – Prudence in Anticipation

The stories above suggest that planning officers 'need by turns to be an expert, a bit of a politician, an assistant negotiator or broker of community differences, a stickler for procedure ("due process"), and a stoic who can accept disappointment with equanimity' (Minson, 1998: 60). In political policy- and decision-making environments, 'clever' planning officers anticipate how the issue at hand might appear both to the local public and to the ERs, and temper their 'expert advice' accordingly. I am obviously unable to suggest any 'universal' strategies as situations are contingent and messy.

The gap between an act being technically 'legal' or 'illegal' under a professional or local authority Code of Conduct and/or 'undemocratic' and yet beneficial to the 'public good' is the space within which the moral and political capacities of planners must be engaged. Clever planners may be able to use Prudence to counter the vagaries of Political Will.

Analysis: 'Questions opened by the gap: ... can we ever hope to possess what we do not now have?' (Taylor and Saarinen, 1994: np)

Most planning decisions where ERs ignore officer advice can be traced to conflicting frames for viewing the issues concerned. When officer reports on development applications etc. come into the wider arena they may take on new meanings and implications as other actors view and respond to them in the light of their own frames. On what basis, though, does one frame become preferable to another in the absence of universals of truth and objectivity?

It appears from the narratives that, apart from any private reasons, ERs attach considerable importance to obtaining help for constituents who may appeal to them. ERs tend to respond to immediate electoral or political pressure and may thereby come into conflict with planners who are professionally required to use a longer-term and wider-ranging frame to view the issue. I regard this as social role taking on the part of ERs rather than deception or corruption. There is a fine balance between the need for ERs to be responsive to the opinions of their constituents and the need for planning decisions to be made according to valid 'planning' criteria. ERs often appear to rely on a feel for the game (habitus) to guide their interpretation of the 'rules' in different circumstances.

Planning practice is a continual interpretation and reinterpretation of what the rules really mean. The relation between rule and practice is reciprocal; various sets of rules (the statutory planning system, cultural traditions etc.) inform practice and practice influences the interpretation of the rules. The rules are, at any given time, what the practice game has made them.

If planning officers are to practice 'good planning',[16] phronetic practical wisdom could be valuable in deciphering the hidden transcripts of their ERs. 'Without some access to the hidden transcript, planners will see only the bouncing ball, missing the forces that make it bounce' (Briggs, 1998: 9). Intuition and anticipation are key elements of being able to catch the ball: 'you can tell which decisions will be hot' (ex-planning officer, metropolitan LA).

Experienced practitioners should be able to reflect in action on the frame conflicts which might arise in relation to various development applications or policy suggestions. Schon and Rein (1994) stress the importance of practitioners 'getting into the heads' of likely actors (ERs, local residents, developers etc.) to understand their habitus and to anticipate their reactions. This should then facilitate practitioners in designing their own actions (moral improvisation) so as to communicate the lessons they wish the other actors to draw; shaping their attention accordingly.

As Forester (1999a: 3) writes, 'planners must develop an astute practical judgement to deal with far more than "the facts" at hand'. He emphasises the need to anticipate 'the plural and conflicting stories of differently affected citizens and stakeholders, ... to recognise in detail the perspectives of others, their stories and accounts, their feelings and stakes, ... (and to) respect, rather than to dismiss, the human emotions of anger and fear, impatience and suspicion'(1999a: 12).

Of course there will be events which planners cannot anticipate, especially those instances when private deals and favours may have been struck. Overall, however, I believe that the predictive abilities of 'practical anticipations of ordinary experience' (Bourdieu, 1987: 96) should form a strong basis for 'good' effective practice.

Conclusions: 'We must remain sensitive to the implications of the gap' (Taylor and Saarinen, 1994: np)

> Democracy suggests that the best technical advice in the world is the wrong decision if ERs vote against it (ex-planning officer, metropolitan LA).

Traditional theories of planning policy – and decision-making – tend to conceptualise a unidirectional, incremental, instrumental process in which council decisions follow planning officer recommendations. Such theories bracket the gap which exists in reality between recommendation and decision, a gap containing hidden transcripts of private and public deals, favours, cultural traditions, demagogic posturing and omnipotent acts of benevolence or vindictiveness. The recent theoretical advances of deliberative democracy, consensus-building and agonism also tend to assume that a deliberatively reached recommendation equals the final outcome.

John Forester's stories from planning practitioners begin to fill the gap in demonstrating the vulnerability of planners' efforts to the messiness of politics. My stories from ERs and planning officers serve to both corroborate Forester's material and to add to our understanding of those seemingly irrational decisions when ERs ignore officer recommendations or change their minds between one meeting and the next. I emphasise the contingent nature of relations between planners, the public and ERs and the role of the habitus in helping planners to anticipate actors' reactions to recommendations. By exposing the potentially hidden transcripts of the habitus; the social traditions, presuppositions and strategies of actors' social worlds, their political 'culture', I hope to provide a 'tool of liberation' (Shusterman, 1999: 12) for planning practitioners unable to make sense of the often unarticulated workings of these worlds and the apparently irrational decisions which result.

In presenting a range of possible 'reasons' for ERs, actions, I raise the caveat of intellectualism; the hermeneutic danger that I may have substituted my relation to practice, for the practical relation to practice itself. The picture I draw is 'that practical rationality depends far less on formulas or recipes than on a keen grasp of the particulars seen in the light of more general principles' (Forester, 1999a: 33). Planning decision-making is a complex mixture of hybrid processes – technical, collaborative and political[17] – involving a range of values and ideals competing for decision-makers' attention.

Considering all the above, what, then, would constitute effective planning? It comprises far more than technical skill and includes astute observation, sensitivity to others' habitus, their cultural traditions, their emotions and opinions, anticipation of reactions and reflective strategies to pre-empt or to counter such reactions. Effective planners are not left in frustration merely retrospectively monitoring the exercise of political will. They actively attempt to communicatively channel that will in specific directions.

Effective decision-making in the voices of my practice stories involves trying 'to sort out instances of genuine need from the quick buck'. 'Its greatest challenge is to find the boundaries of legitimate interests' (Mayor, metropolitan LA). However, we should remember that 'any claims to have a "solution" in today's complexity is a bizarre overreach' (ex-planning officer, metropolitan LA).

If we as planning practitioners are to mind the gap of Political Will, we could do well to heed the practical wisdom of Prudence.

Acknowledgements

My thanks to all the planners and elected representatives with whom I talked and without whose stories this paper would not have been possible.

Notes

1. I take as my working definition of Prudence, 'a range of active steps to secure oneself against future misfortune' (adapted from Rose, 1999: 158) noting that 'caution, skepticism, and political capacity are intertwined' (Mandelbaum, 1996: 432).
2. Hillier (1998).
3. See Gyford (1985) and Campbell and Marshall (2000: 304-305) for discussion of increasing assertiveness of British local government councillors over planning officers and the collision of political and professional objectives.
4. I also acknowledge Judith Innes' recent work with Judith Gruber (1999) in which they demonstrate how a collaborative style of decision-making conflicts with a 'political influence' style to pull interests in different directions.
5. Bourdieu (2000: 166) suggests that since symbolic capital 'only exists through the esteem, recognition, belief, credit, confidence of others, (it) can only be perpetuated so long as it succeeds in obtaining belief in its existence'. In this way, ERs who use symbolic capital to enable dominance over their constituents are actually dependent on them for that very symbolic capital.
6. See e.g. Jenkins (1992).
7. Although I depict the process as fundamentally linear for simplicity of representation, I appreciate that it is often extremely messy and non-linear in practice.
8. For a beginning consideration of other gaps, see Dewar (1999) for an example of the gap between full council and Ministerial ratification ('the judges said that the Secretary of State was not bound by his own guidance. ... This means that even after a council

goes through all the correct procedures it is still up to the Secretary of State what he wants to do' (Dewar, 1999: 3)), and Rooksby (1998) for examples of the gap between decision and implementation where landscape architects and engineers seemingly altered details of public, planner and ER consensus decisions to suit themselves. Stiftel and Harkness (1998) would regard this latter as an example of a 'multiple-table problem' and offer some useful insights into why gaps occur here.

9 I use the term Mayor to denote the ER leader of the council or Shire President.
10 Given the nature of the information sought I only approached ERs whom I knew and who felt they could trust me with some ethically controversial material. This resulted in my interviewing only more 'honest' politicians, although I believe their stories of experience of others' dealings have been valuable. I also appreciate that in my position as 'half-learned', that I may not fully realise that those I interviewed 'both know and resist the truth they claim to reveal' and the extent to which they engage in 'games of self-deception which make it possible to perpetuate an illusion for oneself and to safeguard a bearable form of "subjective truth" in the face of calls to reality and to realism' (both quotes Bourdieu, 2000: 190).
11 I would term this 'good practice', although it appears that the definition of good practice currently favoured (in education and in practice) in WA is that of development facilitation (see also Dear, 2000).
12 See Hillier (1998, 2000).
13 The WA Criminal Code, S83, defines an act of corruption as 'any public officer who, without lawful authority or a reasonable excuse:

   a) acts upon any knowledge or information obtained by reason of his office or employment ... so as to gain a benefit, whether pecuniary or otherwise, for any person, or so as to cause a detriment, whether pecuniary or otherwise' (cited in Department of Local Government, 1999, 2000).

   For other definitions see Alatas (1990), Heidenheimer *et al.* (1989), Heywood (1997), Perry (1997) and Rose-Ackerman (1999).
14 Ignatius (2000) presents a long list of countries in which 'crony capitalism' is widespread, not solely in developing nations, but including the Elf scandal in France and Citibank in the USA.
15 The question of what can (and do) planning officers do is the subject of current research and as such is not explored in depth in this paper.
16 I interpret 'good planning' as transformative change for the benefit of the disadvantaged.
17 See Innes and Gruber (1999).

References

Alatas, S. (1990) *Corruption: its nature, causes and functions*, Aldershot, Avebury.
Albrechts, L. (1999) 'Planners as catalysts and initiators of change: the new Structure Plan for Flanders', *International Planning Studies*, 7(5): 587-603.
Allmendinger, P. (1996) 'Development Control and the legitimacy of planning decisions: a comment', *Town Planning Review*, 67(2)
Altshuler, A. (1965) *The City Planning Process*, Ithaca, Cornell University Press.
Astley, T. (1990) *Reaching Tin River*, Melbourne, Minerva.
Bachrach, S. and Lawler, E. (1980) *Power and Politics in Organisations*, San Francisco, Jossey-Bass.
Baxter, R. (1972) 'The working class and Labour politics', *Political Studies*, 20: 92-107.

Blowers, A. (1980) *The Limits of Power*, Oxford, Pergamon.
Bohman, J. and Rehg, W. (1997) 'Introduction', in Bohman J. and Rehg W. (eds) *Deliberative Democracy*, Cambridge, MA, MIT Press: ix-xxx.
Bourdieu, P. (1987) *Choses Dites*, Paris, Editions de Minuit.
Bourdieu, P. (1990) *The Logic of Practice*, (trans. R. Nice). Stanford, Stanford University Press.
Bourdieu, P. (1991) *Language and Symbolic Power*, Cambridge, Polity Press.
Bourdieu, P. (1993) *The Field of Cultural Production*, Cambridge, Polity Press.
Bourdieu, P. (2000) *Pascalian Meditations*, Cambridge, Polity Press.
Bouveresse, J. (1999) 'Rules, dispositions and the Habitus', in Shusterman R. (ed.), *Bourdieu: a Critical Reader*, Oxford, Blackwell: 45-63.
Briggs, X. de Sousa (1998) 'Doing democracy close-up: culture, power and communication in community building', *Journal of Planning Education Research*, 18: 1-13.
Campbell, H. and Marshall, R. (2000) 'Moral obligations, planning, and the public interest: a commentary on current British practice', *Environment and Planning B, Planning and Design*, 27: 297-312.
Clavel, P., Forester, J. and Goldsmith, W. (1980) *Urban and Regional Planning in an Age of Austerity*, New York, Pergamon.
Conger, J. (1998) 'The necessary art of persuasion', *Harvard Business Review*, 76(3): 84-95.
Dear, M. (2000) *The Postmodern Urban Condition*, Oxford, Blackwell.
Debord, G. (1994) *The Society of the Spectacle*, New York, Zone Books.
Department of Local Government (2000) *Report of the Inquiry into the City of Cockburn*, DLG, Perth.
Dewar, D. (1999) 'Minister victorious on County housing', *Planning*, 12/2/99: 1 and 3.
Edelman, M. (1964) *The Symbolic Uses of Politics*, Urbana, University of Illinois Press.
Flyvbjerg, B. (1998) *Rationality and Power*, Chicago, University of Chicago Press.
Forester, J. (1989) *Planning in the Face of Power*, Berkeley, University of California Press.
Forester, J. (1993) *Critical Theory, Public Policy and Planning Practice*, Albany, SUNY Press.
Forester, J. (1999a) *The Deliberative Practitioner*, Cambridge, MA, MIT Press.
Forester, J. (1999b) 'Reflections on the future understanding of planning practice', *International Planning Studies*, 4(2): 175-193.
Gyford, J. (1985) *The Politics of Local Socialism*, London, Allen and Unwin.
Habermas, J. (1998) *The Inclusion of the Other*, Cambridge, Polity Press.
Healey, P. (1992) 'Planning through debate: the communicative turn in planning theory', *Town Planning Review*, 632: 143-162.
Healey, P. (1996) 'The communicative turn in planning theory and its implication for spatial strategy-making', *Environment and Planning B, Planning and Design*, 23: 217-234.
Healey, P. (1997) *Collaborative Planning*, London, Macmillan.
Heidenheimer, A., Johnston M. and Levine V. (eds) (1989) *Political Corruption*, New York, Transaction.
Heywood, P. (ed.) (1997) *Political Corruption*, Oxford, Blackwell.
Hillier, J. (1998) 'Beyond confused noise: ideas towards communicative procedural justice', *Journal of Planning Education and Research*, 18: 14-24.
Hillier, J. (2000) 'Going round the back? Complex networks and informal action in local planning processes', *Environment and Planning A*, 32(1): 33-54.
Hindess, B. (1997) 'Democracy and disenchantment', *Australian Journal of Political Science*, 32(1): 79-92.
Hunter, T. (1999a) 'Call to sack Cockburn councillors', *The West Australian*, 21/12/99: 33.

Hunter, T. (1999b) 'Grljusich defends actions in land row with Council', *The West Australian*, 7/12/99: 37.
Ignatius, D. (2000) 'Beware the pirates seeking to plunder and corrupt', *Guardian Weekly*, 13-19/1/2000: 28.
Innes, J. (1995) 'Planning theory's emerging paradigm: communicative action and interactive practice', *Journal of Planning Education and Research*, 14(3): 183-189.
Innes, J. (1996) 'Planning through consensus-building: a new view of the comprehensive planning ideal', *Journal of the American Planning Association*, 62(4): 460-472.
Innes, J. (1998) 'Information in communicative planning', *Journal of the American Planning Association*, 64(1): 52-63.
Innes, J. and Gruber, J. (1999) 'Planning strategies in conflict: the case of regional transportation in the Bay area', AESOP conference paper, Bergen, 7-11 July.
Ivison, D. (1997) *The Self at Liberty: political argument and the arts of government*, Ithaca, Cornell University Press.
Jenkins, R. (1992) *Pierre Bourdieu*, London, Routledge.
Kitchen, T. (1997) *People, Politics, Policies and Plans*, London, Paul Chapman.
Krumholz, N. and Forester, J. (1990) *Making Equity Planning Work*, Philadelphia, Temple University Press.
Lee, F. (1999) '"We have been given a second chance". A study of Chinese-Australian involvement in mainstream Australian politics and its effects in WA', paper presented to Curtin University 3rd Annual Humanities Postgraduate Research Conference, Curtin University, Perth, December.
MacAlpine, A. (1998) *The New Machiavelli: the art of politics in business*, London, Wiley.
MacAlpine, A. (2000) 'Mac rules', *The Australian Way*, January: 53-58.
Mandelbaum, S. (1996) 'Ethical mandates and the virtue of Prudence', in Mandelbaum S., Mazza, L. and Burchell, R. (eds) *Explorations in Planning Theory*, New Brunswick, Rutgers: 430-447.
Meerwald, A. (1999) 'Chinese subjectivities in liminal limbo', paper presented to Curtin University 3rd Annual Humanities Postgraduate Research Conference, Curtin University, Perth, December.
Minson, J. (1998) 'Ethics in the service of the state', in Dean, M. and Hindess, B. (eds) *Governing Australia*, Cambridge, Cambridge University Press: 47-69.
Mouffe, C. (1996) 'Deconstruction, pragmatism and the politics of democracy', in Mouffe, C. (ed.) *Deconstruction and Pragmatism*, London, Routledge: 1-12.
Murdoch, I. (1970) *The Sovereignty of Good*, London, Ark.
Nolan Committee, (1995) *Standards in Public Life*, Cm 2850-I and Cm 2850-II, London, HMSO.
O'Hagan, A. (1999) *Our Fathers*, London, Faber and Faber.
Perry, P. (1997) *Political Corruption and Political Geography*, Aldershot, Ashgate.
Phelps, N. and Tewdr-Jones, M. (2000) 'Scratching the surface of collaborative and associative governance: identifying the diversity of social action in institutional capacity building', *Environment and Planning A*, 32(1): 111-130.
Philp, M. (1997) 'Defining political corruption', in Heywood, P. (ed.) *Political Corruption*, Oxford, Blackwell: 20-46.
Richardson T. (1996) 'Foucauldian discourse: power and truth in urban and regional policy making', *European Planning Studies*, 4(3): 279-292.
Roelofs, H. (1967) *The Language of Modern Politics*, Homewood, Ill., Dorsey Press.
Rooksby, P. (1998) *Smoothing the Kinks*? Hons Thesis, Department of Urban and Regional Planning, Curtin University, Perth, unpublished.
Rose, N. (1999) *Powers of Freedom*, Cambridge, Cambridge University Press.

Rose-Ackerman, S. (1999) *Corruption and Government: causes, consequences and reform*, Cambridge, Cambridge University Press.
Sandercock, L. (1998) *Towards Cosmopolis*, New York, Wiley.
Schon, D. and Rein M. (1994) *Frame Reflection*, New York, Basic Books.
Scott, J. (1990) *Domination and the Arts of Resistance*, New Haven, Yale University Press.
Shusterman, R. (1999) 'Introduction: Bourdieu as philosopher', in Shusterman, R. (ed.) *Bourdieu: a critical reader*, Oxford, Blackwell: 1-13.
Stiftel, B. and Harkness, C. (1998) 'Overcoming agency ratification obstacles in environmental negotiation: lessons from labour management practice', ACSP conference, Pasadena, November.
Taylor, R. and Saarinen, E. (1994) *Imagologies*, London, Routledge.
Tewdr-Jones, M. and Allmendinger, P. (1998) 'Deconstructing communicative rationality: a critique of Habermasian collaborative planning', *Environment and Planning A*, 30: 1975-1989.
Throgmorton, J. (1990) 'Passion, reason and power: the rhetorics of electric power planning in Chicago', *Journal of Architectural and Planning Research*, 7(4): 330-350.
Throgmorton, J. (1996) '"Impeaching" research: planning as persuasive and constitutive discourse', in Mandelbaum S., Mazza, L. and Burchell, R. (eds) *Explorations in Planning Theory*. New Brunswick, Rutgers: 345-364.
Wittgenstein, L. (1973) *Philosophical Investigations*. Oxford, Blackwell.
Yanow, D. (1996) How Does a Policy Mean? Interpreting Policy and Organisational Actions, Washington DC, Georgetown University Press.
Young, I.M. (1997) 'Asymmetrical reciprocity: on moral respect, wonder and enlarged thought', *Constellations*, 3(3): 340-363.

10 Place, Identity and Governance: Transforming Discourses and Practices[1]

PATSY HEALEY

City Strategies and Transforming Identities

Governance efforts to manage and develop the qualities of cities touch much more than just the physical fabric or the amount and distribution of services. They are about more than jobs, GDP and material opportunities. They impinge also on our daily life worlds and our identities. This chapter tells the story of a city 'against itself', in which both the governance institutions and citizens are struggling to find a way forward from an old and largely shared identity, tied to a Fordist-welfarist nexus, into a differently configured future. Faced with economic and political challenges, the city council has initiated a strategic approach to changing the city's social mix, through the medium of 'masterplanned' area re-modelling.

This is not a new agenda for planners or for citizens. Planners and politicians argued in the mid-twentieth century that cities needed to be re-modelled to provide a better physical environment to produce a citizenry who were healthier and morally more upright, as this was conceived at the time. But this vision was rejected as people experienced the product. It was equated with arrogant paternalism, by both professionals and politicians. It was also, in many European countries, tied up with the development of welfarist governance organisation, which focused on delivery systems for specific sectoral policies (notably, housing, education, social services, transport), rather than on people's overall sense of themselves and their locales. Treated as 'passive recipients of services', those citizens particularly dependent on the state, for housing and social security benefits, took on expectations of such delivery. Local councils, in theory the arena where policies could be 'integrated' as they affected people and places, had their own organisation and cultures shaped by their vertical relations with the functional departments of national government. The result was a double-faceted 'delivery dependency' identify-formation process for both the council and its 'heartland' citizens.

The paternalist and sectoralised delivery of services to people in locales within cities soon had to deal with the emerging reality of increasing socio-spatial segregation. With twenty years of neo-liberal policies in Britain, much of the universal approach of the different welfare services has been dismantled. Those in poverty have had to cope not only with the loss of economic opportunity consequent upon industrial re-structuring. They have had to live with reduced benefits, tied to housing allocation systems which have increased the spatial concentration of those facing economic and social difficulty. Meanwhile, city councils have not only had their general budgets reduced. They have been faced with an avalanche of reform measures.[2] Faced with cuts and a plethora of nationally-driven regeneration initiatives,[3] city councils found their own identities re-shaped into increasing dependency on a still-sectoralised national government. Their capacity to respond to the deepening difficulties in poor neighbourhoods was therefore undermined, and driven by what national government thought was appropriate. The neo-liberal regime had a clear socio-cultural agenda, focused on reducing dependency. Its product was to increase both levels of poverty and the disruptive social alienation associated with it. It thus threatened the resources of family support and cultural capital available in some poorer communities, built up through the experiences of working class poverty earlier in the century.

In 1997, the neo-liberal regime was apparently brought to an end with the election of the Blair New Labour government. It seemed to promise a new positive role for local government, a more integrated and responsive approach to service delivery, and a socio-cultural agenda aimed to reverse the 'exclusion' of so many poorer people from the opportunities available to the wider society (see DETR 1998; Social Exclusion Unit 1998, 2000). City councils have been urged to take a strategic approach to their activities and to focus on the 'well-being' of their citizens. They are exhorted to integrate their various activities in ways which are responsive to how their citizens configure issues, not politicians and professionals, and to introduce community planning and area management. At the same time, the so-called 'entrepreneurialist' neo-liberal agenda lives on in national encouragement to build linkages to business and to private investors who are to provide the capital for major changes. Stakeholder groups and local strategic partnerships are cropping up across the governance landscape of British cities. Finally, the environmental sustainability agenda, as interpreted in the British context, demands that new development should be concentrated within urban areas if at all possible. To do this, cities must be re-presented in policy conceptions and in popular imagery as positive attractors, rather than as problematic locales it is best to move out of if you can. The new talk is of urban 'renaissance' and citywide urban regeneration strategies.[4]

How should city councils respond to this new climate and new pressure to transform their policy agendas, their practices and their identities? To whom should they and can they respond? How far are councils able to find new roles and identities for themselves and contribute to shaping new collective cultural resources for identity-building among citizens, especially those experiencing the most difficulty? If so, how richly encompassing are these and how do they relate to the multiple meanings and manifestations of city life for diverse citizens?

This chapter explores these issues in a city renowned for its distinctive and much-asserted local culture, forged in a historic lived experience of working class neighbourhoods clustered around workplaces. Councillors, many officials and citizens shared in this cultural identity.[5] But through economic restructuring and social adjustments, the bases of this shared identity have ebbed away. During the 1980s and 1990s, with limited 'mainstream' resources to sustain housing services and local environmental maintenance in the city's poorer communities, initiative after initiative was 'drawn down' from national government to be used to refurbish council housing, introduce more varied tenure mixes and foster improved schools, health services and shopping facilities. But this avalanche of area-targeted initiatives has not stemmed the continuing deterioration of economic and social conditions in these areas. Positioning themselves within the New Labour agenda, and with Labour politicians in hegemonic control of the council since the late 1980s,[6] councillors and officers have responded with a bold 'boosterish' growth strategy and specific masterplans for different areas of the city. The city council has been reorganised to produce more integrated directorates, able to focus more coherently on place qualities. But by July 2000, the citizens from some neighbourhoods are waving placards of protest and releasing red balloons of distress about plans to demolish their locales and about failures of consultation (see Figure 10.1). It seems as if the anti-redevelopment politics of the 1960s is being re-enacted, this time by a citizenry with personal memories of this experience and a deep skepticism towards government motives. What can be learned from such a case about the relation between place-promotion strategies, identity formation and governance transformation processes?

192 *Habitus: A Sense of Place*

Figure 10.1   Protest over area master plans: August 2000
Source: The Evening Chronicle, Newcastle upon Tyne.

A City in Transformation

A Great Industrial City

The case study chosen is that of Newcastle, on Tyneside, in the North East of England (Figures 10.2, 10.3 and 10.4). Among the many examples of old industrial cities struggling to re-position themselves in new economic, social and political landscapes, it is a striking case of economic and cultural change, in a situation with a traditionally strong cultural identity. In this context, local political elites have sought to shift government processes into different policy agendas and relations to reflect new local constituencies and address a changed economic and geo-political position in the world (Wilkinson 1992, Tavsanoglu 1998, Byrne 2000). But these efforts have moved slowly and in different directions. Meanwhile, the local economy has been transformed as residents have ebbed away attracted to suburban areas and small towns in the wider region. Levels of deprivation in neighbourhoods in the traditional residential heartlands of the city have continued to attract national attention. The prospect of a US-style

Place, Identity and Governance 193

'doughnut city' presents a troubling possibility for the city. Table 10.1 presents the data the city council itself uses to describe the situation. For the city council, these figures describe its own dilemma – the decline of its tax base; reduced voting numbers, especially in some of the heartland neighbourhoods; rising costs in managing 'low demand' schools, housing stock and local neighbourhoods.

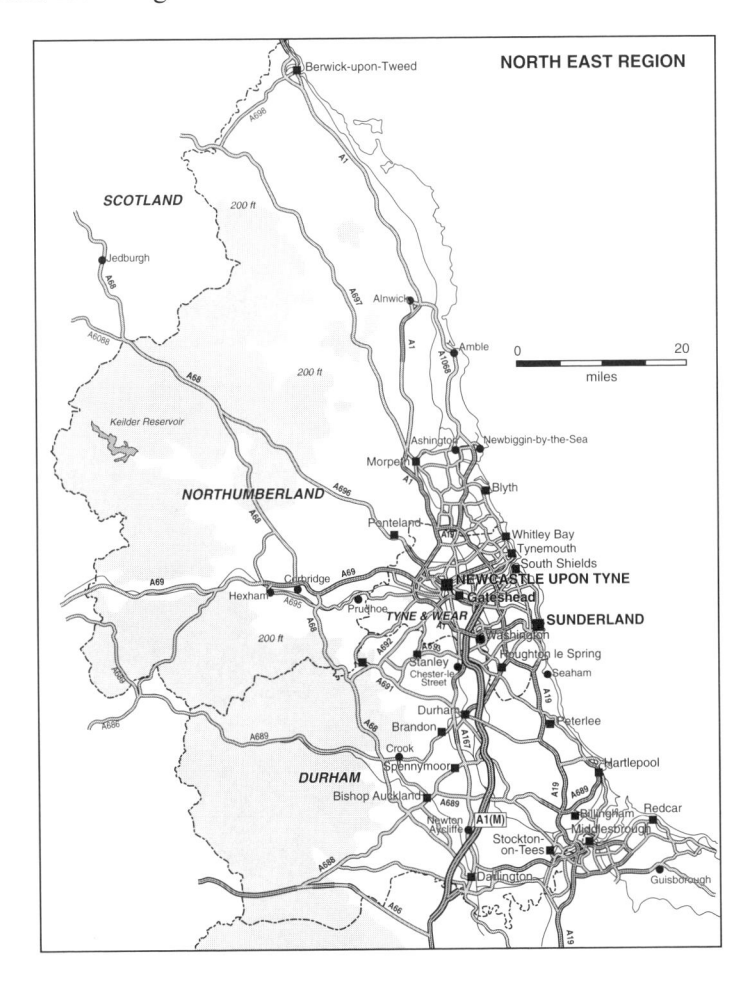

Figure 10.2   Location Map, North East Region
Source: Ann Rooke, Geography Department, University of Newcastle.

194   *Habitus: A Sense of Place*

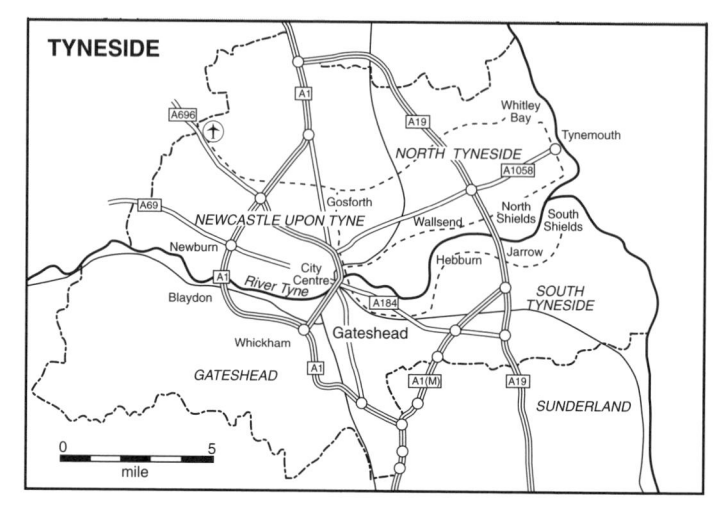

Figure 10.3   Location Map, Tyneside City Centre
Source: Ann Rooke, Geography Department, University of Newcastle.

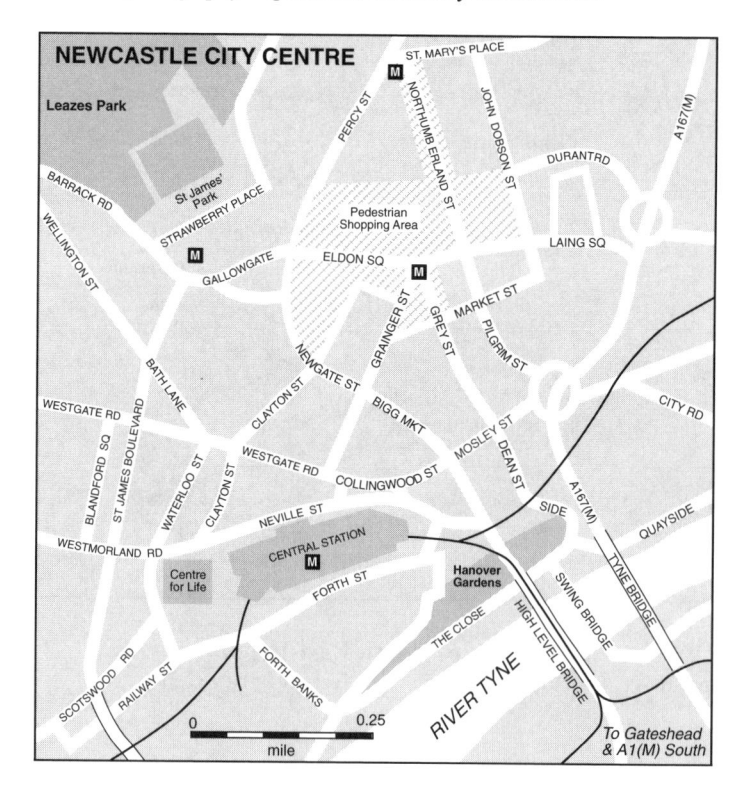

Figure 10.4   Location Map, Newcastle City Centre
Source: Ann Rooke, Geography Department, University of Newcastle.

Table 10.1   Measures of the Decline in the Newcastle City Area

	Situation in 1999	Trend
Population	276,000	1,500 per year net leaving the city
Surplus School Places	3,600	Increasing by nearly 290 per year
Empty/abandoned dwellings	8,600 (7% of stock)	Increasing by nearly 100 per year

Source: NCC, 2000a pp. 4-5. Note that the net population trend is composed of 15,000 people moving out the city and 13,500 moving in per annum, in the period 1971–1998.

The 'story' of Newcastle and Tyneside is repeatedly told in local accounts. Its core referent is the period of economic boom in the nineteenth century, when the city was the third largest in the UK, exporting coal, ships, armaments, glass and chemicals on a global scale. The wealth this generated was then circulated into, among other outlets, building the city and particularly the city centre as the heart of the regional economy. Tyneside's industrial relations were oppressive, almost feudal, linked to the way a landowning class moved into manufacture and vice versa (Benwell CDP, 1979; Tavsanoglu, 1998; Hudson, 1994). The expanding working class thus contested the power of the owners but at the same time shared factory space and sometimes cultural pursuits with them. Living places tended to be very close to work places, sustaining a 'habitus' tied particularly to male factory work. Around this, a culture of place-based community developed, which celebrated the way households helped each other out when times were hard. The trades union movement was strong, but not as hostile to capitalists as in some other parts of the country. The struggles in the first part of the twentieth century were for better working conditions, better education, health and service provision and better housing conditions. The memory of a great industrial past thus came to coexist with memories and experiences of community self-support and of social welfare provided through workplace organisation. These memories were embedded in a view of the working class struggling to win better material conditions for daily life from capitalist bosses.

By the mid-twentieth century, the working class seemed to have achieved a hegemonic position. The welfare state was established at the national level, delivering universal health and education services, and funding major programmes of housing renewal. Local politics was dominated by the Labour Party, with strong links to the unions.

Newcastle's middle class, relatively small in number, tended to move out to the surrounding suburbs and rural areas. After depressed conditions in the major industries in the first part of the century, the economy improved in the 1950s. From the 1950s to the 1970s, the city council undertook major programmes of housing provision and 'slum clearance', transport reorganisation (new roads and a metro system) and city centre redevelopment (Burns 1967). In the 1960s, Newcastle became well-known nationally for innovation in housing policy and city centre renewal, and also for the energy of a charismatic local politician, who championed the cause of the city and then the region in relation to agendas of promoting regional development. In terms of locales, attention was focused on the East and West Ends, the heartlands of working class culture, and the city centre. The city centre, meanwhile, combined, somewhat uneasily, a commercial and elite culture role with that of a working class shopping and leisure destination. The city council emerged from this period of classic 'managerialist' physical reconstruction as a substantial owner of both housing stock and of a large city-centre shopping complex.

The Fordist Nexus Unravels

During the 1970s, however, this impetus fell away. The weakness of the economy reasserted itself, undermined by effective competition in all the traditional industries. The new industries brought in to diversify the economic base had uncertain fortunes. The city council's programmes of physical reconstruction came up against spending constraints. City politics was shaken by corruption scandals. The city itself was both enlarged in the local government reorganisation of the 1970s to include the affluent borough of Gosforth, and then incorporated as one of five boroughs in the wider Tyne and Wear Metropolitan Council. The powers of local government, never strong in centralist Britain, were steadily restricted, especially in the 1980s and 1990s. The political agenda across Tyneside became focused on the search for jobs, as well as the provision of houses. The city centre was promoted as a 'regional capital' in the first structure plan for this area. Meanwhile, in the East and West Ends, housing policy shifted from housing redevelopment to renovation, combined with more emphasis on improving neighbourhood conditions and opportunities. Special teams of officials and ward councillors were set up in these areas to link the city council more closely to local constituents, followed by a stream of regeneration projects focused on particular housing estates and small areas.

The economy continued in decline in the early 1980s. By this time, it became clear that the century-old experience of being in and out of work during a lifetime was to be replaced by the collapse of most work opportunities of the traditional kind, as in many older industrial cities worldwide. The new industries were located away from the old and demanded better skilled labour. Employment opportunities shifted from the industrial sector to the service sector, creating opportunities for women more than men. These shifts not only exacerbated poverty. They undermined the cultural inheritance. Men in particular were displaced from work expectations and from a cultural position, in the home and in the workplace (Campbell, 1993). The political rallying cry used locally was for the provision of 'real jobs', as opposed to service jobs and 'women's work'.[7]

By the 1990s, the service sector was the dominant industry in Newcastle, with the biggest 'companies' being the hospitals and the universities. The traditional working class retained its position primarily through local politics, and the relation between the Labour Party and the unions, though this too was changing. While many of the expanding numbers of middle class and non-manual workers lived outside the city, the city centre remained attractive as a leisure and shopping location and, most recently, as a place to live.[8] The heartland neighbourhoods became labelled in policy initiatives and popular consciousness as 'deprived' areas, full of social problems. This was particularly so in the West End, which had always been a less homogeneous area than the East End. Experiencing significant redevelopment of poor quality housing in the 1960s (Gower Davies, 1972), the area has been the setting for virtually all subsequent urban policy initiatives. The result is that some of the housing stock has been through several rounds of refurbishment. Parts of the riverside have been converted from industrial uses, which in the past sustained local people, into business parks where people from outside the area come in to work, a much-felt symbolic expression of the disconnection between residents and their cultural history. Meanwhile, people continue to leave the area and those still there, while often valuing their local environments, continue to have a hard time. To add to the social stigma of the adverse labelling of their neighbourhoods, there are real and often acute tensions between different groups, reflecting complex social fractures (ethnic groups, family feuds, men versus women, those engaged in criminal activities versus those trying to make it through the mainstream economy, etc.). Those who remain in the area see signs of decay and abandonment around them. The West End was the scene of nationally-reported riots in 1992, and also became associated with car-based and drug-related crime (Campbell,

1993). Meanwhile, those with modest cash sums can buy up low value property to make a living renting out space to low income tenants.[9] Thus, despite continuing efforts at regeneration, the number of empty dwellings increases, leaving void stock in the hands of the city council, the social landlords and mortgage companies who had financed private purchasers. Similar tendencies were also developing in the East End of the city.

Not surprisingly, some city council officials came to believe that small-scale initiatives made little impact in the face of the structural shifts the city was caught up in. A key problem for the city was that the out-migration was selective. Households moved within the social housing stock to areas with better reputations. Households in the majority owner-occupied sector often moved out of the city altogether, to other parts of the conurbation and the small towns and villages in the sub-region. The reputation of the West End in particular, linked to images of low skills, crime and drugs, were constructed in the press and media and in policy reports, and then used to filter applicants by employers and providers of credit, creating negative discrimination to add to people's problems. These shifts, US-style, threatened the viability of the city itself, and certainly threatened the council's financial position and its roles as a substantial social housing landlord, part-owner of the major city-centre shopping centre and provider of education, leisure and welfare services. Its historic self-image as a proud nineteenth century industrial capital, evolving into the twentieth century in the forefront of city planning and welfare provision for a working class community, was now transforming to outsiders as an exemplar of the social alienation and tension of the downside of a post-industrial world. Only in the city centre was this redeemed by a positive image within the world of young people's partying circuits and within the tourist world as a good base from which to visit the region.

Re-Positioning in a Post-Industrial World

Meanwhile, city governance had been living through the 'Thatcher' years, with its deliberate attempts to break the power of local government, and Labour strongholds in particular. Newcastle City Council, held together by a shrewd leader until the mid-1990s, took a pragmatic position, criticising national government in political rhetoric but ensuring that it captured a share of any finance available in government programmes for the city. To do this, it built up links with the private sector through a CBI-inspired partnership (The Newcastle Initiative (Bailey, 1995)), and coexisted with reasonable relations with the Tyne and Wear Urban Development Corporation, which invested large amounts of national government funds in the physical regeneration of the city's Quayside. This has now become a key office locale for major law and accounting firms still based in the city, as well as a leisure location for young professionals, although its success has been in part at the expense of other parts of the city centre, notably the old nineteenth-century core. From the later 1980s, both the city council and the development corporation were vigorous in their attempts to transform the images of the city held by outsiders, particularly potential investors, tourists and government officials. They understood this as displacing the 'Andy Capp' working class image with a concept of a modern, forward-looking city, with good economic prospects (Wilkinson, 1992). In parallel, councillors maintained a public critique of national government and its initiatives, thus playing to the 'gallery' of its working class citizens. This strategy of 'critical pragmatic entrepreneurialism' served to hold the external business audience and the local political base together in some semblance of a shared approach.

But there was little attempt to transform the city council itself and its working practices. Its internal ethos had been shaped in the post-war period, as the deliverer of services to working class constituents. It was organised into departments focused on the different services; housing, social services, transport, planning and economic development, environmental health, etc. In other words, it was a sectoral service delivery machine. Councillors continued to see themselves as delivering services to their wards, fighting over the relative balance between the different wards, and particularly the relative balance between the East and West End wards. These areas were primarily considered as constituencies for a paternalist politics. Councillors expected citizens to approach them with their needs and problems and to see them as their channel to political influence, in clientelistic mode. A Byzantine structure of committees evolved within which councillors could play out a politics focused on competition for resources for their wards. City-wide issues were largely left to the council leader and to officers. Lobby groups, around conservation and environmental issues, were much less well-developed and could be dismissed as minority concerns. The competitive political game was played out with a currency of houses improved, local facilities retained or improved and jobs obtained. With very little active opposition, assured votes at election times and the selection of councillors governed by Labour Party and trades union politics, there was little need to respond to citizens' perspectives. The main challenges were within the Labour council group. East and West End councillors often banded together as opposing blocks.

In the mid-1990s, this tension surfaced in a successful challenge to the leadership, which had been closely associated with the development of the city centre. This new political thrust demanded a more strategic approach to what the council was doing. The business community had also been calling for this for some time. Among the councillors, however, the previous regime was seen as being too close to business. Attacking government investment (under the Tories) as represented in the Tyne and Wear Development Corporation, councillors and officers asserted that the real problems of the city were poverty and lack of jobs, that is, they were 'structural'. This rhetoric was used to justify a focus on future outcomes and dismiss concerns with process, which would have turned attention towards the council's own practices.

The new council leadership, by 1997 basking in a Labour government at national level, brought in new senior officers to develop a more strategic and coherent approach to managing change in the city, although conflicts remained among different factions of councillors. By 2000, this had produced a reorganisation of departments and committees. Responding to the Labour government's 'modern local government' agenda (DETR, 1998), various initiatives were taken to promote new, more 'integrated', policy agendas and develop new processes, including the introduction of 'cabinet-style' government and area committees through which neighbourhoods could contribute to the community plan the city was expected to produce (NCC, 2000c). In parallel, the regional governance landscape was changing, with a new regional development agency, One North East, with control over public funds for urban regeneration and economic development. The national government's office in the region, GO.NE, was also important as a focus for agreeing regional planning strategies for the location of development (industrial and commercial sites, transport routes and housing investment). This strategy, articulated at the end of the 1990s, far from seeking to limit growth, adopted aspirational targets for substantial growth, spread across the region. If Newcastle failed to attract significant amounts of this into its own area, it risked other local authorities providing the dwellings for yet more out-migration from the city.[10]

In the trajectory of half a century, there can be no doubt that the economy, culture and politics of the city are now very different from the heyday of a working class city. The driving forces of these changes are as much from outside as inside and the consequences are both cruel (for many tied into the traditional economic and cultural nexus) and liberating (for those seeking to make their way in the new world of globalised economic and cultural relations). But despite the scale of change, urban governance processes have struggled to find a collective way forward, which can accommodate both the hardship and the opportunity. Instead, the 1980s and

1990s have seen a plethora of initiatives and projects, each promoting something new but caught up in the history of past discourses and practices. The new strategic thrust in the city council has sought to change this. A key tool in mobilising a new approach has been the production of a new strategic vision for the city.

A Political Project for Social Transformation

A New City Strategy: 'Going for Growth'[11]

The city council began consultation on its new city-wide strategy in mid-1999, with public meetings about a broad approach and request for comment. This was consolidated into a more developed discussion document in early 2000, with further meetings and requests for comments, with the final plan agreed in mid-2000. By early 2000, the initiative was already attracting national attention as a new way of addressing the difficult problems of 'northern' British industrial cities. The council had already produced an economic development strategy in 1998.[12] This had positioned the city in global, regional and local economic relationships, adopting the fashionable 'cluster' analysis to identify eight sectors for priority attention. The new, broader strategy, *Going for Growth* (NCC, 2000a), builds on this analysis. It emphasises social demography, located in the context of planning and regeneration policy discourses rather than economic development ones. In early 2000, the city council produced a 'green paper', setting out its vision for Newcastle in 2020. The central problem is presented as the threat of continuing population decline and the selectivity of the movement away from the city. The strategy aims to:

> link growth in population with housing and jobs, and ... with the quality of the urban environment, schools, transport, leisure, health services and community infrastructure (NCC, 2000a, p. 3).

This represents a more 'joined-up' approach to the established 'housing and jobs' agenda of previous years. The fear is that, even if more jobs are attracted to Newcastle, they will be taken by people living in the wider sub-region. If the quality of some residential areas continues to decline, and if services continue to be seen as poor quality, particularly as regards education, then socially selective out-migration will continue, leaving behind those with limited choices, vacant housing stock and a smaller population base to support council services. The council hopes to reduce the leakage by improving the quality of the residential areas and other key city locales. 'Improving' in this context means significant transformation. Not far below the surface of the carefully-crafted text of *Going for Growth* is the implication that improving the quality of the urban environment is not just a task of the physical re-design of areas. It is an effort in social transformation (Byrne, 2000), justified with the vocabulary of social diversity.

> The inner city needs to be transformed. We need more jobs for local people, and those with jobs need to be attracted to live within the City boundary. This means selective clearance, private house-building and improved services like schools, leisure and shopping (NCC, 2000a, 8).

> To be a truly cosmopolitan city Newcastle needs to be a global meeting place where new ideas are generated and exchanged. The dominant local culture needs to embrace and benefit from the diverse range of peoples in the City and thereby attract different cultures to the City (NCC, 2000a, 9).

This social transformation will, it is claimed, be accompanied by a more participative approach to local service delivery:

> Communities will be empowered to participate in the planning and delivery of local services. ... All communities must have the opportunity to play a part in *Going for Growth* (NCC, 2000a, 8).

Going for Growth thus articulates both a new image of the city's social community and a new approach to citizen-state relations, However, while communities are to play a part, the strategy did not involve them in articulating the city-wide vision. The city council, arguing that it is building on a great deal of consultation with people in the neighbourhoods over the years, has given leadership by providing the bare bones of a strategy. Consultees are invited to help fill it out. Here the council presents itself as a leader and a representative of citizens' views. But it also re-enacts top-down paternalism in its processes of articulating and conveying a 'transformative' vision.[13]

The vision seeks to represent the city's qualities and presents a conception of the areas of the city. This is spatialised partly in the vocabulary of wards, to help councillors locate themselves. But it operates with a conception of problematic inner city wards, stable areas and areas where signs of 'weakness' are appearing. This is expressed in a 'traffic light' vocabulary of (see Figure 10.5):

- Red – weak areas
- Amber – intermediary areas
- Green – strong areas[14]

This builds on work underway in the city council for some time on how to forecast when areas might move into an accelerating downward spiral, as property values begin to decline and people move out. The text argues that these distinctions are used to highlight the need for different approaches in different areas. The West and East Ends are referred to by the synonyms 'inner city' and 'riverside'. However, the labelling cannot avoid re-invoking and reinforcing the well-established spatial map of the city.

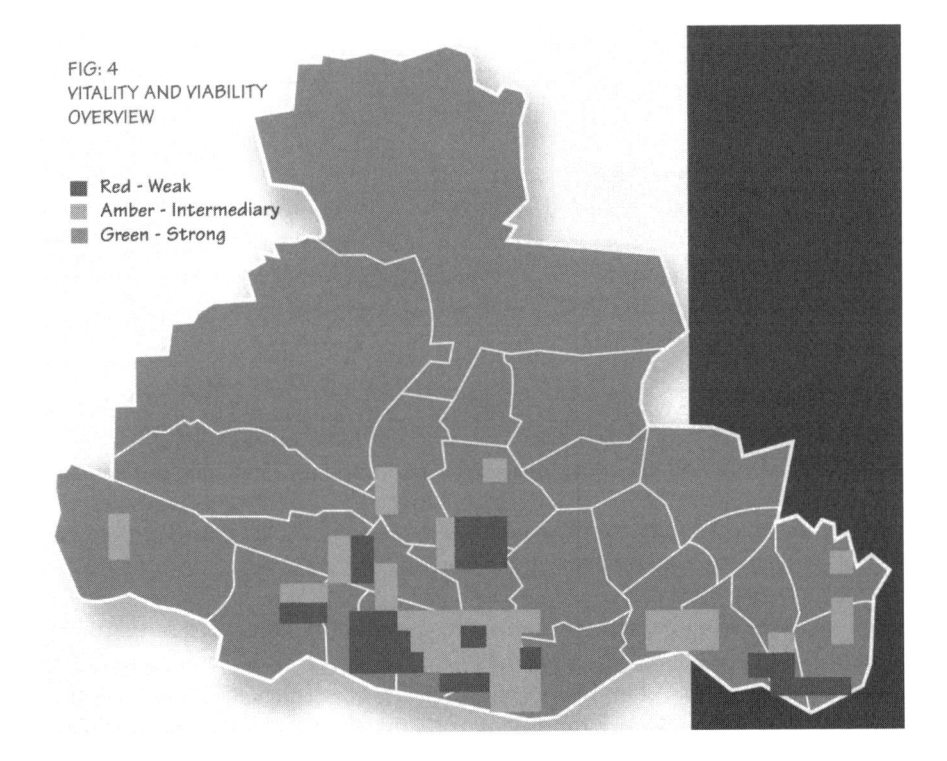

Figure 10.5   Mapping the City's Neighbourhoods
Source: *Going for Growth* Masterplan, Newcastle City Council.

Going for Growth seeks to work with this map in an effort to transform it. This involves combining concepts of an innovative entrepreneurial city developed in the earlier economic development strategy with ideas about place quality in urban design terms. This is to be promoted by area masterplanning, an idea re-introduced into local policy discourse through the national report on *Towards an Urban Renaissance* (Urban Task Force, 1999), produced by the team led by renowned architect Richard Rogers, who had been appointed to advise the government on urban policy. Area masterplans are to be produced for a large new 'greenfield' development site already allocated in the city's agreed *Unitary Development Plan*, for the East and West Ends and for the city centre.

The strategy gives special attention to the creation of a 'New West End'. With job creation projects in the city centre, and on a large former power station site in the west of the city, 'a rejuvenated and buoyant West End' is required 'if citywide population targets are to be achieved' (p. 16). The key tools to achieve this are 'massive investment' and urban design, which in turn will introduce 2000 new households, and 'integrate these successfully with existing communities'. The aim is to create a 'size and diversity of population' to support improved local services.[15] Existing residents will be helped to 'adjust' to all this by a 'multi-agency support team'. The subtext to this ambition is that significant demolition will occur. Thus a classic 1960s 'comprehensive development area' strategy is being re-invented, clothed with the vocabulary of community and diversity current in national urban policy discourse of the late 1990s. The Head of Planning and Transportation, a transport engineer catapulted into the national spotlight in mid-2000, justified this approach in a profile in the national planning press:

> Some of these areas will never have a real chance of success unless they are completely remodelled, renamed and built around viable centres ... There is nothing more difficult than knocking on people's doors and telling them they will have to move ... It is no longer any good undertaking stop-gap measures and pretending that they are going to change the area for good.[16]

There can be no doubt of the complexity and difficulty of the situation the city council faces. It has limited powers and resources, and its constituents, especially in the old working class areas, look to the council to address their difficulties. Key potential assets are the significant resources of council-owned land and property, much of it of low value, and generating considerable costs.[17] Economic and socio-cultural dynamics, in the sub-region and nationally, are working against it. Its citizen base is ebbing away, affecting both its finances and its functions. The city needs to respond to the national policy pressure to 'modernise' itself, somehow combining both streamlined efficiency with much greater involvement with, and responsiveness to, citizens. On top of this, they are expected to introduce new agendas into city management, notably with respect to transport and environmental management. Only by demonstrating commitment to such externally set agendas can city councils expect to capture the resources they need to take new initiatives and even maintain already deteriorating basic services.

The vocabulary of *Going for Growth* thus positions itself primarily in relation to the council's own political and managerial concerns and the agendas of the regional, national and EU funders. Areas are referred to in terms of the presence and absence of problems as faced by public agencies, including the city council as owner of much of the housing and supplier of key services such as education. Despite a great deal of local involvement in neighbourhood management in the West End over the years, the strategy contains no direct reflection of citizens' perceptions and does not speak to them. Rather it pronounces at them. Nor is there any celebration of the distinctive qualities of the city, of the city centre or the locales within it. As a 'place vision', it is very sketchy, largely shaped by the discourse of urban policy professionals, and directed by the immediate preoccupations of the city council as land and property owner and service manager. As others have remarked, the vision of *Going for Growth* floats strangely isolated from a regional context (Byrne, 2000). The place quality invoked replicates a map of the city in terms of 'problem areas', as used so often before.

An Area Masterplan for the West End

The sketchy place vision in *Going for Growth* is filled out in more detail in area masterplans produced in mid-2000. Immediately following the production of the vision, the city council commissioned The Richard Rogers Partnership to produce a strategy for the West End, while council officials produced a masterplan for the East End. Part of the logic for this was that the Rogers Urban Task Force report had asserted that 'low demand' situation areas could be turned around by appropriate area masterplans (Urban Task Force, 1999). There was also a feeling of calling the bluff of the Task Force, by forcing it to take on a very difficult challenge. The two masterplans have been presented as options for consultation based on 'previous and extensive local community consultation' (NCC, 2000b, p. 4). The agenda of both plans is based primarily on housing, jobs and transport, translated into sites and routes, the traditional 'sectoral agenda' of local authority planning in recent years. Within the West End, sites will be generated by substantial clearance. The masterplan argues as follows:

> *Clear untenable housing* There are housing areas near the riverside which have become unpopular and population has dropped below levels

that sustain communities. Reactive demolition is containing the immediate problem, but in many instances it is further fragmenting communities. There must be a very carefully considered proactive strategy to clear untenable stock and change the balance of housing in such areas.

Consolidate existing communities Many residential communities are strong. Within these areas there are empty sites. Gaps that occur along important routes or that adjoin local public places and space, should be priority sites for redevelopment. This will reinforce stability and confidence in these areas. ...

Free up sites for homes and jobs We must strategically plan to free up significant sites for investment. This will help to stimulate market demand to commence vital private investment in housing and jobs. (NCC 2000b, p. 4/5).

This 'radical' approach will provide the sites for 'largescale' housing development, to 'create long-term confidence' by changing 'the housing mix'. This means less council housing, less private rented, more owner occupation and more housing association and shared equity homes. (NCC, 2000b, p. 7).

The masterplan approach is then to break the area up into districts, with clear 'hearts' where services will be focused, presenting communities as neighbourhoods clustered around local centres (see Figure 10.5). These districts, which float somewhat uneasily across current local place maps and ward boundaries, will also be the foci of more devolved neighbourhood arrangements.

The masterplan for the West End thus presents traditional urban design concepts of spatially-contained communities,[18] linked to the currently fashionable rhetoric of consultation and local management. Apart from a nod in the direction of the area's diversity and the overt concern with out-migration and void stock, there is no mention of the area's distinctive characteristics and history. Nor is there any conception of the complex relations through which different communities within the West End area link to other parts of the city and the rest of the world, or vice versa.

Place, Identity and Governance 207

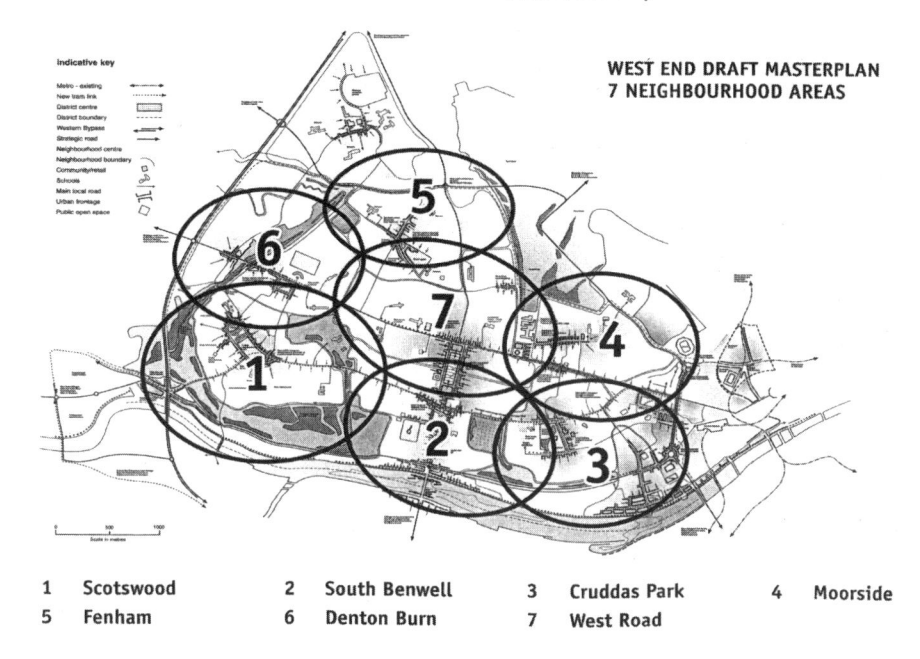

Figure 10.6 Neighbourhood Areas in the West End Draft Masterplan
Source: Draft Masterplan for the East End and West End of Newcastle (NCC 2000b).

Such micro-appreciation of the multiplex realities of daily life[19] in this part of the city is swamped by the focus on physical development, creating 'significant sites' and building 'district communities'. Despite the rhetoric of consultation, participation and neighbourhood management, this plan seems targeted to external audiences, the providers of the 'massive investment', without which very little of the 'radical change' can happen. It sits uneasily with the city council's own parallel initiatives in community development, notably the development of a West End Regeneration Strategy in 1999, and the effort to build a partnership around a government-funded New Deal for Communities strategy, also in the West End, being undertaken in 1999-2000. Both of these promoted more bottom-up approaches to strategy development.

The City's Vision, its Practices and Citizens' Social Worlds

In these various strategic initiatives, the city council has taken up the baton of integrated strategy, focused around urban quality. It has sought, though in a very sketchy way, to articulate a view of the city as a whole and of the various places within it. It presents the past as a problem to be escaped from, while the future is painted in the language of contemporary, professionalised urban policy debate. There is very little effort to articulate any distinctive qualities and meanings of place and identity which belong to Newcastle, except as structured by the agenda of general 'problems'. Nor is there any sense of debate among city stakeholders about qualities of the city. Yet the city council has been talking with these participants in all kinds of arenas over the past twenty years.

The strategy presents a clear transformation agenda, but the past is locked up into a bundle of 'negatives' while the future is expressed as a bundle of 'positives' drawn from national policy talk. Strategic partnerships with stakeholders are to steer the strategy from past to future. There is talk of consultation, even 'empowerment', of local residents to manage their part in it.[20] The lack of specification could even create a space for such consultation to evolve a much richer conception of citizens' perspectives on place qualities, within which community expressions of various identities could be articulated.[21] But the obvious social transformation agenda, played out in *Going for Growth* and elaborated in the visual imagery used in the West End masterplans, resonates with the promotion of 'yuppy takeover', so much criticised by the residents, the city council and the media with respect to the redevelopment of derelict industrial areas in the 1990s. Here is an agenda for planned gentrification and displacement – not just of particular people (especially those in the private rented sector), but of a remembered way of life. It is the very visibility of the social transformation agenda, coupled with the fear and memory of disruption of previous efforts at urban redevelopment and some very real material losses which some groups will face if the proposals go ahead,[22] which brought the marchers and placards in protest outside the Civic Centre in mid-2000 and the red balloons released over the town, one for each dwelling to be demolished. Thus the national government's 'urban renaissance' agenda plays out against its own social exclusion and community development agenda in the terrain of one of the most disadvantaged communities in the country.

In this city, citizens are by now knowledgeable enough to have few illusions about their city council. Their experience of its ways, combined with the general media presentation of local government in Britain, has made citizens quick to suspect self-interested hidden agendas concealed within the council's public face. They hear the council's arguments, in meetings and in the media. But the underlying arguments are not presented to them in much detail – the reality of the weakening position of the council; the difficulties it faces in its social landlord role; its dependence on external financing and the games that need to be played to capture funds; its need to attract developers to invest in the 'brownfield' areas of the city, when there is also a major greenfield development site made available near more affluent parts of the city and the airport; the problems of dealing with situations infiltrated by criminal networks. Senior officials and councillors know that they are taking a calculated risk with the strategy. They know that all kinds of initiatives have been tried in the poorer neighbourhoods and that these have not reversed the decline in employment levels, quality of life indicators and population. They know that citizens in the East and West Ends are very concerned about the deterioration which is happening in their neighbourhoods.[23] They know that they need to mobilise external funding from both the public and private sectors if they are to realise the asset values of the council's land and property, much of it locked up in places where 'markets' as conventionally understood are non-existent. So, they believe, a bold and simple strategy is a move worth making to try to reposition such areas within a city-wide context and to present starkly why, without socio-cultural transformation, the city risks decaying into a classic 'American' doughnut city, with a city centre island, suburban areas beyond and in between a swathe of areas of increasingly stressful living environments. In this context, a commitment to bold socio-physical transformation seems justified, just as it did to their predecessors in the 1960s. But social transformation also means displacement of people from neighbourhoods where they and their families have lived and from their meaningful micro-environments. It means generating a pall of uncertainty over swathes of the East and West Ends which will last until both material conditions and mental imageries have been changed. No amount of multi-agency professional support ('talking the details'), with which many residents are already familiar, will alter this.

Faced with an acute structural challenge, the city council is taking a strategic bet. Its strategy is itself a key tool in its efforts to reposition itself and re-cast its policy discourses. But this 'game of position' is being played out to audiences external to the city, focused on capturing funding and investment attention, as with so much of current British regeneration policy (Oatley, 1998). It is not talking to 'its own', the citizens of the city and especially its heartland supporters. Instead, it speaks to the external audiences about the local processes of participation and partnership which would accompany the development of the strategy. But citizens have a 'been here before' feeling and know that earlier initiatives of this kind, valuable while they lasted, stalled when the initiative funds ran out or some new project distracted councillor and officer attention. The new initiatives in community planning may evolve new processes and practices over time,[24] but for the moment, all is 'on trust', and the social capital of trust is withering away among citizens. The council now finds itself in an increasingly acute 'vice'. Its credentials with national and regional funders depend on the quality of its participation processes as well as on its strategic boldness. Its credentials with citizens depend on rebuilding the basis for some degree of trust. Without these credentials, the strategy will fail to generate either public or private funding, the decline will continue and with it the political and resource base of the council. It is thus caught between the timescales of the politics of capturing funding and the economics of capturing the attention of investors, and the timescale needed for the transformation of its practices and its relations to citizens. Faced with this, not only has the council's commitment to changing its practices been weak. Its bold and radical, externally oriented, top-down strategic discourse, with its boosterist, 'bombastic' style and cosmetic deference to ideas of participation and consultation, serves to reinforce past images of paternalist and unresponsive government. Very quickly the tensions between the 'bold discourse' and local experience of practices have generated an increasingly hostile reception of the *Going for Growth* strategy. The strategic bet may yet backfire in a very short timescale, as residents and local activists mobilise to protest, capturing media attention and spreading their message in ways likely to reach national as well as local audiences. In this mobilisation, the issues at stake are as much to do with process as with policy content, with practices as well as discourses:

> Councillor: 'There's no point in saying "No" to demolitions. We have to go ahead with the radical strategy.'
>
> Local community spokesperson: 'We know there have to be demolitions. We're not completely opposed to what the Council is trying to do. We just want to be included.' (Extract from Radio Newcastle: 3.8.00).

Thus the council's effort to transform its policy discourses is being undermined by the paternalist practices which permeate its own culture. Its spokespeople talk the future but act the past. The council acts the past both in its assumption that, if it gives the strategic leadership, the community can 'fill in the detail', and in the way it continues to play for position on the national stage. One consequence of this is that, in constructing its strategy, it has given little attention to finding out how the city works these days, and how people use and get access to its different resources and locales. Instead, its 'analysis' relates to its own problematic position and its vision draws on national imagery. Meanwhile, the citizens in the West End find, played out across their own everyday worlds, the tensions within the city council's own position and within the 'renaissance' and 'community' dimensions of national urban policy.

Tragic Stories and Limited Transformations

Those involved in city governance face impossible choices wherever they turn. There are always losers and difficult costs to pay. Given the prospects of decline on a US scale which politicians and officials in Newcastle fear, bold moves to generate new bases for hope, to mobilise belief in a new future and to escape from a past grounded in Fordist class relations have some justification. But even as the city council's vision aims to displace the past with new identities for the troubled areas of the city, it incorporates much of the past within both its content and its mode of articulation. Old games of position are played out 'as usual' with an eye to the national stage and national policy agendas. This is not just a result of the city council's own choices. It is 'structured in' by the context, especially the way that national funding for urban regeneration is made available. While national policy stresses that local authorities should become more responsive to their communities, it organises funding for local authorities in ways which serve to reinforce unresponsive practices merely packaged in a rhetoric of responsiveness. City councils are caught in the resultant contradictions. The result of this double-level of 'business as usual' has been that paternalist practices structured with an eye to the national stage continue, merely repositioning themselves in a changing context. Meanwhile, rather than electoral mobilisation, most citizens vote with their feet and their attention, turning away from the city to live in other areas, and turning away from the city's public realm and political engagement.[25]

In the case discussed here, the city council's strategic vision is largely about the council's own search for identity and position in a changing governance landscape. Its emphases and priorities derive from its own preoccupations. Rather than a strategic attempt to develop new cultural resources within which citizens with diverse lifestyles and aspirations could find elements to help build their own forward-looking identities, it uses national imageries and narrowly based conceptions of 'growth' and how to get it. Neither the strategy nor the area masterplans convey a sense of the multiple dynamics and relationships which underpin urban life in the city and generate all kinds of nodes of economic growth and social support, as well as areas of difficulty. There is no richly differentiated conception of what the city is, who lives in and comes to the city, what they enjoy about it as well as what they fear, the memories embodied in the places of the city and the futures that might be in the making. The vocabulary of metaphors and the resonances of meanings are locked into a professional world, rather than the worlds of the diverse citizens of the city. This contributes to the general message of displacement for many in areas such as the East and West Ends – their memories and identities are once again to be wiped out, this time without even the universalistic rhetoric which justified the comprehensive redevelopment of the 1960s. Oriented towards the national government's 'urban quality' agenda, the city council's 'radical strategy' undermines its ability to achieve the same government's community participation exhortations. The resultant tensions are now exploding in the public realm of local TV and radio. Yet, as Stoker (1999) remarks in reviewing trends in British local governance in the 1980s and 1990s, 'disharmony' is not all negative. Maybe it is only through the uncomfortable pressure of citizen mobilisation that councillors and officials can collectively accept and undertake the deep re-thinking which could transform practices as well as discourses in a profound way.

The city council claims it is being radical. The argument in this chapter suggests that it is not being radical enough. Transformative strategies need to penetrate both discourses and practices. They need to touch not just the visible surface of policy rhetoric and public justifications, where identities are displayed. These public performances need to build on real changes in the way interests are configured and political strategies are articulated, in the institutional sites and processes through which identities are played out in coalitions and in conflicts. And these in turn need to be grounded in deeper movements in cultural assumptions and values, the ground upon which identities get shaped.[26] In the case described here, citizens are not taken in by the surface display because they expect this to be a masque for underlying power games. A disillusioned citizenry judges the council with the experience of mistrust rather than confidence in representational leadership.

While acknowledging that the city's position is affected by deep changes in the city's economy and society, councillors and officials have paid too little attention to the underpinnings of its own cultures and practices and how they interlock with the social worlds of those in the city. They have found it difficult to see that their practices merely erode still further the sense of a common fate they once shared with many citizens. Thus the message conveyed in the practices surrounding the articulation and communication of the *Going for Growth* strategy counteracts the language of a hopeful future conveyed in the strategic rhetoric. For many in the most difficult circumstances, the message reinforces their own mental and material sense of displacement from that future. Changing these perceptions is perhaps the most important priority for any city with a history such as Newcastle. A key dimension to transforming such perceptions requires a transformative focus on the governance cultures and practices themselves, a hard task for city councils, with a long timescale for fruition.[27]

The radical move in this context is then not just to have a strategy about the hope for overall 'growth', as if this would somehow transform the city's economy and society in a magic formula. Instead, the really radical move for a city council would be to seek to transform the city's democratic public realm. In their manifesto for a new city politics, Amin, Massey and Thrift (2000) argue:

> What we are searching for ... is an approach which might enable participation and debate (and even disagreement) in a way which recognises the rich diversity of cities and the conflicting claims as well as creative tensions which that throws up ... We (also) believe it (is) important to establish some notion of shared belonging, a sense of common citizenship, an idea that there might after all be such a thing as society. A city politics which could achieve this would be ... a confident democracy based on active citizenship, even when it clashed with 'official' visions of what is right and who has a right (p. 31).

Combined with richer knowledge about the city economy and society – its daily life rhythms, its lifestyles and the triumphs and troubles of its various citizens and stakeholders, such a focus could lead to a distinctive and locally-grounded radical strategy of hope for the city and its future. The red balloons of protest could just be the real basis for building the future.

Faced with the challenges of global repositioning, a really radical strategy could turn its conceptual attention away from the national stage and its funding games to the very local task of building a stronger and richer shared identity among the citizens and stakeholders of the city.[28] If, as Amin and colleagues, Sandercock (2000), Worpole and Greenhaulgh (1999) all argue,[29] we live these days in cities of diversity and difference, then it is difficult to resist the argument that the critical challenge for cities is to transform their governance practices towards more participative and consultative forms. This requires not merely political mobilisation. It also means that the urban professionals and managers, in all sorts of positions, need to transform their own practices, which currently are such a powerful influence on policy discourses and governance practices. Rather than 'ignoring, marginalising or overriding' citizens' 'fears and anxieties, memories and hopes' (Sandercock, 2000, p. 29), city governments should be encouraged to do the slow, hard, conflict-ridden, time-consuming and time-taking micro-level work of reconstructing the relations between citizens and city governance, in ways which can help build on and develop positive identities with place and enrich the diverse social worlds of citizens. This message has implications not merely for individual city councils and their practices, but for regional, national and EU governments who promote new urban agendas and provide the resource and regulatory frameworks to which city governments have to respond.

Postscript

The story of the *Going for Growth* initiative in Newcastle, UK, still provides a good illustration of the tensions in British urban policy between the emphasis on citizen empowerment and the focus on developing the competitive assets of cities (Imrie, 2002; Taylor, 2003). But it also shows how citizen protest and the power of the vote can change local governing regimes. The story in the chapter ends mid-2000. Later in the year, the paper itself was circulating among officers, councillors and activists in the city. As author, I had previously given a copy to the then Chief Executive and discussed the dilemmas of institutional change with him. By this time, councillors and officers were recognising that they needed to pull back from the masterplans and embark on a much deeper consultation with residents. Several different kinds of arenas were created, under the general umbrella of the *Going for Growth* strategy, as was a newly created Local Strategic Partnership, which drew in different public sector activities and business groups at one level, but which also worked closely with residents, discussing street-by-street what should be done.

In 2001, the political situation changed slightly, as some of the key councillors who had resisted such in-depth consultation became national level politicians, which meant they had to give up their role. New local area strategies were produced which drew in funding from the national *Single Regeneration Budget*. By 2004, many of the resultant projects were underway. However, the *Going for Growth* initiative, having lost its main backers in the city council, came under pressure from other departments within the council. Inter-departmental co-ordination was difficult and many councillors found the consultation practices a difficult challenge to their traditional role. More seriously, the councillors were under increasing political pressure across the city, as demands for a new style of politics, different policy agendas and greater co-ordination spread across the city. These demands were increasingly effectively mobilised by the Liberal Democrats, who began to constitute a significant opposition in the early 2000s.

Then, following a reorganisation of ward boundaries due to falling populations in the Labour heartland wards, the Liberal Democrats ousted the Labour Council in a dramatic overturning of the Labour majority, ending thirty years of Labour domination. The first political act of the new majority was to rhetorically cancel the *Going for Growth* strategy. Instead there was to be 'bottom-up consultation'. In effect, the struggle had become one of process. Rather rapidly, the new councillors caught up with the reality that *Going for Growth* was well into implementation and could not simply be cancelled, and that there had actually been a good deal of consultation as the final proposals evolved. What the new majority may actually now take on is the task of developing a new governance culture within the council as a whole, allowing the new governance experiments of the past twenty years to evolve into a new practices.

In retrospect, the story told in the chapter emerges as a significant episode leading to what may be a transformative lurch out of old trajectories. But, as institutionalist analysis emphasises, such changes in trajectory take many years to evolve and always carry some of the old with them. Hopefully, a more empowering governance culture will continue to develop, with the power to sustain attention to the quality of local living environments and life opportunities as well as economic priorities. The social values of the old Labour regime were not misplaced. They just needed to be combined with the new forces and values shaping citizens' lifestyles, life chances and expectations of governance.

Acknowledgements

Our thanks to the *Evening Chronicle*, Newcastle, and Newcastle City Council, for permission to reproduce these figures.

Notes

1. My thanks to Jean Hillier, Margo Huxley and Tim Townshend for helpful comments on an initial draft, to colleagues at Newcastle for discussions on this issue and to Leonie Sandercock and participants at a seminar at Melbourne University for clarifying my thinking on the significance of this story.
2. Stoker (1999) notes three characteristics to management reforms in local governments: the scale of change, its top-down nature and the 'hyperactive quality of the reformers, with one initiative closely followed by another' (Stoker 1999: 5).
3. See Wilkinson and Applebee (1999), Oatley (1998).
4. See Urban Task Force (1999).
5. See Benwell CDP (1979), Campbell (1993), Robinson and Shaw (1991).
6. Over three quarters of the 78 councillors during the 1990s have been from the Labour Party, as is characteristic of much of North East England.
7. During the 1980s and early 1990s, the expanding employment opportunities tended to be in part-time work for women.
8. But numbers of residents are very small, around 2000 in the 1990s.
9. Some properties can be bought for a few hundred pounds. The problem of this kind of 'private investment' is reported from other Northern cities.
10. These issues were debated in the public examination of the draft regional guidance in 1999. In Autumn 2000, national government helped Newcastle by restricting the growth ambitions of surrounding counties and increasing the growth allocation for Newcastle, justified by the argument that new development should be concentrated on 'brownfield' sites.
11. This account is based on the documents produced by the city council, public presentations of the vision, discussions with council officers and councillors, and with colleagues working on various projects in the city, some of whom are also residents, and material accumulated through related projects.
12. Competitive Newcastle NCC (1998).
13. This was very evident in the comments of councillors in the media in mid-2000, as hostility to the strategy built up.
14. When mapped, this metaphor looks static. But the link to traffic lights gives it a dynamic quality.
15. Behind this is the concept of the need to create the conditions within which some kind of 'market' could occur (other than that represented by the buying up of low value properties by the new 'slum landlords').
16. *Planning* 21 July 2000: 11. Profile of John Miller.
17. In national policy debate over housing, areas such as the East and West Ends, long known about in Newcastle, are now referred to as 'low demand' situations (see DETR Housing Signpost Issue, 7 June 2000; see also Power and Mumford (1999), Niner (1999), Holmans and Simpson (1999)).
18. My thanks to my colleague Tim Townshend for his comments on this aspect.
19. See Graham and Healey (1999), and Healey (2000) for this concept.
20. Consultation meetings were undertaken during 2000 across the city on *Going for Growth* and with wards in the East and West Ends on the masterplans.
21. See the city's initiative in community planning and area management. See NCC (2000c).
22. Residents who feel their micro-environments are yet again threatened with government-generated uncertainty, owner-occupiers whose property values may be

written down, the local property operators who have been buying up property for rental business, some of the families involved in criminal networks ('mafia').
23 The Council has been spending money for years on small scale demolition of void property, and improvements to facilities and the local environment.
24 See NCC, 2000c
25 Voter turnout has tumbled to very low levels.
26 For this analysis, see Schon and Rein's (1994) three levels of framing, and the link between this and Dyrberg's re-working of Lukes' (1974) three levels of power (Dyrberg, 1997); see Healey *et al.* (2001).
27 See Schon and Rein (1994) for the significance of this 'third' level of framing.
28 I do not mean by this that the national stage is ignored; merely that the games played to capture resources and regulatory powers are structured by richly-grounded and creative local agendas rather than either local 'politics as usual' or national policy discourses.
29 And as I have argued myself in Healey (1997).

References

Amin, A., Massey, D. and Thrift, N. (2000) *Cities for the Many Not the Few*, Bristol, Policy Press.
Bailey, N. (1995) *Partnership Agencies in British Urban Policy*, London, UCL Press.
Benwell Community Development Project (1979) *The Making of a Ruling Class*, Newcastle, Benwell CDP.
Burns, W. (1967) *Newcastle: a study in re-planning at Newcastle-upon-Tyne*, London, Leonard Hill.
Byrne, D. (2000) 'Newcastle's going for growth: governance and planning in a post-industrial metropolis', *Northern Economic Review*, Spring/Summer (30): 3-16.
Campbell, B. (1993) *Goliath*, London, Methuen.
Department of the Environment, Transport and the Regions (DETR) (1998) *Modern local government: In touch with people*, London, DETR.
Dyrberg, T.B. (1997) *The Circular Structure of Power*, London, Verso.
Gower Davies, J. (1972) *The Evangelistic Bureaucrat*, London, Tavistock.
Graham, S. and Healey, P. (1999) 'Relational concepts in time and space: issues for planning theory and practice', *European Planning Studies* 7(5): 623-646.
Healey, P. (1997) *Collaborative Planning: shaping places in fragmented societies*, London, Macmillan.
Healey, P. (2000) 'Connected cities', *Town and Country Planning*, 69(2): 55-57.
Healey, P., de Magalhaes, C. *et al.* (2001) 'Place, identity and local politics: analysis partnership initiatives', *Policy Analysis for Network Societies*, Cambridge, M. Hajer and H. Wagenaar.
Holmans, A. and Simpson, M. (1999) *Low Demand: separating fact from fiction*, Coventry, Chartered Institute of Housing.
Hudson, R. (1994) *Wrecking the Region*, London, Pion.
Lukes, S. (1974) *Power: a radical view*, London, Macmillan.
Newcastle City Council (NCC) (1998) *Competitive Newcastle*, Newcastle, Newcastle City Council.
Newcastle City Council (NCC) (2000a) *Going for Growth: a citywide vision for Newcastle 2020*, Newcastle upon Tyne, Newcastle City Council.
Newcastle City Council (NCC) (2000b) *Draft Masterplans for the East End and West End of Newcastle: consultation and participation*, Newcastle, Newcastle City Council.

Newcastle City Council (NCC) (2000c) *Community planning paper*, Newcastle, Newcastle City Council.

Niner, P. (1999) *Insights into Low Demand for Housing*, York, Joseph Rowntree Foundation.

Oatley, N. (ed.) (1998) *Cities, Economic Competition and Urban Policy*, London, Paul Chapman Publishing.

Power, A. and Mumford, K. (1999) *The Slow Death of Great Cities? Urban adandonment or urban renaissance*, York, York Publishing Services.

Robinson, F. and Shaw, K. (1991) 'Urban regeneration and community involvement', *Local Economy*, 6 (1): 61-73.

Sandercock, L. (2000) 'When Strangers Become Neighbours: managing cities of difference', *Planning Theory and Practice* 1(1): 13-30.

Schon, D. and Rein, M. (1994) *Frame Reflection: towards the resolution of intractable policy controversies*, New York, Basic Books.

Social Exclusion Unit (1998) *National Strategy for Neighbourhood Renewal*, London, The Cabinet Office.

Social Exclusion Unit (2000) *National Strategy for Neighbourhood Renewal: a framework for consultation*, London, The Cabinet Office.

Stoker, G. (1999) 'Introduction: the unintended costs and benefits of new management reform for British Local Government', in G. Stoker (ed.) *The New Management of British Local Governance*, London, Macmillan: 1-22.

Tavsanoglu, S. (1998) *Transforming the City: capital, state and redevelopment in Newcastle City Centre (1960-1990)*, Newcastle, Centre for Research in European Urban Environments, University of Newcastle.

Taylor, M. (2003) *Public policy in the community*, Houndmills, Hampshire, Palgrave.

Urban Task Force (1999) *Towards an Urban Renaissance*, London, E and FN Spon.

Wilkinson, D. and Appelbee, E. (1999) *Implementing Holistic Government*, Bristol, Policy Press.

Wilkinson, S. (1992) 'Towards a new city? A case study of image-improvement initiatives in Newcastle upon Tyne', in P. Healey, S. Davoudi, M. O'Toole, S. Tavsanoglu and D. Usher (eds) *Re-Building the City: property-led urban regeneration*, London, E and FN Spon: 174-211.

Worpole, K. and Greenhaulgh, L. (1999) *The Richness of Cities*, London, Comedia/Demos.

11 Difference, Fear and Habitus: A Political Economy of Urban Fears

LEONIE SANDERCOCK

Introduction[1]

Discourses of fear pervade contemporary discussions of the city, usually accompanied by or associated with simplistic remedies in the form of urban and social policies and calls for more 'law and order'. Fear dominates public discussion in New York City, whether it be about neighbourhood policing, gentrification, or tourism. In Johannesburg there is endless repetition of the phrase 'crime and grime' in the context of the 'Community Improvement District', itself modelled on New York's Business Improvement Districts (BIDs), which have been all about cracking down on the homeless and 'cleaning up' the neighbourhood. In Paris, fear of violence is the second most significant matter of public concern, according to recent surveys (Bodie-Gendrot 2000). More importantly, it's at the core of how most people think about the physical design of public space and neighbourhoods these days. Consequently it influences not only how planners think about the city, but the projects they are assigned.

Planning and urban management discourses are, and always have been, saturated with fear. The history of planning could be rewritten as the attempt to manage fear in the city: generically, fear of disorder and fear of dis/ease, but specifically fear of those bodies thought to produce that disorder or dis/ease – women, the working classes, immigrants, gays, youth, and so on. At least four generic kinds of 'solutions' have been promoted for the past hundred years: one is policing, that is, more law and order; a second is spatial containment and segregation, keeping certain bodies out of certain areas; a third is moral reform, the attempt to produce certain kinds of citizens and subjectivities, good Melburnians, good New Yorkers, by providing parks and playgrounds, settlement houses, community centres, and other 'civilising' urban facilities. A fourth, more recent approach is assimilation through social policies such as national language requirements and civics classes, to make the Other into one of us. These approaches, which seek to banish fear by banishing or transforming those seen as inducing fear, have surely exhausted themselves in their futility and discrimination.

This paper argues that it is important to look harder at the nature of fear in contemporary cities in order to arrive at more effective and less discriminatory policies for managing our coexistence in the shared spaces of streets and neighbourhoods increasingly characterised by a social heterogeneity which seems inevitably to generate fears and anxieties. I begin by exploring a distinguished line of sociological and social psychological inquiry about fear in the city as it relates to the figure of the stranger, the outsider. In particular, I want to forge links between this historical line of inquiry, Bourdieu's concept of habitus, and a discussion of the homely imaginary of nationalist practices by the Lebanese-Australian anthropologist Ghassan Hage. The descriptive core of the paper focuses on four case studies of contemporary city fears, and their policy consequences. I argue that there is a political economy of city fears (whether these fears are real or imagined), and an unavoidable question is whose fears get legitimised and translated into policy responses, and whose fears get silenced or marginalised. The final section reflects on the potency of discourses of fear, and the threat that these pose to a democratic civic culture and the vibrancy of the urban public realm.

Cities, Habitus and Fear of Change

Lewis Mumford wrote (in *The City in History*) of the need for cities to be more than 'containers' guaranteeing the coherence and continuity of urban culture over time. He warned of the danger of a too-stabilised community, arguing that urban experience is also about mobility and mixture, encounters and challenges. The city multiplies the opportunities for psychological shock and stimulus. Cultural intermixture, he argued, is what makes the city a civilised place to live. For this reason, 'the stranger, the outsider, the traveller, the trader, the refugee, the slave, yes, even the invading enemy, have had a special part in urban development at every stage' (quoted in Robins, 1995: 48). In this aspect of his work, Mumford is part of a larger tradition of sociological writing which has been concerned with the civilising potential of the stranger, beginning with Simmel and continuing in Robert Park's interest in the movement and migration of peoples and the way this loosens local bonds and creates the freedoms of cities (or as the European medieval tag went: 'city air sets one free').

Difference, Fear and Habitus 221

A new generation of urbanists has drawn on this tradition, celebrating the city as 'a coming together of strangers' (Young, 1990), and urban dwellers as people 'always in the presence of otherness' (Sennett, 1990: 123). But Mumford also took seriously the realities of human antagonism and aversion, the fear eating at the soul of the city, the city as a container of disruptive internal forces. He recognised fear and anxiety as the dark side of the stimulation and challenge associated with encounters with strangers. What happens when strangers become neighbours, when the Other moves in next door? What changes with the awareness that we might touch or be touched by a stranger on the street, or when 'the odour of North African barbecues offends noses that are used to other festivities' (Kristeva 1991: 104)? The fears, anxieties, aversions which are thus aroused are, simultaneously, unspeakable, and yet have powerfully shaped urban political discourses and, consequently, the agendas that have been developed around immigration and urban management. We need to look harder at the nature of fear in the city, and the ways in which it is related to notions of home, homeliness, and belonging because, if such fears cannot be legislated out of existence, we will need different approaches to managing our coexistence in the shared spaces of neighbourhoods and cities (Sandercock, 2000).

Interestingly, there has been in the 1990s, a burgeoning of literature about fear, the fear of strangers and foreigners, fear in the city (see Ellin 1997, Kristeva, 1991). To the extent that this literature has infiltrated the planning field, it is pragmatic and design-based, appearing under the rubric of 'crime prevention through environmental design', or its predecessor, 'defensible space', both of which tackle what could be called the hardware of crime prevention rather than the software of fear in the city. I would like to come at the issue of fear in a very different way, recognising, to begin with, that individual identity is often suffused with anxiety, and that these anxieties are projected onto the figure of the stranger, the alien, whose very presence seems to challenge and undermine the known social order. For Robert Park, for example, the fundamental cause of prejudice is the insecurity of relations with the stranger. We hate because we fear (Park, 1967: chapters 11 and 13). Sociologists from Park and Simmel in the early twentieth century to Ulrich Beck towards its end have emphasised this social psychological disturbance stimulated by the presence of strangers. Julia Kristeva's analysis, in *Strangers to Ourselves* (1991), develops an understanding of fear and its relation to the homely, to the socio-spatial ordering of life, which can be linked productively with Bourdieu's 'habitus'. In her opening paragraphs, Kristeva sets out her project:

Strangely, the foreigner lives within us: he is the hidden face of our identity, the space that wrecks our abode, the time in which understanding and affinity founder (Kristeva, 1991: 1).

Her choice of words is revealing – *'the space that wrecks our abode, the time in which understanding and affinity founder'* – resonating with the Bourdieu-ian sociology of *habitus*, and invoking its destruction, the destruction of our socio-spatial and socio-temporal sense of place. In everyday language, we might say that this is the destruction of all that is familiar and homely, all that we have grown up with and take for granted, including the socio-spatial knowledge of our neighbourhoods and indeed, the nation as a whole. Habitus is a field of social relations defined structurally, but that 'field' also has its spatial component, the spaces of the city, as well as the social spaces in which one feels 'at home', where we experience both a positive sense of belonging, as well as a sense of knowing where we belong, in the social order which is also a spatial ordering of the city.

The stranger, the outsider (the rural or transnational migrant, the gay household, the prostitute, the gypsy) threatens to bring chaos into the social order, from the imagined community of the nation to that of the familiar neighbourhood. Individual strangers are a discomforting presence. In numbers, strangers may come to be seen as an invading mass or tide that will engulf us, provoking primitive fears of annihilation, of the dissolving of boundaries, the dissolution of identity. In the face of this unsettling, according to Ulrich Beck, the desire for the logic of order and identity is reasserted. 'We' must secure our centrality and 'they', those who disrupt our homely space, must be pushed out from the centre. Difference is an attribute of 'them'. They are not 'like us' and therefore they are threatening. And yet, the very strangeness of strangers is not only frightening but also enticing (Beck, 1998: 130). Our ambivalence towards strangers expresses both fear and fascination, which is also desire (including erotic desire) fused into one, and is thus doubly unsettling.

Strangers, fear, ambivalence. I want to take this in two directions. First into the work of Ghassan Hage, and his confronting book, *White Nation* (1998), and then into a broader political economy of fear. In doing so, I want to suggest a different way of understanding the history of planning policies – as spatial practices of power deeply implicated in longings and belongings, as the attempt to manage fear in the city.

Hage retells the story from the movie *Falling Down*, in which Michael Douglas plays the role of a man (D-Fens) whose world is disintegrating. His primary experience of disintegration is the breakdown of his family. As the film follows his desperate attempt to rebuild his family, however, we see that to him the experience of breakdown extends also to the breakdown of the neighbourhood, the nation, and the American way of life. The film begins with D-Fens in his car, in a traffic jam, when a fly enters the vehicle. D-Fens snaps as he tries, unsuccessfully, to get rid of the fly, which provides a powerful metaphor for what follows: his attempt to regain control of his 'home space'. Throughout the movie the 'hero' moves within and across overlapping spaces, his car space, his family space, his neighbourhood space, his national space, as he encounters one 'fly' after another – feminists, fascists, bureaucratic mentalities, as well as a variety of ethnic and racial others, all of them uncontrollable 'flies' in his space of being, his 'home'.

Hage uses this film as an illustration of what he calls the mechanics of nationalist practices of exclusion, a way of categorising otherness/ethnicity within a practice of domesticating the social environment in pursuit of a homely space. 'Because of the emotionally charged portrayal of the "hero", the film reminds us that the space of the home that the nationalist is trying to recover is not just a functional space, but also an affective one, a space where he is staging the very meaning of his life' (Hage, 1998: 76). Hage argues that in Australia both white racists and white multiculturalists share a conception of themselves as nationalists and as managers of the national space, a space which is structured around a white culture, and in which Aboriginal people and non-white 'ethnics' are merely objects to be moved or removed according to a white national will. Although his discussion is specifically about contemporary Australia, the argument has broader relevance, in view of the recent intensification of racist and xenophobic sentiments and practices in European countries.

What is interesting for the purposes of this paper is Hage's discussion of the homely imaginary of nationalist practices. I suggest that although 'national space' is an imaginary, it is an imaginary which is actually, literally, embodied in the real local spaces of one's street, neighbourhood and city, where it is either reinforced or undermined. It is an imaginary which involves a sure knowledge that down the street there is, for example, an Aussie butcher's shop, a Protestant or Catholic church, an Aussie pub, and not a Halal butcher, Buddhist temple, or gay bar. When the locality begins to change, one's imaginary of national space is no longer congruent with one's actual experience of local space. And this produces insecurity (when security is equated with the absence of a threatening otherness). Through interviews, Hage talks to people who are deeply unsettled by an immigrant presence in their neighbourhood, but specifically the presence of those whom he describes as 'Third World-Looking People (TWLPs)' like himself, a dark-skinned Lebanese. 'When the nationalist feels that he or she can no longer operate in, communicate in, or recognise the national space in which s/he operates, the nation [via locality] appears to be losing its homely character' (Hage, 1998: 40). Fears are generated. Loss is experienced. 'The other', the stranger, is thought to be taking over, or as having already taken over. One interviewee, a young Australian born of Greek immigrant parents, and self-described university drop-out, said: 'They've come all the way from I don't know where, and they've stolen my dreams' (Hage, 1998: 218).

Hage's analysis helps us to understand that the national issue of migration becomes a struggle which is played out at the level of the locality in terms of an experience of threat and loss, and the desire to reassert control over one's territory, one's spatial habitus. The affective dimension is related to a deep sense of loss and displacement on the part of some residents who, instead of being able to incorporate and adapt to the social changes around them, perceive these changes as a threat, and resist in whatever ways are available – whether through hate crimes or by lodging complaints through the planning system, by behaving offensively or by leaving the neighbourhood. But where does this understanding take us? The point I want to pick up on, returning to the material city, is precisely the issue of social change and people's capacity to adapt to it. In the next section I argue that discourses of fear emerge in different cities and societies at particular historical moments and are linked to profound structural changes of a socio-spatial as well as economic kind.

Urban Political Economies and Discourses of Fear: Four Examples

The American Urban Crisis of the 1960s: Fear of the Ghetto

In American cities since the mid-1960s discourses of fear and of urban decline have been all-pervasive (Beauregard, 1993). The trigger was the inner city rioting that spread across the country from the mid to late 1960s. Long-developing changes like post-industrial transformation become crises when a significant number of people take notice of them, and that usually happens when the consequences of gradual change are displayed all at once in what seems like a sudden, violent disruption. The term 'the urban crisis' usually describes this period of particularly violent social upheaval in inner cities from the mid-1960s to about 1970, and the sources of this urban crisis are generally attributed to the continuing post-industrial transformation of these inner cities: two decades of sustained black migration to the Northern inner city, largely white and middle class exodus to the suburbs, the flight of capital and especially manufacturing jobs from urban neighbourhoods. These structural changes formed the context for the upheavals surrounding the civil rights movement, rising expectations of urban blacks in tension with social and physical conditions in the inner city, and the inadequate responses of the state to the continuing problems of racial conflict, poverty, inequities in housing and education, and increasing criminal violence. As Beauregard puts it in *Voices of Decline*, a single theme emerged from and gave unity to the fevered discourse about urban decline. 'The theme was race, the problem was the concentration, misery, and rebellion of Negroes in central cities, and the reaction was one of fear and eventually panic' (Beauregard, 1993: 169). Thereafter, racial violence (as in the 'race riot') and racially coded violence (as in the figure of the 'mugger', who is always assumed to be either black or hispanic) became rubrics under which to reduce the complexity of urban transformation to sharply representable and narratable form. The widespread tendency to understand the relationship between whites and blacks in the post-industrial city as primarily a problem of too little law and order in the ghetto led to what Sharon Zukin has called 'the institutionalization of fear' as a defining principle of urbanism during and after 'the urban crisis' in America (Zukin, 1995: 39).

The endless repetition and interpretation of images of 'urban disorder' – riots, muggings, police and National Guard responses – chart the sudden shock of Americans' encounter with the slower, duller, more obscure disorder of shifting economic and social arrangements. The racial logic that dominated the discourse gave Americans a way to think about, or not think about, historical processes like the emergence of post-industrial urbanism. One way to understand the urban crisis of the 1960s, Carlo Rotella suggests, is to regard it as the period in which Americans – especially Americans who steered clear of the black inner city – were forced to confront that emergent urbanism (Rotella, 1998: 216). For my purposes, in reflecting on fear and the city, what is significant is the way this discourse of disorder and fear produced a particular politics and set of policy responses. Zukin calls this period a 'watershed in the institutionalization of urban fear'. Voters and policy elites could have faced the choice of approving policies to attack poverty, manage ethnic competition, integrate everyone into common public institutions. Instead they chose to buy protection, fuelling the growth of the private security industry. Employment in this industry tripled from 1970 to 1990 and, as factory jobs disappeared, urban workers – especially minority group members – sought jobs in the security industry, while their white counterparts in small towns sought jobs in the increasing number of prisons being built in or on the edge of small-town America (particularly small-town California, some of whose economies are described (Barthels, 2000) as being 'prison-dependent').

Sao Paulo's Fortified Enclaves: Fear of the Poor

Brazil has experienced an equally powerful set of structural changes in the past decade. Here I draw on the work of Teresa Caldeira (1999) in documenting the emergence of fortified enclaves in Sao Paulo as part of a new urban segregation in this megacity of ten million inhabitants. Caldeira argues that the new pattern of spatial segregation of the 1990s is inseparable from three structural change processes. From the 1940s to the 1970s the middle and upper classes lived in central and well-equipped neighbourhoods, and the poor in the precarious hinterland where many squatted and, over the space of several decades, built their own housing. In the early 1980s, perhaps reflecting the waning control of the military regime, an out-of-control economy produced astronomical inflation, increasing unemployment, and escalating land prices on the periphery put it beyond the reach of a new generation of working class households, who were therefore pushed into the city, into *favelas* (shanty towns of self-built housing). In 1973 *favelas* housed 1% of the city population; in 1993 it was 19.4%, almost two million people. Second, the consolidation of democratic government after almost two decades of military rule brought trade unions and social movements to the centre of politics, and led to increasing investment in infrastructure in periphery neighbourhoods, and the regularisation of land markets on the periphery. These in turn further pushed up land prices, and pushed the poor out of the periphery and into the city's *favelas*, bringing them into close physical proximity with the middle and upper classes. Third, changes in the urban political economy characterised by an expansion in the tertiary sector and a corresponding decline in the industrial sector, saw Sao Paulo for the first time lose its position as number one industrial pole of the country, and there were corresponding changes to the urban fabric, as the oldest areas of the city went through both deterioration and gentrification (Caldeira, 1999: 116-117).

Along with these structural changes came an increase in violent crime, insecurity, and fear which has seen citizens adopting new strategies of protection that, over time, are changing the city's physical landscape, patterns of residence and circulation, everyday trajectories, habits and gestures related to the use of streets and public transportation. Fear of crime has contributed to changes in all types of public interaction. A new aesthetics of security shapes all types of construction and imposes a new urban logic of surveillance and distance. Sao Paulo is becoming 'a city of walls', as physical barriers are constructed everywhere. (Just as in Johannesburg, commercial, financial and retail services have moved out of the downtown and into large centres in homogeneous white, middle and upper class neighbourhoods like Sandton, and walled communities are being constructed adjacent to these new centres.) New enclaves of socially homogeneous housing for the middle and upper classes are emerging on the periphery, adjacent to and yet completely separate from self-constructed working class neighbourhoods and *favelas*. The elites have abandoned the streets, no longer using them as spaces of sociability as has been the Brazilian custom, and they now seek, through a variety of design strategies, to prevent street life from entering their enclaves (Caldeira, 1999: 118-119).

Caldeira analyses the advertising for these new gated communities and describes how they elaborate the myth of 'a new concept of residence' shaped by images of security, isolation, homogeneity, and luxurious facilities and services. The advertisements invoke privileged islands to which one can return every day, in order to escape from the city and its deteriorated environment and to encounter an exclusive world of pleasure among peers. The image of the enclaves is opposed to the image of the city as a deteriorated world pervaded not only by noise and pollution, but more important, by confusion and mixture – that is, social heterogeneity. The ads suggest the possibility of constructing a life of total calm and security. 'In a context of increased fear of crime in which the poor are often associated with criminality, the upper classes fear contact and contamination, but they continue to depend on their servants.' Their rising anxiety levels relate to concerns about the most effective way of controlling these servants, with whom they have such ambiguous relationships of dependency and avoidance, intimacy and distrust. 'Total security' is crucial to the 'new concept of residence'. Security and control are the conditions for keeping the others out, for assuring not only isolation, but also happiness, harmony, and even freedom (Caldeira, 1999: 120-122).

This contemporary urban re-segregation is complementary to the issue of urban violence but also reflective of Brazilian ways of negotiating deeper changes, from an industrial to a post-industrial urbanism, and from military to democratic rule. What is of particular interest is how the fear of crime is used, on the one hand, to legitimate increasing measures of security and surveillance, but, on the other hand, how the proliferation of everyday talk about crime becomes the context in which residents generate stereotypes as they label different social groups as dangerous, as people to be feared and avoided. These everyday discussions about crime, as Caldeira argues, create rigid symbolic differences as well as physical distances between social groups. Two issues emerge here. One is the way in which advertising for the new gated communities plays on and uses the discourse of fear of the city and the implied criminality of the poor, in order to create an alternative to the city, a utopia of total calm and security (and yet a utopia which is utterly dependent on the badly paid labours of the working classes). The second is the importance of everyday talk about crime, in generating a climate in which such a rejection of the city becomes first thinkable, then necessary.

Cape Town: Fears of Loss and Change

A similar trend can be observed in post-apartheid Cape Town today. At the level of national discourse in South Africa, integration is on everyone's lips. There is talk of a new spatial framework at the level of the urban, of a new rationality for future planning, which includes initiatives to integrate urban spaces, like parks, and to showcase different cultures in an attempt to reduce fear.[2] But the dominant official discourse coming from the Cape Town Council, and more specifically from its economic development branch, is fear of inner urban decay.[3] Here, the endless repetition and interpretation of images of 'urban disorder' – deterioration, pollution, filth, decay, waste, illegal immigrants, violence and crime, anarchism – is a coded way of talking about the arrival and presence of non-whites in the inner city, and particularly of groups considered to be marginal, the street vendors, the parking attendants (referred to as 'parking terrorists'), the homeless. The Cape Town Partnership, an initially informal but now formalised alliance between the city council and the business sector, is the driving force behind this discourse of fear of inner urban decay. They see the inner city as the economic heart of any world class city, which must compete with the greater safety of the shopping mall. And Cape Town aspires to be a world class city. Simultaneously it fears becoming an African city (and, interestingly, is the only major city which is refusing to adopt an African name).

These fears are an expression of white Cape Town's ambivalence towards changes in society since the ANC came to power in 1994. Their response is to try to manage the fear by marginalising and defining as a threat certain social groups, like the informal traders, the parking attendants, the illegal immigrants, and the homeless, by controlling them, reducing their numbers, introducing codes of conduct relating to their economic activities. The desire is to create a clean and safe city, with the shopping mall as one model, and New York's Business Improvement Districts (BIDs) as another. This approach, which seeks to restructure urban space into a sophisticated consumption environment (with an eye on the tourist market) has a focus on security and law enforcement, with 8.5 million rand recently allocated for surveillance equipment, rather than focussing on addressing the social problems of the inner city. In other words, official discourse transforms a generalised white anxiety about social change into specific fears about the decay of the inner city, and responds with policies which institutionalise that fear by enhancing security and surveillance. No doubt, this will soon translate into a whole new architecture of fear along the lines now well-established in Los Angeles and Sao Paulo.

Lest these three examples seem selectively apocalyptic and far removed from more 'normal' cities, let me very briefly suggest manifestations of these mechanisms of fear and desire in the very placid west coast Australian city of Perth. Then follows some conclusions about what's really dangerous about fear and its discourses.

Perth's Central Area: Fears of 'Youth'

Perth's Central Area, like that of other Australian cities in the 1980s, was re-made, given a new corporate skyline in an explosion of office building, only to find itself after the property crash with an over-supply of office space and anxieties about attracting new investment. Planners and designers embraced the idea that a 'sense of place' had to be created to encourage shoppers, tourists, residents and employers back to the Central Area and, accordingly, a range of public space improvement projects, medium density housing developments, and renovations of public buildings and the cultural precinct were undertaken by the city council in collaboration with the state government's Department of Planning and Urban Development (Iveson, 2000: 228-229).

But, as the city was made over by the planners' vision of diversity and vitality, some people were made to feel increasingly unwelcome in these new spaces. Groups of young people from the northern suburbs (read as low income) had benefited from the completion of the Northern Suburbs railway line in 1993 in that the inner city had become more accessible to them. But their presence in the city was troubling to some, and, under pressure from politicians, retailers and councillors, police used their powers under child welfare legislation to remove young people not accompanied by their families from the Central Area. The JAG Team (Juvenile Aid Group) mounted operations in 1994 under code names such as Operation Sweep and Operation Family Values in their attempt to 'make the streets of the city and Northbridge safe for families' (McNamara, 1994, quoted in

Iveson, 2000: 230). Policing operations both 'moved on' young people who might constitute a threat to 'families' and also targeted potentially vulnerable 'family members'. That is, young women were detained for being in areas where Aborigines were thought to congregate (Iveson, 2000: 230). By 1997 the JAG team was targeting anyone who looked under 18 and might be wandering the city malls and Northbridge neighbourhood, and herding them onto the last train out of town. One of the catalysts for such police practices was the anxieties of shopkeepers, who regarded young people as undermining perceptions of the safety of the city.

Such is the increasingly sterile (and menacing) planners' and business community's version of diversity – al fresco dining, shoppers and workers and tourists intermingling, jazz bands and farmers' markets – that certain bodies are marked as undesirable in and indeed a threat to the public-private spaces of the re-made city. If the presence of these 'youths' (code 'troublemakers') was unanticipated and unwelcome in the official imaginary of the re-created city, the response was nevertheless predictable. A closed circuit television camera surveillance system was installed throughout the area, in part to reassure potential residents and visitors that something was being done. The Perth City Council's report stated that the cameras were installed to address the 'perception of violence', to respond to the 'media hype', despite the fact that 'the real facts of the situation' were unknown (Iveson, 2000: 232). Other voices urged that the train system ought to be more strictly policed; and one suburban mayor called for parents to discourage their teenage children from catching the train to the city at all (Iveson, 2000: 232). Here is a case where a discourse of fear *creates* a problem which, in turn, marks certain urban bodies as undesirable, and as the target of policy intervention, and in so doing, no doubt goes some way towards producing the undesirable subjectivities which it fears. In the final section I want to tease out the common themes in these four examples of fear in the city and their implications for the practices of planning and urban management.

Conclusions

If urban political economy, in dealing with the material city, asks the question 'whose city?', in the sense of who gets what and where in the distribution of urban goods, services, and locational advantages, then the political economy of fear asks 'who's afraid of whom?' and where in the city is fear concentrated and acted out.

I have provided two lines of inquiry into the question of fear in the city, one sociological/social psychological, the other political economic, and I now want to suggest that these are mutually reinforcing. I also want to suggest that the existence of fear in the city is not a simple reflection of social reality but is a complicated production of that 'reality' through the power of discourse (from everyday talk to advertising, to official documents about the city). The social psychological reading in Part One suggests that the capacity to be drawn into urban fearing lives within us all: that we are all vulnerable to being unsettled by the presence of Others who are different. The political economic reading developed in Part Two suggests that such fears tend to be collectively mobilised as a response to historical moments of profound structural/social/cultural change. These moments or epochs produce urban transformations, re-shapings of the city which give rise to new contestations over whose city it is, who belongs where in the city, which groups are benefiting, which are being pushed out.

These contestations over the re-shaping of the city are in turn accompanied by and partially conducted through a discourse, actually by multiple and competing discourses, and these discourses seek to define who and what is to be feared in the process of change, and in so doing, to influence the management and direction of change in ways that privilege the rights of some at the expense of others, the sense of place of some at the expense of others, one group's homely imaginary at the expense of others. These discourses draw upon, even as they transcend, the material conditions that govern the realities and prospects of cities, and thereby they mediate among espoused values, future possibilities and current dilemmas. Discourses of fear function ideologically to shape our attention, to convey a comprehensible and compelling story of the fate of the city, and to provide reasons for how we should act in response to perceived problems (Beauregard, 1993: 8).

Discourses of fear are maps of a social reality perceived as problematic in moments when we are unsure what direction to take: whether to fight or flee, where and how to live, where to invest. The reality of city fear is always mediated by these discourses or representations of it. Portraying parts of cities as sites of physical and/or moral decay, of economic and/or social disorganisation, as places to avoid, has intended or implicit policy consequences – clearance, clean-up, redevelopment. Portraying certain groups in the city as people to be feared – blacks, gays, youths, the homeless, immigrant youths, Aborigines, Jews, and so on – also has intended policy consequences, from police sweeps, to increasing the hardware of surveillance, to defensive architectural and design practices. What is less explored, and therefore less clear, is that portraying certain groups as fear-inducing surely serves to some extent to produce the very behaviours that are dreaded, while also increasing the likelihood that such groups will be victimised (through hate crimes and/or official brutality) with relative impunity. Rising levels of police violence against minorities in the US, and against the poor in Sao Paulo, attest to this, as do increasingly harsh policies directed at the homeless in New York or Johannesburg, or 'youth' in many cities.

Discourses of fear, then, are potent: they have potency. One of our tasks, as urban intellectuals, is to deconstruct these discourses, and to provide counter-discourses. Official urban discourses (those produced by city councils, departments of planning, police departments, mainstream media) tend to legitimise and privilege the fears of the bourgeoisie, their fears of those Others who might invade or disrupt their homely spaces, their habitus. We rarely hear from those folks whom official discourse classifies as Other, about *their* fears: the fear, for example, of being hungry, homeless, jobless, of having no future in the city, of being unable to provide for one's children, the fear of not being accepted in a strange environment, the fear of police or citizen violence against them.[4]

If we accept that fear, like death and taxes, will always be with us, then we do need to think about how to manage fear in the city, but we need to think about this in a very different way than we have in the past, different from the Perth City Council, different from the Cape Town Council, different from the urban development industry in Sao Paulo or Johannesburg. Because those approaches are killing the city. The consequences of the totalising approach to managing fear include changes in the character of public space and of citizens' participation in public life. One of the most tangible threats to public culture, as Zukin has argued, comes from the politics (and discourses) of everyday fear (Zukin, 1995: 38). As urban public spaces have included more strangers – those who look and talk so differently that they are considered Others – those WASP Americans who used these public spaces before have abandoned them, leaving them to a generalised ethnic Other, a victim of the politics of fear. Anthropologist Merry (1981) concluded her study of 'urban danger' in Philadelphia by arguing that people tend to think Others are criminals; eventually, crime becomes a device, an idiom, for thinking about the Other. When public space is perceived as too dangerous to venture into, then the principle of open access, of a civic culture, is utterly destroyed. Johannesburg may be on the verge of such destruction as a city, as too is Sao Paulo, according to Caldeira (1999).

Among the conditions necessary for a modern democracy is that people acknowledge those from different social groups as co-citizens, that is, as people having similar rights. Cities which become increasingly enclaved are not environments which generate conditions conducive to a democratic way of life. The new urban socio-spatial segregations increase the difficulty of engaging a variety of social groups in political life, in which common goals and solutions would have to be negotiated.[5] This enclaving of the city builds on particular discourses of fear which seek to cleanse and purify the city as a moral order, as well as to make the city safe for consumption, and so to protect the economic order. Rather than being swept under the carpet as undiscussable, or tackled as an issue of increasing urban fortification, urban fears need to be *communicated and negotiated* if we are to keep alive the idea of the city as a vital public sphere.[6] And urban inequalities need to be addressed directly, rather than through policies of enclaving, spatial containment and law and order, if poverty-induced crime is not to produce the new walled cities of the twenty-first century.

Notes

1   Many thanks to Bob Beauregard and John Friedmann for comments on earlier drafts.
2   Phil Harrison, 'The role of planners in shaping urban spaces', Urban Futures Conference, Johannesburg, July 2000.
3   Here I'm gratefully drawing on PhD research by Antje Nahnsen of Carl von Ossietzky University in Germany, as presented at the Urban Futures Conference in Johannesburg, 10-14 July 2000.
4   At a workshop that I was involved in at the University of Iowa in June 2000 on the social sustainability of American cities, one participant, a private detective who works in Oakland, described the fear displayed by tough kids from very tough neighbourhoods, once they are outside their own turf. They are very aware of being perceived as 'alien' and as threatening, and therefore of the likelihood of attracting 'preemptive violence', or of being stopped by police 'for being black while driving a car' (Barthels, 2000).
5   For a more hopeful story from Brazil, see Abers (2000), who describes just such an approach, under the leadership of the Workers Party, in the Brazilian city of Porto Alegre, specifically its participatory municipal budget process.
6   See Sandercock (2000) for an extended discussion of such dialogical/therapeutic approaches to resolving conflicting fears and desires in the city.

References

Abers, R. (2000) *Inventing Local Democracy: grassroots politics in Brazil*, Boulder, Colorado, Lynne Rienner Publishers.
Barthels, J. (2000) 'The meanest streets, Or wake up, Muggles!', paper presented at the Oberman Institute for Advanced Studies, University of Iowa, June, Symposium on Stories and Storytelling and the Sustainability of America's Cities.

Beauregard, R. (1993) *Voices of Decline: the postwar fate of US cities*, Cambridge, Blackwell.
Beck, U. (1998) *Democracy Without Enemies*, Cambridge, Polity Press.
Bodie-Gendrot, S. (2000) *The Social Control of Cities?*, Cambridge, Blackwell.
Caldeira, T. (1999) 'Fortified enclaves: the new urban segregation', in J. Holston (ed.) *Cities and Citizenship*, Durham, Duke University Press.
Davis, M. (1990) *City of Quartz*, London, Verso.
Ellin, N. (ed.) (1997) *Architecture of Fear*, Princeton, Princeton University Press.
Hage, G. (1998) *White Nation: fantasies of white supremacy in a multicultural society*, Sydney, Pluto Press.
Iveson, K. (2000) 'Beyond designer diversity', *Urban Policy and Research*, 18, 2, 219-238.
Kristeva, J. (1991) *Strangers to Ourselves*, (Trans. Leon S. Roudiez.) New York, Columbia University Press.
Merry, S. (1981) *Urban Danger: life in a neighbourhood of strangers*, Philadelphia, Temple University Press.
Park, R. (1967) *On Social Control and Collective Behaviour*, Chicago, University of Chicago Press.
Robins, K. (1995) 'Collective emotion and urban culture', in P. Healey, S. Cameron, S. Davoudi, S. Graham and A. Madani-Pour (eds) *Managing cities. The new urban context*, Chichester: John Wiley and Sons.
Rotella, C. (1998) *October Cities*, Berkeley, University of California Press.
Sandercock, L. (2000) 'When strangers become neighbours: managing cities of difference', *Planning Theory and Practice*, 1,1, 13-30.
Sassen, S. (2000) 'Globalization and telecommunications', *Urban Forum*, 11, 2, 185-200.
Sennett, R. (1990) *The Conscience of the Eye*, New York, Norton.
Young, I.M. (1990) *Justice and the Politics of Difference*, Princeton, Princeton University Press.
Zukin, S. (1995) *The Cultures of Cities*, Cambridge, MA, Blackwell.

12 Spectral Cities: Where the Repressed Returns and Other Short Stories

STEVE PILE

Ghosts of the living and dead alike, of both individual and collective spirits, of both other selves and our own selves, haunt the places of our lives (Michael M. Bell, 1997: 813).

The experience of ghosts in particular places, whether these ghosts be sacred or profane, individual or collective, dead or alive, mine or yours, human or animal, past or present or future, is not happenstance. Ghosts have good reasons to haunt the specific places they do (Michael M. Bell, 1997: 831).

The ghost is not simply a dead or a missing person, but a social figure, and investigating it can lead to that dense site where history and subjectivity make social life. The ghost or the apparition is one form by which something lost, or barely visible, or seemingly not there to our supposedly well-trained eyes, makes itself known or apparent to us, in its own way, of course. The way of the ghost is haunting, and haunting is a very particular way of knowing what has happened or is happening. Being haunted draws us affectively, sometimes against our will and always a bit magically, into the structure of feeling of a reality we come to experience, not as cold knowledge, but as a transformative recognition (Avery Gordon, 1997: 8).

Mood is everything (Michael Taussig, 1997: 145 and 188).

Introduction: A Sense of Place

It is sometimes unfair to cite 'private' documents, such as book proposals. However, I hope the editors won't mind if I risk being unfair in this instance. Jean Hillier clearly set the tone for this volume when she wrote:

Habitus: A Sense of Place

> Habitus is loosely concerned with the social sense of place. It is a concept developed by the French philosopher, Pierre Bourdieu, as 'a sense of place [...] a sense of the other's place'.

In this chapter, I would like to loosen this sense of place – and of a sense of the other's place – enough to incorporate a sense of the spectrality of places. By this, I do not simply mean that places have a ghostliness to them, although places clearly are ghostly in many ways.[1] I am more interested in the entanglements of place and affect; and, therefore, in what ghosts can tell us about the role of affect in social senses of place – and about other senses of place, and other senses of the other's place. The agenda of this chapter is to install affect at the heart of what we might refer to as habitus. This is to argue strongly, in other words, that we cannot understand social senses of space unless there is a place for feelings, emotions and affect.

In this chapter, I will focus on ghosts and cities to allow me to talk about the ways in which feelings such as anxiety, fear, trauma, wounding, dread, fright, grief, mourning and melancholia are active constituents in the production of cities (as spaces and places). Before going on, I must make the parameters of this argument clear. I am not saying that ghosts are the only ways to talk about these feelings, emotions and affects. Even less am I saying that these are the only feelings, emotions and affects worth talking about or exploring. Nor am I arguing that these other feelings, emotions and affects might not 'haunt' the city in some way: I can see, for example, that cities might be haunted by pleasures past, present and future. These intriguing ideas will be set aside, however, in order to focus on that structure of feelings, emotions and affects that ghosts call forth, and symbolise.

There is another aspect to this argument about the entanglement between affect and sense of place – and this is to do with the spectrality of the city. In other words, I am interested in exploring a particular affect (ghostliness) in relation to particular places (cities). However, thinking about the relationship between ghosts and cities does raise some awkward questions. In the first place, can we think of cities as haunting people? It is, perhaps, easier to see how ghosts might haunt cities: imagine, for example, of all the ways people in cities might be haunted. However, I would like to speculate that cities do indeed haunt people. This might be harder to establish: cities are simply passive backdrops to social life, aren't they? Perhaps not. I have always been struck by the way in which very large buildings (of the kind that only cities can sustain) – whether we know what they're for or mean – inspire in people a sense of awe or wonder. If such buildings can make people feel – whatever the variety of such reactions – then what of cities? I would like to pursue this question by exploring how it is that cities themselves might produce certain affects – specifically, in this chapter, how they might produce a sense that places (and spaces) are haunted.

To allow me space to explore these issues, I will not go into the concept of habitus here, partly also because this has already been examined in detail in this volume: see, instead, the introductory chapter by Jean Hillier and Emma Rooksby, chapter 1 by Pierre Bourdieu and chapter 17 by John Friedmann. Another synergy exists, within this book, between some arguments presented here and the discussion of the relationship between fear and city life in Leonie Sandercock's chapter (this volume). In particular, Sandercock draws on Freud's notion of the uncanny – an idea which implicitly informs the analysis of ghosts presented here.[2]

Now, let me begin this task of conjuring up the ghosts of city life with an everyday story of London folk: for there are ghosts in this story; ghosts that speak of the return of fear to the city, and also of other stories.

Fear Returns: London, 20 September 2000

According to 'anti-terrorist' officers, at 10.46pm on Wednesday 20 September 2000, there were reports of a blast at Vauxhall Cross, on the south bank of the Thames, in the vicinity of a spectacular building (see Figure 12.1 for an account of this eye-catching building, see Pile, 2001). Other official police sources indicated that the blast (only one) could have been a bomb. Informally, ordinary police officers were pointing to the damage high up on the side of a conspicuous office block and, not unreasonably, speculating that something might have been fired at, and hit, it.

The news media (press and television) were less circumspect about what had happened and whom it had happened to. After the official statements, they reported eye-witness statements. While there was not agreement about the time – some putting it as early as 9.45pm, others certain it was more like 9.55pm – they all agreed that there were two explosions: the sound of one running into the other. Photographs of the damage were included: a small hole could clearly be seen below an office window on the eighth floor of the building. The building was now clearly recognisable as 85 Albert Embankment, Vauxhall Cross. The conclusion was clear: there had been a terrorist attack on the building. It was speculated that the terrorists had used a 'barrack buster' mortar to fire two missiles. It was added, as a matter of fact, that the target was the headquarters of the British Secret Intelligence Service. It was popularly concluded that the 'Real' IRA had attacked 'MI6 headquarters': an obvious target.

238 *Habitus: A Sense of Place*

Figure 12.1 The Office Block at 85 Albert Embankment, Vauxhall Cross

It matters, of course, which secret intelligence service was attacked. Officially, only MI5 exists.[3] MI5 is tasked with countering threats to national security: their remit has been extended since the end of the Cold War beyond counter-espionage to include combating 'terrorism' (mainly the IRA), the drug trade and other threats.[4] However, this was not their headquarters. The building, matter of factly, is home to MI6. Now, if MI5 is about spy-catching, then MI6 is about spying – not something governments generally own up to, and the British Government is no exception. MI6 agents are recruited to infiltrate foreign groups and governments that are perceived as a threat to national security. After the Cold War, this remit has also been extended – extended, in particular, to cover the IRA (and other terrorist groups). In the press reports, significantly, it was MI6's role, alongside MI5, in countering the Irish terrorism that was highlighted – thereby casting a long dark shadow over MI6's main responsibility for spying activities outside the United Kingdom.

It is this sense that two secret organisations were involved in this murderous 'cry for freedom' that makes me suspicious that something ghostly was going on. On that fateful night, I would like to speculate that what could be seen was the life-after-death of two ghosts, still slugging it out. A dead and deadly war is still being conducted – in the heart of London, within sight of the Houses of Parliament.[5] Ghosts? Fighting a dead war? We can think of it like this: after the Cold War, after the peace process, we might imagine this particular anti-colonial struggle would be an anachronism. The attack, in this sense, was a real blast from the past. So, here we are, at the intersection of past, present and future; but also, in the presence of not-present and not-absent entities – in the presence, that is, of two ghostly figures: the first embodied in the Irish Republican Army (provisional, real or otherwise); the second comes under the popular name of 'spooks'. Let's look to the ghostly IRA first.

Though the news media could not be sure whether it was the IRA, provisional or real, that had done it – since there had been no word on the matter from any 'official' source, IRA or not – the ghosts of IRA attacks past, present and future readily gathered at Vauxhall Cross. Recent attacks within London were listed as 'evidence' that this was the work of Irish dissidents. There was, for example, the (successfully detonated) bomb at Hammersmith Bridge in June 2000 and the (unexploded) bomb at Ealing Broadway tube station on 19 July 2000 (which disrupted celebrations of the Queen Mother's centenary). Unsurprisingly, fears were expressed that this marked the start of a mainland bombing campaign, especially in the lead-up to Christmas. So, not only IRA ghosts (provisional and real) became visible at the bomb site – the kinds of ghosts who can lay explosives, but are never seen, and are certainly never captured – but also the ghosts of IRA victims began to gather. For London has often been witness to the pain and grief of acts of terror. And London is haunted by those who have died, or been wounded, as in the most dreadful of recent attacks:

- the Hyde Park bombing of 20 July 1982 that killed eleven soldiers and 50 others;
- the Harrods bomb that killed six and wounded 90;
- the huge explosion that rocked the City of London on 10 April 1992, killing three;
- the Bishopgate attack of 24 April 1993, where a truck was used, killing one and injuring 44;
- the bomb on Canary Wharf in London's prestigious Docklands on 6 February 1996 that ended the provisional IRA's cease-fire by killing two people.

Twenty-three ghosts to add to the living ghosts of the Real IRA: 'ghosts', because the peace process was supposed to kill off the armed resistance to British colonialism in Northern Ireland; but these ghosts are real, the past will not be buried (even by the painful process of peace). Ghosts living and dead told of the pain and grief that cities – or cities like

London – hold close to their hearts. More than this, this is also about the city and city-ways. For, alongside the terror and grief, there is also a story of ordinary indifference, of calm curiosity and of people choosing just to get on with their lives. For the eye witnesses seemed relatively untroubled: their reports were calm, many simply keen to see what had happened and to learn what had caused the two loud bangs that they had heard (they were really ear witnesses, for they hadn't actually seen anything!).

By mid-November, stronger fears of yet another IRA Christmas bombing campaign were being expressed. This time, ironically, in the wake of better news from the security services. On Sunday 12 November, according to official sources, a plot to detonate a 500-pound bomb (somewhere) had been foiled. The huge bomb was comprised of nuts and bolts wrapped around an explosive core made of fertiliser. Once again, the spectre of the IRA had returned to London. The bomb was similar in size to the one that had rocked Canary Wharf and – despite the fact that it was also of similar size to the Omagh bomb that had killed 29 people in 1998 – it was immediately assumed that the bomb was destined for a prestige target in London and, moreover, because of its size, that the (Real) IRA's intention was to kill as many people as possible. To bolster this assumption, it was also speculated that the explosive device would travel by a route similar to that used to attack Canary Wharf. There's an agitation to London's ghosts now: accounts of the present were being ordered around the presumed motivations, methods and outcomes of past deeds (and supposed futures). There is reason to fear ghosts, for they were looked after in neither life nor death.

On Saturday 25 November, in news that both confirmed and allayed fears, the discovery of an arms cache in Londonderry was announced. The Sunday papers carried warnings of a terrorist offensive. By Monday, television news programmes were carrying the official message – be afraid. Londoners, meanwhile, were far more concerned about train derailments, delays on the tube and a climate of violence in its poorest housing estates (especially in the wake of a series of child murders). The ghosts of the (Real) IRA needed to be mobilised, it seems, by both the terrorists/freedom-fighters and the authorities. Whatever: London has become accustomed to its ghosts, for it is home to more ghosts than those of its Irish colonial past. For London has been witness to killings that have raised other spectres from its imperial legacy. In recent years, the conflicts between Pakistan and India, between Palestine and Israel, between the Muslim-world and the Western-world have led to violence on the streets of London.

Far from it being obvious that it was the Real IRA that had attacked MI6, London can gather in many other people wishing to use it as a place to find justice for their dead. Perhaps other people's spooks had spooked the spooks? Of course, everyone 'knows' about MI6 spooks and their Thames-side haunt. Thus, for example, despite a British Government ban on filming the exterior of the Vauxhall Cross offices, James Bond is seen launching a power boat from the MI6 HQ in the 1999 movie, *The World is Not Enough*. In fact, Vauxhall Cross had already appeared in a previous Bond movie, *Goldeneye* (1995), and in Patrick Keiller's film, *London* (1994). MI6, in fact, have a dramatic structure for their headquarters – easily one of the most prominent of all the buildings on the Albert Embankment, on the south side of the Thames. Of course, the building itself attracted controversy at the time – not simply because it was so obvious a place for the British secret service, but also for its high cost. Much of this cost, it was assumed at the time was due to the high security requirements, including not just anti-surveillance and bomb-proofing but also deep shelters within. These secret security added-extras, apparently, did not deter the Real IRA, nor did they help catch the attackers. So much for Mr Bond.

Indeed, as far as Bond stories go, this wouldn't make the grade: there were no heroes and no villains, and no world-class bad guys got their come-uppance. Instead, the two sets of ghosts seem to have slid past each other, each with barely a scratch. Indeed, these two ghosts seem more concerned with appearing in public than with actually defeating one another. For the IRA, MI5 would seem to be the better target, militarily. After all, it is MI5 that is most directly involved in anti-terrorist operations against the IRA, provisional or real. However, their offices are more scattered (and also more secret and, therefore, less easy to attack or likely to gain much publicity). MI6, though they do not exist, stand out like a sore thumb. It was an obvious propaganda target – an unmissable office block, that is lit up at night like an elaborate Christmas tree – how could they miss? Ghosts are, as we can see, all about show. Ghosts are also about disappearance: the spooks, in this story, were never really there. Officially, there is no MI6. Therefore, officially, the attack was launched at no-one – and there is, therefore, no 'official' reason to attack that lovely building and its anonymous workers.[6] Suddenly, the real (whether IRA or official) shimmers as if a ghost had walked across the city, in front of our very eyes.

So, now we can begin to outline some of the ghostly presences in the city: we have terrorists, freedom-fighters and victims; 'foreigners', locals and Londoners; spies, the police and official sources; commuters, eyewitnesses and residents; news reporters and film-makers – and an audience ('us' city-dwellers). But, as I said, I am interested in the way (these) ghosts might reveal something about people's senses of place – about the way affect is woven into the fabric of place; part and parcel of the processes that produce places as places. To be sure, violence and trauma –

whoever is the perpetrator – exist outside the city, whether London or any other city. Indeed, we can also observe that such events only touch small parts of cities. Nevertheless, it can be argued that cities haunt people differently than other places. What this means, of course, warrants further investigation – and I will be able to say more about how cities haunt people in the next section – but it is possible to make some preliminary observations based on the stories we have already heard.

The assault on 85 Albert Embankment demonstrates how cities (as places) become dense sites of history and subjectivity, where people make public their political demands, symbolically and sometimes violently. It also tells us something of the ghosts that violent events set loose on the world, and the ways these ghosts intensify the feelings and emotions which underpin our understanding of those events. These ghosts, moreover, do not simply go away once the catastrophe is over: they hang around, haunting the places where they made their appearance. Ghosts, then, live after, amongst us, all the time. Cities, to this extent, are places where ghosts gather. And it is this density of ghosts that hints at the urbanity – or cityness – of these events.

The city haunts, then, because it gathers ghosts both in greater numbers of ghosts and in a wider variety than elsewhere. There is more to it. The city also commemorates those ghosts in more intense ways, in part by making the dead endure in its physical architecture, and in part by juxtaposing the dead and putting them into relation with one another. London, of course, has its fair share of actual memorials (with more being added all the time: see also Kerr, 2001), but each new trauma creates a vernacular sacred architecture capable of calling forth the dead. It is not simply headline events at landmark buildings that do this: every now and then road-sides sprout sad bunches of flowers – and those who pass by know someone has passed on. Cities haunt, then, at least in the sense that they force us to recognise the lives of those who have gone (before). In this sense, the physicality of the city itself shimmers as it becomes a flexible and durable place of memory (see also Curtis, 2001).

London does not just house the dead, its dead crowd its streets. For the most part, however, few pay them any attention. Cities are not just places where ghosts can gather, intensely, spookily, they are also places of grieving and forgetting, where the ordinary violences of everyday life are simply lived through. Simmel, of course, caught something of this in his study of the city and mentality (1903). However, we can also perceive aspects of this in the accounts of the attack on MI6. The newspapers were full of stories from bystanders, revealing people's indifference to trauma and of their feelings of safety; something also of people's curiosity and in their willingness to see something that could not be seen; something too of

Schadenfreude, of the desire to witness the trauma, without experiencing its consequences. If anything, then, the city is a place of work for grief and also mourning – of the collection and the dispersal of feelings of dread and fear; of the pleasure-in-danger and danger-in-pleasure of the streets.

Cities, if they are ghostly places, are thoroughly ambivalent places: constitutively, and dynamically, ambivalent. What might this involve? Certainly, cities 'accommodate' affect, but the sense of entanglement, between pasts, presents and futures, between the living and the dead, between bodies and souls, between spirits, implies more than this: more than about the coexistence of different affects; more than about the production of spaces for the full range of human affect; so, it is more about the entanglement of opposing and interplaying affects; more about the entanglement between affect and physical space; more about the city as an intense site for the spectral gathering of affects. Even if this makes sense, puzzles remain. It is easy enough, I think, to see how certain feelings – and their ghostly presences – might appear in cities. Of course, people feel things and if those people are in cities, then they are going to feel them there. And, just as surely, cities might make people feel things: all those strangers, all those dark alleyways, and all those stories of violence (see Sandercock, this volume). But this hardly means that cities are ghostly – and it certainly doesn't mean that we have a sixth sense in our encounters with places, does it?

The Dead and the Life of the City: The Sixth Sense of Place and the Return of the Repressed

Starring Bruce Willis (as Dr Malcolm Crowe, a child psychologist) and Haley Joel Osment (as Cole Sear, a very disturbed little boy), *Sixth Sense* (written and directed by M. Night Shyamalan) was one of the most successful films of 1999. This is one of those movies that relies on the kind of plot twist that makes you replay the movie and re-think the entire plot. Its popularity had much to do with the 'mysterious and unforeseen consequences' that the blurb on the back of the retail video-tape talks about. For most people, this was a successful movie: for them, the twist was both mysterious and unforeseeable. The film is a supernatural chiller, focused initially on Dr Crowe's attempts to learn what is disturbing the boy by winning his trust, and then on his strategy for exorcising Cole's ghosts. In the final few scenes, the true ghost is revealed – not just to the ghost itself, but at the same time to the audience. There are many creepy moments in the movie, usually associated with the uncanny affect associated with haunted children (and haunted children's spaces and times).[7] However, the twist at the end seems to rely on a different kind of creepiness; one that seems to have something to do with the identification of the audience with the desires and motivations of the ghost. The film itself remains true throughout to the emotional perspective of each of the characters: in many ways, 'we' are meant to see through 'their' eyes – feeling Cole's world as he feels it; feeling the discovery of the truth at the moment the character discovers it. The audience, it might be further speculated, is 'creeped out' when it discovers its identification with the project and unfinished business of the dead (perhaps because this is something we already know to be true).

From the beginning of the movie, the plot twist seems to involve the question of whether Cole (the child) can see ghosts or not and, therefore, whether he is suffering from a mixture of visual hallucinations, paranoia, schizophrenia and other kinds of emotional disorder. Though Cole seems to have every psychological disorder under the sun, the potential accuracy of the diagnosis is emphasised by Dr Crowe's status as an award-winning child psychologist. The question of Cole Sear's ability to be a seer[8] of the dead, however, is dissipated. Not only do we see ghosts as Cole sees them, but we also see the physical impact of ghosts on Cole's body. So, if Cole can see ghosts, then the question becomes whether Dr Crowe is himself a ghost – and this is the central concern of the plot twist.

Amazingly, after Cole has fainted and ended up in hospital, the film makes it very clear that the ghost is indeed Dr Crowe. The clue is transparent (perhaps too transparent, the film-makers worried). As a result of ending up in hospital, traumatised, Cole chooses to tell Dr Crowe his dark secret. Cole then tells Dr Crowe that he sees dead people, and that these dead people walk around like regular people, not realising they are dead because they see only what they want to see. During this 'confession', the camera fixes unblinkingly on the face of Dr Crowe. The message is unambiguous: Dr Crowe is a ghost, but he does not (yet) know it because he sees only what he wants to see.

What interests me is how most people were able to suspend their disbelief long enough to be thrown by the plot twist. In many ways, the film is constructed to 'fool' people: Dr Crowe is placed alongside living characters, such as Cole's mother and Dr Crowe's grieving wife, to suggest that he is as alive as they are. Here is an effective demonstration of how the mere juxtaposition of people is enough to convey interaction between people. This cunning, I think, is not the end of the story, however. The fact is that the lack of interaction between Dr Crowe and the other characters should itself have been a clue, so the question becomes why it is not. The answer to this question, I would argue, has a lot to do with what 'we' (unconsciously) 'know' about cities and city life. Let us take a closer look at the cityness of *Sixth Sense*.

The film clearly situates itself in the city – not just any old city, but a particularly old American city: Philadelphia. A caption informs the audience that, in a gesture that works as much to locate as to authenticate, the story will unfold in South Philadelphia. We see Dr Crowe going over some case notes, about a patient with severe emotional problems. The street is quiet, and cold, there are few people around. Exactly as we would expect, no-one is paying any attention to Dr Crowe. Then, as Cole leaves his house, running, frightened, to a church, Dr Crowe follows. We are not surprised when no-one takes any notice, either of the boy or the man following him. The streets are emptied of both people and traffic. The church itself is seemingly empty, as Dr Crowe makes his first contact with the haunted child. Throughout the film, the street scenes appear cold and empty. In this sense, there are no 'eyes on the streets' – as Jane Jacobs might observe (1961), the contemporary American city is dead and deathly. There is no-one to, or who would, notice – let alone stop – a stranger following a frightened boy;[9] or, more in keeping with the film's reality, no-one to help a small boy apparently talking to himself, as if deep in a conversation with someone else. The streets, far from being places of mixing and meeting between people, are evacuated of human contact (as Simmel might have recognised, 1903) – evacuated, that is, except, ironically, for that between the living and the dead.

The choice of Philadelphia as the location for the story is no accident. One of the characters in the film, the schoolteacher 'Stuttering Stan', explains:

> Philadelphia is one of the oldest cities in the country. A lot of its generations have lived here and died here. Almost any place you go in this city has a history and a story behind it. Even this school and the grounds it sits on.

He goes on to ask whether anyone can guess what the school buildings were 100 years ago. Cole answers that they hanged people there. The teacher becomes annoyed: this was a place where laws were made, where law-makers gathered; where the very rule of law began in America. Cole is adamant: it was a courthouse, in which people were tried and hanged.[10] Of course, the point is clear: there are many stories behind any place you go in the city – and some of those stories are about violence and death, even at the hands of the law-makers. Cities, then, are places – and have places within them – that have a shadowy density about them.

246 *Habitus: A Sense of Place*

Visually, the film itself makes great use of shadows to convey this otherworldliness; this underlay of death, grief and trauma that pervades – but is actively forgotten in – the course of city life. Indeed, some of the ways in which Dr Crowe is misrecognised as living have to do with this forgotten deathliness of city interactions. I would suggest that it is no surprise that Dr Crowe might travel by bus and yet not have to interact with anyone; nor that Dr Crowe would have to interact with anyone at a funeral – because the city's unnoticed strangers are everywhere; and everywhere forgotten. What this suggests is that city life is made and remade in the context of an everyday forgetting and the ordinary misrecognition of people by people. Now, it would be easy to think that these were inevitably bad things – the studied indifference and cynicism of the urban dweller – yet what becomes apparent is that these are also part of the ways in which people deal with the troubles and griefs of their lives and in the lives of those around them. Because, and this is the problem, in any city reminders of death and strife are all around.

Figure 12.2 **City of the Dead: St Louis Cemetery No. 1, New Orleans.**

The city itself has its own ghostliness: the light and stones of the city embodying lost souls. Some sequences in *Sixth Sense* seem to bring statues to life: their seemingly timeless bodies seem to grieve, seem to smile, seem to have a life of their own. And Cole shivers and turns away as he goes past a cemetery. Now, of course, modern city dwellers are more careful about their dead: they are segregated from the living, placed in 'slumber villages' outside the city or cremated and potted like eternal plants. Every city has its own different relation to the dead (for example, see Roach, 1996, on New Orleans: see Figure 12.2). Nevertheless, as *Sixth Sense* implies, the city's dead are always liable to return. For ghosts, as Derrida points out, begin by returning (1993, pages 10-11). Indeed, this is what ghosts do, they return. In the case of *Sixth Sense*, they return for help from the living; to help settle their unfinished business.

However, the dead can return in other ways too.[11] Sometimes, this has something to do with the return of the repressed – and, to exemplify this, I would like to turn to another 1999 film, *Bringing out the Dead*. Instead of looking at the narrative structure of the film, however, I will examine two moments, in the original book, when the dead are most present. *Bringing out the Dead* (1998) was written by Joe Connelly, who spent nine months as a medic at St. Clare's Hospital in New York City. The story concerns a paramedic, called Frank Pierce, who is working in New York's Hell's Kitchen. Frank, it might be said, is on the edge of a breakdown: running on alcohol and pills to keep at bay the grief, dread, fear, trauma and guilt he feels; he is also seeing ghosts. Frank, moreover, is ready to give up the ghost precisely because he is so haunted; haunted in particular by Rose, the ghost of someone he feels that he killed.

Early on in the book, Frank's 'special relationship' to the dead is graphically presented. He and his partner, Larry, attend an emergency to find an old man, apparently dead, surrounded by his distressed family. The two paramedics immediately prepare to revive Mr Burke. As Frank opens Mr Burke's mouth, he feels a cool breath of air on his fingers:

> I'm sure it was just gas built up in the stomach from CPR, but in the last year I had come to believe in such things as spirits leaving the body and not wanting to be put back, spirits angry at the awkward places death had left them, and though I understood how crazy I was to think this way, I was also convinced that if I looked up at that moment I would see the dead man standing at the window, staring out over the tar-paper plots and gray ditches of his birthplace (page 3).

The sense that the dead haunt the living pervades the story. In the end, Frank will 'help' Mr Burke's spirit to leave his body, so that his spirit will not be angry and resentful at being kept in the pain of intensive care. However, Frank's belief in spirits begins with his failure to help Rose. Her death haunts the other deaths in the book: it haunts every emergency Frank attends; Rose haunts Frank, and she haunts the city; the city also haunts Frank. And it is this doubleness of haunting that I would like to dwell on a little further. The spirits of the dead become a part of the very fabric of the city, woven into its physicality, such that the sidewalk and stairs become spectral; attached, in some way, to the spirits of the spirits – like a shadow glued to the heel of reality. More than this, the living themselves carry around with them a double hauntedness: for they are also the not-yet-dead, and always in contact with death. Ghosts then are both alive and dead, such that the living become ultimately indistinguishable from the dead. As the story unfolds, we witness the jeopardy that results from this (never less than) double aspect – material and spectral; living and dead; present and absent; traumatised and numb; fearful and indifferent – of life in Frank's torn world.

Larry and Frank had taken a patient, Noël, to the Our Lady of Mercy ER. However, No. 1 was impatient and fled the hospital. While driving around, Frank glimpses No. 1 walking amongst the traffic, then a ghost arrives.

> In the mirror I watched Noël's green camouflage turn left into the yellow-lit ashes of Forty-fifth, and from that place a girl appeared, a teenager, tripping over her high heels as she walked toward me. I couldn't see her face, but I knew the yellow raincoat she wore, the black stockings with a hole in the knee where she fell down once because she couldn't breathe. It was Rose, the girl I had helped to kill. We all make mistakes, but some things cannot be forgiven [...] Rose was getting closer. Maybe it wasn't Rose [...] I crossed my arms on the steering wheel, and holding my breath I pressed my forehead on my hands until they were numb. One of the first things you learn on the job is how to block out the bad calls. In the same way that cops fence off a murder scene, you wall these memories up in the deepest cave in your brain. I used to be an expert, but lately I'd found some big holes (53).

Far from being safe in the caves, memories – bad memories – were perfectly capable of finding their way out into daylight, past the police lines. There would have to be escape routes, however. The sight of a yellow raincoat; a faceless girl; a street scene; a sound – almost anything could allow the ghosts safe passage out of the deep, fenced-off cave. The spirits are angry enough to keep returning, for returning is what they do. Apologies don't appease ghosts: they keep coming back.

> These spirits were part of the job. I always knew that. I had worked Hell's Kitchen for years, and it was impossible to pass a building that didn't hold the spirit of something: the eyes of an unloved corpse, the screams for some loved one. In the violent eruption of life that is death, all bodies leave their mark. You cannot be near the new dead without feeling it. I have seen even the quietest night passing fill a room the next morning with a dense fog of life's remains, and after the air has cleared, the mark lingers, in a pillow that never regains its shape or a stain on the wall that never comes clean (54).

The city bore the traces of trauma, indelibly. The city, moreover, cannot be cleansed of the remains of the dead. If it isn't bodies that leave their mark, then it is also the escaping spirit that fills rooms, looks back on a life departed. And the dead are as heterogeneous as the living ...

> What haunted me now was more savage: spirits born half finished, homicides, suicides, over-doses, and all the other victims, innocent or not, still grasping at lives so abruptly taken away. Rose's ghost was only the last and most visible of many who seemed to have come back solely to accuse me – of living and knowing, of being present at their deaths, as if I had witnessed an obscene humiliation for which they could never forgive me (55).

Frank is haunted, not just by Rose, but the angry accusations that ghosts make against the living. In Freud's discussion of ghosts, he describes the ways in which a belief in ghosts is associated with the sense that the dead are angry that they are no longer living. For Freud, ghosts represent the living's ambivalent relationship to the dead (see Freud, 1913: 92-93 and 107-122; see Freud, 1917, for a development of these themes). He describes the kinds of ritual practices that are involved in keeping the dead at a distance, and of appeasing the dead precisely so that they do not return to haunt the living. For Frank, however, there is no appeasing the dead. In New York City, the infrastructure to keep the dead at bay is at breaking point: everywhere the ghosts of the dead accuse the living, everywhere death is an injustice. And Frank knows he is not well, but the certain modern knowledge that ghosts are just tricks of the mind is not enough to keep the trauma and pain at bay:

> It was a sickness, of course, the mind playing tricks. That's what I told myself, for that was the only way out. I'd been down before and always come back, but never before had I been so closely tied to someone's death. There were times when Rose could look as real to me as Larry (55).

Cole, it would seem, is not the only person who sees dead people wandering around like regular people. Cole is not the only person who sees the dead standing at the window – looking in, accusingly, on life. It is not just that ghosts haunt people, in these tales, for both Cole and Frank are haunted by the city itself: by the souls that fill the very foundations of the city; by its monuments; by the remembrance of times past and future. The city haunts them because it gathers together so many ghosts, so many reasons to be haunted, so many accusations against the living. In both these tales of ghosts and the city, grief explodes like a bomb that shatters the immediate physicality of the city, that sends shock waves through the living, that leaves the traces of bodies in the softest and hardest parts of the city: in its pillows and in its monuments. The problem, then, is not so much that the dead return; more than about redressing the injustices and repressions of the past, it is also about creating a space for the return of the living.

Avery Gordon (see above) is right to suggest that the ghost is a social figure through which something lost or barely visible can be made to appear in front of our eyes. It is possible to read *Sixth Sense* and *Bringing out the Dead* in this light: through a sense of the loss of love or caring or understanding or recognition or reparation or forgiveness in the city, through the deathliness of life on the streets, through the ordinary indifference of city life. Gordon is right, also, to point out that ghostliness is an epistemology: a way of coming to know the traumas and violence that accompany life, even while they are not acknowledged (repressed or oppressed). The ghost, finally, is a way of bringing back these stories, of making the injustices of life walk amongst the living – a way of calling for justice. It is on this (most important) point that I wish to move towards a final word.

Finally ... Possessing Spirit(s)

The central accusation of the dead is one of justice: that they are no longer alive, that death itself is an injustice. The dead, however, are more than some general accusation that life is unfair: ghosts, as Michael Bell says (see above) have a reason to haunt – the injustice is palpable, specific. If the dead haunt cities; if cities haunt the living; if the living are caught up in death – then some work will need to be done with the dead, if there is to be justice amongst the living.

Justice for the living is intimately bound up with justice for the dead and for the not-yet-born: it is bound up with the present as it might have been, had there been justice for the dead; bound up, too, with the possibility of redemption for those yet to come.

So, when Richard Wilkes – a local first nations Australian, on whose land Perth (where the conference that spawned this book took place) now stands – welcomed the delegates to the country, he meant specifically to the land of his nation. It was an ambiguous welcome, though: for he reminded – and told – us, the audience, of the ways in which his nation and other first nation Australians had been massacred by white British settlers. He returned, again and again, to this theme of violence, ignorance and racism amongst the new arrival Australians (in the past and more recently): how they had spread diseases, pathologised, criminalised, marginalised, displaced and disappeared the first nations. Again and again, the conference hall would be populated by the ghosts of dead first nations peoples, arriving not just from Perth and its surrounds, but from all over Australia (on these issues, see Jacobs, 1996, Gelder and Jacobs, 1998, and, Shaw, 2001) ... and even from the rest of Empire (for this was not an unfamiliar tale of colonial conquest and settlement), including the United States (where the expression 'First Nations' has also been used). For Richard Wilkes, then, calling on the ghosts of the pasts is a way of naming and shaming contemporary Australia: of marking a possession that has been dispossessed;[12] of claiming the right to claim possession of a land that has been taken away from them.

Such claims are not confined to post-colonial nations. The life-after and after-life of colonialism continues to return to the heart of Empire: London. When the Real IRA fired missiles from a Russian-made RPG-22 rocket-launcher at MI6 headquarters, they were also making a claim for the possessions of the dispossessed. They also fired a time-space weapon: the then-and-there exploding, somewhat (un)spectacularly, over the here-and-now. Ghosts, then, can easily be recognised as possessing a world that they do not have. Therefore, as Avery Gordon (see above) suggests, a haunting calls forth the emotional truth of the situation: the spirits rise in the act of politics. Transformation (as the future), then, requires an attuning and adjustment to the feelings and affects of the present and the past, in search of a way of appeasing and giving justice to the accusing dead, in search of a form of justice that does not put the not-yet-born through the same injustices.

But cities are awkward places for justice to thrive in these terms: with so many ghosts, would there be space left for the living? Can Perth simply give the land back? Richard Wilkes wondered as much, even joked about it, suggesting that his people might rent the city back to the new nations Australians at a fair price! Could London simply disavow its imperial connections? London is now the heart of a 'post-colonial Empire' and does not control or own territory (even Northern Ireland) in (exactly) the same way. When the Real IRA attacks Londoners, it attacks a multicultural, cosmopolitan and heterogeneous population that is as likely to respond to events in Jerusalem or Lahore or Amritsar as in Belfast or Dublin or even Windsor. Through many and variable routes, cities gather together ghosts, all with claims on the living. If there are to be democratic ways of acknowledging ghosts, then, there also have to be ways of acknowledging that the haunting affect of ghosts may not let us bury the dead and move on; even less, because of the desire to use the dead politically, will the dead be allowed to bury the dead.

The key question, then, is how to exorcise the city's ghosts, but without losing sight of their accusations of injustice, both past, present and future – lest the ghosts and spooks bury us! In his work on grieving, Freud was clear to draw a distinction between mourning and melancholia. In mourning, 'reality-testing' confirms that there has been a loss and that loss is gradually recognised and new attachments are formed (as attachments to the loss are gradually abandoned). In melancholia, the grief turns inwards and begins to take over: as the loss is internalised and there is a strong identification with the loss itself. Whatever one might make of such a distinction,[13] it does suggest the necessity for a more and less ambivalent relationship to ghosts. To deal with their traumas and injustices, cities – as they have always done – will be machines that produce, and work on, social forms of memory and grief. Cities, then, will have to both accommodate their ghosts, and also help some ghosts disappear into the past. Grieving cities will cherish the dead, mourn the dead, and, in their wake, leave them behind and be full of life (with all its pleasures and woes, conflicts and alliances).

Cities, themselves, have their places of melancholia: their statues and churches, places where the dead cast their shadow over the living. Indeed, the Real IRA did their best to make their other-worldly shadow darken the lives of Londoners. On the other hand, if there is to be a democracy in which there is justice amongst the living and the dead, then the threat of death and violence should give way to appropriate expressions of grief and injustice. There are no proper amounts of ghosts, and it may not be good enough (or possible) to exorcise ghosts from city life, but there must be better ways to accommodate all the ghosts that cities bring together – and possess – in the pursuit of a better city life. And perhaps this would be as much a grief process as a peace process. Otherwise, it will be the spooks that take possession of city life.

Postscript

Habitus, it is often said in this volume, is a set of predispositions. Predispositions that are practical, structured, markers of distinction.

Predispositions like those in handwriting, or in force of habit. I still wonder whether these predispositions extend to examples such as mood – the predisposition to feeling a range of emotions and feelings. Does habitus have an emotional 'field'? I continue to suspect that introducing the emotional, the fantastic, the phantasmatic into discussions of habitus has a troubling effect. What if we think of habit as being ghostly, as a haunting of the body by the past? Is the habit of habitus still in the same place if it is haunted, haunting?

On 11 September 2004, the city of New York once again lit The Tribute in Light: two twin towers of light, beamed into the heavens as if marking the route taken by the lost souls of 9/11 2001. Pictures of The Tribute in Light showed the beams dispersing through the rain clouds above, as if it were the clouds produced by an explosion, high in the sky. Meanwhile, outside the American Embassy in London, 67 white roses were laid to commemorate the British victims and a wreath laid in the memorial garden to honour all the dead. (All, I assume, except the terrorists themselves.)

It is possible that the concept of habitus can be extended to incorporate the structure of feeling of New York, before or after 9/11. But it is a crude term, for New York has no one single mood; 9/11 does not evoke a set of predispositions towards a narrow range of emotions and feelings. Indeed, quite the opposite: it seems to intensify very different, sometimes antagonistic, feelings. Anger. Sadness. Hope. Anxiety. Resolve. Loss. Bewilderment. All and none of these. They have just begun to build on the site (Figure 12.3), the proposed Freedom Tower's 1776 marking in feet the year America freed itself from British colonial rule (see Huyssen, 2003 and Sorkin, 2003). The site of such tragedy converted into something quite else. Freedom. Redemption (Figure 12.4).

Yet, New York remains haunted by the events of 9/11, and this matters. Three points. First: at the moment, the towers are ever-present in New York, but only through their absence. Postcards and maps confirm the location of where the towers used to be. Meanwhile, the sky seems emptier, as if a vacuum existed downtown. Second: New York's self-assured position as the world's premier city is now marked forever by a vulnerability, for the world knows where New York is and how easy it is to attack it. New York is a spectral city, haunted not just by past deeds, but by the terror yet to come. Third: New York also haunts the world. Then there was Bali and Madrid. When will it be London's turn? All the while, people die in Israel and Palestine, in Afghanistan and Iraq. When will something even worse happen? The fingers of terror that stretched from the Middle East to the eastern seaboard now draw other parts of the world into its deadly grip.

254 *Habitus: A Sense of Place*

Figure 12.3   Ground Zero: the Widowed Building Looks Down on Lost Ground

Figure 12.4   The Rebuilding Continues

Yet, these points seem to cut across the idea of habitus. Habitus seems to be about what is done, yet these hauntings seem to be about absence, the impractical, the not-done. Habitus defines a field, yet there is no one 'field' of New York that produces a repertoire of social reproduction; instead social reproduction and change seem to be better associated with circulations of various kinds: money, people, ideas, commodities, information ... emotions, fantasies ... terror. And New York itself moves through the world, occasionally appearing, like a ghost, in other places: clanking and wailing, as if warning of an indiscernible, yet frighteningly close, horror.

To understand the haunting of New York means honouring its grief, and tracking its ghosts. For these ghosts of New York – the ghost of New York – now haunt global geopolitics. The dead have not been allowed to bury the dead. Instead, there are simply more dead. Unless the ghosts are recognised, and dealt with properly, it seems as if the repressed will continue to return – in horrific ways.

Acknowledgements

I would like to thank Jean Hillier for giving me the opportunity to air these arguments at the conference and for inviting me to contribute to the book. Two anonymous referees stimulated me to engage with their useful and challenging questions. I have also benefited greatly from conversations with Wendy Shaw, Dydia DeLyser and Karen Till. This paper would be worse but for Jenny Robinson, who commented on earlier versions of this paper.

Notes

1 See Nigel Thrift (1999), who has suggested that 'the ecology of place is a rich and varied spectral gathering' (316), while drawing on the work of Avery Gordon (1997, page 206).
2 This chapter draws on three key works by Freud: 'Totem and Taboo' (1913); 'Mourning and Melancholia' (1917); and 'The "Uncanny"' (1919). Freud is interested in ghosts mainly as a form in which the repressed returns to haunt people. His discussions range from thinking about the figure of the ghost in Hamlet and Macbeth, to the return of repressed childhood anxieties (where ghosts represent the mother in her night-gown[!]), to the expression and representation of fears of the dead throughout modern and pre-modern societies.
3 MI is short for Military Intelligence.
4 I have put terrorism in scare quotes here because we all know that one person's freedom-fighter is another person's terrorist. Part of the point of thinking through the

ghostliness of places is to uncover the affect that constitutes the ambiguity (or switching) of the morality of events like this.
5 Perhaps paradoxically, the ghosts of democracy have been in the habit of gathering at the Houses of Parliament (see Pile, 2004).
6 MI5 is listed in the telephone directory (with an address: 12 Millbank, just over the river from MI6), but there is no listing for MI6. However, the Government Communications Bureau is listed as being at 85 Albert Embankment: the telephone number is to a mobile phone, presumably in order to keep the whereabouts of Britain's secret agents secret.
7 As Freud would not be surprised to see (see Freud, 1919). For him, the uncanny was strongly associated with the return of repressed childhood experiences.
8 C. Sear: geddit?
9 The stranger, of course, is a highly ambiguous, and dare I add ghostly, figure – someone both to rely on, and to be afraid of: see Jacobs, 1961; Young, 1990; Wilson, 1991; and also Pile, Brook and Mooney (eds) 1999.
10 The law and death row in America are uncannily linked: witness the return of 'the executioner' (Texas-style) to the Presidency in the not-quite-present form of George W. Bush.
11 It is worth remembering, as implied above, that not all 'returns' are scary or associated with the dead.
12 To be clear, this was made possible precisely because of the invention and imposition of British notions of law, land, the body, ownership, property and rights.
13 And its place within Freudian thought and specifically its relationship to his account of narcissism.

References

Bell, M. (1997) 'The ghosts of place', *Theory and Society* 26: 3-836.
Connelly, J. (1998) *Bringing out the Dead*, London, Warner Books.
Curtis, B. (2001) 'That place Where: some thoughts on memory and the city', in I. Borden, J. Kerr, J. Rendell and A. Pivaro (eds) *The Unknown City: contesting architecture and social space*, Cambridge, Mass., MIT Press: 54-67.
Derrida, J. (1994 [1993]) *Spectres of Marx: the state of the debt, the work of mourning, and the new international*, London, Routledge.
Freud, S. (1985 [1913]) 'Totem and taboo', in *The Origins of Religion*, Volume 13, Harmondsworth, Penguin Freud Library: 49-224.
Freud, S. (1984 [1917]) 'Mourning and melancholia', in *On Metapsychology: the Theory of Psychoanalysis* Harmondsworth, Volume 11, Penguin Freud Library: 251-268.
Freud, S. (1985 [1919]) 'The "uncanny" in art and literature: Jensen's "Gradiva"', *Leonardo Da Vinci and other works*, Volume 14, Harmondsworth, Penguin Freud Library: 339-376.
Gelder, K. and Jacobs, J.M. (1998) *Uncanny Australia: sacredness and identity in a postcolonial nation*, Melbourne, Melbourne University Press.
Gordon, A. (1997) *Ghostly Matters: haunting and the sociological imagination*, Minneapolis, University of Minnesota Press.
Huyssen, A. (2003) *Cultural Memory in the Present: urban palimpsests and the politics of memory*, Standford, Standford University Press.
Jacobs, J.M. (1996) *Edge of Empire: postcolonialism and the city*, London, Routledge.
Jacobs, J. (1961) *The Death and Life of Great American Cities*, Harmondsworth, Penguin.

Kerr, J. (2001) 'The Uncompleted Monument: London, war, and the architecture of remembrance', in I. Borden, J. Kerr, J. Rendell and A. Pivaro (eds) *The unknown city: contesting architecture and social space*, Cambridge, Mass., MIT Press: 68-89.

Pile, S. (2001) 'The Un(known) City ... or, an urban geography of what lies buried below the surface', in I. Borden, J. Kerr, J. Rendell and A. Pivaro (eds) *The Unknown City: contesting architecture and social space*, Cambridge, Mass., MIT Press: 262-279.

Pile, S. (2004) 'Ghosts in the city of hope', in L. Lees (ed.) *The Emancipatory City: paradoxes and possibilities*, London, Sage:210-228.

Pile, S. Brook, C. and Mooney, G. (eds) (1999) *Unruly Cities? order/disorder*, London, Routledge, in collaboration with the Open University.

Roach, J. (1996) *Cities of the Dead: circum-atlantic performance*, New York, Columbia University Press.

Shaw, W. (2001) Ways *of Whiteness: negotiating settlement agendas in (post)colonial Sydney*, PhD Thesis, University of Melbourne.

Simmel, G. (1995 [1903]) 'The metropolis and mental life', in P. Kasinitz (ed.) *Metropolis: centre and symbol of our times*, Basingstoke, Macmillan: 30-45.

Sorkin, M. (2003) *Starting from Zero: reconstructing downtown New York*, New York, Routledge.

Taussig, M. (1997) *The Magic of the State*, London, Routledge.

Thrift, N. (1999) 'Steps to an ecology of place', in D. Massey, J. Allen and P. Sarre (eds) *Human Geography Today*, Cambridge, Polity: 295-322.

Wilson, E. (1991) *The Sphinx in the City: urban life, the control of disorder, and women*, London, Virago.

Young, I.M. (1990) Justice and the Politics of Difference. Princeton, Princeton University Press.

13 Crime and the Design of the Built Environment: Anglo-American Comparisons of Policy and Practice

TED KITCHEN AND RICHARD H. SCHNEIDER[1]

Introduction

We believe that the complex relationships between crime, the fear of crime and the design of the built environment merit far more attention from planners and other professionals concerned with the quality of place than hitherto they have received. Many arguments could be advanced in support of this view, but for us one of the most significant comes from the typical reactions of local communities when asked to identify the things that matter most to them in determining their perceptions of the quality of life in the places they live. If planning is to be successful in helping to create places of quality for people, then it must engage with those things that people say about their places that really do make a difference; it cannot simply rely on the views of planners about these matters or on the intervention of police, who by themselves have limited ability to deter crime in large urban societies like Britain and the USA. Crime and the fear of crime (and particularly violent crime) consistently score very heavily in local quality of life studies,[2] and there can be little argument that there are significant environmental components that influence (for good or ill) both the opportunity for crime and people's fear that a crime is likely to be committed. And yet, without suggesting that the cupboard is entirely bare, planning literature and practice do not tend to place a major emphasis on the relationships between crime and the design of the built environment. We believe that this needs to change, and our joint work is designed to contribute to the achievement of this objective.

We also believe that Anglo-American comparisons of policy and practice are of particular value because of the insights that they can offer in order to improve the ways in which planning theory and practice address this neglected area. In a world where information flows ever more readily between countries and continents, ideas, policies and practices can move around very quickly; and they do. This is particularly true of the range of issues surrounding concerns about crime; for example, 'zero tolerance' has virtually entered the English language as a particular type of approach, and yet we would suggest that only a small proportion of the people who bandy the concept around have any sort of understanding of where it comes from and the circumstances of its initial application. We believe that if we are to learn effectively from the experience of trying out other people's ideas, we need to understand the cultural and the socio-economic contexts which led to the emergence of those ideas in the first place, the specific circumstances in which they were applied, and the outcomes that materialised. Far too often, however, both politicians and professionals in various fields in need of 'quick fix' solutions to problems that to date have been stubbornly resistant to their ministrations, or maybe who just feel that they need to be seen to be doing something different, pick up ideas from elsewhere without regard to this contextual framework and seek to apply them in the hope that this time the problem will be solved. And there will be no shortage of people standing on the sidelines urging them on, because the field has rather more protagonists of particular viewpoints than it has an accumulation of credible evidence about what works well, where and why. This is not merely a rhetorical stance on our part, but is also one of the major conclusions reached in a recent review of State and local crime prevention programmes funded by the United States Department of Justice (Sherman *et al.*, 1998). This puts the matter as follows, in the opening sentences of the National Institute of Justice research brief summarising the results of this study:

> Many crime prevention programs work. Others don't. Most programs have not yet been evaluated with enough scientific evidence to draw conclusions (Sherman *et al.*, 1998: 1).

Exactly so. Looked at like this, Anglo-American comparisons have obvious potential for developing the kinds of understandings being argued for here, not least because as well as having many problems and responses in common, the two countries also have some important differences.

This statement of where we are coming from should help to explain why we think this field matters to the development of planning thought and why we think a comparative approach offers much to this endeavour. Limitations of length inevitably mean that this present contribution must approach this large subject area in a highly selective manner, and so we have chosen herein to restrict ourselves to five tasks:

- to say something both about overall crime patterns and about the geography of crime in the two countries;
- to say a little about what we know about public perceptions of the significance of this as a 'quality of life' concern as compared with other key issues in both countries;
- to comment briefly on the key ideas that have contributed to thinking about the relationships between crime and the design of the built environment, which we think are broadly common as between the two countries; but in passing, to point out some significant differences in the ways in which ideas get used notwithstanding this broadly common intellectual tradition;
- to focus on what we see as quite a major difference between the organisational structures which enable the two societies to set about tackling these issues, which is partly a function of the very different perceptions of the roles of central government in Britain and of the federal government in the USA and partly a result of some different policy contexts adopted at this level;
- to say something from these analyses about what we think the way forward in this area might be.

Crime Patterns in Britain and the USA

Crime data are replete with difficulties in terms of being sure of their reliability (Walker, 1995; Coleman and Moynihan, 1996). Data derived from police statistics of recorded crime are likely to carry at least the following difficulties with them:

- people's willingness to report crimes to the police varies considerably between localities, as to types of crime, and in terms of the socio-economic characteristics of people themselves;
- police procedures for recording what is reported to them vary both between localities and over time There is also some recent British evidence (Povey, 2000) to suggest that a significant number of reported incidents do not get recorded by the police for reasons that can readily be explained, which then leaves open the possible interpretation that this represents a deliberate act in order to make performance figures (expressed in terms of the percentage of recorded crimes that get cleared up) look better;
- there is a sense in which police statistics can be a self-fulfilling prophecy, in that they reflect operational decisions. This can be either direct or indirect. An example of a direct effect would be a decision to tackle a problem of illegal car parking in an area, which would be likely to

result at least for a time in more illegal car parking offences getting recorded. An example of an indirect effect would be the possibility that an increased police presence on the streets of an area or the installation of closed circuit television (CCTV) cameras in an area might result in the deflection of crimes that might otherwise have taken place in that area to other areas.

Data derived from social surveys, either of the population at large or of victims of crimes carry with them the standard problems of sample surveys, plus a concern that data dependent upon human memory of sensitive incidents might be prone to unreliability, either because of an unwillingness to talk about the subject or because of exaggeration or even forgetfulness.

If these statements are true as generalisations about crime data within individual countries, they make for particular difficulties when cross-national comparisons are attempted. Nevertheless, a recent study for the US Department of Justice (Langan and Farrington, 1998) has compared the positions in both the United States and in England and Wales over the period 1981-1996, using both types of data and with an explicit understanding of the difficulties that are attached to each. Its key findings are as follows:[3,4]

- Over the period in question, *robbery* (when measured in terms of the crime rate per 1000 population) and *burglary* (when measured in terms of the crime rate per 1000 households) both started at much lower levels in England and Wales than in the USA but in both cases went above the USA level in the early 1990s. So in each case England and Wales have seen a rapidly rising crime rate (robbery from just over 4 per 1,000 population in 1981 to just over 7.5 per 1,000 population in 1995, and burglary from about 40 per 1,000 households in 1981 to just over 80 per 1,000 households in 1995), whereas the USA has seen robbery rates fall steadily over the period (from just under 7.5 per 1,000 population in 1981 to just over 5 per 1,000 population in 1996) and burglary rates fall more spectacularly (from about 105 per 1,000 households in 1981 to under 50 per 1,000 households in 1996).
- Throughout the period in question, England and Wales saw higher rates of *assault* (measured in terms of crimes per 1000 population) and of *motor vehicle theft* (measured in terms of the crimes per 1000 households) than did the USA. In both cases, the gap widened over the period. The rate of assaults was very little different between the two in 1981 but the rate for England and Wales was more than double the USA rate by 1995 (20 per 1000 people in 1995 in England and Wales as against just under 9 per 1000

people in the USA in 1996). Motor vehicle theft rates remained broadly unchanged in the USA at around 10 per 1000 households, but rose from just over 15 per 1000 households in England and Wales in 1981 to just under 24 per 1000 households in 1995.
- The *murder* rate in the USA has been much higher than that in England and Wales throughout the period, with the latter remaining fairly steady at just over 0.01 per 1000 people and the former falling from just under 0.1 per 1000 people in 1981 (i.e. nearly ten times the rate for England and Wales) to about 0.075 per 1000 people in 1996 (i.e. nearly six times the rate for England and Wales). The homicide rate in the largest American cities (those with a population of over one million) has, however, declined significantly since 1993, thereby reducing the overall national homicide rate in the USA.
- *Firearms* are much more involved in crimes of violence in the USA than in England and Wales, with police statistics showing in 1996 that they were used in 68% of USA murders and 41% of USA robberies as compared with 7% and 5% in England and Wales respectively.
- When *all crimes* are looked at in the round, the general pattern in the USA was of crime falling in the early 1980s, then rising until around 1993, and then falling again. For England and Wales, the broad pattern is of a more or less continuous rise over the period in question, although the 1998 British Crime Survey did show falls for most types of crime over the period 1995-1997 (Home Office, 1998) and these were continued in the results of the 2000 British Crime Survey (Home Office, 2000).

Some of this may well be seen in some quarters as being surprising. To look at this in terms of British perspectives, the general perception that may still exist of Britain as quite a law-abiding country and of the USA as a place where crime rates (and particularly violent crime rates) are much higher is not supported by these figures, except in respect of what they say about the (related) issues of murder and the use of firearms. Similarly, the fact that crime rates were falling in the USA for a significant part of the 1990s whereas in Britain they were rising (and in relation to some kinds of crimes, quite rapidly) more or less continuously throughout the period 1981-1996 doesn't sit well with this comfortable image of Britain.[5] What may well have made this more difficult still was the apparent phenomenon in Britain of rising crime rates but falling clear-up rates. So, for example, Smith (in Herbert and Smith, 1989: 271) shows that recorded crimes in England and Wales rose by 63% between the mid 1970s and the mid 1980s but that clear-up rates fell from 45% in 1970 to 31% in 1985. This must have had an effect on public confidence in the police, especially since it was occurring at a time when British police operations were often substituting the (unpopular) 'officers in panda car' for the (popular) 'bobbies on the beat'; and even if there is an element of post hoc rationalisation in this fuelled by nostalgia, we think it is not a coincidence that at this same time the traditional view that dealing with crime was something best left to the police was being challenged by views about broader approaches to crime prevention including various kinds of community involvement (Locke 1990: 245 and 246; also Walklate, in McLaughlin and Muncie, 1996: 293-331). The interest in environmental dimensions of crime prevention can also be seen as part of this process.

It is also possible that the phenomena described above have had an effect on the ways in which crime-related stories are presented in the media, which in turn almost certainly affect people's fear of crime. By this we do not mean the process of reporting stories about individual crimes, because these (and particularly those at the violent end of the spectrum) are always likely to receive intensive and extensive media coverage. What we are talking about here is the attention given to the periodic publication of crime statistics and to new initiatives to tackle crime. These matters have developed a very high profile in Britain in recent times (higher, we would judge, than in the USA, perhaps because crime rates there are seen to be more 'under control' recently), to the point at which whether crime rates have gone up or down is seen as a test of the success or failure of a government. There is also recent British experience to suggest that bad news in these terms is likely to be accompanied by intensive attempts at media management in order to try to soften the impact of that news plus new initiatives (that, of course, may be very valuable in their own right) to try to deflect attention from it.[6] All of this means that issues about crime and crime prevention are constantly 'in the news' in Britain, and we would hypothesise that the frequent reporting of this as a problem that is getting worse, even when the most recent statistics do not actually support this interpretation, in turn contributes to growing public fears of crime. It seems probable as a consequence that the task of reducing public fears of crime in a country like Britain is likely to be a long-term one, with no guarantee (and perhaps even no likelihood) that statistical reductions in crime will trigger a concomitant reduction in public fears. This, after all, appears to have been the experience in the USA, despite years of falling crime rates. This leads us to suggest that tackling crime and tackling the fear of crime should be regarded both locally and nationally as two separate but related problems each worthy of their own programmes, with the former having a specific action focus and the latter containing careful and targeted publicity. As part of this process, there is probably also merit in deconstructing what 'fear of crime' actually means amongst different segments of society, because it may well prove to be a euphemism for many different things.

Overall crime rates mask huge variations in the geographical distribution of crime. What the 1998 British Crime Survey describes as 'unequal risks' (Home Office, 1998: 27-43) is in fact about the variable likelihood of being on the receiving end of a crime according to factors such as age, employment status, geographical location or the type of property one lives in. As an example, the following pairs pick out the percentages of households in England and Wales in 1997 who were victims of burglary at least once during that year, against a national average of 5.6% (Home Office, 1998, Tables 5.1 and 5.2):

Age of head of household 16-24	15.2%
Age of head of household 65-74	3.5%
Head of household in employment	5.4%
Head of household unemployed	10.0%
Detached house	4.1%
Flats/Maisonettes	7.2%
Inner city location	8.5%
Rural location	3.4%
Municipal housing area	8.1%
Non-municipal housing area	5.1%
Main road location	6.6%
Cul-de-sac[7]	4.3%

The most significant point about this in terms of the subject matter of this present paper, of course, is that these pairings do relate to particular circumstances on the ground in individual localities, which is precisely what the relationship between crime and the design of the built environment is all about. In particular, they reinforce what we already know about the relationships between crime and relative poverty; if one is young, unemployed, living in a flat, in a municipal housing estate in the inner city, which fronts a main road, then the chances of being on the receiving end of burglary are much greater than would be the case if the description contained the opposites of these characteristics; and this description also fits many of the classic descriptors of contemporary poverty (Social Exclusion Unit, 1998: 13-33).

Arguably, the situation is if anything still more extreme in the USA because of the social polarisation to be found in the structures of many of its urban areas (Kelso, 1994; Logan, in Marcuse and van Kempen, 2000). Some headlines from the USA National Crime Victimisation Survey for 1998 underline this point (US Department of Justice, 2000):

> The likelihood of an individual aged 12 or over being on the receiving end of a crime against the person appears to increase with the size of the core city in a Metropolitan Statistical Area until the core city gets larger than 1 million people. The rates per 1000 people aged 12 or more are 44.4 for a city in the population range 50,000-249,999; 47.9 for a city in the range 250,000-4999,999; and 56.1 for a city in the range 500,000-999,999. Taking all central cities together and classing them as 'urban' areas, the overall rates for the USA on this same basis are 48.7 for urban areas, 36.7 for suburban areas and 28.2 for rural areas (US Department of Justice, 2000, Table 52).

> The figures for property crimes per 1,000 households on this same basis are fairly similar, being 274.2 for urban areas, 204.5 for suburban areas and 173.5 for rural areas. (US Department of Justice, 2000, Table 53)

> When property crimes are looked at according to whether the house in question is owned/being bought or rented, the figures in terms of the rates per 1000 households are as follows:

	owned/being bought	rented
Urban	256.2	291.9
Suburban	181.8	262.9
Rural	149.9	237.6

> This noticeably higher risk arising from renting also has some racial differences associated with it, with white renters more at risk in urban and rural areas and black renters more at risk in suburban areas. The figures quoted above relate to all races (US Department of Justice, 2000, Table 56). The rates also vary quite considerably according to geographical regions in the USA, with urban dwellers in the West being nearly twice as likely as urban dwellers in the North-East to be on the receiving end of property crime (US Department of Justice, 2000, Table 58).

> Family income is also a key differentiator of risk of being on the receiving end of crime in the USA. If the average annual family income is less than $7,500 per annum (and nearly 12 million people aged 12 or over fall into

this group), the risk of being on the receiving end of a crime against the person is 65.5 per 1000 people aged 12 or over, whereas for those from families where the average annual income exceeds $75,000 (and there are just under 30 million people aged 12 or over in this group) the risk drops to 34.1 per 1000 people aged 12 or over, or little over half of that for the poorest group (US Department of Justice, 2000, Table 14). These differences are very much less marked in respect of property crimes, however (US Department of Justice, 2000, Table 20).

What we can probably conclude from all of this is that, whilst there are differences of detail in these terms between the two countries, the broad demography and geography of crime in Britain and the USA are actually fairly similar. Basically, the risk of being on the receiving end of crime goes up substantially for the poorest urban dwellers living in rented rather than owned accommodation. If we wish to have a real impact on crime rates through environmental measures (to the extent that this can be achieved via this route, singly or in combination with other measures), the greatest scope for doing so must therefore exist in these areas at any rate in a statistical sense; and probably the greatest challenge is to be found there as well. This may be illustrated by the extraordinary impact that New York City's declining crime rate has had on reducing overall American crime rates in recent years, especially for violent crimes like murder.

Crime and the Fear of Crime as a 'Quality of Life' Issue

By its very nature, planning seeks to manipulate the physical variables which impact upon the quality of people's lives in a locality, and other aspects of public policy seek to impact upon a wide range of social and economic variables in similar ways. Sitting beneath this huge volume of public activity is a set of implicit assumptions to the effect that the professionals who shape and then implement these policies and practices know what is needed to achieve the target of improving the quality of people's lives, know what works to this end, and have a good level of understanding of local people's perceptions and wishes in respect of these issues. We would suggest, however, that the evidence that planners are fully aware of public concerns about crime and the fear of crime in localities and are reflecting this in their priorities for local action is not particularly strong, otherwise this issue would be much higher up the planning agenda than it appears to be. There must also be a concern about whose views about these matters within urban society planners are actually responding to when they do this at all, since it can be argued that the most strident 'fear of crime' views are those in effect expressed by the 'haves' against the 'have nots'.

A major study reviewing the effectiveness of roughly 20 years' worth of 'urban policy' in Britain included a sample survey of 1299 residents in 15 different areas of Greater Manchester, Merseyside and Tyne and Wear, asking them to rank 20 variables according to their importance to the quality of life in their areas. The percentages of that sample ranking variables as 'very important' (Robson et al., 1994: 342) were as follows:

- Violent crime 79.3%
- Quality of healthcare 73.7%
- Cost of living 71.9%
- Non-violent crime 67.2%
- Quality of housing 64.2%
- Quality of welfare services 61.7%
- What the area looks like 61.3%
- Employment prospects 59.2%
- Pollution 58.2%
- Unemployment levels 58.0%

This finding (that violent crime comes out top of the list, and that non-violent crime also rates very highly) has been broadly replicated in several British local studies. For example, studies asking local people what they think are the things in their local environment that have the greatest impact on the quality of their lives have shown crime and the fear of crime at the top of the lists in Nottingham (Nottingham City Council, undated), in the Dearne Valley in South Yorkshire (Dearne Valley Partnership, 1996) and in Salford (Salford Crime Reduction Partnership, 1999).

A CBS News public survey conducted by telephone in the USA in October 1999 tells a very similar story. Just over 1000 voters were asked what they felt would be the most important problem facing the USA in the twenty-first century; so this was a different question to those asked in the British surveys quoted above, although with a similar focus, not least because American respondents could only class one issue as 'most important' whereas British respondents could use the 'very important' category several times if they wished. The top responses in this American survey were as follows:

8%   crime
7%   moral values
5%   healthcare, poverty
4%   economy, education, environment, drugs, jobs and unemployment, overpopulation, war
3%   racism/race relations, technology/computers
2%   social issues, terrorism

Source: the 'Public Agenda Online' website at: www.publicagenda.org/issues/pcc.

It should be remembered in interpreting these figures that actual crime levels in the USA had been falling for several years when this survey result was obtained, so the fact that statistically crime rates were becoming less of a problem was not reflected in this evidence about people's fears of crime. This is confirmed by the results of the 1999 National Crime Prevention Survey in the USA, the headlines of which were:

- one in eight of Americans said they were more fearful of walking in their neighbourhoods this year than last;
- one in five people said that to varying degrees they had curbed their activities out of fear of crime over the past year;
- three in ten survey participants said that to varying degrees violence was a problem in the neighbourhoods where they live, work and shop.

Source: National Crime Prevention website at: www.ncpc.org/rwesafe3.htm.

This perhaps serves to reinforce the point that in both societies crime and the fear of crime are very major public concerns, and that local crime prevention initiatives have to try to deal both with actual crime rates and with public fears without it always being clear that the second follows from the first. Moreover, in both societies crime prevention planning has fallen largely to the police, an ironical situation since historically of all public agencies, they have had the least control over the design and construction of the built environment, yet have been the most responsible for seeing that it is safe.

Crime and the Design of the Built Environment – Some Key Ideas

There is almost certainly a very long history to the relationship between criminal activity and the ways in which the built environment is laid out

Crime and the Design of the Built Environment 269

(see, for example, Mumford, 1961; Chesney, 1970; Kostof, 1991). But many of the ideas that suggest that the approaches we take to the physical organisation of our urban areas should be influenced by a sophisticated understanding of these relationships are much more recent. They are often conventionally attributed to Jane Jacobs (1964), although she is careful to list the large number of influences on her thinking. Above all else, what we get from her work is the idea that urbanity itself, and the range of human activity, interaction and natural surveillance of others that go with it, can deter crime and make cities safer places. This in turn had a major influence on the work of Oscar Newman (1973) in seeking to utilise human territorial behaviour in designing (particularly) residential areas to reduce opportunities and incentives for crime through the creation of 'defensible space'. A critical component of this thinking was that it was about community (that is to say, collective) responses rather than about individuals seeking to protect themselves in isolation, and this particular tension (that between community and individual action) has been much debated in the literature that has followed over what is now nearly three decades.

Out of all of this has come the notion of 'situational crime prevention' (Clarke, 1980; Clarke and Mayhew, 1980) and the closely related concept of 'CPTED' (Crime Prevention Through Environmental Design: Jeffrey, 1977; Crowe, 1991), which apply to all types of environments and not merely residential areas but are essentially locationally specific. Clarke and Mayhew see situational crime prevention as:

- being directed at specific crimes;
- managing, designing or manipulating the immediate environment in which crime occurs;
- ensuring that the measures that are put in place in this context are both systematic and permanent; and
- reducing overall opportunities for crime.

The six inter-related sets of strategies that comprise the modern CPTED approach can clearly be seen to be based upon this thinking. These six are:

- access control, to decrease crime opportunities;
- surveillance, to tackle real and perceived risks;
- territoriality, to encourage a sense of ownership;
- activity generation, which seeks to place inherently 'unsafe' activities (such as those involving money transactions) in 'safe' locations (those with high levels of activity);

- maintenance, to ensure that the physical environment continues to work well and does not send out negative signals; and
- planning/organisational arrangements, to ensure that all these things can actually be done.

There isn't an enormous amount of rigorous empirical research that can be seen to be offering conclusions about the nature and scale of the contribution made by these sorts of approaches, although there certainly is work which suggests that 'design disadvantagement' (design features which by their nature encourage anti-social behaviour including crime) exists and is capable of being overcome through making design changes (Coleman, 1990). There are also some useful studies which have looked carefully at practical experience rather than concentrated on making cases for particular theoretical stances (Poyner, 1985; Clarke, 1992). A recent review of place-specific crime prevention in the USA provides some qualified support for these kinds of approaches (Feins, Epstein and Widom, 1997). This summarises its findings as follows:

> The most effective place-specific crime prevention strategies are those that take into account the geographic, cultural, economic, and social characteristics of the target community. Thus, the selection of place-specific crime prevention strategies and tactics should be made in close collaboration with the community, after sustained observation of its current patterns of use. The experiences of the study sites reveal two major lessons:
>
> - Physical design modifications, management changes, and changes in use should be tailored to specific locations and co-ordinated in their planning and implementation.
> - The most effective security and crime prevention efforts are those that involve a coalition of different players working together to define the problem and then seek solutions.
>
> By emphasising that crime prevention is not a 'one size fits all' effort, and that some communities may require more attention and ingenuity than others in crafting effective strategies, this report stresses the importance of a thorough analysis of the problems and needs of a given community, as well as ongoing monitoring and evaluation of the place-specific strategies selected. (Feins, Epstein and Widom, 1997: xi, xii).

We agree very much with this approach, and endorse in particular what it has to say both about working with communities rather than imposing views on them and about tailoring what is attempted to the local situation and people rather than imposing pre-determined and inevitably standardised prescriptions. This kind of careful and balanced judgement based upon the evidence has not typified by any means all of the work in this field, however, and as a result there are several major areas of uncertainty. Taylor and Harrell (1996: 22-23) identified four such areas after a review of the literature:

- the sequence of relationships between physical change, crime events, fear of crime and perceptions of place vulnerability;
- the contribution of social, cultural and organisational features to the success of crime reduction through physical environment modifications (see also Fleissner and Heinzelmann, 1996);
- the effect of the larger social, political and economic environment on the risk of crime, and the relationships between these broader issues and the process of modifying the physical environment (see also Taylor, 1999, for an interesting longitudinal study of some of these issues in Baltimore between 1981/82 and 1994); and
- the relative importance of key variables such as housing disrepair and vacancy, land use patterns, vandalism, physical layout, and patterns of traffic and pedestrian circulation.

As well as issues such as this where knowledge is limited, there are other parts of the field covered by this paper where controversy has arisen as a result of strongly held opinions. A good example of this relates to the concept of 'target-hardening', which is action designed to make premises that might be the target of a crime as secure as possible and also to make both access for criminal purposes and escape after a crime has been committed as difficult as possible. In its own terms, this is clearly one component of the actions that might be expected as a result of situational crime prevention or of the application of CPTED principles as defined above, and this is indeed the normal usage of the term in the USA. There are clearly some perfectly sensible things that can be done in relation to individual properties that make them more rather than less secure (Crouch, Shaftoe and Fleming, 1999), and there is recent work in the USA to suggest that landlords ought to be concerned about this because of premises liability (the possibility that they will be taken to court by tenants who are the victims of crime because they failed to take reasonable steps to make their property secure; see Gordon and Brill, 1996). But there is also concern in some quarters that this approach can be taken so far that it creates what is in effect a 'fortress mentality', and thereby results in a kind of place which is the antithesis (it is argued) of the kind of urban environment that makes cities attractive to people (Rudlin and Falk, 1995: 56). This has led to the explicit rejection of this approach in some quarters in favour of an approach based upon the principles of 'new urbanism' (Rudlin and Falk, 1999), which include relatively high densities, mixed uses, a relationship between the design of buildings and the design of streets which creates as many 'eyes on the street' as possible in order to achieve natural surveillance, and the creation of a permeable environment to and through which people can readily move. This approach has probably been given its fullest expression in Britain in the guidelines for the redevelopment of Hulme in Manchester (Hulme Regeneration Limited, 1994), although it is too soon to draw firm conclusions as yet about the success or otherwise of the practical application of these guidelines since at the time of writing the redevelopment of the area is far from complete and the longitudinal studies of residents' reactions have not yet been undertaken. In this British literature, 'target-hardening' has almost become a term of abuse, presented as the polar opposite of 'new urbanism', although it is important to remember that this usage is not reflected in much of the remaining literature where, as we have already said, target-hardening is simply one component of a range of situational responses to crime.

Another major difference between British and US practice in terms of target-hardening has been the widespread acceptance of closed circuit television (CCTV) in the former as compared with the suspicion of it in terms of civil liberties concerns in the latter (Graham and Marvin, 1996: 225-227). Whilst civil liberties concerns about this in terms of its 'big brother' elements have been around in Britain, the available research suggests that the general public's reactions to CCTV in areas such as city centres have been 'broadly positive' (Honess and Charman, 1992), and that the installation of CCTV cameras appears to work in both deterring some crimes and achieving subsequent arrests (Brown, 1995). As a result, Oc and Tiesdell (1997: 130-142), in looking at the role of CCTV in helping to create safer city centres in Britain, have concluded that this policy is 'here to stay'. Public policy has supported this view in Britain, with public funding support being made available for the continued development of initiatives of this kind. The picture in the USA, on the other hand, has been one of much less extensive disposition in public places because of the concern about civil liberties noted above, and as a consequence there has been no equivalent of either the widespread or the government funding support for CCTV initiatives in the USA's public places; although CCTV is more common in privately owned and protected places in the USA such as shopping malls. This difference perhaps illustrates the significance of cultural acceptability as the basis for policy initiatives in a democratic society. Without public consent, policies can be extremely difficult to implement in such situations, and indeed governments may well be unwilling to push an idea in such circumstances.

This has only been a brief review of some of the key ideas in the field, but the significant point is that it represents what is broadly a common intellectual tradition for the USA and for Britain. Ideas have moved between the two, and research studies carried out in the one (where this has taken place at all) have been influential in the other. There have been some differences of interpretation and understanding, such as the example of the different ways in which the concept of target-hardening have been used, and also some differences in practice which we suspect (such as the differing approaches to CCTV) have a cultural basis to them. In the next section, we look at what we see as a major difference between the two countries, which is the organisational frameworks for implementing actions in this field and their related policy contexts.

Differing Organisational Structures in Britain and the USA

One of the most significant differences that we perceive in this field between Britain and the USA is the approaches adopted to organisational structures and the policy frameworks that sit behind them. To put it in very simple terms, Britain has seen the emergence both at local and at national levels of relatively formal arrangements for working in this area, which have no real equivalent in the USA. Whereas it is possible to describe the arrangements that exist in Britain in terms of a broad national pattern (albeit with some significant local variations), it is scarcely possible to see any real patterns at the national level in the USA and at the local level there is a huge amount of variety. To describe the former as a single system and the latter as a fragmented approach is probably in both cases to exaggerate somewhat, but the differences between the two are broadly of this order. In turn, this affects the policy framework that both supports and shapes these systems, with the approach in Britain being increasingly one that sees crime and the design of the built environment as part of some very wide-ranging public policy developments which again have no real equivalent in the USA.

There isn't the space here to map the development of these arrangements, although we have tried to do this elsewhere.[1] All we can do here is to outline what we believe the current situation to be, and offer one (no doubt amongst several) explanations of why we think this difference exists. Our explanation is really very straightforward. It relates to the power of central government in Britain, as compared with the limited powers in this field at any rate of the federal government in the USA when taken together with the jealous safeguarding of the rights of other jurisdictions (States and more local levels of government) emanating from the particular nature of the United States Constitution. Thus, whilst the kind of edifice we describe can readily be built in the British situation because of the largely unconstrained powers of the British government, that is simply not the case in the USA; and thus it is no surprise that the kinds of organisational structures that we see in Britain today not only are not replicated in the USA but (even if it were felt to be desirable that this should be the case) scarcely could be.

At the local level in England and Wales, formal and informal liaison on matters to do with crime and the design of the built environment exists between the local planning authorities and the Architectural Liaison Officers (or equivalent title) established in each police force. This arrangement is formally supported through government guidance in the form of DoE Circular 5/94 (Department of the Environment, 1994), where paragraph 9 urges local planning authorities to consult with police Architectural Liaison Officers in carrying out their development control policies.[8] A great deal of this now happens on a day-to-day basis as part of British local planning practice, with the precise nature of these arrangements being left to local discretion. This process has been taken further through the Crime and Disorder Act, 1998, which places an equal duty (that is to say, it is not discretionary) on local authorities and the police to join together and work with others to review crime and disorder problems in their area, publish and seek views on their findings, and put in place a strategy taking account of these views which sets targets for reducing crime and disorder in their area. The first fruits of this approach in the form of local strategies are now becoming visible throughout England and Wales, and what these strategies are clearly attempting to do is to set issues associated with crime and disorder (including environmental actions) in the context of the wide range of other local strategies about the future of the place in question which are often extant (Crime Concern, undated). In addition, Section 17 of the Crime and Disorder Act, 1998, imposes a new duty on local planning authorities to exercise their functions (which means both development plan-making and development control) with due regard both to the effect on and the need to do all they can to prevent crime and disorder. The full impact of all of this has probably not yet been grasped in British planning circles, but what it does mean is that the relationship between crime and the design of the built environment does now have an established place in British planning at the local level.

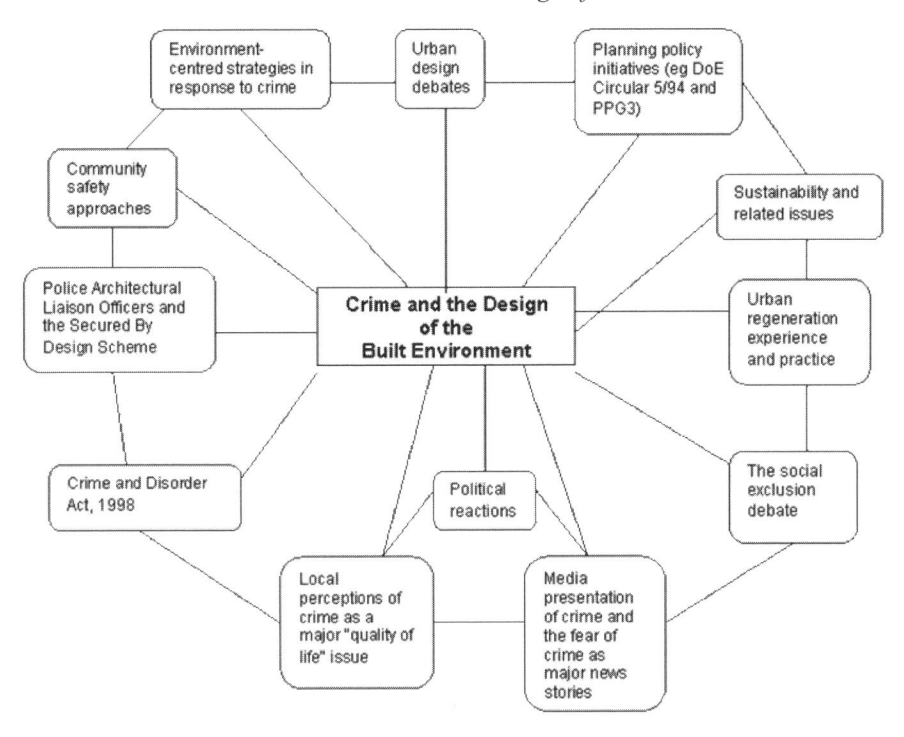

Crime and the Design of the Built Environment 275

Figure 13.1 Key Influences on Recent British Debates about Crime and the Design of the Built Environment

If the process of broadening the policy context, so that crime and disorder issues are not seen to be free-standing but as intimately related to a wide range of other policy concerns, has been happening at the local level in Britain, this is even more true at the national level. We have tried to give expression to this by developing a diagram (Figure 13.1) which illustrates the key influences in recent British debates about crime and the design of the built environment. Although many of the elements of the diagram would probably be expected as influences, some may be rather less obvious. Examples of this from recent British practice are:

> [T]he debate about sustainability, which in Britain has had as a major element in recent years a Government policy thrust to meet at least 60% of the housing requirement arising from new household formation through developments on previously-used land in urban areas (Department of the Environment, Transport and the Regions, 1998).
>
> [T]he debate about urban regeneration practice, where it is now increasingly being accepted that successful regeneration requires an

holistic approach to managing major changes in urban areas, within which measures to combat crime and the fear of crime are an important component (Urban Task Force, 1999).

[T]he social exclusion debate, which is about those communities and people who do not share in the general wealth and good quality of life experiences of much of the rest of the country and who, as we have already seen, are likely as part of these processes of exclusion to be disproportionately on the receiving end of crime (Social Exclusion Unit, 1998).

DoE Circular 5/94 and the revision of the Government's Planning Policy Guidance note on housing (PPG3; Department of the Environment, Transport and the Regions, 1999) both appear to accept the argument that human activity can have a significant impact upon crime, and thus argue that it is the job of the planning system to promote mixed uses, mixed communities and (in some cases) higher densities, all of which are seen as generating desirable human activity in residential areas.

It is probably fair to say that Britain has a distance to travel before it sees the full benefits of this kind of very broadly based approach; the systems and the thinking are in place, but delivery remains a hope rather than something that has already happened. It could also be argued that this widening of the agenda reflects the failure of conventional approaches to crime prevention in Britain (that it is mainly the responsibility of the police and of the criminal justice system), as exemplified by the rising tide of crime discussed earlier, and the consequent search for alternative approaches. Nevertheless, the British system is characterised at present by both a very extensive policy agenda and a plethora of initiatives at both national and local levels.

Having described the British situation at some length, we can perhaps best describe the situation in the USA as not being like this. An equivalent formal, national and local structure does not exist, and although there are a large number of initiatives taking place at different levels and via different methods of funding, they tend to be relatively ad hoc or to be dependent upon individuals or groups wanting to try something rather than to derive from a comprehensive attack on the problem. Whilst there is undoubtedly a very sophisticated understanding in the USA of the relationships between crime and a wide range of social, economic and physical factors, as evidenced by federally-supported initiatives such as 'community-oriented policing' and 'weed and seed' programmes, both of which offer grants at the local level in response to competitive applications, there is also no equivalent of the comprehensive public policy agenda that we see in Britain today which tries to put crime-related activities into a broader context. Indeed, whilst the British approach could perhaps be caricatured as 'more government', much of the general thrust of American national politics in the 1980s and 1990s seems to have been around the theme of 'less government', which is why it is difficult to see British types of initiatives taking place via a national policy drive in the contemporary USA, even if this were felt to be desirable. It could, of course, be argued that there is no need for such an approach to be adopted in the USA because, given its recent history of falling crime rates, it is possible that existing methods and practices are largely working, whereas the innovations to be seen in Britain stem from the failure of pre-existing polices. We think there may well be some truth in this, in the sense that the political urgency generated by the need to respond to rising crime rates has simply not been present in the USA in recent years whereas it undoubtedly has in Britain. The argument for the British approach in terms of whether or not it actually works has also yet to be established, and it might well be premature for other countries to seek to borrow and adapt that approach until this is demonstrably the case. For the present, therefore, we will simply record the view that the two approaches in terms of their organisational structures are very different, which we think is at least in part a function of the very different views taken in each country about the roles of central/federal government.

This conclusion needs to be seen as recording an important cautionary note about transplanting initiatives from the USA to Britain and vice versa without thinking carefully about these very different organisational contexts within which such initiatives will have been initially applied.

Some Ways Forward

This review has suggested to us nine broad propositions, which we would wish to advance tentatively as part of the way ahead:

- Issues related to crime and the fear of crime matter very much to local people in their communities, and if planning is to address the 'quality of life' issues that local people identify, then it must address this concern more effectively than it has done to date. Place-based crime prevention is far too important to be left to the police alone or to any other agency that does not have a grasp of comprehensive design, planning and development issues.

278 *Habitus: A Sense of Place*

- The design of the built environment does impact both upon opportunities for crime and the fear of crime, but it does this in complex ways often involving a range of intervening variables rather than in ways that generate universal rules about what works.
- Whilst crime and the fear of crime intuitively ought to be related to each other, in practice this relationship appears to be very complex. As a consequence, rather than assume that action in the one area will automatically bring benefits in the other area as well (as many contemporary initiatives do), it is better to see these as two separate but related problems which each need to be tackled via tailored programmes with clear objectives which are co-ordinated with each other.
- There needs to be a much more rigorous approach to the careful evaluation of initiatives in this field so that we learn what works well where and why, rather than the over-reliance that we have seen to date on sets of ideas often advanced by true believers in the absence of such a research base.
- Approaches need to be tailored to specific local circumstances and to the people whose daily lives are framed by those circumstances, because the likelihood that there are standard formulae that can be universally applied with a guarantee of success is remote. The role of theoretical ideas and of experiences from elsewhere is to provide some starting points for this process, rather than to pre-determine it.
- Issues around crime and the design of the built environment do not exist in isolation, but are intimately bound up with all the other cultural, social, economic and physical forces that impinge upon people's lives. Whether or not the formal approach to this is the very structured one to be found in Britain or the rather less structured one to be found in the USA, the intellectual approach to the task ought to be an holistic one rather than one that sees crime-prevention measures as free standing.
- In turn, this inevitably means that planners have to work closely not just with the police but also with many other professionals in developing possible solutions to these sorts of problems. This process must also be one of working with local communities to this end, rather than believing that solutions can be imposed on local communities. This represents a real challenge to planning professionals, not just to improve their inter-professional working skills but also to improve the ways in which they work with local communities over the long term, to shape, implement, monitor and if necessary modify initiatives.
- Statistically at any rate, some of the greatest potential gains to be had from initiatives to reduce crime and the fear of crime by environmental measures sitting alongside other types of initiatives are in some of the poorest and most deprived communities in our urban areas, simply because

these are the areas where crime rates are likely to be the highest. They may also, of course, be the hardest initiatives to mount and to sustain, as compared for example with initiatives in suburban areas with very active local communities.
- When looking at ideas from other places that may appear to be attractive, it is important to understand the context in which they have been applied and also whether or not robust evaluation has taken place. The failure to study both context and outcome can all too easily lead to ideas being imported which are imperfectly understood from the outset, and as a consequence can increase significantly the likelihood of failure when they are attempted elsewhere. In a world where knowledge in all its forms is not only constantly growing but is able to be moved around ever more rapidly, the risk of this is probably growing, especially where a 'quick fix' or 'something different' is being sought.

We believe that these principles have the capability to improve planning practice in this field quite considerably. We also believe that there may well be many others that are capable of being distilled from comparative studies of this nature, and this is work that we intend as a consequence to continue. We do, of course, reserve the right to modify some or all of these principles in the light of emerging evidence, and indeed this is probably our major plea. We wish to see the field become more evidence-driven than to date it has been, and a very good start would be a recognition of the need for all initiatives to be carefully specified and objectively monitored.

Notes

1   Many of the ideas in this chapter together with the background to them, are set out in more detail in Schneider and Kitchen (2002).
2   Although it needs to be acknowledged that the concept of fear of crime covers a multitude of responses, and is in turn just one of the many types of fear that may well have a profound effect on people's perceptions of cities. Some of these ideas are explored more fully in the chapters of this book contributed by Leonie Sandercock and by Steve Pile.
3   For the purposes of this summary, survey data rather than police records have been relied upon for information on rates of robbery, assault, burglary and motor vehicle theft. Data based upon police records have been used for information on murder rates. Data based upon police records are also presented in the study by Langan and Farrington in respect of rape (the other major crime of violence), but these are not reproduced here because of the potential unreliability of the statistics in terms of the debate around whether women report rape cases to the police because of fears as to how they will then be treated; but for the record, these figures show the rate as being

several times higher in the USA than in England and Wales, but broadly static in the former and growing in the latter. The reason for preferring survey results over police records for these comparative purposes where they both cover the same ground is that there is clear evidence that the police in the USA are much more likely to record crimes once they are reported to them than is the case in England and Wales (Langan and Farrington, 1998: 11). A further difficulty is that police definitions of what falls into what categories of crime are not always identical between the USA and England and Wales, and in the case of assault they are not even very similar. These effects almost certainly explain why police records (as distinct from survey results) show robbery in the USA to be at a higher rate than in England and Wales throughout the period in question, although converging at a rapid rate, and rates of assault in the USA to have been higher than in England and Wales throughout the period in question until 1995. Both of these findings differ from the findings emerging from survey results.

4   The specific sources for the comparative data summarised here are as follows (all Langan and Farrington, 1998):
points 1 and 2 – page 2 and Appendix 1, page 67.
point 3 – page 4 and Appendix 2, page 68.
points 4 and 5 – page iii.

5   A very good example of this phenomenon is provided by a full-page article in *The Sunday Times*, 11 January 1998, by Jon Ungoed-Thomas entitled 'A Nation of Thieves'. The summary of that article just beneath this banner headline makes our point well for us:

> 'More than one in three British men has a criminal record by the age of 40. While America has cut its crime rate dramatically Britain remains the crime capital of the West. Where, asks Jon Ungoed-Thomas, have we gone wrong?'

6   The following sequence of major articles from *The Independent* during a three-week period in July and August 2000 should serve to show this relationship:

- 11 July 2000 – 'Blair raises stakes with Commons showdown' – major story showing how the political parties are perceived in terms of law and order issues, and relating this to forthcoming 'bad news' on crime statistics.
- 17 July 2000 – 'Planners and police surrender city centres to Britain's Mass Volume Vertical Drinkers' – near-full page spread reporting the rise of violent (alcohol-related) behaviour in city centres that have fully embraced policies of promoting 'the night-time economy'.
- 18 July 2000 – 'Robberies rise by more than a quarter in a year' – full-page spread reporting new crime statistics and some local initiatives.
- 26 July 2000 – 'Ministers identify 47 crime hot spots' – near full-page spread showing Ministerial reactions to crime problems by 'cracking down' on 'hot spots'.
- 1 August 2000 – 'Crime figures sham as police fail to report 1.4m offences' – front page main story, reporting a research study on the difference between reported and recorded crime, which concentrates on the explanation that this was about massaging the figures to make the police appear more successful.

7   This particular statistic relates to one of the most contested ideas in this field, with the cul-de-sac often being favoured by those who believe in 'target-hardening' (making access to premises for the purpose of committing a crime more difficult and restricting the available escape routes) and this approach being explicitly rejected because of the kind of suburban environment it creates by 'new urbanists' who believe in permeability. The statistic does at least offer a basic rationale for the first of these two stances.

8   DoE Circular 5/94 has been formally replaced by Planning Policy Statement 1 (Office of the Deputy Prime Minister, 2005) in tandem with a 'good practice' guide on planning for crime prevention (Office of the Deputy Prime Minister and Home Office, 2004). The basic message about the importance of police-planner co-operation has been carried forward into this new documentation.

References

Brown, B. (1995) 'CCTV in town centres: three case studies', *Crime Detection and Prevention Series Paper 68, Police Research Group*, London, Home Office.
Chesney, K. (1970) *The Victorian Underworld*, London, Temple Smith.
Clarke, R.V. (1980) 'Situational crime prevention: theory and practice', *British Journal of Criminology*, Volume 20, Number 2: 136-147.
Clarke, R.V. (1992) *Situational Crime Prevention: successful case studies*, Albany, New York, Harrow and Heston.
Clarke, R.V. and Mayhew P. (1980) *Designing Out Crime*, London, HMSO.
Coleman, A. (1990), *Utopia on Trial: vision and reality in planned housing*, Revised Edition, London, Hilary Shipman,
Coleman, C. and Moynihan J., (1996) *Understanding Crime Data: haunted by the dark figure*, Buckingham, Open University Press.
Crime Concern (undated), *Reducing Neighbourhood Crime: a manual for action*, Swindon, Crime Concern for the Home Office's Crime Prevention Agency.
Crouch, S., Shaftoe, H. and Fleming, R. (1999) *Design for Secure Residential Environments*, Harlow, Longman.
Crowe, T. (1991) *Crime Prevention Through Environmental Design: application of architectural design and space management concepts*, Boston, Butterworth-Heinemann.
Dearne Valley Partnership (1996) *City Challenge: final review*, Wath-upon-Dearne, Dearne Valley Partnership.
Department of the Environment (1994) *Planning Out Crime*, DoE Circular 5/94, London, HMSO.
Department of the Environment, Transport and the Regions (1998) *Planning for the Communities of the Future*, London, DETR.
Department of the Environment, Transport and the Regions, (1999) *Revision of Planning Policy Guidance Note 3: housing*, London, DETR.
Feins, J. D., Epstein, J.C. and Widom, R. (1997) *Solving Crime Problems in Residential Neighborhoods: comprehensive changes in design, management, and use*, Washington, US Department of Justice, Office of Justice Programs, National Institute of Justice.
Fleissner, D. and Heinzelmann, F. (1996) *Crime Prevention through Environmental Design and Community Policing*, Washington, US Department of Justice, Office of Justice Programs, National Institute of Justice.
Gordon, C.L. and Brill, W. (1996) *The Expanding Role of Crime Prevention Through Environmental Design in Premises Liability*, Washington, US Department of Justice, Office of Justice Programs, National Institute of Justice.
Graham, S. and Marvin, S. (1996) *Telecommunications and the City*, London, Routledge.
Herbert, D. T. and Smith, D. M. (1989) *Social Problems and the City*, Oxford, Oxford University Press.
Home Office (1998) *The 1998 British Crime Survey: England and Wales*, Home Office Statistical Bulletin 21/98. London, Government Statistical Service.
Home Office (2000) *The 2000 British Crime Survey: England and Wales*, Home Office Statistical Bulleting 18/00, London, Government Statistical Service.

Honess, T. and Charman, E. (1992) *Closed Circuit Television in Public Places: its acceptability and perceived effectiveness*, Crime Prevention Unit Series Paper 35, Police Research Group. London, Home Office.

Hulme Regeneration Limited (1994) *Rebuilding the City: a guide to development in Hulme*, Manchester, Manchester City Council.

Jacobs, J. (1964) *The Death and Life of Great American Cities*, London, Pelican.

Jeffrey, C.R. (1977) *Crime Prevention Through Environmental Design*, Beverley Hills, Sage.

Kelso, W.A. (1994) *Poverty and the Underclass: changing perceptions of the poor in America*, New York, New York University Press.

Kostof, S. (1991) *The City Shaped*, London, Thames and Hudson.

Langan, P. and Farrington, D. (1998) *Crime and Justice in the United States and in England and Wales, 1981-96*, Washington, US Department of Justice, Office of Justice Programs, Bureau of Justice Statistics.

Locke, T. (1990) *New Approaches to Crime in the 1990s*, Harlow, Longman.

Marcuse, P. and van Kempen, R. (2000) *Globalizing Cities: a new spatial order?* Oxford, Blackwell.

McLaughlin, E. and Muncie, J. (1996) *Controlling Crime*, London, Sage.

Mumford, L. (1961) *The City in History*, Harmondsworth, Penguin.

Newman, O. (1973) *Defensible Space: crime prevention through urban design*, New York, Macmillan.

Nottingham City Council (undated), *Nottingham City Challenge, 1992-1997: a story of renewal*, Nottingham, Nottingham City Council.

Oc, T. and Tiesdell, S. (1997) *Safer City Centres: reviving the public realm*, London, Paul Chapman.

Povey, K. (2000) *On the Record: Her Majesty's Inspectorate of Constabulary*, London, Home Office.

Poyner, B. (1985) *Design Against Crime: beyond defensible space*, London, Butterworth.

Robson, B. et al., (1994) *Assessing the Impact of Urban Policy*, London, HMSO.

Rudlin, D. and Falk, N. (1995) *21st Century Homes: building to last*, London, URBED.

Rudlin, D. and Falk, N. (1999) *Building the 21st Century Home: the sustainable urban neighbourhood*, Oxford, Architectural Press.

Salford Crime Reduction Partnership (1999) *Salford's Crime and Disorder Reduction Strategy, 1999-2002*, Salford, Salford City Council.

Sherman, L.W. Gottfredson, D.C., Mackenzie, D.L., Eck, J., Reuter, P. and Bushway, S.D. (1998) *Preventing Crime: what works, what doesn't, what's promising*, Washington, National Institute of Justice Research in Brief, US Department of Justice.

Social Exclusion Unit (1998) *Bringing Britain Together: a national strategy for neighbourhood renewal*, Cm. 4045. London, HMSO.

Taylor, R.B. (1999) *Crime, Grime, Fear and Decline: a longitudinal look*, Washington, US Department of Justice, Office of Justice Programs, National Institute of Justice.

Taylor, R.B. and Harrell, A.V. (1996) *Physical Environment and Crime*, Washington, US Department of Justice, Office of Justice Programs, National Institute of Justice.

Urban Task Force (1999) *Towards an Urban Renaissance*, London, Spon.

US Department of Justice, (2000) *Criminal Victimisation in United States, 1998: statistical tables*, Washington, US Department of Justice, Office of Justice Programs, Bureau of Justice Statistics.

Walker, M.A. (1995) *Interpreting Crime Statistics*, Oxford, Clarendon Press.

14 The Silent Complicity of Architecture

KIM DOVEY

Introduction

> The most successful ideological effects are those that have no words, and ask no more than complicitous silence (Bourdieu, 1977: 188).

We experience architecture primarily in states of distraction; we live in it first and look at it second. Our contemplative gaze falls upon 'architecture' within a spatial world we have already silently imbibed and embodied. How do we reconcile this unreflexive embodiment with the production of architectural imagery; everyday life with architecture as discourse? This is a key task for architectural theory and Bourdieu can be a useful ally.

The 'habitus' and the 'field' are two key concepts which form threads through Bourdieu's sociology. The 'habitus' is a set of embodied dispositions towards everyday social practice; divisions of space and time, of objects and actions, of gender and status. The habitus comprises forms of 'habit' and of 'habitat'; it constructs both the sense of 'place' and the sense of one's 'place' in a social hierarchy. But the habitus is taken for granted, its ideological effects lie in what Bourdieu calls its 'complicitous silence'.

Bourdieu's later work on 'fields' of cultural production expands into the discursive critique of language. Overlapping 'fields' of discourse, such as art, architecture and urbanism, are like game boards with certain forces prevailing and resources at stake. The definition of the 'field' is often at stake – can a urinal become 'art'? Is a bicycle shed 'architecture'? For Bourdieu fields of cultural production, such as architecture, are structured in a manner which sustains the authority of those who already possess it, those with the 'cultural capital' and the 'feel for the game' embodied in the habitus. And attempts by the *avant garde* to overturn this alliance of architecture with authority play a key role in re-invigorating the existing 'field' of privileged practices – conservatism reappears in the guise of the ever-new. While Bourdieu's critique has its limits, it offers considerable hope for re-thinking architectural theory and for a re-engagement of architecture as social practice.

Habitus

The term 'habitus' emerges from Bourdieu's early work where it frames the ways in which the everyday world of social practice is constructed and learned in early childhood (Bourdieu 1977, 1990a, 1990b). Habitus is a term borrowed from architecture, specifically its use in Panofsky's 'Gothic architecture and scholasticism' which interprets architecture as a form of knowledge, and for which Bourdieu was the French translator (Panofsky 1967). His early structuralist account of the Berber house (Bourdieu 1973) was the base for the theory of the 'habitus'. For Bourdieu, the habitus is a way of knowing the world, a set of divisions of space and time, of people and things, which structure social practice. It is at once a di-vision of the world and a vision of the world (Bourdieu 1990a: 210). Social practice is a form of 'game' within which the habitus is learnt, not as a set of fixed categories but as a set of dispositions to act; it is the 'feel for the game' of social practice (Bourdieu, 1993: 5). The habitus is taken for granted rather than consciously conceived; a form of ideology in the sense of a socially constructed vision perceived as natural; culture seen as nature. Its importance derives largely from its thoughtlessness or *doxa* – its silence.

The habitus is not cognitively understood but rather internalised and embodied. Bourdieu refers to the dialectical relationship between the body and space as a form of 'structural apprenticeship' through which we at once appropriate our world and are appropriated by it (Bourdieu 1977: 89). As Bourdieu (2000: 141) puts it: 'We learn bodily. The social order inscribes itself in bodies ...'. One of his concerns is to cut across the divisions of subject and object, reflected in philosophical divisions between phenomenology and structuralism (Swartz, 1997). The focus on the dialectic of body and space recalls Merleau-Ponty's (1962) phenomenology of space, yet for Bourdieu this is a more socially structured lifeworld. Bourdieu deploys the phrase 'structuring structure' to describe the ways in which the habitus shapes but is in turn shaped by social practice. The habitus is both the condition for the possibility of social practice and the site of its reproduction. There are some parallels with Giddens' structuration theory with its dialectic relations of structure to agency (Giddens 1984) and with Lefebvre's (1991) focus on everyday life. While Bourdieu recognises the micropractices of institutionalised bodily discipline articulated by Foucault, he adds 'it would be wrong to underestimate the pressure or oppression, continuous and often unnoticed, of the ordinary order of things' (Bourdieu, 2000: 141).

The connections of habitus to architecture lie in the connection of habitus to habitat; the ways in which space frames social practice. For Bourdieu, space is at once both physical and social: 'Social space tends to be translated, with more or less distortion, into physical space ...' (Bourdieu, 2000: 134). The social divisions and hierarchies of the habitus (gender, class, ethnicity, age) become evident in the ways space is divided into suburbs, kitchens, playgrounds, classrooms, cafes, factories and bathrooms. And it is evident in the ways time intersects with such spatial divisions forming situations or events such as meetings, dinner parties, lectures and festivals. There are some important links here to what Hillier terms the 'social logic of space' (Hillier and Hanson, 1984).

The habitus is closely linked to the phenomenology of 'home' as both a form of unreflexive knowledge and of ontological security (Dovey, 1985, Giddens, 1990).

> The agent engaged in practice knows the world ... without objectifying distance, takes it for granted, precisely because he is caught up in it, bound up with it; he inhabits it like a garment (*un habit*) or a familiar habitat. He feels at home in the world because the world is also in him, in the form of habitus ... (Bourdieu, 2000: 142-3).

The appeal of relatively stable traditions of dwelling are seen by Bourdieu as based in a strong congruence between habitus and habitat. The habitus is subject to constant change, but such revisions are always based on existing social practices – which the habitat may change radically, the habitus evolves (Bourdieu 2000: 161). The habitus has degrees of integration and adaptation to the habitat; the built environment may challenge its dispositions, undermining the 'normal' as *avant garde* design so often does. Bourdieu's theory of the habitus is easily, but falsely, seen as deterministic. While it is limited as a theory of social change, it is useful in understanding the deep conservatism of the field of architecture and its deep complicity with practices of power (Dovey, 1999).

Field

Unlike the habitus which is a 'feel for the game', the 'field' of social practice is like a game board wherein agents are positioned with certain forces available and resources at stake in any given moment (Bourdieu, 1984, 1993). The 'field', however, is a field of endeavour which is not identified with physical space. For our interests here there are overlapping fields of discourse such as art, education, housing, urbanism and architecture. The definition of the 'field' is often part of what is at stake. The field is a social space which structures strategic action for control over resources which are construed as forms of capital (Bourdieu, 1991, 1993). This work extends the concept of 'capital' from economic capital to cultural, social and symbolic capital – significant forms of capital based on the economic but not simply reducible to it. There is a good deal of definitional confusion surrounding these terms in writing both by and about Bourdieu. In one of his clearest accounts Bourdieu (1986: 243) suggests three 'fundamental guises' of capital – economic, cultural and social capital. However, symbolic capital forms such a key part of his later theory that it must be considered a fourth category (Swartz, 1997).

Cultural Capital

Cultural capital is the accumulation of manners, credentials, knowledge and skill, acquired through education and upbringing (Bourdieu, 1993). There are three main kinds – embodied, objectified and institutionalised (Bourdieu, 1986). *Embodied* cultural capital is the component of the *habitus* which lends us the capacity to act in a way that shows class or manners. The confidence of bodily language and facial expression that engenders authority in social situations is central here. Such capital is subject to hereditary transmission in the sense that it is often acquired so young that it appears to be innate or natural. *Objectified* cultural capital is the kind of capital that is objectified in things such as art objects, food, dress and buildings. But it is more than the ownership of them – it is the capacity to choose and consume them – the objects can be bought but this capacity cannot. *Institutionalised* cultural capital is the kind of capital that is certified in institutionally recognised educational degrees and academic titles. University fees transform economic capital into cultural capital as an investment in socially valued knowledge.

Social Capital

Social capital is a resource which inheres in social relations or networks of family, friends, clubs, school, community and society. For Bourdieu social capital is based in class membership, institutionalised in the form of exclusive club membership and titles of nobility. Social capital is a collectively owned resource based on reciprocity. It differs from cultural capital by being collective rather than individual; if you leave the group you lose the capital. What is often called 'networking' can be construed as building this kind of social capital; when architecture commissions are won through social connections, social capital is transformed into economic capital. While Bourdieu depicts social capital primarily in terms of the power of dominant groups, the concept also has a growing currency as a positive resource base of all community networks (Portes, 1998; Putnam, 1995). Trust, solidarity, community and class are all forms of social capital while fear, alienation and isolation indicate its absence. Social capital is embedded in the built environment where it is sustained and reproduced by architectural programmes as spatially structured patterns of social encounter. Buildings and neighbourhoods both ground and structure social networks, enabling and constraining the development of social capital whether in housing enclaves, shopping precincts, sporting venues, community centres or university departments.

Symbolic Capital

Symbolic capital is the most problematic form of capital to define and there is considerable slippage in Bourdieu's use of it. In his early work (Bourdieu 1977) it is defined as the symbolic component of goods which demonstrate the aesthetic 'taste' of the owner. Thus it is a form of honour which is largely subsumed under objectified cultural capital as a resource which accumulates in objects and individuals. In later Bourdieu 'symbolic capital' appears to break out of any definition of cultural capital as an individually held resource:

> Every kind of capital (economic, cultural, social) tends (to different degrees) to function as symbolic capital ... symbolic capital is not a particular kind of capital but what every kind of capital becomes when it is misrecognized as capital ... and therefore recognized as legitimate. More precisely, capital exists and acts as symbolic capital ... in its relationship with a habitus predisposed to perceive it as a sign ... (Bourdieu, 2000: 242).

Symbolic capital circulates through the 'fields' of cultural production and aesthetic discourse where it melds into practices of 'symbolic domination' and what he calls (rather loosely in my view) 'symbolic violence' or 'symbolic domination'. Symbolic domination is the power to frame the field in which symbolic mastery will be determined so that the criteria of taste favour those who have already imbibed a basic disposition towards it through the habitus (Jenkins, 1992). To enter a field with any success one must possess the cultural capital and the 'feel for the game' of investing it. Yet symbolic capital is not something one possesses so much as something which infuses the field, similar in some ways to the Foucaultian (1980) notion of power with its capillary actions and micropractices.

Symbolic domination involves the power to establish the legitimacy of a particular symbolic order within a given field. In such a context, according to Bourdieu, aesthetic 'taste' is 'misrecognised' – first as a universally legitimate criteria and second as an inner quality of the individual rather than a function of the discursive field. A key part of the definition of symbolic capital is that it is 'denied capital'; it is not seen as a form of capital (Swartz, 1997: 43). Its potency in practices of power lies in this masking effect of aesthetic autonomy. Thus the slipperiness of the definition of symbolic capital is not coincidental. The production of symbolic capital is a kind of 'alchemy' through which social class divisions become naturalised (Bourdieu, 1984: 172). The base of this alchemy in the everyday dispositions of the habitus is masked – yet if it could be easily 'unmasked' then the misrecognition would not work. Like social capital, symbolic capital infuses a field rather than simply accumulating in individuals. Unlike social capital, of which more or less may be produced, symbolic capital is a fixed resource, a zero/sum game. There is only so much distinction and prestige to be distributed. If everyone gets 'good' architecture, no one wins the symbolic capital.

For Bourdieu, all forms of capital are closely linked and partially convertible into each other. An architect will inherit a certain disposition towards architecture through the habitus, will develop cultural capital through education and social capital through family, profession and other networks (Stevens, 1998; Rüedi, 1998). This will enable the architect to play the field wherein the production of symbolic capital is the architect's key market niche.

Aesthetic Distinction

So how is symbolic capital produced and distributed in the field of architecture and what is the role of cultural producers in this field? Bourdieu's (1984) book *Distinction* is an oblique attack on the primary canon of aesthetic philosophy, Kant's *Critique of Judgement* (Kant, 1974, 1979). For Kant, aesthetic value is transcendent and universal. Art is not that which simply gives pleasure or serves any personal interests – aesthetic experience transcends human interest to a higher truth which entails a certain 'disinterest' in merely human affairs. Within such a conception the aesthetics of architecture must transcend function and human interest. For

Bourdieu the ideal of aesthetic experience identified as universal truth is a paradigm case of ideology – the social misperceived as natural; a conflation of 'taste' with 'truth'. He wants to expose the Kantian view as based in class domination. 'A work of art has meaning and interest,' he argues, 'only for someone who possesses the cultural competence ... The "eye" is a product of history reproduced by education' (Bourdieu, 1984: 2-3).

For Bourdieu, a primary social function of art is to divide its audience into those who do and don't understand and appreciate it. Aesthetic judgements which appear to mark distinctions between things turn out to mark distinctions between people (Featherstone, 1991: 18). The struggle to establish and reproduce status is often based in a series of conceptual oppositions – difficult versus easy, unique versus common, original versus reproduction and form versus function – wherein the first term is implicitly privileged over the latter. Symbolic capital in a given field is established through difficulty to understand and scarcity. Legitimate taste is characterised by a privileging of form over function – a contemplative distance that only some people can afford. For Bourdieu (1984: 469) these are structures of domination wherein distinctions between people, based in cultural capital, are made to appear as pure aesthetic judgements. Interest is seen as disinterest.

The Avant Garde

The traditional role of the *avant garde* is to overturn codes of aesthetic taste. To place a urinal on display as sculpture, or chain link fence as architecture, is to invert the schemas of unique/common, original/reproduction and form/function. One of Bourdieu's key arguments is that such inversions can only achieve success within the field as already constituted. Thus the urinal becomes 'unique' when framed for formal contemplation, the chain link becomes 'difficult' as architecture. Within such a discursive field the scorn which falls on those who 'fail' to understand reinforces the social distinction.

For Bourdieu the *avant garde* fulfil a key role of keeping the images within a field from becoming stale; they change and enliven the field without disturbing its foundations. The prerequisites are a separation of form from function and a reduction of architecture to text. Popular, vulgar and common imagery can be re-valued, the order of social privilege is upturned but only on paper, framed for contemplation and consumption (Bourdieu 2000: 35). The history of 'deconstructive' architecture is a good example. Derridean designs which appear to be under collapse or erasure, aesthetic attempts to defy the alliance of architecture with authority and social order, were very swiftly appropriated into the architectural canon with considerable symbolic capital. Architects as diverse (and talented) as Eisenman and Gehry graduated to a corporate market and the clashing forms of early deconstruction lost their symbolic capital to be replaced by the fluid and folded Deleuzian images of the new *avant garde* (Jencks, 1988; Lynn, 1993). The purpose of these examples is not to denigrate any particular social theorists or their architectural followers; the point is that any imagery produced in resistance to dominant aesthetic codes can be framed, emptied of subversive power and appropriated. Those who deploy the relative autonomy of aesthetic discourse as a form of resistance to privileged codes of domination must recognise that the field is structured to appropriate semantic inversions or radical images and to use them to reinforce social distinction (Bourdieu, 1984: 254).

Bourdieu does not, to my mind, refute Kantian aesthetics so much as he shows its complicity with the production of symbolic capital. The relative autonomy of the *avant garde*, its symbolic opposition to the mainstream, is structurally necessary to its role as the primary source of new symbolic capital. Once the market embraces the product, the architect's reputation as *avant garde* is in doubt and a gap re-emerges in the 'meaning market'. The apparent autonomy of the *avant garde* is geared to its structural role in keeping the field supplied with a stream of new images. While the *avant garde* have the key role of overturning arbitrary aesthetic codes, finding or forging art out of that which had been considered artless, they can do this only within the field as already constituted.

Re-thinking Architecture

From Bourdieu's perspective aesthetic producers such as architects seem inextricably enmeshed in practices of symbolic domination. Any architecture which catches the imagination is available for appropriation as symbolic capital. What then is the scope for an architecture of social change – imagining and building a better world? I suggest there are two key questions which are not answered by Bourdieu. The first is about the relative autonomy of the *avant garde* – does the 'shock value' of the *avant garde* not have a certain surplus value beyond that which is appropriated (and cashed) as symbolic capital? Is there not a residual effect of opening cracks and breaches in the symbolic order of the kind that Delueze and Guattari (1987), Certeau (1984) and others understand as opportunities for new forms of practice? How does one account for social change and for the role of artists in the initiation of new ways of seeing? The second question is about the universality of aesthetic judgement. Bourdieu's works appears to rule out any kind of universal aesthetic but is less than convincing. To show that taste is socially produced and implicated in symbolic domination is one thing; to show that this exhausts the aesthetics of architecture is another.

Noisy Complicity

I suggest that the potential of Bourdieu's work for architectural theory and practice lies in an acceptance and articulation of the deep complicity of architecture with social order – the complicity without the silence; a noisy complicity. As the practice of imagining and building a new world, architecture will always be political. A primary imperative is that architecture be stripped of the illusion of autonomy; there is no zone of neutrality in which to practise. Architects must enter into and understand some necessary complicities.

Architecture is the practice of 'framing' the habitat of everyday life, both literally and discursively (Dovey, 1999). In the literal sense everyday life 'takes place' within the clusters of rooms, buildings, streets and cities we inhabit. Action is structured and shaped by walls, doors and windows; framed by the decisions of designers. As a form of discourse, architecture constructs the representational frameworks, the narratives of 'place', in which we live our lives. Like the frame of a painting or the binding of a book, architecture is mostly cast as necessary yet neutral to the life within. This relegation of built form to the unquestioned frame is its 'silent complicity'. The more that the structures and representations of social practice can be embedded in the framework of everyday life, the less questionable they become and the more effectively they work. This 'complicitous silence' of architecture is the source of its deepest power, in both the worst and best senses of the term 'power' – oppression and empowerment; privilege and resistance.

Buildings necessarily both constrain and enable certain kinds of life and experience – they are inherently coercive in that they enforce limits to action and enable social practice to 'take place'. The control over access to the tutorial room or the bedroom enables freedom of debate or of sexual behaviour, which an open plan would constrain. Designers who believe they are engaged in an architecture of liberation by refusing to segment space or a random segmentation may be engaged in a different form of coercion – an 'enforced' subjection to uncontrolled encounter and disciplinary gaze. The segmentation of space enables and constrains the production of social capital – the resources made available by participation in socio-spatial networks. Enclaves, security zones and boundary control techniques often generate privileged forms of social capital. But social capital can be read in a more positive sense than Bourdieu suggests – as a form of community trust, solidarity and community health (Portes 1998, Putnam, 1995; Hawe and Shiell 2000). The task of design is an inherently social practice of negotiating socio-spatial structures, space allocations, boundaries and formal expressions of identity. If social responsibilities were taken more seriously by the profession then it would gain legitimacy for the production of both symbolic and social capital. Architects inevitably manipulate modes of spatial encounter – the issue is not whether but how they do so.

Architects also necessarily shape a representational world wherein certain forms of identity and place are stabilised and authorised through built form. Architecture engages in imaginative play with our dreams of status, sexuality, security and immortality; our fears of violence, death and difference. While we may articulate theories of fluidity, transparency, virtuality and ephemerality, architecture has great inertia – it inevitably 'fixes' a great deal of economic capital into built form. As Hollier (1989) puts it, architecture is 'society's superego' in the sense that it enforces a social order. Again the issue is not 'whether' but 'how' it does so. The complicities of architecture with social order are to be understood, recognised, theorised, critiqued and debated. But the attempt to avoid such complicity is often fraught with new forms of deception.

Theory, Education and Practice

Once the silence is broken and the complicity accepted, new opportunities for architectural theory, education and practice flow from Bourdieu's work. Architectural theory and criticism can be undertaken as a form of 'field analysis' which generates an understanding of the fields in which architects are enmeshed. The task is to interpret and articulate the various interests at stake, particularly those which are hidden within the 'disinterest' of aesthetic discourse (Bourdieu, 1991: 16).

Such research must include discursive analysis of the primary circuits of symbolic capital within the field – architecture magazines and monographs, where the dominant architectural narratives are constructed and sustained. A primary task is to deconstruct the way photographs, drawings and text excise buildings from their habitus and re-package them for the field of architectural discourse. These forms of discourse construct a virtual habitus of desire, the illusion of an artful life of freedom where the traces of everyday life and human labour have been erased (Dovey, 2000).

The field of architecture with its focus on the struggle for symbolic capital between a shifting hierarchy of professional stars has a tendency to reduce academic debate to the issue of how the available symbolic capital is to be distributed – critique becomes reduced to booing and cheerleading. Architectural monographs are often funded by architects who exercise editorial control over their own critique through tame academic 'authors' (Baillieu, 1994). Photographic images are often supplied and controlled by the architect, stripped of the traces of everyday life except when used to signify forms of social capital. These books and magazines with their prices discounted by subsidy and their ideas filtered to match the ideology of aesthetic autonomy, are crucial to the production of symbolic capital within the field of architecture. And this field becomes increasingly oriented to the pursuit of symbolic capital and disconnected from the lifeworld of everyday experience. Such symbolic capital circulates across coffee tables within privileged social settings, connecting the field of architecture to the dominant social classes which are its primary market (Zukin, 1991: 47).

The values of the field also permeate architectural education with an increasing specialisation in the production of symbolic capital. Why is it that so many architects follow the footsteps of their parents (Stevens, 1998; Rüedi, 1998)? What values saturate design juries and which of our students have already imbibed those values? Why is it so difficult to generate rigorous engagement with social and environmental issues in architecture? Students are urged to produce socially and environmentally responsive work, but little of the symbolic capital within the field is distributed on those criteria unless they produce new imagery. To what extent do architecture schools hire and promote on the basis of social and cultural capital to produce graduates with more of the same to invest in the production of symbolic capital?

The early history of modernity in architecture can be read as an heroic but failed attempt to engage architecture as a social practice – a radical attempt to reinvent the habitus in both formal and functional terms. There is not scope here to pursue this history but it was based upon simplistic notions of 'function', easily reduced to imagery and co-opted to the reproduction of privilege. Social questions in architecture appeared again and again during the twentieth century yet were either resisted or co-opted into new forms of social control. The 1960s unleashed a round of promise for a more socially responsive architecture through research in human-environment studies (Alexander *et al.*, 1977; Altman, 1975; Rapoport, 1982). While such research continues it is increasingly marginalised within architecture schools and is often more useful for the questions it begs than those it answers. If buildings are shaped to match human needs, interests or desires, then whose interests are to prevail and how have they been constructed? Architecture will not progress by getting better and better at the spatial reproduction of the habitus. The reduction of architecture to any kind of programme can begin to approach social engineering. Yet the cleavage between function and form serves ideological purposes. Architecture has found a role for itself whereby the definition of the field is largely reduced to the production of imagery while control over programming is ceded to the commissioning client (Markus 1993). The illusion of 'changing the world' is maintained through the production of ever-new imagery while the reproduction of social practice continues unchallenged.

Bourdieu's work punctures this illusion and suggests that designers who seek a retreat from codes of aesthetic domination in radical forms of representation are engaged in a misrecognition of the field. Architecture is the least autonomous of the arts and even its most radical products operate to supply new images for appropriation. The only way through this nexus seems to be a re-engagement with social practice. And this will require a broad and deep understanding of both the field and the habitus of architecture.

Architecture has long lived with the tensions of being both an art and a profession – it is the most social of arts and the most aesthetic of professions. As an art it carries the obligation to imagine a future world; as a profession it carries the obligation to practise in the public interest. The idea of the 'public interest' irritates many architects with its implications of participation, populism and comfortable consensus. Yet many of the same architects conveniently forget that architecture has always served the interests of those who commission it – participation is a name we use for power when it is distributed evenly. Yet engagement with questions of the public interest need not lead to comfortable consensus at all. Real communities are shot through with differences of identity, ethnicity, age, class and gender. A socially engaged architecture entails the deconstructive and reconstructive tasks of exposing and giving voice to real public interests; unpacking and restructuring the habitus. Such a programmatic deconstruction would entail a systematic engagement with the ways in which the lifeworld has been sliced, its functions categorised, coded, juxtaposed and omitted. The key role of architects is to join design imagination to the public interest; it is to catch the public imagination with visions of a better world. The task, albeit in a small way, is to 'change the world'. It is to keep alive the liberating spirit of design without the illusion of autonomy. We cannot erase the complicity of architecture but we can render it less silent.

Postscript

As outlined in this original paper, Bourdieu's work cannot be easily incorporated into architectural critique without generating a shift in the field of practice, a field that is at once formally innovative and socially conservative. Bourdieu's work remains a powerful intellectual framework for understanding this field, yet it is notable that it is only ever used as a basis for architectural critique and not for critical approaches to architectural practice. The book by Stevens (1998) remains the most potent and sustained of such critiques but the reviews are highly polarised and he remains a marginalised figure within the field (www.archsoc.com). A key problem is that such a critique is seen as a denial of aesthetic values in architecture, a denial that is at odds not only with the way the field of practice is constructed, but also with the importance of aesthetic practices in everyday life. The response from within the field of design practice is to acknowledge yet ignore Bourdieu's work because it does not offer an easy way forward.

Within the field of architectural critique it is a different story because the intellectual framework of habitus and field offer a fertile ground for research questions on topics ranging from the formal critique of the *avant garde* to studies of everyday spatial practice and the marginalisation of environmental and social issues. The debates will surely continue and will not be easily resolved; Bourdieu's passing leaves us with more questions than answers but they are very good questions indeed.

References

Alexander, C., Ishikawa, S. and Silverstein, M. (1977) *A Pattern Language*, New York, Oxford University Press.
Altman, I. (1975) *The Environment and Social Behavior*, Monterey, Brooks Cole.
Baillieu, A. (1994) 'Vanity fare', *RIBA Journal*, January: 6-7.
Bourdieu, P. (1973) 'The Berber house', in M. Douglas (ed.) *Rules and meanings*, Harmondsworth, Penguin.
Bourdieu, P. (1977) *Outline of a Theory of Practice*, London, Cambridge University Press.
Bourdieu, P. (1984) *Distinction*, London, Routledge.
Bourdieu, P. (1986) 'The forms of capital', in J.G. Richardson (ed.) *Handbook of Theory and Research for the Sociology of Education*, New York, Greenwood.
Bourdieu, P. (1990a) *The Logic of Practice*, Cambridge, Polity.
Bourdieu, P. (1990b) *In Other Words*, Cambridge, Polity.
Bourdieu, P. (1991) *Language and Symbolic Power*, Cambridge, Polity.
Bourdieu, P. (1993) *The Field of Cultural Production*, New York, Columbia University Press.
Bourdieu, P. (2000) *Pascalian Meditations*, Cambridge, Polity Press.

296 Habitus: A Sense of Place

de Certeau, M. (1984) *The Practice of Everyday Life*, Berkeley, UC Press.
Deleuze, G. and Guattari, F. (1987) *A Thousand Plateaus*, Minneapolis, University of Minnesota Press.
Dovey, K. (1985) 'Home and homelessness', in I. Altman and C. Werner (eds) *Home Environments*, New York, Plenum: 33-64.
Dovey, K. (1999) *Framing Places: mediating power in built form*, London, Routledge.
Dovey, K. (2000) 'Myth and media', *Journal of Architectural Education*, 54 (1): 1-6.
Featherstone, M. (1991) *Consumer Culture and Postmodernism*, London, Sage.
Foucault, M. (1980) *Power/knowledge*, New York, Pantheon.
Giddens, A. (1984) *The Constitution of Society*, Cambridge, Polity.
Giddens, A. (1990) *The Consequences of Modernity*, Stanford, Stanford University Press.
Hawe, P. and Shiell, A. (2000) 'Social capital and health promotion', *Social Science and Medicine*, 51(6): 871-885.
Hillier, B. and Hanson, J. (1984) *The Social Logic of Space*, Cambridge, Cambridge University Press.
Hollier, D. (1989) *Against Architecture*, Cambridge, Mass., MIT Press.
Jencks, C. (ed.) (1988) *Deconstruction in Architecture*, Architectural Design Profile 58.
Jenkins, R. (1992) *Pierre Bourdieu*, London, Routledge.
Kant, I. (1974) *Critique of Judgement*, (Trans. J. Bernard), New York, Hafner.
Kant, I. (1979) 'A theory of esthetic experience', in M. Rader (ed.) *A Modern Book of Esthetics*, New York, Holt, Rinehart and Winston: 336-346.
Lefebvre, H. (1991) *The Production of Space*, Oxford, Blackwell.
Lynn, G. (ed.) (1993) *Folding in Architecture*, Architectural Design Profile 102.
Markus, T. (1993) *Buildings and Power*, London, Routledge.
Merleau-Ponty, M. (1962) *Phenomenology of Perception*, London, Routledge.
Panofsky, E. (1967) Architecture Gothique et Pensée Scholastique, (trans. P. Bourdieu), Paris: Minuet.
Portes, A. (1998) 'Social capital', *Annual Review of Sociology*, 24: 1-24.
Putnam, R. (1995) 'Bowling alone: America's declining social capital', *Journal of Democracy*, vol.6: 65-78.
Rapoport, A. (1982) *The Meaning of the Built Environment*, Beverly Hills, Sage.
Rüedi, K. (1998) 'Curriculum vitae: the architect's cultural capital', in J. Hill (ed.) *Occupying Architecture*, London, Routledge: 23-38.
Stevens, G. (1998) *The Favoured Circle*, Cambridge, Mass., MIT Press.
Swartz, D. (1997) *Culture and Power: the sociology of Pierre Bourdieu*, Chicago, University of Chicago Press.
Till, J. (1998) 'Architecture of the impure community', in J. Hill (ed.) *Occupying Architecture*, London, Routledge: 61-76.
Zukin, S. (1991) *Landscapes of Power*, Berkeley, University of California Press.

15 Belonging: Towards a Theory of Identification with Space

NEIL LEACH

Architecture is often linked to questions of cultural identity. For what sense would discourses such as critical regionalism or gender and space make unless they assumed some connection between identity and the built environment?[1] And yet the manner in which people actually identify with buildings has hardly been broached within architectural theory, which has been preoccupied almost exclusively with questions of form.

It is clear, however, that if theoretical commentators are to link architecture to cultural identity they must extend their analysis beyond any mere discourse of form to engage with subjective processes of identification. It is perhaps by following Homi Bhabha's concept of the nation as 'narration' – of identity as a kind of discourse – that we can grasp the importance of understanding form as being inscribed within a cultural discourse. The nation, for Bhabha, is enacted as a 'cultural elaboration'. To perceive the nation in this way in narrative terms is to highlight the discursive and contested nature of such identities: 'To study the nation through its narrative address does not merely draw attention to its language and rhetoric; it also attempts to alter the conceptual object itself. If the problematic "closure" of textuality questions the "totalisation" of national culture, then its positive value lies in displaying the wide dissemination through which we construct the field of meanings and symbols associated with national life.'[2]

Of course, it would be wrong to reduce the nation to mere narration as though form were totally unimportant. Rather we have to recognise the nation as being defined within a dialectical tension. It is a tension, for Bhabha, between the 'object' and its accompanying narrative: 'signifying the people as an a priori historical presence, a pedagogical object; and the people constructed in the performance of narrative, its enunciatory "present" marked in the repetition and pulsation of the national sign'.[3] If then the nation is a kind of narration, it is never an abstract narration, but a contextualised narration inscribed around certain objects. And it is precisely here within this field of objects which have themselves become the focus of narrative attention that we must locate architecture, as a language of forms not only embedded within various cultural discourses, but also given meaning by those discourses.

This brings us close to Bourdieu's concept of habitus, as a non-conscious system of dispositions which derive from the subject's economic, cultural and symbolic capital. Habitus, for Bourdieu is a dynamic field of behaviour, of position-taking where individuals inherit the parameters of a given situation, and modify them into a new situation. As Derek Robbins explains: 'The habitus of every individual inscribes the inherited parameters of modification, of adjustment from situation to position which provides the legacy of a new situation'.[4] Such an approach supposes an interaction between social behaviour and a given objectified condition. It is here that we could perhaps locate the position of architecture in Bourdieu's discourse.

Architecture, in Bourdieu's terms, can be understood as a type of 'objectivated cultural capital'. Its value lies dormant and in permanent potential, but it has to be reactivated by social practices which will, as it were, 'revive' it. In this respect, architecture belongs to the same category as other cultural objects: 'Although objects – such as books or pictures – can be said to be the repositories of objectivated cultural capital, they have no value unless they are activated strategically in the present by those seeking to modify their incorporated cultural capital. All those objects on which cultural value has ever been bestowed lie perpetually dormant waiting to be revived, waiting for their old value to be used to establish new value in a new market situation.'[5] In other words, what Bourdieu highlights is the need for praxis to 'unlock' the meaning of an object. In a sense this comes close to the Wittgensteinian model wherein linguistic meaning is defined by use. Just as words can be understood by the manner in which they are used, so buildings can be grasped by the manner in which they are perceived – by the narratives of use in which they are inscribed.

This opens up a crucial problematic within an architectural discourse that has traditionally been premised almost solely on questions of form. It is as though narratives of use stand largely outside architectural concerns. As a result, there is no accepted framework for exploring how people make sense of space and relate to it. Without this, the relation of architecture to cultural identity can hardly be addressed. In order for architecture to be understood in terms of cultural identity, some kind of identification with architecture must have taken place. But how exactly does this identification occur? Architectural theory is silent on this issue, while Bourdieu – for all his incisive thinking on the question of habitus – did not really address this question.

This article attempts to sketch out a schematic framework for a tentative theory of identification with space by bringing together three discreet theoretical models. Starting with a theory of how we 'territorialise' and make sense of space through a process of narrativisation, it goes on to explore how a sense of belonging to that space is achieved through 'performativities', before finally suggesting how eventual identification with a particular space is forged through a series of 'mirrorings'.

Narrativisations

In *The Practice of Everyday Life*, Michel de Certeau has developed a theory of territorialisation through spatial tactics. Through habitual processes of movement, by covering and recovering the same paths and routes, we come to familiarise ourselves with a territory, and thereby find meaning in that territory.[6]

De Certeau draws the distinction between 'place' (*lieu*) and 'space' (*éspace*). Somewhat confusingly de Certeau inverts their usual relationship such that space becomes a contextualisation of place. Space is for de Certeau, place made meaningful – 'awakened' – by practices that contextualise it: 'Space occurs as the effect produced by the operations that orient it, situate it, temporalise it, and make it function in a polyvalent unity of conflictual programs or contractual proximities. On this view, in relation to place, space is like the word when it is spoken, that is, when it is caught in a proximity of an actualisation, transformed into a term dependent upon many different conventions, situated as an act of a present (or of a time), and modified by the transformations caused by successive contexts ... Space is a practiced place. Thus the street geometrically defined by urban planning is transformed into a space by walkers.'[7]

The problem of space is, for de Certeau, ultimately a problem of representation. With Maurice Merleau-Ponty he draws the distinction between 'geometrical space' and 'anthropological space', famously observing the impossibility of grasping the 'concept' of space as a map, with his description of New York, as seen from the top of the World Trade Centre. De Certeau is close to Fredric Jameson's concern for 'cognitive mapping' in his quest for various tactics that overcome this problem.[8] Hence he formulates a 'rhetorics of space' which amounts to an individualised process of spatial demarcation, based on a linguistic model of narrativity. 'The opacity of the body,' de Certeau notes, 'in movement, gesticulating, walking, taking its pleasure, is what indefinitely organises a here in relation to an abroad, a "familiarity" in relation to a "foreignness".

A spatial story is in its minimal degree a spoken language, that is, a linguistic system that distributes places insofar as it is articulated by an "enunciatory focalisation", by an act of practicing it.[9] The city turns into a theatre of actions, narratives of space, pedestrian speech-acts: 'It is a process of appropriation of the topological system on the part of the pedestrian (just as the speaker appropriates and takes on the language); it is a spatial acting out of a place (just as the speech-act is an acoustic acting out of language).'[10] It is about 'tours' and not 'maps'. If any 'map' is achieved, it is not some abstract map, but an individualised 'cognitive map' to use Jameson's terminology. In other words it is borne of a strategic engagement with the city, and does not reside in the city itself as a collection of buildings.

'To walk,' notes de Certeau, 'is to lack a place. It is the indefinite process of being absent and in search of a proper.'[11] As Ian Buchanon observes, this opens up the reliance of de Certeau on Lacan.[12] For it is the traumatic mirror-stage – and the seemingly paradoxical attempt to overcome that alienation through repetition, as demonstrated in Freud's example of the child playing the *fort-da* game – that establishes the primordiality of Lacan in de Certeau's work. Space must be theorised by means of the mirror-stage, and spatial practices are none other than repetitive gestures aimed at overcoming the alienation of all conceptual, abstract space. As de Certeau comments: 'In the initiatory game, just as in the "joyful activity" of the child who, standing before a mirror, sees itself as one (it is she or he, seen as a whole) but another (that, an image with which the child identifies itself), what counts is the process of this "spatial captation" that inscribes the passage toward the other as the law of being and the law of place. To practice space is thus to repeat the joyful and silent experience of childhood; it is, in a place, to be other and to move toward the other.'[13] What de Certeau articulates, then, is a model for how we make sense of space through walking practices, and repeat those practices as a way of overcoming alienation.

By basing his model of spatial appropriation on linguistics, de Certeau emphasises the narrative aspect to spatial stories. Spatial tactics offer ways of making connections, and finding meaning in otherwise abstract places. But de Certeau says little about the actual identification with those spaces, being more concerned as a theorist with 'otherness' than with assimilation.[14] If then we wish to extend de Certeau's theory for making sense of place into one which establishes a mode of identification, we must also consider how these 'spatial tactics' help to forge a sense of identity.

Belonging

Here we should turn to the work of Judith Butler, who has famously elaborated a vision of identity which is based on the notion of 'performativity'. Butler is a theorist of lesbian politics, and her concern is to formulate a notion of identity that is not constrained by traditional heterosexual models and to offer a radical critique of essentialising modes of thinking. According to Butler, it is precisely our actions and behaviour that constitute our identity, and not out biological bodies. Gender, she argues, is not a given ontological condition, but it is performatively produced. It is 'a construction that conceals its genesis, the tacit collective agreement to perform, produce and sustain discrete and polar genders as cultural fictions is obscured by the credibility of those productions'.[15] By extension, without wishing to collapse sexuality, class, race and ethnicity into the same category, all forms of identity can be interpreted as dependent upon performative constructs.[16]

As such we may effectively rearticulate our identities and reinvent ourselves through our performativities. Here it is important to note that identity is the effect of performance, and not vice versa. Performativity achieves its aims not through a singular performance – for performativity can never be reduced to performance – but through the accumulative iteration of certain practices. For performativity is grounded in a form of citationality – of invocation and replication. As Judith Butler explains: 'Performativity is thus not a singular "act", for it is always a reiteration of a norm or set of norms, and to the extent that it acquires an act-like status in the present, it conceals and dissimulates the conventions of which it is a repetition.'[17]

This has obvious ramifications for a theory of identification with architecture. Butler's incisive comments on gender – gender identity being defined not in biological terms, but in performative terms as an identity that is 'acted out' – can be profitably transposed to the realm of identification with place. This opens up the possibility, as Vikki Bell has explored, of a discourse of performativity and 'belonging'.[18] 'The repetition,' she notes, 'sometimes ritualistic repetition, of these normalised codes makes material the belongings they purport to simply describe.'[19] It suggests a way in which communities might colonise various territories through the literal 'performances' – the actions, ritualistic behaviour and so on – that are acted out within a given architectural stage, and through those performances achieve a certain attachment to place.

Central to this latter notion is the idea that just as communities are 'imagined' communities, so the spaces of communities – the territories that they have claimed as their own – are also 'imagined'. 'Imagining a community,' as Anne-Marie Fortier observes, 'is both that which is created as a common history, experience or culture of a group – a group's belongings – and about how the imagined community is attached to places – the location of culture.'[20] Fortier has explored how, through ritualised repetition of symbolic acts, often conducted within an overtly religious context, these 'imagined' communities can 'make material the belongings they purport to describe'.[21] Crucially these acts are performed within specific architectural spaces.

What then happens though these stylised spatial practices is that these spaces are 'demarcated' by certain groups by a kind of spatial appropriation. Through the repetition of those rituals the spaces are 're-membered', such that those participating reinscribe themselves into the space, re-evoking corporeal memories of previous enactments. The rituals are naturalised through these corporeal memory acts, and the spaces in which they are enacted become spaces of belonging: 'Belongings refer to both "possessions" and appartenance. That is, practices of group identity are about manufacturing cultural and historical belongings which mark out terrains of commonality that delineate the politics and social dynamics of "fitting in".'[22]

What is so suggestive about the concept of 'belonging' as a product of performativity is that it enables us to go beyond the limitations of simple narrative. It privileges the idea not of reading the environment, as though its meaning were simply there and waiting to be deciphered, but rather of giving meaning to the environment by collective or individual behaviour. 'Belonging' to place can therefore be understood as an aspect of territorialisation, and out of that 'belonging' a sense of identity might be forged. The attraction of Fortier's application of performativity to space is that it resists more static notions of 'dwelling' emanating from Heideggerian discourse that seem so ill at ease with a society of movement and travel. What Fortier is proposing is not some discourse of fixed 'roots', but rather a more transitory and fluid discourse of territorialisation – in the Deleuzian sense – which provide a complex and ever renegotiable model of spatial 'belongings'. Fortier's model is essentially a rhizomic one of nomadic territorialisations and deterritorialisations. For territorialisation belongs to the same logic as deterritorialisation. What we find, then, is that the very provisionality of such territorialisations colludes with the ephemerality of any sense of belonging. Just as territorialisations are always shifting, so too identifications remain fleeting and transitory, while all the time leaving behind traces of their passage. As Bell comments: 'The rhizome has been an important analogy here, conveying as it does an image of movement that can come to temporary rest in new places while maintaining ongoing connections elsewhere.'[23]

Butler's discourse is effectively an extension to Pierre Bourdieu's debate about habitus. But what Butler brings to that debate is the possibility of political agency, and of subverting received norms. It is through its repetitive citational nature that performativity has the power to question and subvert that which it cites. For mimicry, as Homi Bhabha has illustrated, is invested with the potential to destabilise and undermine, as in the case of political satire. Performativity, in this sense, is not some uncritical and ultimately nihilistic acceptance of the given, but rather a mode of operation charged with a certain political efficacy. Moreover, whereas Bourdieu stresses the production of the subject through culture, for Butler, social structures have themselves been 'performed'. Hence performativity offers an obvious mode of challenging such structures. In an age, moreover, colonised by 'fictional worlds', as Marc Augé has described our present era, Butler importantly locates performativity at the heart of our cultural identity today.[24]

Yet if we are to understand 'belonging' as a product of performativity we must still construct an argument to explain exactly how this comes into operation. For the argument above merely assumes that a sense of belonging will emerge as a consequence of progressive territorialisation, without fully accounting for this process of identification.

Identification

Here it might be useful to consider psychoanalytic theory, which has long been preoccupied with such questions.[25] For while both de Certeau and Butler engage with psychoanalysis, it could be argued that they do not follow through its full ramifications in their work. According to psychoanalytic theory identification is always specular. It is always a question of recognising – or mis-recognising – the self in the other. There has been little discussion of this within architectural theory, but within the context of film theory, Christian Metz has outlined a series of mirrorings that occur within the cinema that constitute the basis of identification.[26] These mirrorings depend upon the nature of vision itself. Vision operates with a 'double-movement'. It is both projective and introjective. As one casts one's eye (in a projective fashion) one receives and absorbs (in an introjective fashion) what has been 'illuminated', as it were. Consciousness therefore serves, in Metz's terminology, as a 'recording surface':

> There are two cones in the auditorium: one ending on the screen and starting both in the projection box and in the spectator's vision insofar as it is projective, and one starting from the screen and 'deposited' in the spectator's perception insofar as it is introjective (on the retina, a second screen). When I say that 'I see' the film, I mean thereby a unique mixture of two contrary currents: the film is what I receive, and it is also what I release. Releasing it, I am the projector, receiving it, I am the screen; in both these figures together, I am the camera, which points and yet records.[27]

What happens, then, in the process of viewing is a series of mirror-effects. 'Am I not myself looking at myself looking at the film?' asks Metz.[28] As a result, the spectator is both absent from the screen 'as perceived', but so too present there 'as perceiver'. 'At every moment', Metz notes, 'I am in the film by my look's caress.'[29] There are, in other words, a series of specular identifications that take place in viewing a film, identifications that are connected with the mirror as the original site of primary identification.

For identification to take place with an architectural environment we should look for an equivalent process of 'mirrorings'. This process would itself be dependent on the 'introjection' of the external world into the self, and the 'projection' of the self on to the external world, such that there is an equivalence – the one 'reflects' the other – and identification may take place.

The sense of 'introjection', of the absorption of the external world, described by Metz, is echoed within an architectural context in the work of Benjamin, who presents the mind as a kind of camera obscura, a photosensitive 'plate' onto which certain interiors are etched in moments of illumination. But this occurs only at certain moments when a particularly memorable event serves as a kind of flash bulb, flaring up like magnesium powder to imprint that interior on the mind:

> Anyone can observe that the duration for which we are exposed to impressions has no bearing on their fate in memory. Nothing prevents us keeping rooms in which we have spent twenty-four hours or less clearly in our memory, and forgetting others in which we have passed months. It is not, therefore, due to insufficient exposure if no image appears on the plate of remembrance. More frequent, perhaps, are the cases when the half-light of habit denies the plate the necessary light for years, until one day from an alien source it flashes as if from burning magnesium powder, and now a snapshot transfixes the room's image on the plate. Nor is this very mysterious, since such moments of sudden illumination are at the same time moments when we are beside ourselves, and while our waking,

habitual, everyday self is involved actively or passively in what is happening, our deeper self rests in another place and is touched by the shock, as is the little heap of magnesium powder by the flame of the match.[30]

We should perhaps extend Benjamin's suggestive model of the camera to that of the camcorder. For spatial experiences are seldom static. As such the photograph 'still' gives way to the video 'movie' as the primary model for understanding how memories of spatial experiences are 'etched' on to the mind.

The second part of the 'double-movement of vision' in Metz's terminology is the projective one. This remains a crucial aspect of the process of identification which involves a twofold mechanism of grafting symbolic meaning onto an object and then reading oneself into that object, and seeing one's values reflected in it. The environment must therefore serve as a kind of 'screen' onto which we would project our own meaning, and into which we would 'read' ourselves. As was observed by Robert Vischer in the context of empathy theory, we need to project something of ourselves on to the other in order to recognise – or misrecognise – ourselves in the other:

> At this point, however, our feeling rises up and takes the intellect at its word: yes, we miss red-blooded life, and precisely because we miss it, we imagine the dead form as living. We have seen how the perception of a pleasing form evokes a pleasurable sensation and how such an image symbolically relates to the idea of our own bodies – or conversely, how the imagination seeks to experience itself through the image. We thus have the wonderful ability to project and incorporate our own physical form into an objective form, in much the same way as wild-fowlers gain access to their quarry by concealing themselves in a blind. What can that form be other than the form of a content identical with itself? It is therefore our own personality that we project into it.[31]

This projection of personality or intentionality on to an object is one that is overlooked by much mainstream architectural commentary. The investment of meaning not only explains the creative potential of seeing oneself in the other in moments of identification, but it also explains the problematic foundation of any discourse of authenticity that, as it were, 'projects' authenticity on to an object.[32] In the hermeneutic moment one tends to read that projection as though it were a property of the object. And yet in reality, intentionality, authenticity and all kinds of content are merely projections. Buildings, according to Fredric Jameson, do not have any inherent meaning. They are essentially 'inert', and are merely 'invested' with meaning.[33]

Walter Benjamin, however, adds a crucial gloss to these processes of introjection and projection:

> Buildings are appropriated in a twofold manner: by use and by perception – or rather, by touch and sight. Such appropriation cannot be understood in terms of the attentive concentration of a tourist before a famous building. On the tactile side there is no counterpart to contemplation on the optical side. Tactile appropriation is accomplished not so much by attention as by habit. As regards architecture, habit determines to a large extent even optical reception. The latter, too, occurs much less through rapt attention than by noticing the object in incidental fashion. This mode of appropriation, developed with reference to architecture, in certain circumstances acquires canonical value. For the tasks which face the human apparatus of perception at the turning points of history cannot be solved by optical means, that is, by contemplation, alone. They are mastered gradually by habit, under the guidance of tactile appropriation.[34]

In Benjamin's terms, buildings are 'appropriated'. They are introjected – absorbed within the psyche not just through vision, but also through touch. We should perhaps extend this to include the full register of senses. Moreover, for Benjamin, these 'appropriations' are reinforced by habit. Here memory plays a crucial role. Over a period of time the sensory impulses leave their mark, traces of their reception. These traces are themselves not forgotten, but constitute a type of archive of memorised sensory experiences. Indeed life itself can be seen to be conditioned by these impulses, such that it is these that constitute our background horizon of experience. In this sense, identification might be understood as an ontological condition that is consolidated through memory. We could therefore reflect upon the model of the oneiric house offered up by Gaston Bachelard in 'The Poetics of Space'.[35] It is precisely the odour of drying raisins – parallelling Lefebvre's equally evocative description of the sound of singing echoing through the cloisters – that points to the very Proustian way in which the oneiric house is itself a type of introjection of previous experiences.[36]

Identification with place could be therefore perceived as a mirroring between the subject and the environment over time. Here we might understand the subject, in Metz's terms, as both 'screen' and 'projector'. For in moments of identification we effectively see ourselves in objects with which we have become familiar. At the same time we have introjected them into ourselves. The registering of impulses as a kind of introjection leads to one type of 'reflection' – the recognition of the other in the self. Meanwhile the projection of the self on to the external world leads to a second type of 'reflection' – the recognition of the self in the other. In either case what results is a type of mirroring. From this two-way process a fusing between self and other is achieved. And here we can recognise a second order of mirrorings. For mirrorings occur not only in the engagement between the self and the environment, but also between that engagement and memories of previous engagements. There is an originary experience that is repeated in all similar such experiences. And in that process of repetition there is a reinforcement of the original moment of identification. In this sense habit – as a ritualistic replication of certain experiences – is, as Benjamin observes, precisely that which consolidates the process of identification.

The seemingly static model of identification forged through a 'reflection' – as though in a mirror – appears at first sight to contrast markedly with the more dynamic notion of identity based on performativity. And yet, if we perceive the former as being grounded in a certain intentionality, we should recognise the actative dimension to the gaze itself. For performativity is not merely a question of physical performance. It extends also to modes of perception, such as the gaze. Butler has already addressed how the gaze should be seen as the site of performativity in the context of race: 'I do think that there is a performativity to the gaze that is not simply the transposition of a textual model onto a visual one; that when we see Rodney King, when we see that video we are also reading and we are also constituting, and that the reading is a certain conjuring and a certain construction. How do we describe that? It seems to me that that is a modality of performativity, that it is radicalisation, that the kind of visual reading practice that goes into the viewing of the video is part of what I would understand as the performativity of what it is "to race something" or to be "raced" by it. So I suppose that I'm interested in the modalities of performativity that take it out of its purely textualist context.'[37]

This can be extended to the gaze as the potential site of an identification with place, since any act of viewing may be charged with a conscious moment of politicised reading. Visual attachments might therefore be read as containing an actative, performative moment. And what applies to the gaze may equally apply to the other senses. What we find, then, is that identification based on a process of mirroring is but a variation on the actative identification with place embodied in ritualistic patterns of behaviour. It is through the repetitive performativities of these various modes of perception that a mirroring can be enacted and a sense of identification with place can be developed and reinforced through habit.

308 *Habitus: A Sense of Place*

Conclusion

Identity, Freud once remarked, is like a graveyard of lost loves and former identifications. Among these identifications we could include architectural ones. Through a complex process of making sense of place, developing a feeling of belonging and eventually identifying with that place, an identity may be forged against an architectural backdrop. As individuals identify with an environment, so their identity comes to be constituted through that environment. This relates not only to individual identity, but also to group identities.

Architecture therefore offers a potential mechanism for inscribing the self into the environment. It may facilitate a form of identification, and help engender a sense of belonging. From this point of view, architecture may be seen to play a potentially important social role. The significant factor, however, – beyond the nature of the environment – is our engagement with that environment. For identification is a product of the consciousness by which we relate to our architectural surroundings, and not a property of the architecture itself. Nor does matter – in Butler's terms – exist outside of discourse. As Mariam Fraser observes, following Butler: 'Matter does not "exist" in and of itself, outside or beyond discourse, but is rather repeatedly produced through performativity, which "brings into being or enacts that which it names".'[38]

All this helps us to reassess the relationship between architecture and cultural identity. The message is clear: we should focus not only on architectural forms themselves – for we would be wrong to dismiss these forms as irrelevant – but also on the narrative and performative discourses that give them their meaning.[39] Indeed, with time architectural features tend to lose their prominence, and slip into becoming an unnoticed and marginal background landscape. If identity is a performative construct – if it is acted out like some kind of 'filmscript' – then architecture could be understood as the 'filmset'. But it is as a 'filmset' that it derives its meaning from the activities that have taken place there. Memories of associated activities haunt architecture like a ghost.

Notes

1   The implication that critical regionalism may contribute in some way to cultural identity is made, at least, in one of the chapter titles, 'Critical Regionalism: Modern Architecture and Cultural Identity', used by Kenneth Frampton in his seminal study, *Modern Architecture: A Critical History* (1992). But it would appear that Frampton himself has explored this connection just once – and even then only very briefly:

'Among the preconditions for the emergence of a critical regional expression is not only sufficient prosperity but also a strong desire for realising an identity. One of the mainsprings of regionalist culture is an anticentrist sentiment – an aspiration for some kind of cultural, economic and political independence.' Frampton (1983).
2 Bhabha (1990a).
3 Bhabha (1990b).
4 Robbins, D. (2000) *Bourdieu and Culture*, London, Sage: 30.
5 Robbins (2000): 35.
6 De Certeau, M. (1984) *The Practice of Everyday Life*, Stephen Rendell (trans.), Berkeley, University of California Press.
7 De Certeau (1984: 117).
8 Famously Jameson analyses the homogenising placelessness of late capitalism through the confusing spatial layout of the vast atrium of the Bonaventure Hotel in Los Angeles. He goes on to explore the process of what he terms 'cognitive mapping' as a means of inscribing oneself in the environment, and overcoming this placelessness. In capitalist society everything is co-opted into signs, images and commodities, and the world threatens to become increasingly depthless. But aesthetics also promises a way out of this condition. The domain of aesthetics can therefore be seen to play a Janus-faced role. On the one hand it contributes to the aestheticisation of the world. On the other it promises to counter that tendency by offering a mechanism of identification. If we are to follow Jameson's arguments, what we need today is a viable aesthetic practice that reinserts the individual within society. Aesthetics may play this role and serve as a form of cognitive mapping. As such, we might recognise the primary social role that architecture may play.
9 De Certeau (1984: 130).
10 De Certeau (1984: 97-8).
11 De Certeau (1984: 103). 'Proper' here would appear to be referring not to 'propriety', but to a sense of 'appropriation'.
12 Buchanon, I. (2000).
13 De Certeau (1984: 109-110). 'Captation' might equally be translated 'appropriation'.
14 See, for example, his book on 'otherness': Certeau, M. de (1986) *Heterologies: discourse on the other, trans*, Brian Massumi, Manchester: Manchester University Press.
15 Butler, J. (1990: 3).
16 Bell discusses the possibility of understanding Jewishness in this light in Bell (1999). See also Gunew (1996: 159-171).
17 Butler, J. (1993) *Bodies that Matter*, London, Routledge: 12.
18 Bell (1999).
19 Bell (1999).
20 Fortier, Anne-Marie (1999) 'Re-membering places and the performance of belonging(s)', in Vikki Bell (ed.), *Performativity and Belonging*, London: Sage, 1999: 42.
21 Bell (1999: 3).
22 Fortier (1999: 42).
23 Bell (1999: 9).
24 Augé, M. (1999) *A War of Dreams*, trans. Liz Heron, London, Pluto.
25 For Butler's engagement with psychoanalysis, see especially Butler, J. (1997) *The Psychic Life of Power: theories of subjection*, Stanford, CA, Stanford University Press.
26 Metz C. (1982) *Psychoanalysis and the Cinema*, Celia Britton, Annwyl Williams, Ben Brewster and Alfred Guzzetti (trans.), London, Macmillan: 48.
27 Metz (1982: 51).
28 Metz (1982: 52).

29 Metz (1982: 54).
30 Benjamin, W. (1979) *One-Way Street*, London, Verso: 342-3.
31 Vischer, R. (1994) *Empathy, Form and Space*, New York, Routledge: 104.
32 If we are to look for a model of the way in which content might be understood as a kind of 'projection' we could consider the work of the Polish-Canadian public artist, Krzysztof Wodiczko, who literally projects politically loaded images on to buildings as a commentary on the politics of use of that building. In 1985 Wodiczko projected the image of a swastika onto the pediment of South Africa House in Trafalgar Square, London. This act was intended as a political protest against the trade negotiations then underway between the apartheid government of South Africa and the British government under prime minister, Margaret Thatcher. The projection of the swastika onto the building raises some interesting questions about the relationship between buildings and politics. In particular it highlights the condition of buildings which have been blemished with the stain of evil. His projection of 'content-laden' images on to monuments and buildings echoes the process by which human beings 'project' their own readings onto them, as though on to some blank cinematographic screen. On the work of Krzysztof Wodiczko, see 'Public Projections' and 'A Conversation with Krzysztof Wodiczko', *October*, 38: 3-52.
33 'I have come to think that no work of art or culture can set out to be political once and for all, no matter how ostentatiously it labels itself as such, for there can never be any guarantee that it will be used the way it demands. A great political art (Brecht) can be taken as a pure and apolitical art; art that seems to want to be merely aesthetic and decorative can be rewritten as political with energetic interpretation. The political rewriting or appropriation, then, the political use, must be allegorical; you have to know that this is what it is supposed to be or mean – in itself it is inert.' Jameson (1996: 258-59).
34 Benjamin, W. (1969) *Illuminations*, New York, Shocken: 233.
35 The notion of oneiric space is also central to de Certeau's concept of space. As he observes: 'From this point of view, after having compared pedestrian processes to linguistic formations, we can bring them back down in the direction of oneiric figuration, or at least discover on that other side what, in spatial practice, is inseparable from the dreamed place.' De Certeau, M. (1984: 103).
36 Bachelard, G. (1996: 92); Henri Lefebvre (1996: 142).
37 Judith Butler, 'On Speech, Race and Melancholia', (interview with Vikki Bell) in Bell (1999).
38 Fraser, Mariam, 'Classing Queer,' in Vikki Bell (ed.) (1999).
39 Thus regionalism, for example, should be more properly understood in narrative terms as a 'discourse' of regionalism.

References

Augé, M. (1999) *A War of Dreams*, trans. Liz Heron, London, Pluto.
Bachelard, G. (1996) 'The poetics of space (extracts)', in Neil Leach (ed.), *Rethinking Architecture*. New York, Routledge: 86-97.
Bell, Vikki (ed.) (1999) *Performativity and Belonging*, London, Sage.
Benjamin, W. (1969) *Illuminations*, New York, Shocken.
Benjamin, W. (1979) *One-Way Street*, London, Verso.
Bhabha, H. (1990a) 'Introduction', in Homi Bhabha (ed.) *Nation and Narration*, London, Routledge: 1-9.

Bhabha, H. (1990b) 'DissemiNation', in Homi Bhabha (ed.) *Nation and Narration*, London, Routledge: 298-299.
Buchanon, I. (2000) *Michel de Certeau*, London, Sage.
Butler, J. (1990) *Gender Trouble*, London, Routledge.
Butler, J. (1993) *Bodies that Matter*, London, Routledge.
Butler, J. (1997) *The Psychic Life of Power: theories of subjection*, Stanford, CA, Stanford University Press.
Certeau, Michel de (1984) *The Practice of Everyday Life*, Stephen Rendell (trans.), Berkeley, University of California Press.
Certeau, Michel de (1986) Heterologies: discourse on the other, Brian Massumi (trans.), Manchester: Manchester University Press.
Fortier, Anne-Marie (1999) 'Re-membering Places and the Performance of Belonging(s)', in Vikki Bell (ed.) (1999) *Performativity and Belonging*, London, Sage: 41-64.
Frampton, K. (1983) 'Prospects for a critical regionalism', *The Yale Architectural Journal*, 20.
Frampton, K. (1992) *Modern Architecture: A Critical History*, London, Thames and Hudson, 3rd edition.
Fraser, Mariam, 'Classing Queer', in Vikki Bell (ed.) (1999). *Performativity and Belonging*, London, Sage.
Gunew, Sneja (1996) 'Performing Australian Ethnicity: 'Helen Demidenko', in W. Ommundsen and H. Rowley (eds) *From a Distance: Australian Writers and Cultural Displacement*, Geelong, Deakin University Press: 159-171.
Jameson, Fredric (1996) 'Is space political', in Neil Leach (ed.) *Rethinking Architecture*, New York, Routledge: 255-269.
Lefebvre, H. (1996) 'The production of space (extracts)' in Neil Leach (ed.), *Rethinking Architecture*, New York, Routledge: 139-146.
Metz C. (1982) *Psychoanalysis and the Cinema*, Celia Britton, Annwyl Williams, Ben Brewster and Alfred Guzzetti (trans.), London, Macmillan.
Robbins, D. (2000) *Bourdieu and Culture*, London, Sage.
Vischer, R. (1994) *Empathy, Form and Space*, New York, Routledge.
Wodiczko, K. (1986) 'Public Projections' and 'A Conversation with Krzysztof Wodiczko', *October* 38 (Winter 1986): 3-52.

DECOLONISING SPATIAL HABITUS

16 Place-making as Project? Habitus and Migration in Transnational Cities

JOHN FRIEDMANN

The work of Pierre Bourdieu, particularly his central and twinned concepts of habitus and social field, has not, to my knowledge, been widely applied to the study of built forms, the city, or that elusive but related notion of place. In the following remarks, I would like to explore this application and, more particularly, explore the potential usefulness of Bourdieu's sociology for the city-building professions. After elucidating the mutually contingent meanings of habitus and field, I will look at five ways by which Bourdieu's theory of the habitus, which is essentially a theory of social reproduction, may be extended to illuminate also processes of social change. Continuing with some observations on Bourdieu's interpretation of the typical dwelling in Kabyle village society in Algeria, I proceed to a more general discussion of habitus and the built environment in the contemporary, increasingly transnational metropolis. I conclude by asking whether and under what conditions localities whose habitus has been severely strained by the settlement of transnational migrants can become proactive on their own behalf and, in this way, attempt to heal the wounds they have sustained.

Habitus and Field Defined

Pierre Bourdieu is somewhat reluctant to give an explicit account of his theoretical framework. He prefers to let theory emerge from actual field investigations. Still, from time to time, he has felt obliged to expound his theoretical approach, and it is from these sources that I have drawn my own understanding of habitus and field (Bourdieu, 1990, 2000; Bourdieu and Wacquant, 1992. See also Calhoun, 1989).

The habitus of concrete social practices does not exist in a vacuum of social relations; rather, its discovery requires that we first delineate the social field that has both structured the habitus specific to it and, in turn, been structured by it. Societies are composed of a large number of relatively autonomous, linked, and overlapping social fields, and it is these fields that, Bourdieu believes, should be the principal focus of a reflective, self-critical sociology.[1] Some fields, such as a specific social class or, for that matter, the village society of the Algerian Kabyles, are vast and encompassing, while others are more narrowly, though still quite broadly defined.[2] Examples would be the social worlds of the university, artistic production, science, medicine, the military, business, and religion. Each of these fields is structured by relations of power among individuals and institutions that occupy strategic positions within it. The object of these power holders is to keep the 'game' going. The game itself is understood as a form of agonistic competition among all of the players deployed in the field for the accumulation of 'symbolic capital', another key term in Bourdieu's lexicon. It is this constant striving for influence and power which, he argues, are the real stakes of the game. Specific rules must therefore be strictly enforced to prevent the game from deteriorating into chaos.[3]

Corresponding to each social field is a characteristic habitus which gives each player a 'pre-reflective, infra-conscious mastery' of the field (Bourdieu and Wacquant, 1992: 19). Bourdieu defines the habitus as the *durable, transposable, structured (and structuring) dispositions* of individuals (Bourdieu, 1990: 53). Specific to a given field or, more precisely, specific to identifiable positions within the field, the habitus has to be learned. It manifests itself as a pattern of practices so tuned to the rules of the game that, to be in the field and take part in the ongoing game is to feel comfortable and 'at home' (Bourdieu and Wacquant 1992: 128). By the same token, social practices tolerated and even appreciated in one field, say in a Melbourne working man's pub on a Saturday night, would be shockingly out of place in a nearby upscale restaurant, where they would make everyone feel ill at ease.

The term 'dispositions' is critical to the definition of habitus and needs clarification. We could say that the habitus serves as a kind of template which generates strong, normative *propensities* of actual social practices that are considered normal, acceptable conduct within a given field. According to Bourdieu, the habitus serves as a 'generative principle' that makes possible, but also *sets limits to*, the 'free production of all the thoughts, perceptions, and actions inherent in the particular conditions of its production' (Bourdieu, 1990: 55). Thus the blanket term 'practices' covers forms of behaviour, speech, bearing, posture, manners, eating conventions, aesthetic preferences, as well as ways of seeing and interpreting the world.

The habitus is always gender-specific and sometimes age-specific as well. Acquired in early childhood, it evolves throughout one's lifetime on the basis of new experiences. Though inscribed in the individual human body, it is a collective phenomenon in the sense that a certain habitus is and, indeed, must be shared or, at least, implicitly understood and accepted by all the players in the game. The tendency is therefore for the collective habitus to be preserved over relatively long periods of time. But because the field is subject to multiple influences, both from within and outside itself, it inevitably undergoes a slow process of change, so that what were acceptable practices, say, three or four decades ago, would not necessarily be acceptable conduct now, or at least would seem odd, quaint, or old-fashioned.[4]

As a collective phenomenon, the habitus enables social practices to be 'objectively harmonized', like the sounds of a 'conductorless orchestra' (Bourdieu, 1990: 58). It may happen and, indeed, it happens to most of us, that we are forced (or may choose) to enter another field than the one in which we are 'at home'. This involves learning a new set of rules, a process that is slow and painful and which we experience, Bourdieu asserts, as a kind of 'second birth' (ibid.: 68). In some cases, this process may be seen as a 'natural' extension of one's basic class habitus, as when young men of Prussian Junker background choose a military career instead of going into business; but for most of us, living in turbulent times, what economists would call a path-dependent choice has become an increasingly untenable option, and we find it necessary to transit from field to field more than once over the course of our lives.

Habitus and Social Change

Listening to Bourdieu's voice, one senses that his interest is firmly focused on practices that ensure the social reproduction of fields. His construct is a loose, time-sensitive *structural* theory; it admits of 'strategic actions', for example, but only in a restricted sense, that is, not as a voluntaristic, existential choice, but as 'objectively oriented lines of action which social agents continually construct through practice' (Bourdieu and Wacquant, 1992: 129). The habitus is not explicitly tied to a theory of social change.[5]

It is not my intention here to enter into a lengthy debate about Bourdieu's complex relation to the Parisian structuralist school (Lévy-Strauss, Althusser, Foucault, etc.). Above, I referred to Bourdieu's acknowledgment, in conversation with Loïc Wacquant, that in certain circumstances, we can experience a 'second birth', as we enter a new field with its attendant habitus. But, the impression one has is that the deep structure of the first habitus is never quite erased. Here is Bourdieu's thinking in his own words:

> Habitus is not the fate that some people read into it. Being the product of history, it is an *open system of dispositions* that is constantly subjected to experiences, and therefore constantly affected by them in a way that either reinforces or modifies its structures. It is durable but not eternal! Having said this, I must immediately add that there is a probability, inscribed in the social destiny associated with definite social conditions, that experiences will confirm habitus, because most people are statistically bound to encounter circumstances that tend to agree with those that originally fashioned their habitus (Bourdieu and Wacquant, 1992: 133).[6]

Social destiny, statistical probabilities ... terms such as these suggest the maintenance of structurally generated dispositions. But there are many situations, and I would insist on their relevance and importance, where both individual and collective habitus are fundamentally altered, with major consequences for social life generally. Let me briefly refer to some of them.

Escaping the habitus Many people in modern class societies are socially mobile, usually upward, but occasionally also in the other direction. You are born into a working class family, but because of education and/or marriage, you gradually move out of your class background into a new field where different rules prevail. You change your speech patterns, your eating habits, your clothing, your way of looking at the world. Even your bodily form and bearing may undergo a change (say, by a change in diet or by exercise), and you prefer not to be reminded of the field you have left behind as you have moved on and disappeared into a new world. Perhaps this is what Bourdieu meant by 'second birth'. But it is more than an overlay on first dispositions. Your first dispositions were left behind, leaving their traces only in your memory.

Forcing the habitus through migration That we are living in an 'age of migration' is no longer headline news. But whether it's from the countryside to the city, or across national boundaries, migration typically involves a massive readjustment of migrants' habitus. Migrants who move from a rural village into the metropolis, looking for work in building construction or in factories have to learn not only new skills but also a new work discipline, a new rhythm of life, a new sense of time. They may struggle with a new dialect or language. Their senses are bombarded with a range of new impressions which have to be absorbed and interpreted. The children of adult migrants will have an easier time to learn the habitus appropriate to their new station in life. For a while, they may learn to adopt one set of practices in school at the same time that another, more traditional habitus, is enforced by parental authority at home. But sooner or later, migrant children will opt for the class habitus of the metropolis, and this may lead to serious conflicts with their parents, particularly as it concerns the conduct of young women. If their mothers should also be working in the economy, they, too, will undergo a change of habitus, but if they are not, they will remain staunchly settled in the old ways of their village, which is the only way they know how to make sense of the world. There are many variations of this story, but the kernel of all of them is always the same: how to make a more or less successful transition from one habitus to another as a matter of economic survival.

Challenging the habitus Migrants' adjustment of their habitus as a matter of survival or escaping one's class habitus by choice through education and/or marriage are both individual achievements. But in the final decades of the twentieth century, major challenges of shared, collective habitus have been launched by social movements, most notably the feminist movement. In all parts of the world, women's habitus has been defined (and enforced) by a patriarchal ideology that places women in a subordinate and dependent position to men. The feminist movement has rebelled against these restrictions on the power of women, with some considerable success in the Western industrialised regions of the world, though even here the patriarchal hegemon is far from having been defeated. In other parts of the world, most notably Afghanistan, he has roared back with a vengeance and sought to exclude women from public life altogether, confining them to their servile, reproductive roles in the home. So the struggle over a gender-specific habitus continues and, because it involves a *collective* habitus, it is, in the first instance, a social struggle which, of course, has also an individual dimension (as in the case of escaping the habitus into which one is born).

Accelerated change of habitus Although Bourdieu's concept of the habitus is a dynamic one which allows for certain change, the impression one gets is that any changes are apt to proceed at a somewhat leisurely pace. While this may well be true of traditional Kabyle society, it is blatantly not the case as soon as we focus on the modern metropolis. Here life is speeded up, and not only life, but also the changes it imposes on one's habitus. Is this a mere illusion, or is it actually the case? The influences on one's habitus multiply in the large city. There is more variety, more exposure to different experiences. Relative to rural folk, urbanites are more literate, more alert to change, more open to changes in fashion – not only in clothing but also in preferences for food, speech patterns, religious cults, popular culture. In the post-Fordist world, it is the rare person who enjoys the privileges of a life-time job. Young people try their hand at many things. Even later in life, flexi-time arrangements allow one to experiment with a variety of work and occupations, including self-employment which may expose one to different fields. Pierre Bourdieu is entranced by the notion of play or game (*ludus*), to the point of using 'field' and 'game' indifferently for each other. In fact, however, life in the metropolis may increasingly be experienced as ludic or 'playful', an aspect also noted by Henri Lefebvre. This may have been made possible by the generous safety net provided by a welfare state that is still largely intact, at least in Australia and the countries of the European Union. Or it may be the colourful multiplicities of possible worlds that confront one in the city (except for those considerable numbers who are economically excluded from participating in this meta-game).[7] All of this, however, may lead one to greater awareness of one's original habitus, to confront it more openly in what Bourdieu calls self-analysis, and to experiment with a variety of roles throughout one's lifetime.

The breakdown of habitus   The breakdown of habitus manifests itself not only in societies where the social order has collapsed – as it has at various times in Rwanda, Liberia, Somalia, Kosovo and Chechnya – but also in such reputedly stable societies as the Japanese. In a recent article by David Esnault, winner of Japan's 1998 Reporter prize, we learn of widespread voluntary prostitution among schoolgirls who are 'well educated and not from particularly poor families', of children who beat up their parents, of a type of bullying, prevalent especially in junior schools, called *ijime* that is a form of psychological torture and may lead to suicide and occasionally the murder of one's tormentors, and of a sharp rise in the number of assaults and violent crimes committed by juveniles, many of them committed by very young adolescents often for no particular reason or on only the slightest of pretexts (Esnault, 1999). Whatever the reason for this apparent upsurge in 'dissident' behaviour (to put a positive spin on a story that others have linked to the breakdown of traditional Japanese society), it is clear that for those perpetrating these acts, the habitus of their early upbringing has all but collapsed or, at the very least, been badly damaged. It reminds one of similarly disoriented youngsters who go on 'wilding' expeditions in New York City's Central Park, or of 'drive-by' shootings in Los Angeles. This breakdown of habitus in otherwise 'normally functioning' societies is pathology not envisioned in Bourdieu's theoretical vision.

The foregoing examples are not meant to question the role of habitus in social reproduction. Bourdieu is absolutely right in stressing its stabilising role. But it is not the whole story. Whether the culprit is called modernisation, urbanisation, globalisation, complex dynamics capable of disrupting the existing social order and to transform it into something else, the evidence suggests that the twinned concept of habitus/field is a great deal more malleable than Bourdieu suggests.

Habitus and the Built Environment

With this in mind, I would now like to look more closely at how the concept of habitus/field can be used in the study and practice of the built environment and, more specifically, in a perspective of social change. Bourdieu himself has not concerned himself with this question. When he resorts to metaphors of space, he has almost always a social space in mind.[8] The major exception to this is his well-known essay on the Kabyle dwelling, reproduced as an appendix to *The Logic of Practice* (Bourdieu 1990), and which in *Pascalian Meditations* he cites as a 'quasi-perfect coincidence between habitus and habitat' (Bourdieu, 2000: 147).

Bourdieu undertook extensive anthropological studies of Kabyle society during the latter half of the 1960s, a work that resulted in his first major book, published in French in 1972 and, five years later in an English translation, the *Outline of a Theory of Practice* (Bourdieu, 1977). The Kabyles are an ancient, predominantly agricultural, tribal people of North Africa, whose centre is the rugged Kabylia region of Algeria. Forming one of the larger divisions of the Berbers whose culture is known to be more than four thousand years old, they are known for their fierce resistance to the successive conquerors of the region and were in the forefront of the struggle to drive the French colonial government out of Algeria. Slow to adopt the Muslim religion and Arabic speech, they still retain their vernacular language, at least in the central and southern parts of Algeria.

In Bourdieu's account, the Kabyles are a phallocentric, highly regulated society which finds its legitimacy in a cosmic world view based on the binaries of light and darkness, outside and inside, and dominant/virile and subordinate/receptive. I would like to quote a few short excerpts from Bourdieu's masterful essay 'The Kabyle House or the World Reversed', to give both the flavour of his writing and a glimpse into the world of the Kabyles in their southern mountain strongholds.

The interior of the Kabyle house is rectangular in shape and divided into two parts, at a point two-thirds of the way along its length, by a small openwork wall half as high as the house. The larger of the two parts, some fifty centimetres higher and covered with a layer of black clay and cowdung which the women polish, is reserved for human use. The smaller part, paved with flagstones, is occupied by the animals. A door with two wings gives access to both rooms (Bourdieu, 1990: 270).

*

The lower part of the house is the place of the most intimate secret within the world of intimacy, that is, the place of all that pertains to sexuality and procreation. More or less empty during the daytime, when all the (exclusively female) activity in the house is centred on the fireplace, the dark part is full at night, full of human beings and also full of animals, since the oxen and cows, unlike the mules and donkeys, never spend the night outdoors; and it is never fuller than in the wet season, when the men sleep indoors and the oxen and cows are fed in the stable. The relationship that links the fertility of the humans and the fields with the dark part of the house ... is here established directly (Bourdieu, 1990: 274).

*

At the centre of the dividing wall, between 'the house of the humans' and 'the house of the animals', stands the main pillar, supporting the 'master beam' and the whole framework of the house. The master beam (*asalas alemmas*, a masculine term) which extends the protection of the male part of the house to the female part, is explicitly identified with the master of the house ... (Bourdieu, 1990: 274-5).

*

In contrast to man's work, which is performed outdoors, women's work is essentially obscure and hidden ...: 'Inside the house, woman is always on the move, she bustles like a fly in the whey; outside the house, nothing of her work is seen'. Two very similar sayings define woman's estate as that of one who can know no other abode than the tomb: 'Your house is your tomb'; 'Woman has but two dwellings, the house and the tomb'.

Thus, the opposition between the women's house and the men's assembly, private life and public life, the full light of day and the secrecy of night, corresponds exactly to the opposition between the dark, nocturnal, lower part of the house and the noble, brightly lit, upper part. The opposition between the external world and the house takes on its full significance when it is seen that one of the terms of this relation, that is, the house, is itself divided in accordance with the same principles that oppose it to the other term. So it is both true and false to say that the external world is opposed to the house as the male to the female, day to night, fire to water, etc., since the second term in each of these oppositions splits, each time, into itself and its opposite.

The house, a microcosm organized on the same oppositions and homologies [qualities of similarity in structure, form, or function] that order the whole universe, stands itself in a relation of homology to the rest of the universe. But, from another standpoint, the world of the house, taken as a whole, stands in a relation of opposition to the rest of the world, an opposition whose principles are none other than those that organize both the internal space of the house and the rest of the world and, more generally, all areas of existence. Thus, the opposition between the world of female life and the city of men is based on the same principles as the two systems of oppositions which it opposes to one another. The application to opposing areas of the same *principium divisionis* that establishes their opposition ensures economy and a surplus of consistency, without involving confusion between those areas (Bourdieu, 1990: 276-7).

The world of the Kabyle house is indeed a World Reversed!

I would now like to ask you to join me on a mental journey, and to imagine a number of Kabyle families as they move from their mountain eyries to the city. To make the contrast as stark as possible, let that city be Frankfurt, Germany. At first, only the men made the move at a time, in the early 1960s, when Germany was importing large numbers of *gastarbeiter*. The work and the pay were good, and after some years, the men decided to bring their families from Kabylia to join them. Once in Frankfurt, their families had to move into *Mietskasernen* or tenement flats that had absolutely nothing in common with their dwellings back home. The cosmic order that had always given meaning to their lives had been shattered for good.

The men worked on construction jobs and had picked up enough German phrases to get by in their daily work. Their children, if they were old enough, were sent off to school where they soon became fluent in the Frankfurt vernacular, although at home they continued to speak their own language, increasingly peppered with German expressions. But what about the women? What was their place in the new setting?

The tenements where the newcomers lived were in an old Frankfurt neighbourhood of older working class Germans intermixed with a sprinkling of Moroccan and Turkish guestworker families. A few local food shops catered to the *Ausländer* or foreign migrants, but to get to a mosque, they would have to take public transport to a suburban location. Initially, what was to grow into a small Kabyle community had found accommodations through personal contacts, but once a beachhead had been secured in the neighbourhood, others soon followed. The Kabyles tended to cluster together, as did the Moroccans and Turks, glad to find people like themselves, similarly disoriented, to whom they could pout their pain, recall familiar scenes from the old country, and who would help each other cope with their new life. Occasionally, their kids would come home from school with tearful tales of chicanery and harassment inflicted upon them by their German schoolmates. But who was there to complain to and to set matters right? Their children's teachers spoke no Arabic, their menfolk had to report to work every morning, and the women, cowed and vaguely fearful, or maybe just shy, couldn't even begin to contemplate contacting the authorities – and what authorities, after all? – to protest the rowdy waywardness of their children's tormentors. It was difficult enough for them to venture out onto the street to buy ingredients for their next meal, in an area where hardly anyone spoke their language and where they, themselves unable to read Arabic not to mention incomprehensible German, might easily lose their way. Come evening, their menfolk, tired from work, would return home, expecting the familiar dishes of their village, but they would often be obliged to make do with whatever was set before them. The flavour had gone out of their food.

One day, a young woman will appear on their doorstep, accompanied by an interpreter. She has come from the city's Office of Multicultural Affairs to invite the Kabyle women to a welcome festival for newcomers to be held at the Römer, the city's main square. Would they please come dressed in their 'native costume' and perhaps perform some village dances for the audience in the interest of furthering cultural understanding. This would be a popular event, drawing thousands to the festivities. The Kabyle women scarcely knew how to reply to this invitation which, though spoken by the skilled interpreter in mellifluous Arabic, asked them to dance before the eyes of thousands of strangers. And perhaps they thought to themselves: 'Woman has but two dwellings: the house and the tomb'.

I trust that this imaginary journey has been sufficiently instructive to raise a number of questions. We have seen that Kabyle habitus is strongly gendered, defining very clear roles and physical spaces for both male and female. It is also evident that their habitus is deeply integrated with a particular view of the world, and indeed of the universe as a whole, which, though deeply patriarchal, confining women's place to the enclosure of the house, is a world view so complete in itself that even the dwelling reflects it symbolically in its layout, domestic space being tightly controlled in the sense of who may occupy it at what times and for what purposes. For all of its rigidity, it provides a strong sense of order and security for all members of the clan. The world is as God has ordained it. Outside forces are repelled, sometimes fiercely, and the culture remains intact. The great turning point in Kabyle life came with the Arab conquest in the eighth century, when Kabyles converted to Islam and began using Arabic as the new *lingua franca* of the region while retaining their own vernacular. Their strictly enforced habitus guaranteed that the social order of Kabyle peasant society would be reproduced down through the centuries, from generation to generation. Cultural changes no doubt have occurred over the past twelve hundred years, but we know little about them from Bourdieu's account.[9]

Migration to Germany disrupted this habitus once and for all, at least for those who made the move.[10] (We know nothing about the flow of influences back to Kabylia villages, though some has undoubtedly occurred over the past forty years as migrants returned, new technologies were imported, remittances from abroad raised living levels, etc.). The tenement flats in cosmopolitan, multicultural Frankfurt allowed none of the practices which had been central to life in Kabylia to be maintained. It is nevertheless interesting to note that transnational migrants in Frankfurt (as indeed in all transnational cities) tend, at least initially, to cluster in what we may call *affinity environments*. As distinct from ghettos, affinity environments represent a voluntary clustering of migrants in certain districts that, by virtue of migrants' proximity to each other, offer material and cultural support and eases the psychological pain of coping with the strains of surviving in a city where none of the familiar cultural cues are present. Absent these cues, situations arise that can lead to a serious misreading by both newcomers and older resident populations of practices that, harmless and even well-intentioned in themselves, may easily be interpreted as hostile, leading to flare-ups of passion.

The adjustment of migrant families to their new life is mediated through gender, age, and education. The men work, leaving their dark, airless, and overcrowded flats in the morning, to return only at night. In this way, they maintain their dignity as Kabyle men: they are not house husbands, 'who brood at home like a hen in its nest' (Bourdieu, 1990: 276).[11] Men's place is out of doors, women's place is inside the home. But Kabyle women cannot remain completely shut in, not in a city like Frankfurt. They have to run errands, use public transport, look after their small children, perhaps become involved with a Kabyle women's group. In this wider range of contacts, they must venture out into public space, learn its geography, its opportunities and pitfalls. Their inability to speak German, let alone read it, proves to be a major handicap.

Kabyle children growing up are the real problem, however, especially the boys, since girls are more under the supervision of their mothers and likely to be more inclined to accept – a gender-specific habitus – the rules of the patriarchal order in 'exile'. Marriage in the traditional manner may be arranged for them, with bridegrooms from their home villages coming to Germany; alternatively, on reaching adolescence, some of the girls may be sent home to relatives in Kabylia to get them out of harm's way. But the boys assimilate rather quickly to their new surroundings and are powerfully attracted to the material youth culture of Germany. This brings them inevitably into conflict with their parents, who may still harbour thoughts of eventually returning to an ever more idealised Kabylia, and are likely to be 'in denial' about the very real cultural disruption they have suffered.

And there is this further consideration. Many of the Kabyles' German neighbours are not particularly friendly towards the newcomers or, indeed, towards the other *Ausländer* living in their midst, Turks and Moroccans. There are so many barriers to mutual understanding: physical appearance, religion, language, dress, the smell of their food and even of their bodies. But there is also a feeling of resentment, because many Germans, especially among the unemployed, believe, rightly or wrongly, that it's the *Ausländer* who are taking their jobs away. The Kabyle kids experience this resentment physically, hence their many tales of woe. Children want desperately to belong, but in the end, Kabyle boys have only each other. And so they form gangs that are up to all sorts of mischief, from graffiti to drugs, and fight with (perhaps) local Turkish and Moroccan gangs that have come into existence for much the same reasons: rejection by Germans, poor performance in school (language, cramped quarters at home), frustrated material dreams, the need for some recognition by one's peers.

Youth gangs add a reality dimension to the neighbourhood, where older German residents now have an objective reason to feel insecure and perhaps even threatened by muggings and street violence. Police presence is increasingly visible, and boys quickly learn that the German police are likely to see things, not surprisingly, from a German perspective. The result is that the number of Kabyle, Turkish and Moroccan arrests is disproportionately large in Frankfurt.

In the opinion of many Germans, the Kabyles are intruders. Originally, they may have been invited to Frankfurt as guestworkers, but that was then, and this is now. It's true, they may have had the legal right to bring their families, but no one asked them to stay put and disrupt the peaceful neighbourhood with its homey *Biergarten*, small groceries, and butcher shops. The character of the neighbourhood has changed and, in the opinion of the German residents, much for the worse. Their grown-up children no longer want to live there, and are likely to move into 'nicer' (and safer) suburbs as soon as they are able. And what began as a mixed neighbourhood and an affinity environment for Kabyles, Turks and Moroccans may, in the longer term, turn into a foreign ghetto.[12]

How are places, like our imaginary Frankfurt working class neighbourhood, severely strained by their insertion into the global economy, most powerfully by transnational migration, to be reconstituted? And is reconstitution, assuming it is desirable, a genuine possibility? This is the question which I should like to explore next.

Place-making as Project?

In a first-rate theoretical reflection on the 'politics of place', Arif Dirlik argues the case for conceiving of 'place as a project' somewhat along the lines of what the 'modernist project' was in its dimensions of development, social analysis, and culture, only in a very different direction (Dirlik, 1999: 43ff). For Dirlik, place is a topographically and ecologically situated, inhabited space, a locality whose boundaries are porous, but even so, a particular world, with its own historical memory and shared understanding of itself. I want to pick up on Dirlik's proposal, using my imaginary Kabyles in Frankfurt to further explore the meanings of habitus. In this next stage of our journey, I will give a more precise definition of 'place' and a pragmatic meaning to 'project' that differs significantly from Dirlik's use of the term.

I have already referred, if somewhat obliquely, to the transnational character of Kabyle migration. What I mean by this is simply that the Kabyles, in their (temporary?) and voluntary exile, are living simultaneously in two countries: the Algeria of their origin and the Germany of their present work. In the latter, they earn money and raise their families, but their 'true home' continues to be Kabylia in whose stony and unforgiving ground their culture has its roots, where many of their relatives continue to live, where their remittances go, and where they are politically engaged.[13] In Frankfurt, by contrast, they are socially and politically excluded. Thus we may call Frankfurt a divided city, a place torn apart by migration from outside the European Union.[14]

'Place' and 'place consciousness', terms that have come into increasing use, tend to have a positive connotation, just as 'placelessness' is generally regarded as Gertrude Stein is supposed to have said about

Oakland, California, '*there is no there there*'. In my own vocabulary, however, the subjective quality of a place, what can perhaps usefully be called its character, is neither good nor bad. Always a locality, but of uncertain dimension, its character is simply what it is. To use a terminology derived from Marxism, an Oakland or Frankfurt (or any specific subdivision of these cities) is merely a place *in* itself, not necessarily *for* itself. If it is to become the latter, that is, if it is to begin to think of itself *politically*, it must become a 'project' for a significant part of its population, it must be rescued from anonymity through collective action.

The 'home away from home' which the Kabyles in Frankfurt made for themselves was gained at the expense of the 'affinity environment' of the resident German population which they disrupted by settling into the neighbourhood. It is this disruption of a finely tuned German working class habitus-turned-habitat that many among the local German residents resent, and why they wish the foreigners would 'go back to wherever they came from'. A place so torn apart will have the character that it does, a wounded, conflicted place, but it will never be able to think of itself politically as a place *for* itself, inclusive not only of Germans, but of Kabyles, Turks and Moroccans as well. To become that kind of place, to mobilise itself around common objectives, will require something more than the hollow rhetoric of multiculturalism.

In the late 1980s, a Social Democratic and Green coalition captured the Frankfurt City Council and, under the charismatic leadership of Daniel Cohn-Bendit, established the city's first-ever Office of Multicultural Affairs in Germany (Friedmann and Lehrer 1997). It was a valiant, if underfunded, effort that, by a variety of ingenious means, attempted to institutionalise something like a *local citizenship* for residents 'without a German passport', the new euphemism for *Ausländer* or aliens. I followed the story for a number of years, until a more conservative Council was elected and Cohn-Bendit departed for the European Parliament in Strasbourg. But my guess is that the anti-foreign sentiment among many Frankfurters hasn't changed much over the decade, and that the once so proud designation of *local citizen* has left a bitter aftertaste for a population that continues to be socially and politically pushed to the margins, much as was the case before the municipal experiment with multiculturalism. When, as a result of the recent federal elections in Germany, the Greens joined the SPD, this time in a national 'red' coalition, one of the first moves they made was to launch a proposal that would make it much easier for aliens to gain German citizenship, including even dual citizenship. This brave attempt was hooted down by the conservative opposition even before it reached the *Bundestag* and it was made abundantly clear that, as far as most

Germans are concerned, citizenship is a privilege reserved chiefly for those of German ancestry, however distant, and not for swarthy foreigners.[15]

Despite this, I would maintain that the notion of at least a local citizenship has merit and is actually the basis for what must become a four-pronged approach to integrate transnational migrants both socially and politically at the level of local government. The aim would be to create an environment in which local places (neighbourhoods, city blocks), torn apart by migrant settlement, can be sutured and healed and begin to become proactive on their own behalf. Briefly, the four prongs are these: *special education* to assist foreign kids of both genders to overcome the learning difficulties they experience in their host city, supplemented by adult education programmes, especially for migrant women; *job creation* for both citizens and permanent residents in cities and regions suffering economic depression; *restructuring local governance* in ways that will give presence and voice to the excluded population and get them actively to participate in programs for the betterment of their own neighbourhoods; and *opportunities for inter-ethnic dialogue* through joint sponsorship of collective neighbourhood projects involving volunteer efforts, the joint celebration of festivals, and similar undertakings. None of these programmatic suggestions will be easy to implement, and outcomes are not guaranteed. But, in principle, they should help foster something like local citizenship and pride in one's place of residence that will go a long way towards healing the social body. Short of a multi-layered approach such as this, wounded places will remain wounded, ghetto formation will almost certainly continue, and anti-foreign feelings will seek to find expression in nationalist parties that, like Austria's Freedom Party, thrive on racism and may ultimately inflict great harm on our liberal democratic order.

Concluding Observations

We seem to have travelled far from our initial concern with habitus and the built environment, but even if invisible, the concept of habitus has been with us all along. Bourdieu's master concept needs to be critically examined before it can be applied, particularly in highly dynamic situations such as those we encountered in our hypothetical case study. We saw how the Kabyles' habitus was fatally challenged by their migration to metropolitan Germany where it could no longer be sustained by the physical space of their traditional dwellings which once had ordered the smaller and larger rhythms of their lives.[16] We also saw how, by staying close to each other in the foreign city, they had hoped to create an 'affinity environment' that would help ease the multiple shocks they experienced in facing life in the foreign city. But the very success they had in consolidating their beachhead also disrupted the lifeworld of their German neighbours whose larger environment had been finely attuned to their own habitus that was being torn apart by the newcomers. The result was a severely damaged, conflicted place which, in turn, led Kabyle families to strengthen their transnational relations with the Algerian homeland, even as their adolescent children, particularly the boys, grew further and further apart from them, but in a Germany that, at least until recently, refused to even consider them as potential citizens. The result was a criminalisation of some parts of Kabyle life in the foreign city, and increasing violence at home and on the street.

This, then, is a story without a conclusion. There are other, kinder stories, but the underlying dynamics are much the same. In a general way, we know what needs to be done to bring peace to the city, but it is not clear whether we have the time, or indeed the will, to work through the experiments that hold out some hope in an otherwise bleak situation.

As for Bourdieu's theory of the habitus/field, we concluded that it is perhaps of only limited use for the city-building professions. Most of us live in cities, and our psyches are subject to repeated shocks. Either simultaneously or sequentially, we participate in multiple fields and learn to accommodate our practices to always changing environments and structures of power. Over a single lifetime, most of us change our habitat more than once – in Australia, by some accounts, as many as thirteen times over a lifetime – and some of these moves may even take us to foreign parts, where our immediate neighbours may be quite unlike us in their cultural and class background, and may not even speak our language or share our beliefs. And yet, we somehow survive, as do our neighbours, and on the whole we manage to get on with life.

Notes

1 For Bourdieu, 'a differentiated society is not a seamless totality integrated by systemic functions, a common culture, criss-crossing conflicts, or an overarching authority, but an ensemble of relatively autonomous spheres of "play" that cannot be collapsed under an overall societal logic, be it that of capitalism, modernity, or post-modernity' (Bourdieu and Wacquant, 1992: 17).
2 Bourdieu defines a social class as 'biological individuals who are the products of the same objective conditions, have the same habitus' (Bourdieu, 1990: 59).
3 For Bourdieu, each field is a kind of 'game' whose players have a sort of unwritten understanding among themselves that the game is worth the candle. Bourdieu calls this understanding *illusio*. While this may be an adequate account of 'games people play'

Place-making as Project? 331

in, say, academic life, the concept of game/*illusio* has little relevance in the life of poor people engaged in their daily struggles for subsistence/survival.

4   It is noteworthy that Bourdieu talks primarily of 'practices' rather than 'actions'. His concept of 'strategic action' is part of the struggles for symbolic capital within a given field and is therefore interest-driven. It is thus very different from the Arendtian concept of action which refers to 'setting something new into the world', a new beginning with uncertain consequences (Arendt, 1958).

5   'The social world has a history,' writes Bourdieu (2000: 215), 'and for this reason it is the site of an internal dynamic, independent of the consciousness and will of the players, a kind of *conatus* linked to the existence of mechanisms which tend to reproduce the structure of the objective probabilities or, more precisely, the structure of the distribution of capital and of the corresponding chances of profit.'

6   To this statement, Wacquant adds a revealing footnote: 'Aside from the effects of certain social trajectories, habitus can also be transformed via socio-analysis, i.e., via an awakening of consciousness and a form of "self-work" that enables the individual to get a handle on his or her dispositions, as Bourdieu suggests. ... The possibility and efficacy of this kind of self-analysis is itself determined in part by the original structures of the habitus in question, in part by the objective conditions under which the awakening of self-consciousness takes place. ...' (ibid.: 133, fn 86). One is left with the impression that escaping the vice of one's habitus is a relatively rare occurrence. I propose to argue the opposite case.

7   According to Calhoun (1989, note 17), Bourdieu agreed with commentators at a conference that 'complex' societies are importantly characterised by a multiplicity of fields, by contrast with societies in which the division into fields is minimal.

8   In an essay that was available to me only in a German translation, Bourdieu's understanding of the built environment in relation to social space is made explicit. The structure of social space, he says, is *inscribed* in physical space. Habitus makes the habitat, in the sense that 'it forms specific preferences for a more or less adequate use of habitat'. Or more concretely, a working class habitat is formed by working class habitus, just as upper class habitus shapes the exclusive residential districts in which the upper class, by preference, resides (Bourdieu, 1991; see also Bourdieu, 2000: 134). But the theme is not further elaborated.

9   Bourdieu assumes that the society of the Kabyles which he studied in the 1960s was a uniform society throughout, informed by the same world view and engaged in like practices. But this is a questionable assumption, as the Kabyles do not live in isolation but have continuing contacts both within Algeria and outside, with the Kabyles in Algiers and Frankfurt, for example. Their society is thus undergoing a process of change that may leave it fractured.

10 Please remember that we took the Kabyles on an imaginary journey. In fact, I don't know how many Kabyles went to Germany to work, though many undoubtedly did. But what I describe in the text has happened to other groups of whom we know, for example Moroccans and Turks. The Kabyles' story is useful, because it allows us to link up with Pierre Bourdieu's work about their world view, and how this is reflected in the construction of their homes and the meanings attached to different spaces within them. For relevant information on North African migration to Europe, see Reniers (1999).

11 But when Kabyle men become unemployed, or teenage boys cannot find a job, what happens to their self-esteem? And where do they go to uphold their male code?

12 For some evidence along these lines, see Blom (1999). The foregoing is a composite description from many accounts of migrant settlements in transnational cities. See, for

example, Häußermann and Oswald (1997). The Frankfurt story is in part based on Friedmann and Lehrer (1997). I have purposely left out the growing influence of Islamist organisations among North African migrants in Germany, France and elsewhere in Europe. See the essays by Jonker and Tietze in Häußermann and Oswald (1997).

13 For the concept of transnationalism, see, among others, Basch *et al.* (1994), Smith and Guarnizo (1998), Ong (1999), and Friedmann (1999).
14 Citizens of EU countries are allowed to vote in local elections in Germany and are otherwise privileged. Karpf (1993) wrote a history of immigration into Frankfurt to show that Frankfurt has never been an ethnically homogeneous city, and his book was part of a larger effort to create a political space for new wave immigrants. He therefore did not dwell on the disruptions of habitus and place which this new wave brought about.
15 In May 1999, however, the *Bundestag* did manage to reform Germany's nationality law, which made the acquisition of German citizenship through naturalisation much easier than it had been. (See http://www.bundesregierung.de/english/09-11-1999 The new Nationality Law).
16 Roxana Waterson (this volume) tells a different story but with quite similar outcomes for a community's habitus among the Sa'dan Toraja of Sulawesi. Migration (in this case out-migration) played a role here as well, but so did conversion to a Protestant form of Christianity and the opening up of isolated, closed village societies over a period of several decades.

References

Arendt, H. (1958) *The Human Condition*, Chicago, The University of Chicago Press.
Basch, L. *et al.* (1994) *Nations Unbound: transnational projects, postcolonial predicaments, and deterritorrialized nation-states*, Langhorne, PA, Gordon and Breach.
Blom, S. (1999) 'Residential Concentration Among Immigrants in Oslo', *International Migration*, 37, 3: 617-642.
Bourdieu, P. (1977 [1972]) *Outline of a Theory of Practice*, Cambridge, Cambridge University Press.
Bourdieu, P. (1990) *The Logic of Practice*, Stanford: Stanford University Press. (Orig. 1980).
Bourdieu, P. (1991) 'Physischer, sozialer, und angeeigneter physicher Raum', in Wentz, M. (ed.), *Stadt-Räume*, Frankfurt/New York, Campus Verlag: 25-34.
Bourdieu, P. (2000 [1997]) *Pascalian meditations*, Cambridge, Polity Press.
Bourdieu, P. and Wacquant, L.J.D. (1992) *An Invitation to Reflexive Sociology*, Chicago, University of Chicago Press.
Calhoun, C. (1989) 'Habitus, field, and capital: the question of historical specificity', in Calhoun C. *et al.* (eds), *Bourdieu: critical perspectives*, Chicago, The University of Chicago Press.
Dirlik, A. (1999) 'Globalism and the politics of place', in Olds, K. *et al.* (eds) *Globalisation and the Asia-Pacific: contested territories*, London and New York, Routledge: ch. 3.
Esnault, D. (1999) 'Japan's teenage horrors', *Le Monde Diplomatique*, September, 14.
Friedmann, J. and Lehrer, U. (1997) 'Urban policy responses to foreign in-migration: the case of Frankfurt-am-Main, Germany', *Journal of the American Planning Association*, 63, 1 (Winter): 61-78.

Friedmann, J. (1999) 'Transnational migration and the spaces of incorporation', in Friedmann, J. (forthcoming), *The Prospect of Cities*, Minneapolis, University of Minnesota Press.

Häußermann, H. and Oswald, I. (eds) (1997) Zuwanderung und Stadtentwicklung. Leviathan, Sonderheft 17, Opladen/Wiesbaden, Westdeutscher Verlag.

Karpf, E. (1993) 'Und mache es denen hiernächst Ankommenden nicht so schwer ...': Kleine Geschichte der Zuwanderung nach Frankfurt am Main. Frankfurt, Campus Verlag.

Ong, A. (1999) *Flexible Citizenship: the cultural logics of transnationality*, Durham, N.C., Duke University Press.

Reniers, G. (1999) 'On the history and selectivity of Turkish and Moroccan migration to Belgium', *International migration*, 37, 4: 679-714.

Smith, M.P. and Guarnizo, L.E. (eds) (1998) *Transnationalism from Below. Comparative Urban and Community Research* vol. 6, New Brunswick, N.J., Transaction Publishers.

17 Enduring Landscape, Changing Habitus: The Sa'dan Toraja of Sulawesi, Indonesia

ROXANA WATERSON

Introduction: Landscape, Habitus and the Sense of Place

The worlds of meaning that cultures create grow out of time and space. In their interactions with local environments, humans shape the landscape around them and read into it the traces of ancestral and historical activity. Over time, as meaning becomes sedimented in landscape, so people themselves become embedded, or, to use Peter Gow's (1995: 51) turn of phrase, *implicated* in the landscape, able to understand its meanings. This, Gow emphasises, is not simply a subjective experience of gaining knowledge, 'because implication depends on actively moving around in the landscape, and leaving traces in it'. This emphasis on a physical involvement, on process and movement, is a good starting-point for an understanding of the cultural specificity of people's senses of place. We can connect it, too, to the germinal ideas of Pierre Bourdieu (1977, 1990a) which focus upon the role of practice in social life, as distinct from structures or abstract rules, and his concept of habitus, with its emphasis on embodied dispositions. Bourdieu himself makes use of a topographical image when he contrasts the notion of 'culture' as a map – 'the analogy which occurs to the outsider who has to find his way around in a foreign landscape' – with 'the practical space of journeys actually made, or rather of journeys actually being made'. The sum of these journeys constitutes the practical mastery of the native, a mastery which itself involves an embodiment of orientations (Bourdieu, 1977: 2).

The extent to which social knowledge is vested in landscapes is a matter which has been subjected to close analysis in some recent anthropological studies (Bender, 1993; Hirsch and O'Hanlon, 1995; Fox, 1997). The latter volume focuses specifically on ideas of locality in Austronesian societies. Fox (1997: 8) introduces the concept of *topogeny*, or 'the recitation of an ordered sequence of place names'. 'Like genealogies,' he notes, 'topogenies figure prominently among Austronesian populations but have not been recognised as a distinct means for the ordering and transmission of social knowledge. In so far as a sequence of names can be attached to specific locations in an inhabited landscape, a topogeny represents a projected externalisation of memories that can be lived in as well as thought about.' Especially typical in eastern Indonesia are recitations, often in poetic form, that describe the migrations of a name group or clan from a distant point of origin to their present location. In these accounts, images of pathways and journeys predominate; the entire history of a group and its encounters with others is typically represented as the travels of a single individual, rendered in a first-person narrative. In that volume, I wrote about how Sa'dan Toraja myths and historical memories are inscribed on the landscape and serve certain purposes in terms of how people construct their relationships, both to neighbouring societies and to each other (Waterson, 1997). The claims to precedence embedded in these stories are still deployed for political purposes in the present. While this paper shares the concern with landscape, I shift my focus here from history to ritual practice and the world view generated by the Toraja indigenous religion, which is nowadays known as *Aluk to Dolo* ('Way of the Ancestors') or *Alukta* ('Our Way'). I shall examine some different kinds of narrative recitation, occurring in ritual contexts, which also describe journeys through the landscape – this time, of deities summoned to be present at a rite, or of the spirit of a recently deceased person, who is invited to set out toward the Afterlife. I argue that Toraja religion generated its own distinctive habitus, which for participants involved an ongoing interaction with deities and ancestors whose presence was so much *in nature* that it saturated the landscape itself with meaning. Offerings performed while the rice is growing are held on rice field banks, mountain tops or hillsides, where a bamboo pole hung with offering baskets remains as a marker of the communication established with the locally residing deities who ensure fertility. Family tombs are hollowed out of egg-shaped granite boulders or cliff faces, where from balconies in the rock, the wooden effigies (*tau-tau*) of the deceased look out across the rice fields they once cultivated. The ancestors, too, were once believed to be close at hand, their shades accompanying the living as they went about their tasks of ploughing and harvesting. Since this religion is now in crisis, probably in its death-throes, I am also obliged to ask what happens to this habitus in a situation of profound social transformation? Is the dislocation and disenchantment involved in the conversion to a predominantly Calvinist style of Christianity also causing the landscape itself to become drained of meaning?

Social Transformation and the Transformation of Habitus

The concept of habitus, which Bourdieu derives from various antecedents, has been variably formulated and elaborated in his writings, as he has developed it in his own distinctive way.[1] In *The Logic of Practice* (1990a: 52-65), habitus is defined as 'systems of durable, transposable dispositions, structured structures predisposed to function as structuring structures, that is, as principles which generate and organise practices and representations that can be objectively adapted to their outcomes without presupposing a conscious aiming at ends or an express mastery of the operations necessary in order to attain them' (1990a: 53). 'Dispositions' refers to the values internalised and embodied by individual actors, in processes of socialisation into a culture which begin early in life, and are in large part absorbed without needing to be consciously articulated. Images from his fieldwork among the Kabyles of Algeria – of the house as a 'book' which children learn to read with the body, of the radically contrasting postures and gaits of men and of women – are memorably deployed in the substantiation of this concept, which in its insistence on the not fully conscious nature of much cultural knowledge, can be seen to bear close affinity with Michael Polanyi's (1975) conception of 'tacit knowledge'. Polanyi sets out to characterise a category of 'personal knowledge', particularly the processual knowledge which is concerned with practical mastery of skills. This involves the tacit integration of a complex multitude of elements – an ability which the human brain is able to perform with incredible swiftness, without stopping to make a conscious selection. In performing a skill such as hammering a nail, or riding a bicycle, we do not, indeed, must not, hold in focal awareness everything we are doing; the focus instead is projected on to a subsidiary element (the nail to be hammered, the road ahead). The sense of 'knowing what we are doing' comes precisely when we no longer have to stop and think about it. This integrative ability is also implied in the acquisition of experience which is necessary for excellent performance in any specialisation, whether as a doctor, an athlete, an art dealer, or anything else. Furthermore, Polanyi proposes that it is this kind of knowledge and ability to project our attention which is deployed in our assessment of social situations and our ability to read or intuit others' motives in social interactions.

Suggestive as this is, Polanyi does not pursue the precise extents to which everyday knowledge of all kinds may be held out of conscious awareness. In a recent collection of papers, Bloch (1998) attempts to push further a project to build better bridges between anthropology and cognitive psychology. Trying to explain how it is possible, for instance, for Malagasy farmers to assess at a moment's glance whether a certain hill slope would make a good swidden or not, he argues that such mental feats can only be explained if we assume that the knowledge involved is organised, not in a linear, sentence-like fashion (as has often been proposed), but as a mental model (Johnson-Laird, 1983) or schema (Schank and Abelson, 1977) within which multiple parallel processing can take place (Bloch, 1998: 8, 12-14). He argues that much of our cultural and practical knowledge of different domains or situations (environmental, social or otherwise) must be organised in terms of such schemata, by means of which a whole set of different kinds of information can be almost instantaneously reviewed in such a way as to allow amazingly rapid assessments of a given situation, without the person having had time to make an explicit selection of evidence. In the light of this proposal, it is explicit, linguistically articulated knowledge that begins to look 'peculiar', and Bloch (1998: 16) concludes that 'we should treat all explicit knowledge as problematic, as a type of knowledge probably remote from that employed in practical activities under normal circumstances'.

Bourdieu for his part has left vague the question of how the brain is working at producing tacit knowledge, which might be seen as a shortcoming. However, he discusses habitus in such a way as to make clear that he, too, sees it as encompassing very large areas of social action. This is all the more so since individual habitus is clearly not developed in isolation but as part of social groupings – family, class, gender, and so on. The idea of habitus potentially provides a means to illuminate the interface between individuals and the social organisations in which they participate, and the problem of how cultures are able to reproduce themselves. It is not surprising, therefore, that Bourdieu should show a concern with time, particularly in the way that actions and decisions taken must, he argues, be viewed as *strategies*, which partly depend on time for their effect. The strategy approach, however, generally deals with time in the shorter, rather than the longer, historical term. Strategies represent choices between the available possibilities for action, which, while in no way predetermined by 'culture', are always limited by already existing circumstances. Habitus is thus 'a virtue made of necessity' (1990a: 54). In a somewhat equivocal way, strategies are depicted as being the only semi-conscious outcome of the actors' decisions, formulated without subjective intention. Habitus is 'a spontaneity without consciousness or will' (1990a: 56). People act without necessarily 'knowing what they are doing', producing statistical regularities of which they themselves may be unaware. Although social scientists have always reserved the right (and probably must, of necessity, do so) to discover meanings in social action of which actors are unaware, this aspect of the theory has been criticised by a number of commentators. They consider that Bourdieu's formulations underestimate the ability of actors to analyse their own situations, thus denying them any real agency (Jenkins, 1992:77; Strathern, 1996: 28), while simultaneously generating a far too static vision of social life (Calhoun, 1993: 70). The main difficulty is that habitus is depicted as always tending to reproduce itself; while the *possibility* of innovation, or of disruption in times of crisis, is acknowledged, the image of society actually produced in Bourdieu's writings is an overwhelmingly conservative one, which fails to examine in great depth the potentials for either incompetent performance, resistance or change.

What happened to history? Of course Bourdieu is far too sophisticated not to have considered the historical nature of all human action, as of all sociological data. In fact, habitus is repeatedly defined in terms of history:

> The habitus, a product of history, produces individual and collective practices – more history – in accordance with the schemes generated by history. It ensures the active presence of past experiences, which, deposited in each organism in the form of schemes of perception, thought and action, tend to guarantee the 'correctness' of practices and their constancy over time, more reliably than all formal rules and explicit norms (1990a: 54).

Or again:

> The habitus – embodied history, internalised as a second nature and so forgotten as history – is the active presence of the whole past of which it is the product. As such, it is what gives practices their relative autonomy with respect to external determinations of the immediate present. This autonomy is that of the past, enacted and acting, which, functioning as accumulated capital, produces history on the basis of history and so ensures the permanence in change that makes the individual agent a world within the world (1990a: 56).

And yet, it is strange that 'history' here is conceived solely in terms of 'constancy' and 'permanence'. There is no sense of the tracing of great social transformations in the interface between the individual and the collective, as is so brilliantly pursued, for example, by Norbert Elias (1994) in his study of the evolution of manners in European civilisation. And this is all the more curious, given that the two countries in which Bourdieu has done most of his fieldwork – Algeria and France – have hardly been immune to dramatic social transformations. It seems that in the late 1950s and early 1960s, Bourdieu did write about the social pressures at work in contemporary Algerian society – he could hardly have overlooked them! – but these writings have been less accessible to an English-speaking audience.[2] And yet, discussions of history, conflict and change are largely conspicuous by their absence from his presentation of his fieldwork in Kabylia in either Bourdieu (1977) or (1990a). If he held these concerns apart in his earlier work, presenting them in separate texts, we might see this as maintaining a certain conformity to the ethnographic conventions of the time, though these would soon be transformed by the suddenly increased concern with history that has marked so much anthropological writing of the 1980s onward. Still, the presentation in (1990a) is quite continuous in style with the earlier work. Similarly, the discussion of kinship strategies in Béarn, France (1990a: 147-61) focuses on the duties imposed by tradition while remaining mute on the pressures of modernity that have transformed rural practices all over Europe, and which are vividly depicted in a work such as Collier (1997).

In his most recent book (2000), Bourdieu addresses these criticisms, articulating more clearly his ideas with regard to the transformation of habitus, which, he now emphasises, must often encounter conditions different from those in which it was formed in the first place. He notes that new experiences, and especially education, have the potential to alter the habitus by raising to consciousness aspects of the old habitus. He observes (2000:161) of his Béarn research how it revealed that upper class families of the region were clinging to already dysfunctional dispositions in the face of rapid social change, and how the concept of habitus 'forced itself upon' him as a way to explain the *mismatches* between precapitalist and colonial economic dispositions in the Algeria of the 1960s (2000:159). Still, this would appear to say more about the time lag between economic transformations and a recalcitrant habitus, reluctant to absorb the resultant moral changes, than about how individuals actually adapt their ways in response to new circumstances. The truth is that anybody who has maintained a fieldwork involvement almost anywhere in the world for the space of twenty years cannot help but be – often painfully – aware of the speed of change in the societies they are studying. It would be reasonable to suppose that habitus has been under more stress in the century just closed than ever before in history. Friedmann (this volume) proposes that the pace of change is liable to make habitus itself more dynamic, as it strains to respond to the challenges posed from within a society by those groups which are anxious for change. Versatile as humans are, individuals in these conditions are likely to become ever more self-conscious about what elements of the habitual repertoire they choose to maintain or to reject, and may end up transiting across several habituses in the course of a single lifetime. In what follows, I try to trace some of the changes I have myself had time to observe in Tana Toraja since I first did fieldwork there in 1978 – with some observations on the disintegration of a habitus which itself was already changing even before 1905, when the era of Dutch colonialism began to introduce its own radical transformations into Toraja society.

The Contest of Religions in the Toraja Highlands

The Sa'dan Toraja occupy the present-day *kabupaten* (regency) of Tana Toraja in the northerly, highland region of the province of South Sulawesi (Indonesia). According to the 1990 census, Tana Toraja has a population of around 360,000, though an uncounted number of Toraja have also emigrated beyond their homeland to seek educational or work opportunities in other parts of Indonesia, or beyond. The majority who live in Tana Toraja are subsistence farmers, growing rice in rain-fed hill terraces, and cultivating coffee, chocolate and cloves as cash crops. Tourism also contributes to the economy, and has developed considerably since the late 1970s. Political uncertainties following the fall of Suharto in 1998 did, however, cause a drastic (if no doubt temporary) slowdown in the tourist trade. The Toraja are one of very few groups in Indonesia to have succeeded in winning official government recognition for their indigenous religion, *Aluk to Dolo*.[3] This ensures the right to practise the religion and to claim it as one's faith for bureaucratic purposes, for instance, on one's identity card. In spite of this, Christianity is now the overwhelmingly predominant faith in Tana Toraja.

The name *Aluk to Dolo* does not feature in Kennedy's (1953) ethnographic survey of South Celebes (Sulawesi), and Bigalke suggests it may not have been invented until as late as the 1950s. Even today it is still often referred to by a variety of terms, including *alukta* ('our way') or *pa'kandean nene'* ('feeding the ancestors'). Christianity, first introduced by the (Calvinist) Dutch Reformed Church Mission (*Gereformeerde Zendingsbond*) in 1913, won so few adherents in its first few decades of activity that Bigalke (1981: 227) has described the pace of conversion as 'glacial': by 1930, less than 1% had converted, and the figure was still under 10% in 1950. This may have meant that there was still no felt need to give a name to the indigenous religion. Rather than being perceived as an entity distinct from other possible alternatives, it was still part of the way things were, of what Bourdieu (1977: 167) calls *doxa*, that which 'goes without saying because it comes without saying', and not yet one of a number of competing 'orthodoxies'. All the same, the statistics conceal the actually extensive influence of the mission, which had already taken a leading role in the provision of education and health services, and was thus indissolubly allied in people's minds with the forces of modernity and the new bureaucratic-rational order of colonialism. Large-scale conversion began only from the 1950s, when guerrillas of the Muslim separatist movement *Darul Islam* were active in the highlands, opposing forces of the Indonesian National Army (TNI), and co-opting villagers into their forces. The violence of their behaviour provided a new and pressing motivation for many Toraja to define themselves both as 'not heathen' and also 'not Muslim'. Census figures for ensuing decades show the total of Christians rising from around 40% in 1960, to 79% in 1980, and 83% in 1990, while the adherents of *Aluk* declined from 55% in 1960, to 15% in 1980, and just under 10% in 1990.

Conflicting reports exist for figures in the 1970s. Nooy-Palm (1979: 9) claimed that 'almost 60%' of Toraja were Christian by 1975, but Crystal (1974: 140) proposed that 'a plateau in Christian affiliation seems to have been stabilised over the past 20 years at about 40-45% of the total populace'. Elsewhere (Crystal 1978: 109) he suggests a still lower figure of 35%. His optimism (unfounded, as it now appears) that the rate of defection from *Aluk* was slackening, was an understandable interpretation of the events of the moment. *Aluk* was granted official status in 1969, while at the same time he witnessed the beginnings of a nascent tourism industry, bringing with it what he termed a new 'tourist ethic', which could provide renewed validation for indigenous ceremonial practice (1978: 118). The early 1970s was a period of renewed social, economic and political stability, which also saw the abrupt eclipse, after two decades of local dominance, of the political influence of the Indonesian Christian Party, Parkindo. Parkindo had held 75% of the seats in the local legislature (the DPRD, or Regional People's Representative Council), but suffered a disastrous defeat at the polls in 1971 when Toraja voted en masse for the government party, Golkar. Golkar candidates were drawn from Protestant, Catholic, Muslim and *Aluk to Dolo* faiths, with the result that for the first time there were to be more *Aluk* than Parkindo representatives in the new DPRD (Crystal 1974: 144). With hindsight, the question arises as to why, in fact, *Aluk to Dolo* has not been able to hold its own, in spite of its official status, but has continued to lose adherents rapidly. At the time when I myself began fieldwork, it was clear that there was great variation between the central valley area, around the two towns of Ma'kale and Rantepao, where almost everyone was Christian, and the remoter districts, where converts were fewer. In the most isolated, western region of Simbuang, I was told that only 20% of the people were Christian. In the district of Malimbong, where I took up residence, 60% of the population was recorded in 1978 as still adhering to the *Aluk*. When I returned in 1994, my entire village had converted to Christianity, some only a year or two before.

This is all the more ironic, when we consider a neighbouring example, that of the Pitu Ulunna Salu region, northwest of Tana Toraja, discussed by George (1993, 1996). This is a far more marginal population, who have not been successful in winning official status for their indigenous religion, called *ada' mappurondo*. Yet here we find that a very similar proportion, about 10%, of the population have maintained their allegiance to local practices. Similar pressures are at work here: the challenge from world religions, historically and officially associated with 'civilisation'; the association of a 'proper' religion with the requirements of citizenship (and with urban life, education, modernity, the lifestyle of civil servants, etc.) in the modern nation-state of Indonesia; and the practical difficulties of maintaining traditional ritual obligations once communities become fractured. The pulls of modernity have been extremely powerful for Toraja, who have been active in crafting for themselves a new identity within, first, the Dutch colonial empire and then the independent nation of Indonesia. By contrast, *ada' mappurondo* seems to have survived as part of a culture of resistance and concealment, developed by this more isolated group as a means to cling on to an older identity.[4]

Landscape and World View

Toraja religion, like most indigenous religions of small-scale societies, is both highly localised, and also emphasises ritual practice over coherent theological dogma. Even within Tana Toraja, the different districts, and even groups of villages which formerly organised certain rituals together (traditionally called *bua'*), show a great deal of variation not only in the details of ritual procedure but also in their myths. This is in a sense both the strength and the weakness of the *Aluk to Dolo*. The ritual cycle encompasses two great classes of rites: those of the East, to do with life and fertility, and those of the West, having to do with death, while one or two rites are of a transformative character spanning both spheres, for example those which transform the deceased into deified ancestors. Within the life-enhancing category of rites, some of those most frequently performed were the rites connected with the rice-growing cycle. These rituals are no longer being performed in many areas. This is due partly to the influence of Christianity, and partly to the widespread introduction of high-yield rice varieties which can give two crops a year (thus changing the rhythm of the cycle and making community co-ordination more difficult). But they were still carried out by a majority of villagers in the area where I lived in Malimbong, Saluputti district, during my first two field trips in 1978-9 and 1982-3. The simple offerings of betel, rice and small chickens, held in the fields or on mountain slopes affording (in terms of my perception of landscape) splendid views of the countryside and cultivated lands all around, connect farming families with the land and the rhythms of the agricultural cycle in what seemed to me a singularly appropriate way. After the offerings called *medatu* (made as the rice is ripening), a tall, leafy bamboo pole (*paloloan*), hung with offering-baskets, is erected on a mountainside as a sign that some farming household has been in communication with the *deata*, the deities of nature whose bounty brings successful harvests. Sharing the food cooked on these occasions, in such beautiful settings, provides pleasant moments of relaxation and enjoyment which punctuate the hard work of rice cultivation. The ancestors, too, are envisaged (as in many other agricultural societies) as retaining a beneficent interest in the prosperity and fertility of their descendants. Their spirits, although said to be resident in an afterlife far to the south, called Puya, were traditionally thought to visit the houses of their living descendants too. They might come and sit on the platform of a rice barn to enjoy the shade, or accompany the living when they went to plant and harvest the rice. A little basket (*bi'tak*) was kept above the hearth for them, into which small quantities of food would be placed at each meal time.[5] In chants performed at funerals, the deceased person is described as departing on a journey to the village of the ancestors, travelling south through the familiar landscape, passing through Enrekang (the district on Toraja's southern border) stopping on the way to rest and chew betel, crossing over water, until he or she is so far away as to be just a small dot on the horizon. The dead are described as mounting the rainbow to the sky, resting in the lap of the stars, and eventually returning to earth as rain to make the crops flourish, so that descendants will 'meet them at the edge of the spring'. This cyclical conception provides one particular means of transcending the finality of death. It is an image repeated in surprisingly many small-scale agricultural societies (cf. the Hopi of New Mexico), one which contrasts strongly with the monotheistic conception of a linear progression to an afterlife radically different from this life, from whence no return is possible and no communication with the living is supposed to be countenanced.

In the bigger and more spectacular rituals of the East, participants summon the *deata* to be present, calling them in chants from named mountain tops of a particular locality, or describing their journey from the 'edge of the sky' until they arrive in the village. In a fine piece of oral poetry from the *ma'bugi'* ritual to protect against illness, an elderly man, Ne' Tambing of Sa'dan, describes the *bugi'* (a deity of unknown sex), whose home is at the edge of the sky (*randan langi'*), the place of origin of rain, at the back of the sun and at the base of the moon. The deity observes omen birds and selects a good day for setting out on a journey. S/he is then described travelling, stopping to rest, crossing the sea, and arriving at Palopo (a port town in Luwu', the old Bugis kingdom which lies to the east of Toraja territory), conversing with the ruler of Luwu', and then travelling up into the highlands, moving first east and then turning to the north, passing the mountains of Suso' and Sinadi, and a series of named villages, to arrive at the site of the festival. Here is an extract:

Ba'tu to apa sanganna	Who is that?
Ba'tu to minda to minda	Who can it be?
Ungkaloran sae Bugi'	Who comes bringing Bugi'
Ba'tu tampanglaya tedong	It's probably the buffalo herdsman
To mangkambi' karambau	The herder of the buffaloes
Ungkaloran sae Bugi'	Coming to bring the Bugi'
Umpopa'tete Balanda	Coming to bring the Dutch[6]
Kalo' lempan ri Sinadi	Crossing the irrigation ditches on Mount Sinaji
Ungkaloran sae Bugi'	Coming to bring the Bugi'
Umpopa'tete Balanda	Coming to bring the Dutch
Tibaen lusau' Tampo	Arriving there in the south at Tampo [in Mengkendek]
Marinding na tindukkunni	Arriving at Marinding
Salao'-lao'na mai	Getting closer and closer
Sae mengkannai Limbu	Coming as far as Limbu
Mentunanga' ri Tadongkon	Arriving at Tadongkon
Salao'-lao'na mai	Getting closer and closer
Sae mengkannai Kesu'	Coming as far as Kesu'
Mentunanga' ri Malenong	Arriving at Malenong
Salao'-lao'na mai	Getting closer and closer
Sae mengkannai Rante	Coming as far as Rante
Mentunanga' ri Pasele'	Arriving at Pasele'
Tibaen lulian Limbong	Arriving at Limbong [a place near Rantepao, known for its spring, inhabited by spirits]
Saruran natindukkunni	Arriving at the water-spout
Sae mengkannai tondok	Coming into the village

Mentunanga' ri Pangleon	Arriving at Pangleon
La rampo inde mo te'e	S/he is arriving here
La tasik mengguliling mo	Surrounded by a sea of people
Diballaran mo ko ale'	The mats are already laid out
Dirante-rantean tuyu	The mats have been spread
Mu nai torro ma'pangan	For you to sit and chew betel
Unnesung ma'lea-lea	To sit and refresh yourself with betel

There follows a poetic description of the magical house of the Bugi' deity in the sky, and of how offerings will be made during the ritual, so that sickness will be cured, before the deity is invited to depart and travel home again, with the calling down of blessings and good fortune for everyone. The journey of the Bugi' spirit is thus inscribed in the landscape, and can be imagined by the participants; at the same time, recitation of the verses is intended literally to have an effect, to summon the deity and insure her/his presence, which will be demonstrated when participants enter a trance state and become possessed or 'taken' by the deity (*naala deata*). These Toraja verses and their intended efficacy can be compared with the invocations of Iban bards of Sarawak during the Gawai Antu (final secondary rites of the dead). Their songs recount the journey of the spirits of the dead, led by gods and goddesses of the Otherworld, as they travel to the world of the living. Their presence is thus invoked at the festivities in the longhouse, which itself at this moment becomes 'a symbolically organised landscape', 'thronged with unseen visitors' (Sather, 1993: 103; 101).

Here is another fragment of a chant from the *ma'bugi'* ritual, collected from villagers in Malimbong:

Iko deata i Kallan	You deities of Kallan
Iko puang Buttu Dido'	You lords of Buttu Dido'
Iko puang pa'buaran	You deities of the ceremonial ground
Iko puang bura-bura	You lords of the foam [i.e. water]
Iko deata i londo'	You deities of the land
Iko puang Sarapeang	You lords of Sarapeang
Iko deata ri Messila	You deities of Messila
Iko puang ri Sado'ko'	You lords of Sado'ko'

The names are all those of mountains which are familiar local landmarks; Buttu Dido' and Sarapeang are also the traditional sites of annual offerings made when the rice is ripening (*ma'bulung pare*). The *pa'buaran* is the sacred ground on which the biggest of the Rites of the East, the *ma'bua'*, is held.[7] The last *ma'bugi'* these informants had attended was celebrated in the village of Pasang around 1988; due to the efforts of a local dignitary to hasten the pace of conversion to Christianity, it may well have been the last for this community. At *ma'bugi'*, when the *deata* have been summoned long enough, some of the dancers will enter trance and perform amazing feats, climbing ladders of knives, pulling drawn swords against their abdomens, or dancing on hot coals. The *deata* were believed to protect the people from hurting themselves. Rites involving trance have been opposed more fiercely than any other by Protestants, who regard any such manifestation as demonic. Given their expense, it has become increasingly difficult to organise them in communities where part of the population has converted to Christianity and is no longer supposed to take part in them. As a consequence this part of Toraja ritual life is dying out faster than other, less contentious rites (especially funerals and house ceremonies) which have been actively adapted for continued performance by Christians.

Conclusion: From Local to Global: Transformation and Disenchantment of the Toraja World

One of the most transformative factors acting on Toraja culture at the present time is the very large number of Toraja who have migrated away from their homeland to work or study in other parts of Indonesia. Migrant workers transmit large sums home to their families, or return to spend money at important ceremonies, especially funerals or house ceremonies. This has not only made the Toraja economy more dynamic over the past two or three decades, but has had an impact on the traditionally rather rigid status system. Most young people nowadays hope to spend at least some time outside of Toraja; in some areas (notably Mengkendek in the south, and Sesean in the north) virtually all of them have left, leaving only old people and small children behind. Since very few schoolteachers in Tana Toraja are not Christian, and next to nothing about traditional culture is ever taught in schools, children are already influenced to convert away from *Aluk* to a religion which (as in many other parts of the world) is associated with literacy and modernity. Even those who have not converted, once outside of Tana Toraja, will feel uncertain how to continue to follow the *Aluk*, given its highly localised character, and its lack of places or fixed times of worship. It is easy to see that *Aluk*'s intimate interweaving with local landscape and activities is at once its strength (what made it once so appropriate) and its weakness: it simply does not translate easily to other contexts. This is one reason why migrants continue to show a remarkable loyalty to their homeland, often returning long distances to be present at rituals. The fact that some rites continue to be so prominent in Toraja life, even in a Christianised form, gives some indication, too, of the great social significance of rituals for the maintenance of kin relationships and the building of local political careers. Likewise it is said that an origin-house built in the traditional style would make little sense outside of Toraja itself and could never really become a *tongkonan*. Still, attachment to places and houses of origin remains sufficiently strong that many emigrant Toraja are prepared to make financial contributions to the rebuilding of origin-houses in which they will never reside.[8]

There are among Protestants in Toraja those who are emphatically opposed to the traditional religion and wish to hasten its demise. Some of them enjoy positions of influence in the local administration and have been actively obstructive of *Aluk to Dolo*, in spite of its officially recognised status and a national policy of tolerance of cultural and religious variation within the archipelago. Others, again, converted long ago either to Christianity or (in a few cases) to Islam, yet feel regret at what they perceive to be the inexorable cultural losses that would attend the extinction of *Aluk*. For example, of the increasingly few surviving *to minaa*, or priests, who are the repositories of a rich tradition of ritual poetry, genealogy and cultural knowledge, nearly all are already of advanced age, and not a single one, to my knowledge, has a successor in training. The role has no appeal for young people, and much of their knowledge will be lost with their deaths. This process of attrition has been going on for decades already and is now far advanced. Parents in my village had clearly given up any attempt to pass on their own practical knowledge about the *Aluk*. Their children already know little about it, and will no longer have the chance to learn by participation where and how to make the familiar household offerings, for instance. Schooling provides a quite different way of learning, as well as a different kind of subject matter. As transmission fails, the habitus, in the sense of everyday practices, is rapidly altered. Among some members of the village, who felt there had been unreasonable pressure to make the change, there was a mood of resignation. Now that the village, in the last three years, has received electricity, satellite dishes and television, the plausibility of older cultural practices will soon wither, as Hefner has sensitively documented for another formerly isolated community, the Hindu Javanese of Tengger. As he puts it, 'here, as in most of the developing world, the certainty of appeals to local ways is destined to fade. Issues of community and identity, however, will not' (Hefner, 1990: 244).

The production of community, as it happens, is one very important dimension of habitus. Bourdieu (1977: 163) talks of the *synchronisation* of activities brought about by traditional patterns of agricultural and ritual activities for the Kabyle; and this was certainly true for the Toraja, where a ritual 'Leader of the Land' (*Indo' Padang*) had to commence the cycle by making offerings in a specially designated rice field, while the rest of the community co-ordinated their activities accordingly, ending with the simultaneous celebration of the harvest. Moreover, activities and symbolic elements associated with the rites of the East and of the West, of Life and Death, were formerly strictly separated from each other. Once some members of a community have converted, unity is fractured, and quarrels may even break out when some members begin to ignore former restrictions, mixing categories which formerly were held separate, or performing their own activities out of sync with the rest. At the same time, it becomes increasingly difficult for those who remain within the old religion to bear the costs, alone, of ritual activities which used to be shared. In many areas, adoption of new high-yield strains of rice which can give two harvests a year instead of one has also contributed to the breakdown of a communally orchestrated rhythm of cultivation. Where people sometimes used to exchange their labour in voluntarily organised work groups, the tendency over the past two or three decades has been toward an increasingly individualised pattern of working. The whole process of rice agriculture has become deritualised, and the landscape correspondingly disenchanted. Ironically, it is possible that one highly salient aspect of village habitus could at this point only be rescued by the conversion of the whole community. That is the very strongly valued habit of working together. All the men of the village are expected on certain occasions to work together – for instance, in re-roofing a house, in helping to build temporary constructions to accommodate the hundreds of guests who come to funeral celebrations, or in dividing sacrificial meat. When I returned to the village in 1994 after an absence of over ten years, my family and the rest of the villagers insisted on holding a prayer meeting, while my 'sister' declared that she would not be happy unless she killed a pig to celebrate my return. As I watched the men of the neighbouring households all working good-humouredly together to butcher and cook the pig, I could not avoid the conclusion that socially, the final demise of *Aluk* at least would bring the ironic benefit that now everybody could do things together again. The fractured community could be mended, and there was some comfort in this renewal of co-operation.

Some prominent persons who are sympathetic to the plight of *Aluk* are not prepared to convert back to it because they feel personally already 'set' in their new faith, or dare not appear to treat the matter of religion flippantly. One such person, however, who does feel strongly, declared that what the *Aluk to Dolo* now needs most urgently is a Book. Young people, he argued, needed something to refer to that would explain authoritatively both the beliefs and principles of the *Aluk to Dolo*, and how it should be practised, whether within or beyond the homeland. Furthermore, he was of the opinion that with the passage of time, people would become bored with Christianity and would realise what they had thrown away, and that they would then need something that they could go back to if they wanted to revive the *Aluk*. Such a book, clearly, could not be produced without doing considerable violence to the local variation, flexibility and inconsistency which is an inherent feature of *Aluk* as a set of localised oral traditions and practices. The very idea of compressing *Aluk* into a book reveals most graphically the pressures felt by those who are not adherents of the world religions to reshape their belief systems so as to conform more closely to the model of *agama* that dominates the state's approach to religion, and to the need within the Indonesian context to be seen to have a 'religion' in terms recognisable to the adherents of world religions.[9] However much *Aluk* might be transformed by such a process of literacisation, this informant is probably right that if it is to survive at all, in competition with the 'religions of the book', it may need to embark upon such a course. Disunity among the representatives of *Aluk*, and the lack of an obvious author, not to mention funds, renders it unlikely that this project will be accomplished, however.

In the meantime, with the increasingly rapid dwindling of *Aluk*'s adherents, it is difficult not to see a draining away of meaning from the Toraja landscape, as within this century an older way of life and world view yields to the forces of modernity and homogenisation. It must be said that, while some people seem resigned to the alteration, and a few voice their protests at the losses this entails, there are others who actively welcome this transformation. One close friend put it this way: 'Before, we were afraid to go out at night. The trees looked funny and we heard strange noises and were frightened. That doesn't happen any more. Now [the countryside] is "clean".' This woman, whose conversion came some two decades ago after a number of strange incidents persuaded her that power in the modern era lay with Christianity and not with the deities and ancestors of the old religion, sees I think not simply a sweeping away of superstition, but a more literal disenchantment of the landscape, with the vanquishing of evil spirits. Many Christian converts reclassify all the supernatural beings of the old religion simply as *setan* or demons, in a move that is familiar from the history of monotheisms generally. Thus, even to dream of a dead relative may be said by some to be the work of *setan* and no longer a genuine and comforting communication with an ancestor.[10] One man commented that in the old days, people used to be much more afraid of tomb sites than they are now, and that strange or supernatural occurrences in these places were also more common. At the same time, as I have mentioned, there was an intimacy with the ancestors which may still find echoes at the present time. Another friend, long Christian, still honks his horn in greeting when passing the rock grave of his ancestors, in which he expects to lie eventually. An informant of a progressive bent, whose own father witnessed and participated in many of the social transformations of this century, and who himself has recently withdrawn from Gereja Toraja in order to be 'born again' and join a new evangelical sect, sees the final eradication of *Aluk* as both inevitable and beneficial. 'You must understand,' he urged me, 'this is a [the?] time of transition (*masa transisi*, Ind.).' His own son had never attended any *Aluk* rituals and showed a combination of ignorance and anxiety when talking about *Aluk*. His daughters, after attending universities in Java, barely speak Toraja any more, and cannot name the mountains visible from their own front door.

Still, given the literalist approach to the Bible of a Calvinist version of Christianity, Torajans might be seen as having abandoned one set of indigenous myths, intimately associated with their own, familiar landscape, in favour of another set, evolved in an alien landscape belonging to the ancient Hebrews. People struggle to make sense of Old and New Testament stories, searching for points of connection with the landscape they know, and sometimes coming up with bizarre associations in the attempt. One person compared the twelve disciples with the twelve *pangalukan bua'*, the ritual functionaries within the aggregation of villages (*bua'*) who each have different tasks to perform in certain rituals. He compared the ten commandments to the ten *sukaran aluk* or rules of the *aluk* (their number actually differs widely in different accounts). The tower of Babel he identified with the *eran di langi'* or 'stairway of heaven', a stone stairway which according to myth used to join the earth to the sky. Puang Matua, the 'Old Lord' of the heavens, was angered at the actions of the ancestor Londong di Rura, who chose to marry together his four sons and four daughters, and hurled the stairway to earth, causing a great flood which drowned everyone at Rura. The supernatural founding ancestors of some aristocratic houses, the *to manurun di langi'* and *to kendek diomai liku*, he equated with the Lost Tribes of Israel. Like some other Toraja, his attention was also attracted by Old Testament descriptions of animal sacrifice, which seem to have at least some resonance with current Toraja practice.

This effort to link the known world to the unfamiliar one depicted in the texts of a world religion is far from unique. The reference to the Lost Tribes of Israel is a manoeuvre designed to create a 'historical' and kinship connection with the adopted world religion, an effort at integration, perhaps, which can also be read as indicating an inexorable logic in the eventual conversion to Christianity. On Nias island (west Sumatra), the Rhenish mission made heavy inroads from 1865, and the whole population is now Christian, the indigenous religion having totally collapsed. A local historian here, S. Zebua (1984), perceives many parallels between traditional Nias culture and that of the ancient Hebrews, concluding that the Niassans were descendants of Abraham. Woodward (1989: 221) details how in Java, Hindu *wayang* traditions have been integrated into Muslim culture by means of mythical genealogies which make all the *wayang* characters, including the *dewa*, descendants of Adam and Eve, or in other ways encompass them within a Muslim cosmology. A further example can be found among some Chinese converts to Christianity in South-East Asia. According to Wee (1988: 30-31), some overseas Chinese Christians, looking for a way to preserve their sense of 'Chineseness', claim that Christianity had always been immanent in Chinese history and culture. For example, the Chinese fondness for the colour red is interpreted as a harbinger of the blood of the Lamb; some even claim that the Chinese are God's new 'Chosen People'.

The shift from a localised religion, integrated with a local landscape, to a universal faith with its more global landscape is in short something that evokes a variety of sometimes ambivalent emotions in different people. Yet some rituals continue to flourish, linking people to houses of origin, or causing them to participate in mortuary celebrations, even when they may no longer be living in Tana Toraja. Precisely because these rites, and the houses which are the sites for their performance, are seen only to 'make sense' when performed in the Toraja landscape and not elsewhere, they draw Toraja migrants back to their homeland, and play an important role in the construction of a modern, yet still distinctive, Toraja identity. At the same time, there is no denying the cultural erosion represented by the loss of knowledge of the old ways, including a huge store of ritual verse, constituting an oral poetry of great beauty, or the dying away of an intimate relationship with the land which a new faith cannot replace.

Postscript

When Bourdieu wrote about his fieldwork with the Kabyles of Algeria, in spite of his emphasis on practice, he stressed the durability of habitus, which is presented as deeply conservative. He was of course well aware of the ferment of anticolonial resistance in Algerian society at the time but, following what was then a familiar convention in anthropology, he chose to write about this in a completely separate book. His later research on kinship in France likewise emphasised continuity over the pressures of modernity. Bourdieu's development of the habitus concept was most often criticised for not sufficiently addressing the conditions of change, or the conscious agency of individuals in adapting to social transformations or sudden disruption. In later writings he was obliged to address these criticisms. Like other chapters in this section, this one focuses on the question of change. The Sa'dan Toraja of Sulawesi (Indonesia) are subsistence rice farmers whose traditional religion, now in terminal decline, provided a system of meaning closely embedded in the local landscape. Radical social, economic and religious changes began in the early twentieth century with Dutch colonisation and missionisation. The author argues that connections to landscape have been deeply disrupted by conversion to a Calvinist style of Christianity which disvalues indigenous cosmology and prohibits participation in certain types of rituals. Individuals must with increasing self-consciousness select what aspects of their habitus they wish to maintain as aspects of their own identity. This scenario is one that is repeated all over formerly colonised parts of the world, suggesting that habitus has been under more stress in the past century than ever before.

Notes

1   Though the notion of 'habitus' can be traced back to the writings of Aristotle, a more direct anthropological antecedent can be found in Mauss's original, if programmatic, essay on 'Body Techniques' (1979 [1935]: 101). Bourdieu (1990b: 12) also acknowledges its use by Hegel, Husserl, Weber, and Durkheim. Swartz (1997: 115-6) observes that these classical theorists viewed habitual action in a very broad sense, encompassing not only processual skills, but many other areas of life where action may be patterned by implicit or taken-for-granted assumptions. Bourdieu deploys the term in a similarly broad and inclusive manner.
2   See the bibliography published in Bourdieu (1990b).
3   Indonesia's constitutional 'Five Principles,' or *Panca Sila*, stipulate belief in one God as the basis of national values. Although *which* God is not specified, official definitions of religion (*agama*) strongly privilege the world religions. Toraja *Aluk* has been classified under the category 'Hindu-Buddha', an umbrella which also shelters

Kaharingan, the designation successfully claimed for their religion by several peoples of southern Kalimantan in 1980 (Weinstock, 1981, 1987).

4   George also acknowledges the difficulty of making accurate predictions at a given moment in one's fieldwork experience. In 1985, at the end of his first stay in the field, attempts to secure official status for *ada' mappurondo* had failed, even though he had gone with a group of its adherents to Ujung Pandang to try and help them in this endeavour. But the bureaucratic requirements to establish fixed sites for rituals, and offices at each level of the local administration, were beyond the means of this tiny and highly localised group. However, on a return visit in 1994, he found cause to revise his earlier, gloomy prognosis for its chances of survival. After prolonged efforts, one member had succeeded, that year, in obtaining official papers registering it as an *aliran kepercayaan* ('sect', or 'stream of belief'), from the provincial offices of the Department of Education and Culture. Several households had returned to *mappurondo* (when young men raised as Christians had taken *mappurondo* wives), and, with new income available from cash crops, some women's rituals were even beginning to be revived and performed more frequently than before.

5   The household in which I resided in 1978 still kept such a basket; stories were told of the ancestors complaining in dreams if it had not been properly tended. By 1999, only one of the ten children in this family had not converted, and she had taken the basket to her house. A tiny instance of disenchantment: when I inquired after it, she lifted it from its spot on a kitchen shelf; but it was empty except for a toothbrush.

6   The names 'Bugis' and 'Belanda' (Dutch) are commonly paired in verses of *ma'bugi'* chants, possibly because, historically, outsiders really have represented the dangers of introduced diseases.

7   For a description and analysis of this rite, see Waterson (1984a).

8   I have discussed the role of the house in present-day maintenance of Toraja identity in Waterson (1984b, 1986).

9   Cf. also Atkinson (1987) on the Wana of Central Sulawesi.

10 The emotional conflicts some people undoubtedly feel as a result of this transformation in world view are discussed in Waterson (1984b).

References

Atkinson, J. (1987) 'Religions in dialogue: the construction of an Indonesian minority religion', in R. Kipp and S. Rodgers (eds), *Indonesian Religions in Transition*, Tucson, University of Arizona Press: 171-186.

Bender, B. (ed.) (1993) *Landscape: Politics and Perspectives*, Providence/Oxford, Berg.

Bigalke, T. (1981) 'A Social History of "Tana Toraja", 1870-1965', PhD Thesis, University of Wisconsin.

Bloch, M. (1998) *How We Think They Think: anthropological approaches to cognition, memory, and literacy*, Boulder, Westview.

Bourdieu, P. (1977) *Outline of a Theory of Practice*, Cambridge, Cambridge University Press.

Bourdieu, P. (1990a) *The Logic of Practice*, Cambridge, Polity Press.

Bourdieu, P. (1990b) *In Other Words: essays towards a reflexive sociology*, Cambridge, Polity Press.

Bourdieu, P. (2000) *Pascalian Meditations*, Cambridge, Polity Press.

Calhoun, C. (1993) 'Habitus, field and capital: the question of historical specificity' in C. Calhoun, E. LiPuma and M. Postone (eds), *Bourdieu: critical perspectives*, Cambridge, Polity Press: 61-88.
Collier, J. F. (1997) *From Duty to Desire: remaking families in a Spanish village*, Princeton, N.J., Princeton University Press.
Crystal, E. (1974) 'Cooking pot politics: a Toraja village study', *Indonesia*, 18: 119-51.
Crystal, E. (1978) 'Tourism in Toraja (Sulawesi, Indonesia)', in Valene Smith (ed.), *Hosts and Guests: The Anthropology of Tourism*, Oxford, Blackwell: 109-25.
Elias, N. (1994) [1939] *The Civilizing Process*, Oxford, Blackwell.
Fox, J. (1997) 'Place and landscape in comparative Austronesian perspective', in J. Fox (ed.) *The Poetic Power of Place: comparative perspectives on Austronesian ideas of locality*, Canberra: Research School of Pacific and Asian Studies, ANU: 1-21.
George, K. (1993) 'Dark trembling: ethnographic notes on secrecy and concealment in highland Sulawesi', *Anthropological Quarterly* 66/4: 230-246.
George, K. (1996) *Showing Signs of Violence: the cultural politics of a twentieth-century headhunting ritual*, Berkeley, University of California Press.
Gow, P. (1995) 'Land, people and paper in Western Amazonia', in E. Hirsch and M. O'Hanlon (eds), *The Anthropology of Landscape: perspectives on place and space*, Oxford, Clarendon: 43-62.
Hefner, R. (1990) *The Political Economy of Mountain Java: an interpretive history*, Berkeley: University of California Press.
Hirsch, E. and O'Hanlon, M. (eds) (1995) *The Anthropology of Landscape: perspectives on place and space*, Oxford, Clarendon.
Jenkins, R. (1992) *Pierre Bourdieu*, London, Routledge.
Johnson-Laird, P. (1983) *Mental Models: towards a cognitive science of language, inference and consciousness*, Cambridge, Cambridge University Press.
Kennedy, R. (1953) *Field Notes on Indonesia: South Celebes 1949-50*, New Haven, Conn., Human Relations Area Files.
Mauss, M. (1979) [1935] 'Body techniques', in M. Mauss, *Sociology and Psychology: essays*, (trans. Ben Brewster). London, Routledge: 97-119.
Nooy-Palm, H. (1979) *The Sa'dan Toraja: a study of their social life and religion*, Vol 1, The Hague, Nijhoff.
Polanyi, M. (1975) 'Personal knowledge', in M. Polanyi and H. Prosch, *Meaning*, Chicago, University of Chicago Press: 22-45.
Sather, C. (1993) 'Posts, hearths and thresholds: the Iban longhouse as a ritual structure', in J. Fox (ed.), *Inside Austronesian Houses: perspectives on domestic designs for living*, Canberra: Research School of Pacific Studies, ANU: 65-115.
Schank, R., and Abelson, R. (1977) *Scripts, Plans, Goals and Understanding*, Hillsdale, N.J., Erlbaum.
Strathern, A. (1996) 'Habit or habitus? theories of memory, the body, and change', in Strathern, A., *Body Thoughts*, Ann Arbor, University of Michigan Press: 25-39.
Swartz, D. (1997) *Culture and Power: the sociology of Pierre Bourdieu*, Chicago, University of Chicago Press.
Waterson, R. (1984a) 'Rites of East and West: ritual, gender and status in Tana Toraja', in R. Waterson, *Ritual and Belief among the Sa'dan Toraja*, University of Kent Centre of Southeast Asian Studies, Occasional Paper no. 2: 3-34.
Waterson, R. (1984b) 'Taking the place of the ancestors: ethnic identity in Tana Toraja in the 1980s', in R. Waterson, *Ritual and Belief among the Sa'dan Toraja*, University of Kent Centre of Southeast Asian Studies, Occasional Paper no. 2: 34-72.

Waterson, R. (1986) 'The ideology and terminology of kinship among the Sa'dan Toraja', Bijdragen tot de Taal-, Land- en Volkenkunde, 142/1:87-112.
Waterson, R. (1997) 'The contested landscapes of myth and history in Tana Toraja', in J. Fox (ed.) *The Poetic Power of Place: comparative perspectives on Austronesian ideas of* locality, Canberra, Research School of Pacific and Asian Studies, ANU: 63-90.
Wee, V. (1988) 'What does Chinese mean? An exploratory essay', National University of Singapore, Dept. of Sociology Working Paper no. 90.
Weinstock, J. (1981) 'Kaharingan: Borneo's "oldest religion" becomes Indonesia's newest religion', Borneo Research Bulletin 13/1:47-48.
Weinstock, J. (1987) 'Kaharingan: life and death in Southern Borneo', in R. Kipp and S. Rodgers (eds) *Indonesian Religions in Transition*, Tucson, University of Arizona Press: 71-97.
Woodward, M. (1989) *Islam in Java: normative piety and mysticism in the sultanate of Yogyakarta*, Tucson: University of Arizona Press.
Zebua, S. (1984) Sejarah Kebudayaan Ono-Niha. (Cyclostyle; published by the author.)

18 The Endurance of Aboriginal Women in Australia

FAY GALE

The Drover's Boy

They couldn't understand why the drover cried
As they buried The Drover's Boy,
For the drover had always seemed so hard
To the men in his employ.
A bolting horse, a stirrup lost
And The Drover's Boy was dead.
The shovelled dirt, a mumbled word
And it's back to the road ahead,
And forget about, The Drover's Boy.

They couldn't understand why the drover cut
A lock of the dead boy's hair.
He put it in the band of his battered old hat,
As they watched him standing there.
He told them 'Take the cattle on,
I'll sit with the boy a while'.
A silent thought, a pipe to smoke,
And it's ride another mile,
And forget about, 'The Drover's Boy'.

They couldn't understand why the drover and the boy
Always camped so far away.
For the tall white man and the slim dark boy
Had never had much to say.
And the boy would be gone at the break of dawn,
Tail the horses, carry on
While the drover raised the sleeping men,
Daylight, hit the road again,

And follow, The Drover's Boy.
Follow The Drover's Boy.

In the Camooweal Pub they talked about,
The death of The Drover's Boy.
They drank their rum with a stranger who'd come
From the Kimberley run, Fitzroy.
He told them of a massacre in the west
Barest details, guess the rest.
Shoot the bucks, grab a gin,
Cut her hair, break her in,
Call her a boy, The Drover's Boy
Call her a boy, The Drover's Boy.

So when they build that Stockman's Hall of Fame
And they talk about the droving game,
Remember the girl who was bedmate and guide,
Road with the drover side by side,
Watched the bullocks, flayed the hide,
Faithful wife, never a bride,
Bred his sons for the cattle runs.
Don't weep ... for The Drover's Boy
Don't mourn ... for The Drover's Boy
But don't forget ... The Drover's Boy.[1]

(reproduced with the permission of Ted Egan)

Ted Egan's song, *The Drover's Boy*, epitomises the role so many Aboriginal women played in developing the pastoral industry in Australia. Let me tell you the story of one such drover's boy.

When the drover first came to this pastoral station in northern Australia he was given a girl, a gin as he called her. The girl was a young traditional Aboriginal who in time gave birth to a baby girl who was, in those days, labelled a half-caste because of her mixed parentage. Eventually the drover moved on and left his 'boy' behind. She was then, in customary style, given a man from her own group and they settled on a cattle station, where he worked as a stockman. They had a son, a 'full blood' Aboriginal, and her daughter remembers a happy childhood playing with her young brother in the camp near the station homestead. But that happy and secure childhood was shattered when she became one of some 100,000 children taken, or rather kidnapped, because they were deemed to be of lighter colour than their mothers.

She was a young girl when the police eventually took her away but she was old enough to remember the trauma well and still weeps as she recalls that dreadful day the police came for her. She remembers life on the station as very happy and carefree, but mostly she remembers the love of her mother and her aunties. She was of course one of those children now known as members of 'the stolen generation' and her mother just a statistic of the thousands of women who had their children forcibly taken because they were of lighter colour skin than others on the station.[2]

Mostly the mothers never saw or heard of their children again. This girl's name was changed and she was taken over a thousand kilometres away to make sure she was never traced. In spite of the fact that the station was isolated and hundreds of kilometres from the nearest town, the police sought her out and came several times before they actually were able to capture her and I use the word 'capture' quite consciously. She remembers bitterly how the police drove into the station and grabbed her as she was playing and threw her into the back of their utility. She remembers sadly that she was not even allowed to give her mother a hug or say goodbye. She was told nothing, just silently grabbed. Her story of her lonely and frightening journey of several days seems impossible to comprehend. How could such cruelty to small children have been tolerated and so carefully planned? It was said to be, as Anna Haebich so appropriately entitled her book, 'For Their Own Good'.[3] What appalling, misguided paternalism.

How did those mothers survive and often become strong people in their communities? How did those 'stolen' girls get over such trauma and go on often to become leaders and mentors to others. Let me tell you of one such mother who, in spite of agonising attempts, was never able to trace her child and died not knowing what had happened to her. In spite of such cruelty she did not succumb. She became a leader of women and worked hard in her community to gain opportunities for healthcare. In particular she saw the benefits to children of Aboriginal diet rather than the same poor handout on the mission of white bread and tinned jam. She devoted herself to land rights claims believing that only ownership of traditional lands would give access to healthy and nourishing natural food for children. She said that she really cared for the land, as did most women, but the men, she said, so often only cared for the 'grog'.[4] She saw the improvement in the health of the children when their mothers had access to traditional foods following a successful land claim. Some time later she told me with great excitement, when her group had won a land claim and gone back onto their homelands, 'our babies don't die any more'.

I speak as an observer and admirer of the survival and emotional strength of Aboriginal women over decades. I cannot, of course, speak directly as an indigenous woman. I can speak only as an observer. Today there are many strong women who can and do speak out with great courage for their people and in protest at their inequitable treatment. Many voices can now be heard from those who suffered the trauma of being removed from their mothers and their land and cultural roots that are so embedded in that land. But when I first started my studies in the 1950s no one would listen to the Aboriginal women on any issue. If the views of Aboriginal people were considered worth hearing at all by the various authorities it was only the men who were heard. Indeed why would the servants of the past governments want to hear the complaints of the traumatised mothers whose babies were snatched from them. Certainly they were deaf to the cries of the children. Ignoring the women whether on child welfare, land rights, traditional food and medicines, marriage rules or any other issue has led to the compounded problems we now face as a nation.

But then nor was I, a white woman, listened to on the issue of taking children, now such a politically alive and controversial issue. Maybe if I and others had been listened to, or if those police and welfare officers and missionaries, so much servants of the government policy, had listened to the heartache of the mothers, or the critics like myself, our Prime Minister would not be in the situation of being regularly asked to say 'sorry' to those known now as the 'stolen generation'. During my postgraduate student days in the late 1950s I spoke about what I had seen of children being forcibly taken. On one occasion this was reported on the news and immediately I had a call from the head of the Welfare Branch of the Northern Territory saying that because of my ill-informed statements I would be prohibited from entering the Northern Territory to study. What arrogance, what power! I was deeply affected by this, not only because it upset my studies and I had to change my thesis topic, but also because it made me realise what power he and his staff could wield over the lives of Aboriginal women in his jurisdiction. I had no comeback, so what an impossible position were they in?

I never cease to be amazed at the resilience of the women in the face of such treatment. Their strength came from the land and their place in the eternal Dreaming and the sense of spatial belonging. It was a great sadness to them that their stolen children would grow up without these essential roots. We have seen all too well the dreadful social destruction resulting from that loss of place and the power of the cultural forces and the security attached to it. With the loss of land came the loss of religion so closely embedded in the land. Without their firm foundation in one place with its religious sites and cultural history, they lost all sense of meaningful identity. With the loss of land came the loss of traditional foods and medicines. We have seen all too well the resulting decline in Aboriginal health and the high rate of infant mortality and morbidity. To Aboriginal people their very being is tied to their land. In the past, the Dreaming as it is usually called, ancestral beings walked the land and created all of the present day features. Aboriginal people must care for those features, the water, the plants and the animals and respect and reinvigorate the ancestral beings to ensure the land and its bounty continue. Habitus, as applied to Aboriginal people and their land, has such a deep and unifying meaning covering every aspect of life. As one Aboriginal woman said to me, in essence, you whites think you can own the land but you are wrong, it is the land that owns you. Our cultural arrogance, personal greed and complete misunderstanding of the ties that bind people to land are now costing this nation dearly.

Women in traditional society were the carers and nurturers of country and people. Country, as they say, had to be cared for and its deep links to people's lives protected. Yet those women's voices, calling out about land and their spiritual affinity with it, were ignored. Male anthropologists wrote of male ceremonies and Aboriginal men's role in recreating their sites, but because they did not have access to the women's sacred life they wrote as though it did not exist. Certainly this has been corrected at least academically, but not listening to the women has been at a cost.

When in the early 1980s it was decided to build a recreation lake at the former Telegraph Station on the Todd River, five kilometres upstream from Alice Springs, there was considerable discussion and consultation. By this time in our history it was recognised that Aboriginal people should be consulted about developments on traditional land. However, the government representatives and the engineers were male planners. Whilst they consulted with some Aboriginal men, they did not think to consult with Aboriginal women. The problem was that this was a women's sacred site and no one thought to ask the women. The men could not speak for the women, it was a women's site and only the female custodians could speak for it, but they were not asked. The traditional owners of the site, known as Welatje-Therre, were women. This was a very important conception site in the spiritual sense and sacred to women over a very large area surrounding Alice Springs. Many Dreaming trails led to this site. One woman giving evidence at an inquiry, which was held later, said they believed that, if the site was flooded to make a dam and the sacred trees drowned, then women would become infertile. Their intimate connection with this particular site and the way it linked people and their land over large areas became evident over the time of the inquiry.

The women did not take the government decision to flood this important piece of land lying down. So crucial was this site to women and their ceremonies and beliefs that when the decision to build the lake was announced in 1982, they took political action. They organised protests, publicised their concerns and attracted support from all over Australia. Whilst totally ignored at the local level, they took national action and even the then Prime Minister's wife, Hazel Hawke, was there at the crucial time to join the protest. It was the local Aboriginal women who organised these protests and enthused white women to join with them in fighting off the bulldozers.

The publicity was considerable and as a result the Commonwealth and Northern Territory governments jointly funded an inquiry to establish the value of the claims and, they hoped, gain the clearance to go ahead with the construction of the lake. I was a member of that inquiry and I saw first hand what ignoring the voice of women could cost the taxpayer. I saw the fight the women put up, the evidence they produced and the support they gained. With the weight of such evidence, both oral and written, the three members of the inquiry team unanimously recommended that the building of the lake should not go ahead. It was the first time in Australia's history that the women were heard and their political action successful in preventing a development that would be harmful to them and their beliefs. To this day the lake has not been built. This is a clear example of the fact that even after decades of suppression, they have not given in and continue to fight for their land, the source of their identity and future existence.

That passionate caring for their land and the strong ties some women feel with it have been well in evidence in the whole conflict over the building of the Hindmarsh Bridge in South Australia. There, however, the results have been quite the opposite. In spite of their action, pleas and protests they have not been successful in halting development on a site they believe to be crucial to their spiritual well-being. In 1991 the then premier of South Australia announced that a bridge would be built across the River Murray to an island, Hindmarsh Island, which was used mainly for holiday houses and access was only by ferry. But there was concern that the wait for the ferry was too long and the building of a bridge was made a condition for the development of a marina on the island. Some Ngarrindjeri women with historic connections to this site protested to the Federal Minister for Aboriginal Affairs who, following advice from a confidential consultancy, recommended that the site be acknowledged and the bridge not go ahead. Later a Royal Commission was established by the State government. In 1995 that Commission found against the women and indeed pronounced that the women's evidence had been fabricated. The women challenged this finding and another Federal Inquiry was set up in 1996. But a High Court challenge then ruled the appointment of the commissioner to be ineffective. For the Australian taxpayers this bridge has already cost over $30 million. The bridge was opened in March 2001, ten years after the initial decision to build it.[5]

In March 2000 the developers lodged a claim in the Federal Court of Australia for AUS$20 million in damages over the delays in the construction of the bridge. The case was heard by Justice J. von Doussa. Once again the Ngarrindjeri women who were the proponents for the protection of this site were brought before the courts. Their endurance through this long process was amazing. From the time the decision to build the bridge was announced until they were finally vindicated in 2001, they suffered enormous pressure, insult and media spotlight and misrepresentation. The use and abuse of this small group of women in the interests of 'white' development was reminiscent of the colonial era. Yet through all the pressure and negative publicity they remained true to their beliefs and commitment to their land. In the final case the judge found against the developers' claim for compensation and the Aboriginal women were at last vindicated:

> From the Aboriginal perspective late emergence of tradition would not be indicative of fabrication: on the contrary, it is to be expected in the case of genuine sacred information of importance (2001, para. 336).
>
> I am not satisfied on the evidence before this Court that the applicants have established on the balance of probabilities that restricted women's knowledge as revealed to Dr Fergie and Professor Saunders was not part of genuine Aboriginal tradition (2001, para. 12).

I for one have been overawed by the endurance of these women who attested to the conviction of the spiritual significance of this piece of land believed by them to have been sacred to Ngarrindjeri women for generations. It is clear they believe they have a sacred trust and will fight against all odds to remain true to that. Our society's inability to understand the sensitive cultural issues involved and to appreciate the intensity with which some Aboriginal women can hold their spiritual beliefs in their sites has led, in this case, to enormous costs to the taxpayer.

I remember when the Pitjatjantjara lands were being negotiated for return to Aboriginal ownership, there were photographs, published in *The Advertiser* newspaper, of the Aboriginal men camped at the Victoria Park race course in Adelaide for a meeting with the South Australian Premier. The men, the assumed elders and sole spokespeople, had been flown down at government expense. The women were not consulted but they were not daunted. They pooled their money and got a bus to bring them to Adelaide. Their voice in securing the land rights and the protection of their sites was crucial in the final negotiations. But for their initiative and drive they would have been overlooked and a much less successful agreement worked out.

I was in Alice Springs at a hearing of the Liquor Licensing Commission at the time of the opening of the motels at Yulara, the new tourist village at Uluru, known until then as Ayers Rock. The owner of one of the motels was seeking what is known as a 'take-away licence'. That is one that meant they could not only sell to persons in the motel or those who came into the bar, but could also sell unlimited amounts to be taken away. Women from the area had come into Alice Springs to present a case against the licence for Aboriginal men. The women were very concerned that, if a take-away licence were given, then their menfolk would bring alcohol back to camp, become drunk and violent fights would erupt. They said women would pay the price. The women lost the case and the white licensee gained an open licence. Only a few weeks later I was out at Yulara and to my horror found that one of the women who had come in to plead had her arm in plaster. It had been broken when her husband attacked her while he was drunk on the alcohol he had been able to bring home from that newly licensed hotel. Why are the women never heard?

The history of white suppression substantially changed the traditional roles of Aboriginal men more than those of the women, particularly in southern and eastern Australia where lands were taken and traditional lifestyles squashed as Aboriginal people were taken off their land and segregated onto missions and reserves. White missionaries largely took over the roles of the men in religious and educational matters, but the women's roles as carers of children and healers of the sick were largely unaffected. That women often were able to remain in contact with their land and much of the knowledge that went with it meant that they became custodians when men were forced to go away droving or shearing. That role of women and the degree of the knowledge they have maintained even after generations of white occupation and segregation has been ignored by most people in the general community.

The level of concern for their ties to their traditional land, even in southern and eastern Australia, where they no longer had any legal ownership was demonstrated in a conference held in Adelaide in 1980. Aboriginal women came from all over Australia to talk about their land and its significance in their lives and their communities. A book of the proceedings was published under the title of *We are Bosses Ourselves*: *the status and role of Aboriginal women today.*[6] It was a title given by one of the women from the north as she spoke about her land, the land rights claims and the fact that women did not need men to speak for them as whites assumed. In fact women had their own land and place-related stories and beliefs and needed to speak for it themselves.

So many times I have seen women take on issues that their menfolk were afraid to tackle. One woman testifying to the Alice Springs Lake Inquiry said her brother, who should have been fighting for the protection of a site to the north, was too busy with white men's things to care. She meant drink and football and just being away from country, as they call it. So she said she had to take on the fight for the sake of the future generations, even though it was really her brother's job.

Petrol sniffing is quite a serious concern on some remote communities and authorities seem at a loss to deal with it. On one such community the senior women, so concerned for their young boys, got together and told their men they must not bring petrol-driven vehicles into the community. To demonstrate this when the men ignored them, they burnt one of the cars. But that was not a method of enforcement favoured by the white authorities and the women got no back-up or support of any kind. Indeed they were badly treated by their menfolk who can become extremely violent when drunk. Yet knowing this they were prepared to try to stand up and do something when no one else would. It was a demonstration and of course they could not enforce it. Nobody seemed to listen to women's concerns about petrol-driven vehicles being used in the outback communities. It is now, much later, well recognised that petrol sniffing has become an increasingly debilitating, brain destroying and highly addictive activity that has become widespread amongst teenagers in desert communities.

One publication of which I am a joint author, *Aboriginal Youth and the Criminal Justice System: the injustice of justice,*[7] was the result of a request from some Aboriginal mothers who were concerned at the frequency with which their sons were jailed. It was finally when one mother pleaded for greater understanding after her son committed suicide to avoid jail that she asked us to study the situation. These mothers have agonised, gone to court, fought for their children when so often the men have walked away. In doing the work for this study we sat in on various court appearances in the Children's Court. Mothers and often grandmothers would accompany the youth to court and give the guarantees and support. I did not once see a male do so.

Just recently, *The Advertiser*, the local South Australian newspaper published a photograph of an Aboriginal girl in court on a serious assault charge and there was her grandmother beside her. I thought things have not changed much in all the years I have been observing. I have asked what happens when those grandmothers die or become too ill to continue their essential roles of support and cultural maintenance, but I see there are younger women coming on with the same strength to take their place.

I have never ceased to be amazed at what control many of these strong women exert over their households, irrespective of where they are living. I remember on one occasion driving an older women home to her city house when she suddenly called out to me to stop and turn around. She had seen a son-in-law on the other side of the street. I did as I was told and as we drew up alongside him, she jumped out and demanded money. She later explained it was his pay day and if she did not get his money for her daughter and their children, he would drink it all or blow it at the races. I was surprised at the authority she wielded as he meekly handed over much of his money, even though he did not live in her household.

On another occasion I was taken out of town to look for plants to make a herbal medicine for a sick child. This woman had spent all her life on the mission and it was assumed there was no traditional knowledge remaining but she certainly knew her plants and where they could be found. More recently it has been shown that those same plants do in fact possess healing properties. The very women's knowledge we have tried to squash in the past is now being sought by medical researchers from many countries. What is so encouraging is the ability of so many women to speak up against all odds and to ensure that their ties to land are not forgotten or ignored.

Time and again it is apparently powerless women who are fighting for recognition of their traditional sites or organising protests against developments at sites important to them. No matter how much non-indigenous Australians consider that indigenous people in southern and eastern Australia have no traditional knowledge left, the descendants still assert their ties to particular pieces of land. For them the highly significant association with their land has not been annulled by European occupation.

It has been a history of women misused, ill-treated, ignored. Though they have spoken out about their relationship with their land, they have not been heard. Yet their locational abilities and spatial knowledge were well used on the frontiers where they worked as stockmen, as cooks and sexual partners for white men. I met one group of women in the 1950s who had shown great ingenuity. They and their families had been moved off the station onto a mission. During the war, when Aboriginal people were not allowed petrol ration tickets, the group were unable to use the one old truck they had in the community. It was the women who thought during the war, when many of the men had enlisted, that they could get the engine out of the truck. It was of course no use without fuel. So the engine was removed and it was a rather odd looking truck I first saw. The women had broken in some feral donkeys and used these to pull the engineless vehicle. They used it go rabbiting as this was paying reasonably well. After the war when I first met them, they continued to use the truck with the donkeys as an economical means of transport.

In 1985 Isobel White, Diane Barwick and Betty Meehan edited a collection of Aboriginal women's life histories. The book is aptly called *Fighters and Singers: the lives of some Aboriginal women*.[8] In the introduction they sum up much of what I am saying. 'We solicited these life histories from a circle of women researchers who share our belief that the dignity and strength of Aboriginal communities could be more widely understood through reading about the women who contribute so much to the maintenance of those communities' (White, Barwick and Meehan, 1985: xvii). They are great histories from all over the continent depicting the strength of women in very different circumstances.

Let me tell you of one fighter who is not in that book. I met her first the year she left school. She had grown up in a fringe camp out of town in the scrub where Aboriginal people could live if they kept clean and out of sight. She walked some six kilometres into the town to the local school. Later the family was able to move to a small cottage on a property nearer town where it was not so far to walk to school. Her commitment was rewarded and encouraged by her mother and her intelligence and wide ranging abilities shone through. I need hardly say she had a very strong mum.

I was interviewing the headmaster of the high school, where she had just completed the highest level they had. She had topped the class and he was concerned about her future because of the racial discrimination in the town. She wanted to go into the local bank and the headmaster said he tried hard to get her in as he knew the bank manager well. But his friend had said he was sorry but it was not possible to have a coloured girl dealing with customers. She was able to get a job as a housemaid at a local hotel and later in a shop, not serving customers, but out the back where she would not be seen, weighing up the goods.

Later she moved to the city and got a job as a telephonist at the exchange, a job again out of sight. But she spoke well and was highly intelligent and was appreciated but not seen. She told me that when she was on night shift it was really scary coming out of the building, as there would always be men waiting at the door to grab the dark girls whom they saw as easy sexual targets. She had to leave this job because she could get no protection from these predatory males nor any sympathy from management in changing her shifts.

Eventually she found the opportunity to meet other Aboriginal women and to help develop support groups for them. Through a number of avenues working with Aboriginal people, she became a renowned leader and supporter of women and young people. She gave public lectures and did much to educate the public about the plight of Aboriginal people. Her bravery was remarkable and her commitment endless, yet I had seen enormous suffering in her youth and early adulthood. It was as if she did not want other Aboriginal women to suffer that kind of discrimination so she worked hard to change attitudes.

The daughter of the drover's boy is now a grandmother. In spite of an early life that most of us would find destructive, she is a very strong head of her family. After the trauma of being taken from her mother and her security and moved between institutions and situations as government policy dictated, she has emerged without bitterness and with an enormously positive outlook on life and the importance of her Aboriginal heritage. Her daughter is very proud of that background and I have no doubt will go on to be a fighter like her mother for Aboriginal people. I only hope we in the broader Australian community will make it easier for her than we did for her mother.

Postscript

Indigenous women in Australia have occupied a space both physically and socially quite different from that occupied by non-indigenous women and also different to a large degree from the changed habitus in which indigenous men find themselves.

Since the first Europeans came to settle in Australia and take over the land of the original inhabitants, Aboriginal women have been used and abused. They were robbed of their roles as carers of their children and protectors of the spiritual continuity of their land. Aboriginal men also had their lives and roles greatly changed in the colonising process but in ways often different from that of the women.

The chapter opens with a ballad about the murder of indigenous men and the removal of their women to become sexual partners of European men on the frontiers. Their children born in such liaisons were then often removed from them under government legislation. Such women lost their homes, their families, their beliefs so closely tied to their land and, as a final insult, their children were taken from them without redress.

368 *Habitus: A Sense of Place*

These children were usually snatched from their mothers who never saw or heard of them again. The pain, as so many stories attest, was unbearable. They seem to have lost everything of meaning to them. But their strength and their spiritual beliefs could not always be taken from them. They could not practise their beliefs in a foreign land, but they remembered many of the stories of the Dreaming as the beliefs have come to be called. Wherever possible these were passed onto their children.

One decade long contemporary saga over the building of a bridge by developers illustrates the enormous endurance of these women in the face of seemingly impossible hurdles. In the end their veracity was upheld, but the bridge that destroyed important women's sites was still built.

This chapter gives numerous illustrations from the personal experience of the author of the strength of Aboriginal women in the face of enormous pressures. They were forced to occupy a space dominated by the usurpers of their land. Even their men were given a higher status, albeit still in dominated space. When gradually other Australians, at least officially, came to realise the importance of indigenous knowledge of the Australian environment it was the men rather than the women who were taken notice of and consulted. In such a culturally isolated space they still remained firm to their long traditions and personal strength wherever possible. Even after generations of dominance they are emerging as women of strength and purpose.

Majority Australia still finds it impossible to understand how, after removal and time away from country, Aboriginal women can still hold firm to their beliefs and fight for their recognition and continuance.

Notes

1   Marchant, Bob, *'The Drover's Boy' Series of Paintings*, Bob Marchant, Bundeena, NSW, 1995.
2   There are many case studies of these 'stolen children' described in a report carried out by the Australian Human Rights and Equal Opportunity Commission. It tells heartbreaking stories of so many Aboriginal children removed under government policy and so cut off from their families, their land, their language and their culture. For more detail see Wilson, Ronald, (1997) *Bringing Them Home: national inquiry into the separation of Aboriginal and Torres Strait Islander children from their families*, Human Rights and Equal Opportunity Commission, Canberra (1988).
3   Haebich, Anna, (1988) *For Their Own Good: Aborigines and government in the southwest of Western Australia 1900-1940*, Nedlands, University of Western Australia Press.
4   In Aboriginal communities alcohol can have devastating effects. In the past unscrupulous whites often sold coloured, usually with cochineal, methylated spirits. I have seen young children drinking such burning liquids with horrifying consequences. In towns where alcohol is now readily available, some Aboriginal men who are already

addicted spend their pension money on alcohol when their families are desperately in need of food. In more remote areas there are still white men trafficking in flagons of wine at exaggerated prices. Many Aboriginal communities have now declared themselves to be 'dry' to prevent 'trouble' and it is usually the women who police the rules and refuse to allow in those with alcohol. So now on the road leading to these 'dry' communities, it is possible to see many tins and casks discarded on the road side but usually empty as the contents had been hurriedly drunk.

5   This case has had enormous publicity and greatly damaged a number of people. The story, largely from the women's point of view, has been written up in a comprehensive book by Diane Bell (1998) entitled *Ngarrindjer Wurruwarrin: a world that is, was, and will be*, Melbourne, Spinifex Press. A shorter and later article by Diane Bell is in Brock, Peggy (ed.) (2001) *Women and Silences: Aboriginal women, politics and land*, Sydney, Allen and Unwin.
6   Gale, Fay, (ed.) (1983) *We are Bosses Ourselves: the status and role of Aboriginal women today*, Canberra, Australian Institute of Aboriginal Studies Press.
7   Gale, Fay Bailey-Harris, Rebecca and Wundersitz, Joy (1990) *Aboriginal Youth and the Criminal Justice System: the injustice of justice*, Cambridge, Cambridge University Press. Further material on Aboriginal deaths in custody can be found in: Royal Commission into Aboriginal Deaths in Custody (1991) *National Report*, Volumes 1-5, Canberra, Australian Government Publishing Service. Also see: Federal, State and Territory Governments (1992) *Response by Governments to the Royal Commission into Aboriginal Deaths in Custody*, Canberra, Australian Government Publishing Service.
8   White, Isobel, Barwick, Diane and Meehan, Betty (eds) (1985) *Fighters and Singers: the lives of some Aboriginal women*, Sydney, George Allen and Unwin.

References

Bell, D. (1998) *Ngarrindjer Wurruwarrin: a world that is, was, and will be*, Melbourne, Spinifex Press.
Brock, P. (ed.) (2001) *Women and Silences: Aboriginal women, politics and land*, Sydney, Allen and Unwin.
Federal Court of Australia. Thomas Lincoln Chapman, Wendy Jennifer Chapman and Binalong (Receivers and Managers Appointed) (In Liquidation) v Luminis Pty Ltd, Deane Joanne Fergie, Cheryl Anne Saunders, Robert Edward Tickner and Commonwealth of Australia (2001) Federal Court of Australia, No. SG 33 of 1997, Reasons for Decision, Aug, 2001, para 336 and para 12.
Federal, State and Territory Governments (1992), *Response by Governments to the Royal Commission into Aboriginal Deaths in Custody*, Canberra, Australian Government Publishing Service.
Gale, F. (ed.) (1983) *We are Bosses Ourselves: the status and role of Aboriginal women today*, Canberra, Australian Institute of Aboriginal Studies Press.
Gale, F., Bailey-Harris, R. and Wundersitz, J. (1990) *Aboriginal Youth and the Criminal justice system: the injustice of justice*, Cambridge, Cambridge University Press.
Haebich, A. (1998) For Their Own Good: Aborigines and government in the southwest of Western Australia 1900-1940, Nedlands, University of Western Australia Press.
Marchant, B. (1995) *'The Drover's Boy' series of paintings*, Bob Marchant, Bundeena, NSW.

Royal Commission into Aboriginal Deaths in Custody (1991) *National Report*, Volumes 1-5, Canberra, Australian Government Publishing Service.

White, I., Barwick, D. and Meehan, B. (eds) (1985) *Fighters and Singers: the lives of some Aboriginal women*, Sydney, George Allen and Unwin.

Wilson, R. (1997) *Bringing Them Home: national inquiry into the separation of Aboriginal and Torres Strait Islander children from their families*, Canberra, Human Rights and Equal Opportunity Commission.

19 Belonging, Naming and Decolonisation

VAL PLUMWOOD

Land of Paradox

There are many good reasons to conclude that a rich, deep connection with land and place is a key part of a healthy human culture, a source of human wisdom and sustainable living, of caring for the land and ensuring a healthy future.[1] Australian schoolchildren recite verse from a national literature that lays a strong claim to love of the land: 'Core of my heart, my country, a wilful, lavish land, all you who have not loved her, you will not understand' writes Dorothea McKellar. A major task for Australian environmental philosophy and history is then to explain why people from a settler culture who make such claims to love their land have been engaged in destroying so much of it. What is it that has given non-indigenous Australia some of the worst vegetation clearance, land degradation and biodiversity extinction rates in the world? Does the very size of the continent give us a frontier sense of inexhaustibility? Has the colonial heritage of Australians, which positions us on both sides of the colonial relationship as both colonised (in relation to the British) and coloniser (in relation to Aboriginal people) perhaps distorted, stripped and impoverished our relationship to our transplanted home?

Are the key factors our high level of urbanisation and unreal expectations of comfort, linked to our participation in the system of global capitalism? Or is it primarily the failure to develop a rich land culture and through it, to come to know our land deeply, that is the main factor? Have eurocentric expectations, knowledges and standards appropriate to a different kind of landscape and climate contributed to our dismal record of land management? If so, how can Australians deal with this inheritance and develop a sense of belonging in and to this continent? It is a paradox that in Australia what seems to be one of the most land-sensitive human cultures the planet has ever seen confronts what statistics attest to be one of the most wasteful and land-insensitive. If settler land management[2] has perhaps brought out some of the worst in the traditions we inherited from our largely Western-European origins, can we also hope that non-indigenous Australians perhaps may now have the potential to develop a type of land sensibility that, hybridising with that of indigenous culture, may yet bring something new and valuable into human land relationships?

In an important new book that is relevant to some of these questions, Peter Read explores an important left/right division in Australian society over belonging. Many non-indigenous Australians express a sense of doubt about belonging to this continent in the context of their sorrow and guilt about the dispossession and murder of Aboriginal people.[3] This sensitive (some might say over-sensitive) response is mainly articulated by non-indigenous people active on indigenous issues. On the opposite side of indigenous politics, One Nation supporters can be heard stridently asserting their own belonging, their very over-emphasis belying their assurances that it is unproblematic. As Read shows, by analysing for example country music, much contemporary Australian culture can be read as a response to the strength and endurance of Aboriginal cultural ties to the land, powerfully articulated even through the white legal system in judgements like Mabo and Wik and now impossible for non-indigenous Australians to ignore. Indigenous land ties are seen by some in the settler culture as threatening, so they stress in return non-indigenous belonging and land love, often in a way that idealises rural lifestyles and land relationships.

The idealised rural ideology and culture of One Nation is not likely to be much help to many of us. If we Australians are one of the most mobile and urbanised nations in the world, moving on average 13 times in our lifetimes, and leading lives for which rural sources of identity are increasingly unlikely, the countryman image can provide a decreasingly useful definition of identity. One Nation's response on the land issue seems to be based on denial and envy as much as its response to Aboriginal welfare: we are to take no responsibility for the dispossession of Aboriginal people, admit no connection with our own possession of the land, (which is unproblematic), and of course we have nothing to learn from them. There are much better non-indigenous responses, for example aiming to develop a close bond to the land to parallel the indigenous one, but even these seem to me to need to do more to come to terms with the failures of the past and present. An important part of being convincingly sorry is being able to give a good account of where past mistakes lie (a point Philip Ruddick should note) and only to the extent that this is done thoroughly might one reasonably expect better behaviour in the future. So a thorough attempt to change would seem to me to need to consider the facts with which I began this paper. A similar denial or incomplete sorry appears in the response to feminism of some forms of the men's movement (an interesting parallel

Read's discussion suggests but does not develop), where the oppressor not only denies their own group's oppressive role, but attempts to appropriate for themselves (and even to claim superiority in) the very characteristics they have made the basis for the Other's oppression.

Read himself adopts the parallel approach of affirming the need of non-indigenous Australians for a deep connection with the land. In interviews and accounts of various lives, he illustrates how love for the land on the part of non-indigenous Australians can go along with respect for Aboriginal people and acknowledgement of their rights. What is more controversial, however, is his demand that this development be not only parallel but separate, that it should not be copied from, motivated or informed by Aboriginal culture, but be established by a completely independent route. '*Let's intuit our own attachments to country independently of Aboriginals. We can belong in the landscape, on the landscape, or irrelevantly to the landscape*,' Read writes (Read, 2000: 204). A spiritual relationship to land, yes, but one that he sees as optional and articulated without reference to indigenous traditions and practices. This is one of several places where I feel deeply dissatisfied with Read's approach and conclusions.

Despite this clear conclusion, Read seems in many places ambivalent in his advocacy of independence, since he also seems to acknowledge the superior richness of Aboriginal relationships to place, and occasionally, it seems, the need for indigenous culture to take a leading and teaching role. Read appears similarly ambivalent about the way non-indigenous Australians love their land. Thus he feels the need to make in several places a curious qualification to his claims for this love: 'we loved the land,' he says 'but nevertheless we ruined it.' Can a different culture of the land from the dominant one which 'ruined it' really be seen as just optional, merely part of the individual's psychological need to belong, or is rather it a necessity, born of our culture's need to find a way to live sustainably in the land we continue to love and continue to ruin? Do we really have the option, in the long term, of an identity that treats the land as irrelevant, as Read seems to suggest?

The metaphor of moving from an abusive to a non-abusive love is an attractive one as a way to picture the dominant culture's need to transform its land culture and relationships, denying neither the love, the abusive practice, or the need to heal. Nevertheless the abusive love metaphor involves another paradox that requires rather more in the way of explanation and unpacking than Read seems willing to give it. How could it be possible for a parent, for example, to say, 'I loved this child but I abused her'. One can imagine explanations for some cases – the parent is deeply conflicted, or does not know the damaging outcome of their actions. (Neither of these seem to fit the case of many current abusive land relationships; consider, for example, land clearing in Queensland and in many other parts of Australia, where outcomes like salination are well known.) These caveats may allow the parent to maintain their claim to love, as an exceptional case to be explained by special circumstances, but such cases could hardly be the normal case.[4]

It is a mistake to think of love simply in terms of private relationships or episodes of internal emotion, like feeling strongly when you see a beautiful sunset. Love involves dispositions, including practices of caring for the loved one, and attempting to ensure that others' actions also exhibit that care. In these dispositional terms, abusive love is a very doubtful form of love. Love of the land can be expressed at the public as well as the private level; at the public level also (indeed especially) love requires that we take care of the land, and see that others do as well. While public policies tolerate and even encourage abusive practices such as land clearance, our love of the land does not deserve the name. As abusive love is only doubtfully love, so Read's assumptions about non-indigenous Australians' love for the land must be seen as doubtful or at least as requiring much more elaboration and discussion.

Independence or Convergence?

Read's overall approach, which seems to form the basis of his interview choices and selection of life narratives, is to posit an existing form of non-indigenous land or place attachment (equated with spirituality) that can be developed independently of indigenous Australians, without reliance on any form of direct or indirect guidance from them. This approach enables Read to avoid any systematic comparison of the two cultures in relation to land sensibility along with any critical assessment of mainstream Australian or indeed Western land ethics and cultures. It avoids the comparisons of land cultures based on self-derogation, hand-wringing and envy that Read rightly wants to avoid, but this advantage comes at a rather large price, that of avoiding any self-critical or comparative reflection on land cultures in general on a larger-than-individual scale. It bypasses any systematic discussion of land ethics, and the major critiques of Western models of land culture and ethics developed in disciplines such as environmental philosophy and critical anthropology. In doing so it privatises the issues and lends covert support to the idea that the dominant model is adequate, is getting there or will get there without major challenge. This I find especially problematic.

Read provides few clues as to why he advocates the course of independent development, which he springs on the reader in the concluding pages with little preliminary discussion. It seems as if Read implicitly assumes alternatives of independence versus imitation or appropriation of Aboriginal culture. No doubt such an option can be justified under the slogan 'respecting difference', but so can many others that have more to be said for them. I believe these options to offer all Australians a false choice in relation to Aboriginal society, and that the supposed independence is, and would be, a fake.[5] I agree that non-indigenes should not aim to imitate Aboriginal society and its land culture, if that were possible; to do so would be to ignore the connection between a society's land narratives and its economy, for one thing. I do not agree, however, that non-indigenous Australians should aim to be independent in these areas.

These alternatives seem to me to ignore all the more interesting options of interaction, including dialogue, learning, convergence and hybridisation, dynamically evolving and adaptive forms that are quite distinct from static cultural imitation. There is much to be said for working for cultural convergence, to evolve what Aboriginal philosopher Mary Graham calls 'the embryonic form of an intact, collective spiritual identity for all Australians, which will inform and support our daily lives, our aspirations and our creative genius'. (Graham 1999: 117). It is not after all as if we can realistically divide the country simply into 'ours' and 'theirs', bits to be kept strictly separate and run by totally different systems, and Read himself, in advocating a generalised handover of national parks to indigenous Australians, appears to reject such a separation. If cultural structures must be able to recognise the ecological interconnectedness of land, a degree of cultural dialogue and convergence seems essential. It would be both arrogant and unwise, I think, for a culture that has been in this continent for a mere two centuries and which has, by any standards, done a great deal of damage to the land, to ignore guidance that may be offered by one that has behind it 50,000 years of inhabitation. To be willing to listen and learn is not the same as to imitate or appropriate. It is not only compatible with but requires respect, humility, and self-critique (distinct from self-flagellation). Various levels and kinds of hybridisation are possible: it is a serious mistake to think that our belonging here requires that we appropriate exactly the indigenous names and narratives, the same stories and meanings, and that the land could never come to sing to us except derivatively through these cultural materials of others.[6]

So if, as Read says, approvingly quoting John Mulvaney, 'the greatest gift of Aboriginal society to multi-cultural Australia is a spiritual concept of place' (Read, 2000: 109), why not accept that gift? Well, Read seems to think non-indigenes already have such a concept, and don't need indigenous models or other help to acquire, develop or refine it. We non-indigenes need to have and can get – indeed he seems often to suggest, *have got* – our own forms of spirituality of place. But this assumption I think is deeply problematic on several counts, and is not well supported by his interview material.

First, from the perspective of the urgent practical problem of developing a better land ethic and culture, spirituality is only part of the story, and perhaps not the most important part. A broad and unqualified concept of spirituality is too indiscriminate to be particularly useful in this context – the more important question is: what kind of spirituality? The concept of spirituality frames a quest in very general terms that are not sufficiently clearly directed to ecological forms of land connection, although these are the forms that settler culture so badly needs if it is to stop despoiling the land. True, Western culture has its own forms of spirituality, but its dominant post-Christian forms have often been framed in terms that have opposed it to the earth and to the body, and seen the spirituality of place as something to be overcome or drawn into its larger scheme which figures the value of place accordingly, in the largely instrumental terms of leading us to a higher, non-earthly place.[7] Historical Christianity, as John Passmore remarks, often saw pagan place and nature reverence as its main enemy, and set itself the task of destroying pagan shrines or giving them a contrary meaning as part of its own framework of transcendence.[8]

A spirituality of place is at odds with the Western system of dualisms that have made the particular and immediate, the bodily, the sensory, the experiential and the emotional the inferior 'others' to the abstract, the mental and the rational-dispassionate. A spirituality of place is not then something that will just fall into the laps of people with these kinds of traditions behind them. Because its dominant traditions have been hostile to nature and place, locating the sacred in a transcendent higher world beyond the fallen earth, the development of a non-superficial spirituality of place that locates the sacred as immanent in particular places is highly problematic for Western culture, and requires major rethinking and re-imagining. In logical and structural terms Aboriginal culture has a great deal to teach about these specific forms of land spirituality which challenge Western traditions. At this point Read's objective of cultural independence or separate spiritual development risks losing the plot, since it would deprive non-indigenous Australians of alternative models from indigenous land cultures that can be most helpful and suggestive of how to develop the communicative and dialogical elements that, according to Deborah Bird Rose, are characteristic of indigenous land culture,[9] as opposed to the monological character that adheres to the propertarian and instrumental forms that have typified Western land relationships.

The concept of spirituality appears to provide an easy general solution to the question of how we can find a system that is better for us and for the land only because of two confusions. The first is a confusion between necessary and sufficient conditions; a spiritual relationship to the land may be necessary to a better land culture, but it is not sufficient. If spirituality is defined in a very inclusive way as access to and pursuit of meaning, vision, value and deep purpose, it is clear that very many different kinds of land philosophies count as spiritual in this definition. But this includes some varieties that have been deeply damaging and antipathetic to the earth and its systems of life. For examples, we can consider certain traditional forms of spirituality that are hostile to the body, to other species, to the earth, or to women, or that foster racial or religious hatred. Or we could consider certain types of 'blood and soil' land spiritualities that form the basis for ethnic exclusion and war. The label 'spirituality' by no means lets us off our critical responsibilities to consider the ethical and political content of systems of beliefs and practices. It is crucial to consider what kind of spirituality is in question; but in order to do this you have to go well beyond spirituality as such to outline a philosophy and a politics to go with it.

Of course spirituality may be given a less inclusive meaning, although the apparently inclusive character of the concept is certainly part of its appeal; for example, we could define spirituality itself in dialogical terms, as a certain kind of communicative capacity. But then we would still have to address the question of what kinds of things it applies to, a complex issue. We get a similar outcome if we define spirituality in terms of recognition of the sacred dimension of life. Again, we have to consider concepts of the sacred that define it in an oppositional contrast to the profane or fallen, or which locate value and meaning in the immaterial abstract in a way that devalues the earth and embodiment. From the perspective of a land ethic, setting up a few special locations as 'sacred' may do little by itself to counter the devaluation, degradation and instrumentalisation of ordinary land. Again from the perspective of the land, the problem is not so much that non-indigenous culture lacks a concept of the sacred, as Veronica Brady has claimed, as that it has mostly located the sacred in the wrong place, above and beyond a fallen earth.

Some of the agenda associated with the concept of spirituality, such as the rejection of reductionism, is important, but it is hard to see how the highly inclusive forms of the concept can provide any useful or general solution to problems of environmental ethics. Nor should we endorse the assumption that all forms of spirituality are good and make a positive contribution to our problems of developing place or nature-sensitivity.[10]

I am not rejecting the idea that a spirituality of the land and of place is needed. But although 'spirituality' may be a necessary condition for a better land philosophy, the really important thing is to delineate the kind of spirituality involved and the structural barriers to attaining it. Once these qualifications have been registered, Read's independence thesis is much less plausible because it is at this further point that indigenous land philosophy can be particularly helpful. What this means is that we would have to work a lot harder than Read suggests to show that non-indigenous Australian culture has reached the point of attaining the kind of spirituality or philosophy needed to redress the damage the dominant culture has done to the land, or that it has the basis for developing this quite independently of indigenous culture. But there are further independent reasons for questioning the degree to which Read has established this through his interview methodology.

The Demand for a Place-Sensitive Culture is a Revolutionary Demand

Read tries to show that non-indigenous culture has, independently of indigenous culture, a spiritual concept of and relationship to place. The case for this rests on the narratives of individual attachment to places that feature in the book. But interesting and sensitive though these narratives are, Read's largely anecdotal approach of interviewing selected individuals leaves unidentified and unchallenged the *structural* obstacles to getting a place-sensitive society and culture. This individualisation of the problem enables him to suggest that non-indigenous culture is much closer to realising this goal than I think it is. The key question here – one that Read's discussion leaves entirely unaddressed – is how far the lives whose land spirituality he outlines are typical or are able to be made general or normal. It seems clear to me that in the relevant respects the land attachments Read outlines are not typical; indeed many swim strongly and consciously against the mainstream, and they could not be made typical without very major structural change. If such individual sensitivities exist in the counter-spaces and are unable to be generalised, they may tell us little about the character of the culture as a whole and its structural constraints on and denials of attachment to place.

Granting for the sake of argument[11] that many non-indigenous Australians do have strong attachments to places and parts of the land, there is still a very important structural difference between our respective cultures in the way those attachments are treated. If indigenous society is one where social customs, etiquette and institutions in every way nurture and recognise relationships to place, non-indigenous Australian culture and its institutions conversely and systematically neglect, frustrate and deny these relationships. The survival requirements of economic availability as an employee in the labour market, for example, require each of us to spurn and set aside our place and extended family attachments.[12] They demand that each of us in the normal case renounce our first love, the maternal place, ask us to leave and to forget, and this will be only the first of many such betrayals required of us. Clearly, in these circumstances, it is not enough to produce tales of individuals who have by good fortune been able to ignore or beat dominant structural constraints on place-sensitivity and place relationship.

The concept of a spirituality of place suggests that the problem can be addressed at the purely individual and private level of personal quasi-religious feelings, observances and rituals relating to places. This over-individualised account overlooks the way relationships to place are differentiated and structured through various class, gender and racialised relationships. Read recognises some differentiation of the basis of belonging in the case of gender – although in a rather problematic way. Given that feminism has rejected especially strongly the idea that maternity is central to and defining of women's identity, it is hard to imagine that many contemporary feminists would be happy to endorse a criterion of women's belonging and identity that makes it dependent upon where birth-blood falls and afterbirth is disposed of.[13] But other class constituents of place-making also need to be considered.

Relationships to place are strongly affected not only by gender but also by class and colonial status. Those who are most vulnerable and powerless are most at risk of losing control over their ability to remain in a home place or place of attachment. In the contemporary Australian welfare system, for example, the unemployed are legally required to move on bureaucratic demand: their attachments to place are given no weight at all. Similarly, Aboriginal people as colonial subjects lost their power to maintain their relationships to place and were required to relocate to the places their colonial masters specified, in ways which did not recognise their traditional tribal or place relationships. In the recent past of the West, we may think of the enclosures, which created an unattached urban working class and a labour market precisely by destroying key peasant land and place relationships.[14] Generally speaking, those groups who are already well enough provided for to resist the imperatives of the labour market have the best chance of developing or maintaining a relationship to place, but this relationship then usually suffers from the problem of being framed in the monological terms of property ownership.

To make philosophical progress on the problem of achieving better cultural relationships to land and place, we need to put some effort into identifying and removing structural obstacles to developing mutually enhancing land relationships. Most non-indigenous Australians inherit several background levels of what I would term 'disbelonging' (alienation would be another term) that are part of the general cultural inheritance of the West. This is rather more than a passive state of not belonging. Rather it is an active state or process of denying or rejecting certain kinds of origins and ties, especially ties to the earth and to the embodied and material realm – expressed especially in actively and systematically not seeing or crediting the context of the ecologically situated body. (Denial is an active process of not picking up certain things, backgrounding certain agencies, it is not just a matter of failing to know something.) At the deepest level of disbelonging we are heirs to the ancient dualist dynamic of the West that takes for granted a transcendent view of the self as expressed in the activities of the 'subject' conceived as mind or soul in opposition to the body and the world of surrounding 'objects'. To the extent that these traditions survive at deep levels, bearers of Western culture mostly still have to discover not only that they belong to the particular lands they inhabit but that they belong to the earth at all, and not to the disembodied realms of heaven or that new heaven of disembodied reason, cyberspace.

Other structural obstacles to belonging include also the constituents of modern capitalism that envisage the earth in terms of private property, so that places become interchangeable units of the underlying economic substratum of property. This is a framework that envisages place in instrumental terms, reduces attachment to profitability or other market benefits and reduces the value of land to a potential for accruing these benefits. Other contributing factors widely shared across modern cultures include insensitivity to the more-than-human aspects of place born of human-centredness and human (and especially urban) self-enclosure. High levels of urbanisation and mobility discourage deep contact with the non-human aspects of place. These require time in that place, time for the experience of seasonal change, and time to make contact with its non-human voices. And time is what we increasingly lack.

We have taken a quantum leap further in insensitivity to place with the current form of globalisation, which increasingly demands such a heavy investment of time for the work of survival that attachments of any sort become problematic, and now demands that we prioritise a global standpoint of place which is the standpoint of no place or of abstract, virtual space. To these we must add factors especially associated with neo-European and Australian colonial origin: Eurocentrism and nostalgia for the European homeland, leading to a view of the new country as inferior to or as an extension of the old, to be experienced and judged primarily in relation to the old, or as to be made in the image of the old, rather than as an independent presence to be engaged with on its own terms.

So I propose a start on the problem from the other end than Read, enumerating the structural obstacles in Australian society and related societies to recognising attachments to place. When we do this, I think it is possible to see that, far from Australian society being 'already there', the quest for a nature- and place-sensitive society, like the quest for a better quality working life and a genuinely communicative democracy, unveils a project that is revolutionary in the sense that it challenges the existing order very deeply and fundamentally at many levels.

The Politics of Place Names

Different cultures have different bases for ownership of the land: these differences can be so radical that they amount to different paradigms of land relationship, incomprehensible to those from a different framework. In some cultures it is the paradigm of expenditure or mixing in of human labour that validates the claim to own the land. This Lockean position validating capitalist and colonial models of appropriation and ownership, is, as I have argued elsewhere,[15] basically a one-way, monological form of relationship in which nature's agency and independence is discounted and the land conceived as an adjunct to or resource for human projects. An alternative paradigm is communicative, making ownership out in the essentially narrative terms of naming and interpreting the land, of telling its story in ways that show a deep and loving acquaintance with it and a history of dialogical interaction. In terms of this second paradigm, non-indigenous Australians have a long way to go in achieving ownership and belonging. The namings of non-indigenous Australians tend to be Eurocentric and to register a monological or non-interactive relationship with a land conceived as passive and silent. Aboriginal narrative patterns of naming can help to show us possibilities for a richer dialogical relationship which our dominant conceptual schemes obscure.

I made the close acquaintance of the first paradigm growing up on a small NSW farm whose front gate bore the hand-lettered name 'Wyeera'. The name, my father told me, meant 'to dig the soil'. He said it was an Aboriginal word, although he was unable to say which tribe used the term or from whence they came.[16] If the name did have this meaning, it seems likely that the nature of the digging involved was very different from the digging we practised. Digging and the hard work that went with it was a venerated activity on our land, a piece of low fertility Sydney sandstone my father had to strip of its trees to make our farm. In our pioneering mythology, it was cultivation (interpreted as digging) representing European agriculture, and the exemplary hard work of altering the land to fit the Eurocentric formulae of cultivation and production that supposedly made us European settlers superior to other races and species.

But it is not just the romantic call of another culture that makes me think now that digging and sweating to force the land into the ideal form of the European farm is not the only or the best basis for land relationship and that the kind of narrative basis for ownership typical of indigenous cultures has much more to offer. A communicative paradigm, the reflexive relationship Rose describes in her classic study of the Yarralin of the Victoria River Downs region and their land relationship, *Dingo Makes Us Human*, makes good sense for non-indigenous Australia too in the context of the ecological failure of Eurocentric models in the Australian context. But a narrative project of sensitivity to place requires discarding the mechanist, reductionist and human-centred conceptual frameworks that strip intentionality and thereby narrative subjecthood from the land and from non-humans generally. Human self-enclosure that denies subject positioning to all but the human vastly contracts the range of subjects and possible narratives that give meaning and richness to place. Human-centredness reduces the land to a passive and neutral surface for the inscription of human projects. Capitalist versions of human-centredness reduce the agency and value of the land to a mere potentiality for aiding or realising these projects, e.g. profit-making. These are monological modes of relating that reduce the land to an instrumentalised Other on whom projects are imposed, rather than an interactive and dialogical relationship that recognises agency in the land. Monological modes of relating are dysfunctional, especially in the context of the current crisis. They allow no space for two-way adaptation to the other, for negotiation, attentiveness or sensitivity.

These contrasting paradigms, and much else also, are reflected in our respective cultures' naming practices. The way we name places reflects our land spirituality and the superficiality or depth of our relationship to the land and its narrative embedment. Western philosophy's theories of naming the land illustrate this. Logical positivist philosophers treated names as purely conventional, neutral markers without cultural content, mere pointers or numbered labels. They could not have been more wrong. Names are only conferred in individualistic and therefore arbitrary ways where there is no recognition of the importance of community, in whose absence there is no such thing as meaning. Conventionalism reflects the concept of the land as neutral, passive and silent. Conventionalism is an index of the shallowness of relationships to place: a completely instrumental approach may require only a number as a name, the shortest distance between two points, that of the namer and his purpose, the least possible investment of attention and effort in the other. Naming workers are often required to follow positivist practice. A friend who had worked on creating and registering street names told me of the arbitrary lists they used to select from, lists compiled from dictionary words, first names and surnames. These official namers never saw the places they were naming and knew nothing of their histories, but followed conventionalistic rules like 'a short name for a short street'.

There is an important politics to names and naming. Colonial modes of naming the land normally carry a politics reflecting colonial relationships, and a politics which is often blatantly incorporative as well as a mode of relating which is monological. To illustrate what I mean, consider Frederick Turner's account of Columbus' naming of the New World:

> To each bit of land he saw he brought the mental map of Europe with which he had sailed. Anciently ... place names arose like rocks or trees out of the contours and colors of the lands themselves ... as a group took up residence in an area, that area would be dotted with names commemorating events that took place in it ... where one tribal group supplanted another, it too would respond to the land, its shapes, moods, and to tribal experiences had there. Now came these newest arrivals, but the first names by which they designated the islands were in no way appropriate to the islands themselves. Instead, the Admiral scattered the nomenclature of Christianity over these lands, firing his familiar names like cannon balls against the unresisting New World ... One group was called Los Santos because the Christ-bearer sailed past them on All Saints' Day ... An armoured Adam in this naked garden, he established dominion by naming.[17]

Several things emerge from this account: first, Columbus' naming is an act of power over the land and those who inhabit it, an act of incorporation into what is thought of as an empire. Second, Turner contrasts dialogical indigenous with colonial monological modes of naming that are not a response to the character of the land and are 'in no way appropriate' to the lands themselves. Columbus' naming does not record any of its features or any real encounter with the land, but merely registers its conquest, its incorporation into the empire of the same. Beyond this incorporative meaning, these names invoke no depth of knowledge or narrative, being little more than mnemonic devices holding place for a neutral marker, like the logical positivist labels.

It seems to me that far too many Australian namings are still like Columbus' namings, if we replace Columbus' Spanish Christian saints with the bigwigs of the British Colonial Office. In these same terms I think we should problematise many Australian capital city namings, like Sydney, Melbourne, Brisbane, Adelaide and Hobart, as now-empty power namings.[18] Such namings overlay the land, conceived as neutral, with a grid of bureaucratic or political power that registers obeisance to the empire, or commemorates those in the surveyors' office in 1903.[19] Most of our state capital names and many of their suburb names either locate us in terms of what is now a largely meaningless grid of colonial power or a largely irrelevant nostalgia for European places.

Another group of names exhibits the colonial dynamic in a different way from those commemorating major figures of colonial power. These are the names that refer back to the places of a European homeland, usually bearing no resemblance at all to the new place 'named after' it. ('To each bit of land he saw he brought the mental map of Europe with which he had sailed.') It is now hard to connect Perth in WA, the mining capital, with the small town on the upper reaches of the River Tay in Scotland. Ipswich, Camden and Penrith are places in Britain. The settler societies formed for the purpose of introducing the biota of the homeland were called 'acclimatisation societies'; we can perhaps regard the acclimatised names here as being the equivalent of the feral fauna the colonists tried (sometimes unfortunately successfully) to introduce in their efforts to assimilate the new land to the old, and think of these kinds of acclimatised names in similar terms, as feral names. Feral names, like feral biota, register the colonial dynamic of periphery and centre, the devaluation of Australian landscapes and biota in comparison to 'home'. Thus the acclimatisers believed that Australia had no song birds, and strove to introduce 'real' ones from the homeland. Although an element in what we must construe as their deafness to the many wonderful indigenous songsters was the strangeness and unfamiliarity of the colony, another major part of it was the colonial mindset and Eurocentric conceptual framework that considered Australia as a deficient, empty land, a mere absence of the positive qualities of the homeland, the place at the centre. In the colonising framework, the other is not a positively-other-than entity in its own right but an absence of the self, home or centre, something of no value or beauty of its own except to the extent that it can be brought to reflect or bear the likeness of home as standard, be assimilated or made to share in the Same.[20] Feral names like Perth and Ipswich are pointedly assimilationist in their references to home, their longing inscription of the landscape of Britain and occasionally Europe on the new 'featureless' land. They invoke no shared narratives and provide no evidence of affection for, attention to or even interaction with the land.

A third category of names we should problematise are blatantly monological colonial namings that take no notice of the land when it is nearly impossible not to notice it. ('One group was called Los Santos because the Christ-bearer sailed past them on All Saints' Day ...') The contrast between the empty egoism or passé nostalgia of these monological colonial namings and the rich dialogical practice of Aboriginal narrative namings impressed itself on me strongly in a recent bushwalk in the 'Mt. Brockman' area of 'Arnhem Land'. In this region you encounter fully Kakadu's extraordinary qualities of beauty, power and prescience. The massif we know as 'Mt. Brockman' is part of an extravagantly eroded sandstone plateau weathered to immense, fantastic ruins that bring to mind enigmatic artefacts from some titanic civilisation of the past. In the place where we camped on Baraolba Creek on the second day of our walk, an inchoate sphinx face and a perfect sarcophagus, both the size of battleships, topped the great towers of the domed red cliffs to the south. Everywhere, strangely humanoid figures of shrouded gods and finely balanced sandstone heads gaze out over country formed by a thousand million years of play between the sandstone and the hyperactive tropical atmosphere.

Yet namings like 'Mount Brockman' take no notice at all of this extraordinary place, or of its power and agency.[21] The puzzling, pointless and Eurocentric naming of this great outlier of the escarpment, marked by remarkable and ancient Aboriginal places and rock art galleries, commemorates a European 'discoverer', finding the place notable only for the accident of its falling in the way of a member of the colonial aristocracy travelling by. Such monological namings treat the place itself as a vacuum of mind and meaning, to be filled through the power plays of those in favour with the current political equivalent of the colonial office or the resource activities of mining companies.

In deep naming, names connect with a narrative, as they so often do in Aboriginal patterns of naming, that gives depth, meaning and a voice to the land and its non-human inhabitants. Walking in the upper stretches of Baraolba Creek in Yegge (early dry), I encountered the *kunbak*, a small waterplant whose fine green fronds represent the hair of the Yawk Yawk sisters.[22] The Yawk Yawks live in the slowly moving water along the edges of this little stream that drains a huge area of the stone country. In the narratives of the Kunwinjku people of the western (part of Kakadu) Arnhemland, these sisters are little spirit mermaids with fish tails instead of legs. They dwell in the holes beneath the banks and come out to sing and play where the pandanus grows. From underneath the water they watch women swimming, ever on the lookout for one ready to become their mother, to birth them as human. For a *balanda*[23] woman like myself, the Yawk Yawks offer welcome sisterly and *binitj* travelling company in the landscape, enticing Westerners across the high wall we have tried to build between the human and non-human worlds. Many *binitj* namings invoke narratives like those of the Yawk Yawks. These striking stories function both to impress their meanings cunningly and irresistibly in the memory, and to bind together botanical, experiential, practical and philosophical knowledge, community identity and spiritual practice in a rich and satisfying integration of what we in the West usually oppose – life and theory. *Binitj* stories and namings envelope a journey in their land in a web of narrative, so that one travels through a speaking land encountered deeply in dialogical mode, as a communicative partner.

Decolonising the Naming Relationship

The deeply colonised and colonising naming practices I have discussed still figure too large on the Australian map, and neither they nor their underlying narratives of Eurocentrism and of colonial power are in any way challenged by formal and superficial decolonisation exercises like republicanism. Since in my view it is a much more important decolonising project to work on these cultural modes of naming than to tinker with the head of state, I am tempted to call the project of cultural change suggested here 'deep republicanism'. It is precisely such cultural practices we have to take on if we Australians are ever truly to belong culturally to this land and develop a mode of exchange that attends to and respects the uniqueness and power of place as well as recognising its prior naming and occupation by Aboriginal people. A renaming project of this kind must recognise the double-sidedness of the Australian colonial relationship, in which non-indigenous Australians were historically positioned both as colonisers of indigenous Australians and as colonised themselves (in relation to the British).[24]

An empty and highly conventionalised naming practice is both a symptom and a partial cause of an empty relationship to the land. If we want a meaningful relationship with the land that expresses a healthier pattern than the colonial one, we have to look to naming it in meaningful terms that acknowledge its agency and narrative depth. So I want to propose a renaming project as a project of cultural convergence, cross-fertilisation, reconciliation and decolonisation. It might be helpful to start the cultural decolonisation project from locations and issues that offer the possibility of generating some common culture through involvement and engagement of both indigenous and non-indigenous communities. That is, one that offers possibilities for developing shared spiritual meaning and ritual observance, not just an individual search for privatised spiritual meaning. The project of decolonising our naming relationship is such a project, one in which indigenous and non-indigenous communities could come together to rework their relationship to each other and to the land. So I am proposing we can start by a joint renaming project that is part of remythologising the land and which prioritises for replacement at least the categories of names I have discussed above. To these we should add some other categories.

Perhaps at the top of the list for replacement are those names that commemorate and honour the makers of massacres against indigenous people, like the name for the major highway that runs right through the middle of Perth – the Stirling Highway. We might better call it the Jack Davis Highway, to honour another kind of hero who surely better deserves our commendation. In terms of encounter with the land, such a naming would remain monological. Where nature is dominant over culture, as in Kakadu, we could hope that a dialogical naming practice might attend to or engage to a high degree with the land, but where culture is highly dominant over nature, as in the city, it might be reasonable, to begin with at least, that naming practice draw largely on human cultural engagements and elements. But these urbanised namings could be much more adventurous, witty and less colonial than the 'neutral marker' suburban place names we often have now, and they could connect with real or imaginary narratives of events which have occurred there or people worth remembering.

But, it can be objected, names honouring the colonial office are a genuine part of our history, which would be lost if they were eliminated. So they are, but we do not have to passively remain in the mindset that created them. We can take charge of how our land is named and make it relevant to today. I do not suggest that colonial names should be just thrown away and forgotten, discarded; they may have something important to tell us about where we have come from. But that is not necessarily who we are now, and I believe we need alternatives that do not force us to honour slayers of Aboriginal people and others whose role in our history presents similar atrocities. As a dynamic and evolving society, we should be able to democratise, de-bureaucratise and put up for community cultural engagement, elaboration and contest our processes of naming. This will be a long-term process, but one we need to get started on now. To allow for cultural difference, I think we should aim for the formal possibility of multiple namings, and also for namings that are worked through communities as part of a democratic cultural process in which a broad range of groups can participate.[25]

A further group of names we should reconsider are the many Aboriginal place names, although what mainly needs to be problematised here is the relationship of non-indigenous Australians to these names. For the most part these indigenous names are treated by the dominant white population in logical positivist style as neutral markers, but it is important that non-indigenous communities make an effort to understand their historical and narrative significance. Where these names acknowledge Aboriginal presence, commemorate tribal land, or have other appropriate meanings, non-indigenous communities should learn about them, in co-operation with the relevant indigenous communities. Sometimes these namings form part of the larger cultural practice in which features of Aboriginal culture are appropriated when we need them to provide us with a distinctive national identity, a colonising practice that often leads to inappropriate or paradoxical use. To overseas visitors these names are part of what makes Australia interesting. They mark out our unique Australian-ness, and where we use them shamelessly for this purpose without understanding or respect, we should think of them as stolen names. To escape this meaning, non-indigenous communities should understand them as a precious cultural heritage and treat them appropriately.

To sum up: recovering a popular naming practice that generates meaningful, dialogical names is part of recovering a meaningful relationship to the land. We need to construct new naming practices to replace or provide alternatives for the problem categories of power names, feral names, and monological names, and rethink our relationship to stolen names. In this decolonising project, indigenous patterns, models and practices have much to teach non-indigenous culture, but we need an active, dynamic practice of naming and narrativising that can also incorporate elements from non-indigenous Australian cultures, not a slavish imitation or colonising assimilation or incorporation of indigenous naming and narrative.[26] Such a dynamic outcome could only be possible if we can make the project of renaming the land one of cultural co-operation and convergence between indigenous and non-indigenous communities.

Notes

1   Of course it is always a little more complex than that, and one has to consider the case, increasingly common in commodified and colonial land contexts, where one's land of attachment thrives at the expense of other land which is treated as sacrificial. In this case land attachment does not necessarily lead to positive environmental outcomes.
2   I do not take the term 'settler' to be synonymous with 'non-indigenous', since in compound terms there is a clear difference: 'settler culture' for example connotes something both more invasive and singular than 'non-indigenous culture'.
3   Read, P. (2000) *Belonging*, Cambridge, Cambridge University Press.
4   To put the matter in Wittgensteinian terms, abusive love could not be the paradigmatic case.
5   Many of the lives and land attitudes Read narrates as examples of non-indigenous spirituality, for example, show clear signs of being influenced in various ways by indigenous land culture.
6   Read (2000: 99) writes, 'the bush speaks and sings whenever its spiritual guardians are present, but without an Aboriginal guide Ian knows and can feel only a fraction of its stories'.
7   This instrumental model is apparently endorsed by Read. The idea of spiritualising the land can also be developed in extremely human-centred ways. See Walls, L.D. (1995) *Seeing New Worlds*, Wisconsin, University of Wisconsin Press; see especially the discussion of the spirituality of Coleridge and Emerson, p. 64.
8   Passmore, J. (1974) *Man's Responsibility for Nature*, London, Duckworth.
9   See Rose, D.B. (1992) *Dingo Makes Us Human*, Cambridge, Cambridge University Press. See also Australian Heritage Commission (1996) *Nourishing Terrains*.
10 The approach of treating 'spirituality' in general and inclusive terms as a virtue is dangerously indiscriminate. Thus the concept of a 'spirituality coefficient' that rates spirituality in general terms as invariably better than non-spirituality seems to involve a straightforward distributive fallacy, one discussed by a number of philosophers, e.g. John Stuart Mill. Even if it is true that individuals and societies are better off psychologically with a form of spirituality, defined as a search for meaning and values, it does not in the least follow that the meanings and values they may arrive at are ones they or society in general should endorse. Nor does it follow that because their spirituality is good for them, it is good. The idea of quantifying spirituality as an unequivocally positive dimension of life, and condemning those who supposedly lack it as 'spiritually dumb', implies not only that all spiritualities are good in some general way but that any kind of spirituality is as good as any other – that is, it implies a suspension of critical ethics once an approach has been endorsed as 'spiritual'. But whether individuals or societies are 'better off' with spirituality is not something that can be assessed in any general way, but depends entirely on the character of that spirituality, whose positive ethical content is in no way established just by the 'spirituality' label.

11 Although in fact it seems unlikely that land attachment would be able to develop as strongly in a system which gives no adequate structural recognition to such relationships.
12 This is one basis for the connection between the flourishing of the capitalist market in labour and that of the nuclear family, suitably portable and detachable from place.
13 This highly romantic motherhood-centred account of women's place seems to imply that childless women have no belonging, but also runs into obvious problems about hospital incinerators and rubbish tips.
14 See Polanyi, K. (1974) *The Great Transformation*, Boston, Beacon Press.
15 See Plumwood, V. (2000) 'Deep ecology, deep pockets, and deep problems: a feminist eco-socialist analysis', in A. Light, E. Katz and D. Rothenburg (eds) *Beneath the Surface: critical essays on deep ecology*, Cambridge MA, MIT Press: 59-84. As I argue there, this model of land ownership tends to give little weight to indigenous labour and ownership, treating the land as a *terra nullius* and assuming a Eurocentric account of what counts as labour.
16 In those days, most people supposed there was just one Aboriginal language and tribe.
17 Turner, F. (1986) *Beyond Geography*, New Brunswick, NJ, Rutgers University Press: 131.
18 Of course power namings do tend to become conventionalised, empty and irrelevant very quickly, which is another good reason for avoiding them. An exception might be highly rationalised and systematised power namings, like those of Canberra suburbs commemorating Prime Ministers.
19 The bushwalking community has long contested these colonial power names, and has worked at its own renaming – on their maps names like Mt. Cloudmaker replace names like Mt. Renwick commemorating the survey office.
20 See Plumwood, V. (2001) 'Centrism and the "logic of alterity"', in M. Hass and R.J. Falmagne (eds) *Feminist Approaches to Logic*, PLACE, Rowman and Littlefield.
21 There is no single equivalent Aboriginal name for the area we know as 'Mt. Brockman'.
22 See Nganjmirra, N. (1997) 'Kunwinjku Spirit', in Neil McLeod (ed.) *Gundjiehmi: creation stories from Western Arnhem Land*, Melbourne, Miegungah Press at Melbourne University Press: 172.
23 Some Aboriginal people of Arnhem Land use the terms *binitj* for Aboriginal people and *balanda* for non-indigenous people.
24 On this cross location in the Indian case, see Spivak, G.C. (1999) 'Gender and International Studies', *Millennium*: 809-831.
25 Local councils, schools and community groups might set up literary contests to generate names and narratives, for example.
26 For a wonderful example of such cultural convergence in the field of narrative, see San Roque, C. (2000) 'The Sugarman Cycle' PAN (1): 42-64.

References

Australian Heritage Commission (1996) *Nourishing Terrains*.
Nganjmirra, N. (1997) 'Kunwinjku Spirit', in Neil McLeod (ed.) *Gundjiehmi: creation stories from Western Arnhem Land*, Melbourne: Miegungah Press at Melbourne University Press.
Passmore, J. (1974) *Man's Responsibility for Nature*, London, Duckworth.

Plumwood, V. (2000) 'Deep ecology, deep pockets, and deep problems: a feminist eco-socialist analysis', in A. Light, E. Katz and D. Rothenburg (eds) *Beneath the Surface: critical essays on deep ecology*, Cambridge, MA, MIT Press: 59-84.

Plumwood, V. (2001) 'Centrism and the "logic of alterity"', in M. Hass and R. J. Falmagne (eds) *Feminist Approaches to Logic*, PLACE, Rowman and Littlefield.

Polanyi, K. (1974) *The Great Transformation*, Boston, Beacon Press.

Read, P. (2000) *Belonging*, Cambridge, Cambridge University Press.

Rose, D.B. (1992) *Dingo Makes Us Human*, Cambridge, Cambridge University Press.

San Roque, C. (2000) 'The Sugarman Cycle' PAN (1): 42-64.

Spivak, G.C. (1999) 'Gender and international studies', *Millennium*: 809-831.

Turner, F. (1986) *Beyond Geography*, New Brunswick, NJ, Rutgers University Press.

Walls, L.D. (1995) *Seeing New Worlds*, Wisconsin, University of Wisconsin Press.

CONCLUSIONS

20 Conclusions

JEAN HILLIER AND EMMA ROOKSBY

Since the death of Pierre Bourdieu, his legacy has continued to evolve, and his work to be taken up in new and varied ways by scholars interested in different aspects of his critical sociology. The variety of subject and approach taken in the chapters contained in this volume reflects the richness and complexity of Bourdieu's legacy. The contributors write from a range of disciplinary and interdisciplinary perspectives, and take up many different topics to which Bourdieu's work is relevant, from the habitus of indigenous Australian women to the place of ghosts in the city, from the strategic responsibilities of urban planners to the persistence of colonialism.

Behind the variety of subject and disciplinary approaches, common themes and strategies can be discerned. In the Introduction, we explored some of the themes common to most chapters; themes that have also been taken up in the broader secondary literature on Bourdieu, both prior to and after his death. These include the relationship between habitus and psychoanalysis, and the mutability and plurality of habituses.

The authors demonstrate, by various means, that habitus is not monolithic, immutable or inexorable, as some writers have postulated in the past. Bourdieu himself was clear on this point, writing in *Pascalian Meditations* that it is essential to recognise 'the existence of cleft, tormented habitus bearing in the form of tensions and contradictions the mark of the contradictory conditions of formation of which they are the product' (2000b: 64). The structuralism of some earlier works such as *A Theory of Practice* can, in this new light, be seen more as reflections of the comparative stability of some habitus at the time of Bourdieu's writing, rather than as a statement of the immutability of all habituses at all times.

Bourdieu's sociology of symbolic power describes an important relational dimension between culture, social structure and action, showing how individual actions are produced within social structures and how, in turn, they creatively respond to and alter those structures to suit their own interests. This they can do by drawing on resources (cultural or other capital) acquired in one field, to effect change in another, or by importing 'moves' recognised within one field into others. The authors have illustrated how these relations function in particular social contexts, their theoretical starting points illustrated and informed by the particular fields in which their fieldwork has been conducted.

The chapters explore, for different fields and contexts, how cultural resources, processes and institutions hold individuals and groups in competitive and self-perpetuating hierarchies of domination, illustrating the extent to which individuals are able to respond creatively within such fields and contexts. Chapters by Waterson, Sandercock, Kitchen and Schneider, Plumwood and Friedmann show how cultural socialisation places individuals and groups in competitive (status) hierarchies. The chapters by Mouffe, Laclau, Hirst, Pile and Thompson illustrate how social struggles are refracted through symbolic classifications, and those by Hillier and Gale demonstrate how actors struggle and pursue creative strategies to achieve their interests within particular fields. Finally, the chapters by Leach, Dovey, Painter and Hindess show how actors reproduce the social order(s) within which they are located. Such reproductions and contestations are, the authors show, by their very nature political.

The chapters provide empirically informed and critical pictures of how different types of capital are accumulated and employed, by individuals and by groups, in a range of different and intersecting fields. From the concerted machinations of the Newcastle-upon-Tyne local authorities to the evolving and contested representations of Toraja religion, the chapters show that, not only do individuals and groups compete for different kinds of capital, they also show the fundamental contestability of what counts as capital within any given field. The struggle for social distinction is, the chapters illustrate, a fundamental dimension of social life; even the terms in which such struggle occurs are open to contestation.

True to Bourdieu's relentless insistence on the importance of the empirical, the chapters in this volume all involve both theoretical and empirical work, looking at habitus in particular social contexts, examining the types of capital at stake, the moves in the game, and the players in the field. They also look at the room that agents and groups have to manoeuvre within those fields, exploring the social and political possibilities of different habituses.

Four Questions

In the Introduction to this volume, we highlighted two major debates about habitus that have developed in the years since Bourdieu's death. In one way or another, all the contributions to this volume address one or other of these debates. In closing, we would like to highlight these themes, and to take up two additional themes important to the volume as a whole.

The first theme is the locus of habitus. Does habitus exist at a macro-level? How does the notion of habitus help us to understand international and national political structures and activities? The second theme is that of place and the built environment. Does habitus help explain processes of place-making in fields relating to practices of the built environment?

The third theme is the relationship between the individual and her or his habituses. Does habitus presume a particular account of the individual? Does, and should, habitus draw on a psychoanalytic account of individuals? The fourth, and final, theme is that of the durability of habituses. How durable are habituses? Might habituses undergo transformation in changing circumstances? Do some people's habituses actually *need* to change? In the sections that follow, we will consider each of these questions in turn, drawing on the chapters in this volume

Habitus: Micro and Macro?

The first set of questions raised by the authors in this volume is concerned with the locus of habitus. Does habitus exist at a macro-level? How does the notion of habitus help us to understand international and national political structures and activities?

The contributors who address the first of these questions give one of two answers. Some extend the notion of habitus to cover national and international contexts as well as local contexts, arguing that there is no difficulty in extending the notion in this way. Other contributors follow Bourdieu in discussing habitus at the micro- or local level, but also supplement habitus with other concepts in order to take into account the existence of habitus-like regularities at the macro-level.

Supporters of the affirmative view interpret events and interactions on national or international stages as according with the existence of habitus at the macro level. One such interpretation, made by several contributors, focuses on the legitimation of the exercise of power at regional, national and international levels. The exercise of power, at national and international levels, as at local levels, requires legitimation in some form or other; in some circumstances, legitimation is achieved through negotiation or bargaining, and in others by symbolic violence. Examples of symbolic violence at work to legitimate power are present in the essays by Gale, Dovey, Hindess, Painter and, particularly, Healey and

Plumwood, who discuss the capacity of dominant groups at regional and national levels to maintain their power despite adopting discursive strategies in which they explicitly disavow that power.

Plumwood's chapter illustrates this point in detail, showing how regionally and nationally dominant groups can violently impose their interests on subordinate or marginalised groups while seeming to be, and believing themselves, 'impartial' in their attitudes. The chapter by Hindess covers, among other subjects, aspects of the habitus of colonial administrators, themselves members of liberal societies, but in the position of administering colonised groups often deemed incapable of the autonomy necessary for liberal citizenship. As Healey's chapter shows, the symbolic power of dominant groups (marked both officially by title or uniform, and unofficially by dress, demeanour, accent and so on) has the capacity to skew negotiations in urban planning processes, and to skew attributions of blame when negotiation does not proceed smoothly. Mouffe explores similar issues in relation to a habitus of democratic participation, while Painter considers how the development of Regional Economic Strategies for different parts of the UK involves the construction and legitimation of 'knowledge' about the regions, their economic mix, environmental qualities and so on.

Contributors who continue to focus on habitus at the micro-level and to supplement it with other references to the macro-level include Kitchen and Schneider. Writing about crime and the design of the built environment, they allude to the role of organisational structures and policy frameworks in designing cities for improved quality of life. Such designing, they argue, inevitably takes the views of some people (the 'haves') to matter more than those of others (the 'have nots'), and as such probably involves habitus-like regularities, of the kind explicitly discussed by Hillier.

Bourdieu has called habitus 'a genetic theory of groups' (Bourdieu, 1987). His work explores how groups pursue strategies to produce and reproduce the conditions of their collective existence, at both macro- and micro-levels. Without the reinforcement of groups and institutions, many of which operate at national and (increasingly) international levels, individual actions may have little or no impact. Related positions are articulated in this volume by Hindess, Hillier, Dovey, Sandercock, and Kitchen and Schneider.

Place and the Built Environment

Does habitus help explain processes of place-making in fields relating to practices of the built environment? This question was addressed specifically by several contributors, who explored and articulated Bourdieu's references to the built environment, which are scattered throughout his work and find their fullest articulation in his discussion of the Kabyle house (Bourdieu, 1962).

Bourdieu's view on the role of physical space, and its relation to habitus, is difficult to discern, in part because nowhere in his oeuvre does he treat the subject in detail. Perhaps the most that can be said is that, according to Bourdieu, social space translates into physical space but that the translation is often blurred. Social space appears as the distribution in physical space of different kinds of goods and services, of individual agents and physically situated groups. These groups are endowed with greater or fewer possibilities for appropriating those goods, with the distribution of these possibilities dependent in part on their respective locations.

The chapters in this book show how the disappearance of certain physical or geographical aspects of a habitus can affect that habitus, and/or even destroy it. To the extent, then, that a habitus includes particular actions or practices that are enabled by, or are dependent on, particular physical surroundings (natural or artefactual), that habitus is dependent on this environment, and may be distorted, transformed or destroyed if the surroundings change or disappear. Friedmann's chapter in particular addresses the ways in which habitus may change when physical surroundings may change.

In common with Foucault's analysis of the intrication of physical space with the effects of power, several chapters in this volume illustrate how architectural spaces address mute injunctions directly to the body, in a process that Kim Dovey dubs the 'silent complicity of architecture'. The stateliness of the new Berlin Reichstag, dwarfed by a battlement of logo-plastered skyscrapers, the contrived barrenness of the public housing developments, the enticing cornucopia of the supermarket, the newly-safe city square watched by television cameras – these convey the real effects of symbolic power, as Leach and Dovey argue in this volume. Dovey injects a note of cautious optimism in his chapter with the observation that the '"complicitous silence of architecture" is the source of its deepest power, in both the worst and the best senses of the term "power" – oppression and empowerment; privilege and resistance'.

These issues are also addressed in different ways by several other contributors – by Sandercock, and Kitchen and Schneider in relation to street addresses and the fear of crime, and by Plumwood in relation to conceptions of the Australian landscape. Chapters by Gale and Pile describe how those already deprived of various types of capital are both physically and symbolically held at a distance from the 'rarest' or most valuable social goods.

Struggles over space may assume more collective forms, at international, national and local levels, an issue that is addressed in one way or another by almost every chapter in this volume. While at one level individuals may compete for capital within particular fields, they often also share a common interest in perpetuating the features of the habitus within which they move, and the fields within which they compete. Hirst demonstrates this with particular force in relation to the nation state, disputing claims of its obsolescence in a globalising world. Waterson and Friedmann both illustrate how the opening up of traditional communities to globalisation requires additional work of those communities, to preserve or adapt their habitus. Likewise, the pressures of globalisation make it more difficult for traditional communities to maintain a built environment within which that habitus can function. Nevertheless, as Friedmann observes, displaced communities (such as immigrant Algerian communities in Germany) are also able to adapt their habituses, to some degree, to new and very different built environments.

A major arena for many struggles over space and place is governmental policy formation; government policy wields an immense power over space and spatially-based habituses, through its capacity to change the value of land, and to enable or encourage alterations to the environment, both natural and built. The chapter by Painter provides a 'bridge' between national and local spatial scales, examining the power of Regional Development Agencies in the UK to construct both regions and their regional economies. Healey points out, in addition, how actors who already possess capital, such as developers and other commercial organisations, are in a position to influence disproportionately the planning policy of local and national government, the use of land and the granting of permissions to individuals for such uses. Hillier's chapter gives food for thought to planners who hope to work for community-focused planning, and to prevent the consolidation of capital in the hands of the few. The chapters by Pile and Sandercock also take up this issue in different ways.

The Durability of Habitus

The third set of questions which the essays in this volume address concern the durability of habitus. How durable are habituses? Might they undergo transformation in changing circumstances? Do some people's habituses actually *need* to change?

As we discussed in the introduction to this book, there is an increasing consensus that habitus is both dynamic and transformative, and that habituses interact with each other in a range of ways. The concept of habitus can be used to show breaks in or development of traditional ways of working, thinking and being, as is illustrated with particular force in the chapters by Friedmann and Painter. This implies a certain dynamism of habitus, a dynamism increasingly emphasised in Bourdieu's later work. As he wrote in *Pascalian Meditations*: 'Habitus change constantly in response to new experiences' (Bourdieu, 2000b: 161).

Criticisms of the structuralist inflexibility of notions such as habitus are explicitly rebutted in Bourdieu's recent work:

> In situations of crisis or sudden change, especially those seen at the time of abrupt encounters between civilisations linked to the colonial situation or too-rapid movements in social space, agents often have difficulties in holding together the dispositions associated with different states or stages, and some of them, often those who were best adapted to the previous state of the game, have difficulty in adjusting to the new established order. Their dispositions become dysfunctional and the efforts they may make to perpetuate them help to plunge them deeper into failure. (Bourdieu, 2000: 161).

Such people end up 'clinging to a disappearing way of life' (Bourdieu, 2000: 161) in 'a kind of social death' (Bourdieu, 2000: 161). Many of us are today familiar with the rapid obsolescence of the social ways of our grandparents, of our parents or our peers, and even our own habits and practices. Family structures continue to fragment, community involvement to decrease and take different forms, remote communication (email, SMS) to supplement or displace face-to-face meetings, and corporations to intervene ever more intrusively in the lives and values of their employees. Meanwhile commercial advertising and public announcements encourage constant adaptation and innovation. As contexts and cultures change, so do habituses.

Bourdieu's conceptual mappings of the symbolic and cultural capital of the French class system (Bourdieu, 1977, 1982) may now seem outdated; *vin ordinaire* and *foie gras* paté are hopelessly passé as examples of capital within France. But this observation too works to reinforce the view that habituses change and evolve. It is only the particular brands of cultural capital for which agents compete that have changed, while competition for cultural capital, within very similar general fields, continues. Thus Bourdieu's assessment of the durability of habitus, that it is a fate and not a destiny, accords with the analyses of changing, evolving habituses, and of the mutual influence of habituses on each other, provided by this volume.

402 Habitus: A Sense of Place

To the related question of whether some habituses *ought* to change, Bourdieu's work can be seen to give a resoundingly affirmative answer. His earlier writings, while articulating his own distinctive philosophical and sociological position, expressed doubts about the possibility of producing a theoretically complete or unified formulation of concepts such as habitus. His more recent work, such as *Pascalian Meditations*, provides more substantial argument for the necessary incompleteness of theories about the social world. But, as we stressed in the Introduction, rather than this conclusion pushing theorists back into quietism or passivity, Bourdieu's formulation of the incompleteness of social theory pushes theorists to be *more* practical, *more* political. Bourdieu's work does not simply address the descriptive question of what the world is like. It also tackles the normative question of what is wrong in the world, and the practical, political question of how to make the world more as we would have it be (where 'we' are located at an acknowledged and identifiable critical standpoint).

In addition to descriptive and interpretive analysis of habituses, such a stance enables, though it does not require, the articulation of critiques of particular habituses. Interestingly, though, the stance from which critique might be articulated is not internal to a sociological theory of habitus, but instead imports normative considerations from other disciplines or stances. Bourdieu's vocal alignment of himself with the political left – and specifically with the *gauche de gauche* – left little doubt as to the normative basis of his criticisms of certain habituses, such as those perpetuated in the mainstream media and in the world of academia. His critiques concentrated on the ability of powerful individuals and groups within a habitus to reinforce their power and positions relative to others, and on the amenability of habituses to such co-optation. (Bourdieu, 1998, 2001, 2002). Habituses make moves seem 'natural' or 'automatic', when they in fact embody particular interests and values, often those of a privileged or powerful minority (a point also made more broadly by the pragmatic movement within contemporary philosophy (Smiley, 1992; Walker, 1998; Bowden and Rooksby, 2005)). In addition, Bourdieu considered the corrosive effects of certain habituses taken holistically, as dynamic systems creating and reinforcing some forms of capital over others (Bourdieu, 2000).

Echoes of Bourdieu's focus on the practical aspect of both research and the answers it provides can be seen in all the contributions to this volume. All make at least provisional suggestions, and provide productive practical avenues to explore, for researchers, policy-makers and concerned citizens. But, in a sense, these suggestions also remain very much open. Those avenues that might be explored should be explored collectively – by many of those who share a habitus and not by isolated individuals – for their salutary effects to be felt. Each chapter in this collection, then, might be read as a challenge, directed towards every reader, to think practically about how to improve social and political conditions for people living in cities and in rural areas, in liberal democracies and in post-colonial states. Such questions invite further practical work in the spirit of Pierre Bourdieu, not only from individuals but from groups, alliances and collectivities at all levels of society.

The failings of current habituses may require, as Hillier suggests, the development of new techniques, strategies and improvisations for dealing with practical dilemmas. The positive transformation of unjust or oppressive habituses may, as the chapters by Thompson, Sandercock, and Kitchen and Schneider suggest, benefit from a broadening of dialogue currently taking place in academia (and in some other quarters) on how to tackle the social consequences of widening economic and social inequalities within and among developed and developing nations.

That there is room within Bourdieu's conceptual framework for such developments is uncontestable. The field (ranging from the globalised world at the macro level or the region or locality at a micro level) is continually in a state of dynamic tension, because the relations between positions (what counts as advantage and even where the borders of the field are drawn) are constantly being redefined by the actors who are located within it.

Individuality and Habitus

Bourdieu's articulation of habitus has continually emphasised its capacity to 'leave room' for individual agency within the structuring power of habituses and fields, while at the same time avoiding the extremes of individualism embodied in certain other academic disciplines, such as the *homo economicus* of much economic, and some political and philosophical, theory. What, then, of the individuals whose agency is at stake? How do they come by their agency? How do they use it? And how do they escape the potentially determining power of their habituses?

One suggestion might be that individuals pursue their own interests across the range of habituses in which they are involved, not fully determined by any single habitus, and able to draw on strategies and resources acquired in one field to better their position in others. This suggestion appears to lean heavily on the notion of the individual as, above all, competitively individualistic, and hence threatens to collapse individual psychology back into rational individualism. And indeed, as an account of social structure, Bourdieu's emphasis on competition remains perhaps the single most structuralist aspect of his work. His account of individual motivation has been summarised, rather uncharitably, by Theodore Schatzki as: 'Maximise Capital!' (Schatzki, 1996: 144).

However, given the range of habituses in which agents move, the variety and contestability of the capital for which they compete, and the fact that habitus influences behaviour at a level below that of conscious awareness, this maxim by no means captures the complexity of habitus and its workings. Nor does the maxim make any allowance for the possibility, inherent in Bourdieu's critical stance as well as in his theorising more generally, of solidarity and other alliances among individuals, or of action in pursuit of non-maximising goals, such as the reduction of injustice and inequality. The habitus is consistent with a far wider range of individual psychologies and motivations than that suggested by Schatzki.

Rather than make claims such as these at an abstract level, many of the chapters engage in empirical work, exploring the social and political possibilities of particular habituses. For instance, the chapters by Hillier and Plumwood show that successful exercise of power requires broad social legitimation, and hence various forms of compromise by the powerful. The need for legitimation ensures that the capital for which agents compete is not perceived as having a solely arbitrary value; agents, even oppressed individuals and groups can, to varying degrees, contribute to the determination of what counts as capital.

At the same time, as some chapters stress, the workings of individual psychology have a role to play in the understanding of habituses. Specifically, individual psychology is one of the keys to understanding how individuals come to have a feel for the game (including multiple games, involving potentially conflicting forms of social and cultural capital) at a level below conscious awareness. Bourdieu has stressed the importance of denial, anamnesis and other psychoanalytic concepts for understanding how habituses are formed and perpetuated, and the power relations within them sustained or undermined. His use of psychoanalytic terms and techniques in his socioanalysis is suggestive of his own views on how best to theorise individual psychology, although it is not clear from his corpus how fully he endorsed psychoanalysis as a whole (Fourny 2000). As we emphasised in the Introduction to this second edition, there is still lively debate on the subject of how heavily habitus relies, or need rely, on psychoanalysis for its account of individual psychology.

A pressing question concerning individual psychology arises from the renewed emphasis on the mutability and transformative nature of habitus. How can we claim that there is a habitus, a social-physical structure that provides the framework for spontaneous, prereflective responses to a range of situations if, at the same time, we are – or are becoming – aware of that habitus? This is not a question relevant only to the sociologist or critical theorist who engages, on a professional basis, in reflexive analysis of habituses; it is also relevant to contemporary individuals, and their wider communities, where self-reflexivity and the bringing to awareness of habits, presuppositions, biases and values is becoming increasingly prevalent.

Some responses to this question claim that the reflexivity characteristic of much contemporary social practice consists of an abstracted self looking back at its own habitus. Others treat the reflexivity as another part of the habitus; we spontaneously reflect on the ways in which we act. Perhaps the most plausible possibility here is to develop the notion that habitus includes reflection upon itself, but that no matter what, there will always be some portion of the habitus that is not reflective.

One essay in this collection touches on just this point, although it gives no definitive answer to it. Roxana Waterson draws on the work of scientist-turned-epistemologist Michael Polanyi to develop her account of habitus in Sulawesi. Polanyi's (1958) account of knowledge is one in which all explicit knowledge is underlain by tacit knowledge, which may be either unarticulated propositional knowledge, or bodily know-how. He holds that no explicit knowledge is possible without its base of tacit knowledge; if we move from focusing on some piece of explicit knowledge to the tacit knowledge that underlies it, then what was tacit becomes explicit, and turns out to be based on yet other tacit knowledge. Here, in outline, is a way in which it is possible for people who are enmeshed in a habitus to be aware of that habitus and at the same time to act spontaneously and prereflectively in ways structured by a habitus.

Habitus and Beyond?

This volume illustrates the extent to which Pierre Bourdieu's work is multidimensional and multidisciplinary. While focused primarily on the disciplines of sociology, anthropology and philosophy, his development of habitus also reaches into many other areas including architecture, urban planning, psychology and politics. The related notions of habitus, field, power and capital can be used together to analyse almost any social patterns or practices. As we have suggested here, the notion of habitus is not limited to micro-contexts, but can also be usefully employed at the macro levels of regional, national and international engagement, political and otherwise.

Whereas the field can be described as the objectified state of process, habitus is the embodied state, existing across time as sets of dispositions that generate performances that coalesce into regular but evolving social practices. Together, Bourdieu writes, habitus and field are the means by which 'the dead seize the living' (Bourdieu, 1993). However, as the chapters in this volume have demonstrated, the hand of the dead does not immobilise the living, or condemn them to repeat the same patterns *ad infinitum*. As Pile's chapter suggests, the structuring effected by the enduring nature of habitus can be enabling, rather than simply paralysing.

To conclude, habitus and the conceptual framework within which it sits are valuable for understanding human lives, and particularly for understanding how the regularities of individual lives fit together into larger social units, however defined. Life involves, at all levels, a 'generated principle of regulated improvisations' (Bourdieu, 1977: 78). Habitus and related notions allow us to comprehend the workings of these improvisations, and make conceptual space for the satisfaction of individuals' desires and interests through the (more or less) harmonious co-ordination of larger, national and international, social groups. Careful analysis of habituses also leaves room for informed criticism of those habituses (and of subsets of their occupants); while an empirically engaged grasp of the realities of social practices can, it might be hoped, allow for effective and context-sensitive reform of unjust, inegalitarian or exploitative habituses. The developments and applications of the notion of habitus in the chapters in this volume will, we hope, contribute towards these goals.

References

Bourdieu, P. (1962) [1958] *The Algerians*, Boston, Beacon Press.
Bourdieu, P. (1971) 'Champ de pouvoir, champ intellectuel et habitus de class', *Sociologies*, 1: 7-26.
Bourdieu, P. (1977) *Outline of a Theory of Practice*, Cambridge, Cambridge University Press.
Bourdieu, P. (1982) [1979] *Distinction*, Cambridge MA, Harvard University Press.
Bourdieu, P. (1987) *Choses Dites*, Paris, Editions de Minuit.
Bourdieu, P. (1993) 'Concluding remarks', in Calhoun, C., Lipuma, E. and Postone, M. (eds) *Bourdieu: critical perspectives*, Cambridge, Polity Press.
Bourdieu, P. (1998) [1996] *On Television and Journalism*, London, Pluto.
Bourdieu, P. (1998) *La domination masculine*, Paris, Seuil.
Bourdieu, P. (2000a) *Pascalian* Meditations, Polity Press, Cambridge.
Bourdieu, P. (2001) *Science de la science et réflexivité*, Paris, Raisons d'agir.

Bourdieu, P. (2002) [2000] *The Social Structures of the Economy*, Cambridge, Polity Press.
Bowden, P. and Rooksby, E. (2005) 'Understanding condemnation: a plea for appropriate judgement', in Tabensky, P (ed.) *Judging and Understanding: essays on free will, justice, forgiveness and love*, Aldershot, Ashgate. Forthcoming.
Polanyi, M. (1958) *Personal Knowledge: towards a post-critical philosophy*, London, Routledge and Kegan Paul.
Schatzki, T. (1996) *Social Practices: a Wittgensteinian approach to human activity and the social*, New York, Cambridge University Press.
Smiley, M. (1992) *Moral Responsibility and the Boundaries of Community: power and accountability from a pragmatic point of view*, Chicago, Chicago University Press.
Walker, M. (1998) *Moral Understandings: a feminist study in ethics*, London and New York, Routledge.

Index

Aboriginal women 26, 367–8
  and Alice Springs Lake Inquiry
    political action over 361
    sacred site 360
  and attempts to stop petrol sniffing 364
  as community activists 358
  and endurance of 362
  and failure to listen to 360, 364
  as fighters 366–7
  and Hindmarsh Bridge conflict 361–2
  and household authority 365
  and ignored by authorities 359
  and ingenuity 365–6
  and the land 359–60, 363–4
  and Pitjatjantjara lands 362–3
  and power of authorities over 359
  and protest over alcohol licence 363
  and recording life histories of 366
  and resistance 35
  and the 'stolen generation' 357–8
    loss of land 359–60
  and strength of 369
  and support of youth 364–5
  and traditional knowledge of 365
  and traditional role of 363
Absolutism, Age of 85–6
  and liberalism 86–7
  and sovereignty 86
Actes de la recherce en sciences sociales 4, 5–6
aesthetics 48, 288–9
  and architecture 290
  and *avant garde* 289–90
affect
  and cities 236–7, 242–3
  and dispositions 253
  and habitus 236, 253
  and place 236, 242–3
  and urbanism 236
agonistic pluralism 115
  Albrechts, L 178
Allen, C, and habitus 11
Allmendinger, P 179
Amin, A 212
antagonism, and politics 110
antagonistic pluralism 95, 96
appeasement 37
  and conditions for regime of toleration 102–3
architecture 29
  and aesthetics 288–9, 290
  as art and profession 294
  and *avant garde* 289–90
  and complicity with social order 291–2
  and cultural capital 31, 298
  and cultural identity 297, 298, 308
    and deconstruction 289–90
  and discursive analysis 292
  and experience of 283
  and framing of everyday life 291
  and habitus 43, 285, 298
  and identification with space 308
    mirrorings 301–3
    narrativisations 299–300
    performativity 301–3
  and narratives of use 298
  and oppression 34
  and power of 291
  and professional education 293
  and the public interest 294
  and resistance 35–6
  and social capital 287, 291–2
  and social practice 293–4
  and symbolic capital 32–3, 288–9, 293
  and symbolic power 399

see also built environment
art, and social function of 289
artistic practice, and habitus 48
Association for Reflection on Higher Education and Research 6
associative democracy, and Hirst 4–5
Astley, Thea 169
Augé, Marc 303
Augsburg, Peace of (1555) 92
Australia
　and Aboriginal (Indigenous) people
　　and the Dreaming 360
　　and habitus 360
　　and the land 26–7, 359–60, 379
　　and naming of places 381–2, 386, 388
　　and oppression of 33–4
　and belonging
　　the land 373
　　left/right divisions 372
　　structural obstacles to 380
　and colonialism 251
　　habitus durability 38–9
　　the land 27, 34, 40
　　and naming of places 384–5
　　oppression 33–4
　and fear of youth (Perth) 229–30
　and land and non-indigenes
　　class 379–80
　　cultural convergence 375, 387
　　destructive relationship with 371, 374
　　disbelonging 380
　　failures of the past 372
　　impact of eurocentrism 381
　　independent relationship with 373, 374–5, 376–7, 378
　　land spirituality not typical of 378–9
　　love of 373–4
　　settler management of 371–2
　　spirituality of place 376–8
　　structural restraints on relationship 379, 380
　　structuring of relationship 379
　and One Nation 372
　and place-names
　　decolonising of 386–9
　　politics of 381–6
　see also Aboriginal women; planning decision-making
authoritarianism, and liberalism 118–19
　and colonial autocracy 120–2
　and rationale for 128
autonomy, and liberalism 120–1, 123–6
　and categorisation of populations 126–7
　and promoted by 126
avant garde 289–90
　and value of 290

Bachelard, Gaston 306
Balfour, Arthur J 123–4
Barthels, J 226
Barwick, Diane 366
Baxter, R 177
Beauregard, R 225
Beck, Ulrich 221
　and strangers 222
Bell, Michael 235, 250
Bell, Vikki 301–2
belonging
　and Australia 372
　and identification with space 308
　and performativity 301–2
　and structural obstacles to 380
Benjamin, Walter 15, 304–5, 306
Bhabha, Homi 297, 303
Bigalke, T 340
Blackwood, Arthur 152
Blair, Tony 137, 190
Bloch, M 336–7
Bodin, Jean 69, 71, 73
Bond, James 240
borders, and nation states 76, 80, 94
Bourdieu, Pierre
　and activism of 3–4, 6
　　motivation for 7
　and activity, views of 21

Index 411

and aesthetics 288–9, 290
and architecture 298
and *avant garde* 289
and capital 24–5, 286
and collusion 172–3
and common miscognition 171
and culture as a map 334
and death of 3
and doxa 340–1
and fields 164, 406
and globalisation 8
and habitus 6, 7–8, 406
  acquired nature of 45
  artistic practice 48
  change in 37–8, 45, 338–9, 352, 395, 401–2
  character 45
  definition of 21, 164, 336
  durability of 352
  dynamic nature of 46–7
  embodiment of 284
  generative principle 316
  lifestyle 44–5
  maintenance of 318
  oppression 33
  principle of invention 46
  reproduction of 46, 338
  style 44
  systemacity 44–5
  theory of groups 398
and inequality 5
and intellectual collective 9–10
and interestedness 22
and Kabyle 321
  houses of 322–3
and legacy of 395
and misfits 35, 47
and motivation 20
and neo-liberalism 8
and psychoanalysis 14–15, 404
and receipt of gifts 170, 171
and scholastic thinking 48–9
and scientific research 8–9
and socioanalysis 14, 15
and space 285, 399
and structuration 6

and symbolic capital 176, 287
and symbolic power 25, 395–6
and tacit knowledge 337
and theory/practice dichotomy 21, 48
and time 337
and writings of
  Algeria 60 47
  Distinction 44, 288
  Esquisse pour une auto-analyse 7, 9
  An Introduction to Reflexive Sociology 43
  Logic of Practice, The 38, 321, 336
  Masculine Domination 46
  Outline of a Theory of Practice 6, 321, 395
  Pascalian Meditations 48, 49, 321, 395, 401, 402
  Science de la science de réflexivité 7, 8–9
  Si le monde 7
  Social Structures of the Economy 47
  Sociology in Question 6
Bové, José 3
Brady, Veronica 377
Brazil, and fear of the poor 226–8
Bridge, G, and habitus 12
Briggs, X de Sousa 182
Bringing out the Dead 247–50
British Crime Survey 264
Buchanon, Ian 300
built environment
  and crime 258, 264, 268–73
    British local strategies 274
    British national strategies 275–6
    closed circuit television 272
    crime disadvantagement 270
    Crime Prevention Through Environmental Design 269–70
    'defensible space' 269
    limited knowledge 271
    new urbanism 272
    place-specific crime prevention 270

planning principles 278–9
situational crime prevention 269
target hardening 271–3
and habitus 321, 398–400
Kabyle houses 322–3
see also architecture
bureaucracy, and habitus 131
Business Improvement Districts (New York City) 219, 228
Butler, Judith 15, 301, 303, 307

Caldeira, Teresa 226, 227
Calhoun, C, and social life 25
Capetown, and fear of loss and change 228–9
Capetown Partnership 228
capital 286, 396
  and fields 24
  and power 25
  and types of 24
  see also cultural capital; economic capital; social capital; symbolic capital
capitalism, manic 96
Catalan Company 73
centralisation, in United Kingdom 133–4
Certeau, Michel de, and spatial appropriation 299–300
Césaire, Aimé 120
change, and habitus 37–40, 43, 45, 317, 338–40, 352, 395, 401–3
character, and habitus 45
Charter 88 3
China, and trade unions 11–12
Christianity
  and Sa'dan Toraja people 340
    associations with indigenous myths 350–1
    conversion to 341, 342, 346, 351
    influence of mission 341
  and spirituality of place 376
cities 37
  and affect 236–7, 242–3
  and ambivalence of 242–3
  and building shared identities 212–13
  and cultural intermixture 220
  and the dead 247–50
  and democratic public realm 212
  and funding of urban regeneration 210
  and ghosts 236, 241–2, 252
    exorcising of 252
  and grief and mourning 242, 246, 252
  and habitus change 40, 319–20
  and haunting by 241, 242, 250
  in medieval period 72–3
  and migrants' affinity environments 325
  and migrants disruption of 328
    local citizenship 328–9
  and *Sixth Sense* (film) 244–7
  and the stranger 220–1
  see also fear, and the city
citizenship, local, and migrants 328–9
city councils (UK)
  and dependency on central government 190
  and development 189
  and New Labour agenda 190–1
  and socio-spatial segregation 190
  and welfare service delivery-dependency 189–90
  see also Newcastle City Council
city-states, of ancient Greece 69–70
civil society 125–6
civilisation, and Western standard of 117–18, 128
Clarke, R V 269
class
  and cultural capital 31
  and habitus 11, 318
  and oppression 34
  and social capital 31, 286
closed circuit television, and crime prevention 272
Cockburn, Inquiry into the City of (Australia, 1999-2000) 169–70
Cohn-Bendit, Daniel 328
Cold War 95, 96

collaborative planning 161
collective security 97–8
colonialism 27
  and habitus durability 38–9
  and liberal autocracy 120–2
  and oppression 33–4
  and politics of place-names 384–5
  and post-colonial liberal condition 127–8
  and state system 77
  and symbolic capital 32
Columbus, Christopher 383–4
communicative action, Habermasian 162–3
communities, imagined 301–2
Community Improvement Districts (Johannesburg) 219
confederal public powers, and the international order 94–5
conflict, and democracy 111
Conger, J 168
Connelly, Joe 247
consensus, and politics 110–12
corruption, and planning decision-making 168–9
crime 28
  and Anglo-American comparison
    American approach 276–7
    British local strategies 274
    British national strategies 275–6
    Central/Federal Government power 273–4, 277
    crime rates 261–3
    demographical distribution of 264–6
    differing organisational structures 273–7
    geographical distribution of 264–6
    quality of life 266–8
  and built environment 258, 264, 268–73, 278
    British local strategies 274
    British national strategies 275–6
    closed circuit television 272
    crime disadvantagement 270
    Crime Prevention Through Environmental Design 269–70
    'defensible space' 269
    limited knowledge 271
    new urbanism 272
    place-specific crime prevention 270
    situational crime prevention 269
    and target hardening 271–3
  and crime data
    police statistics 259–60
    social surveys 260
  and crime prevention programmes 268
    context of 279
    evaluation of 259, 278
    local tailoring of 278
    poor/deprived areas 278–9
  and fear of 258, 268, 277
    need to tackle separately 263–4, 278
  and media reporting of 263
  and poverty 264–5, 265–6, 278–9
  and quality of life 258, 266–8, 277
  and zero tolerance 259
Crime and Disorder Act (UK, 1998) 274
Crime Prevention Through Environmental Design 269–70
Crossley, N
  and habitus 12
  and influences on individual action 14–15
Crystal, E 341
cultural capital
  and architecture 31, 298
  and class 31
  and definition of 24
  and Kabyle 31
  and regional development 32
  and Toraja 31–2
  and types of 286
cultural identity, and architecture 297, 298, 308
cultural production, fields of 283
culture, and planning decision-making 173–5

Darul Islam 341
Davies, Norman 133
dead, the
  and cities 247–50
  and justice 250
Dean, M 141, 153
Debord, G 175
decentralisation, and regional development 39
decision-making, *see* planning decision-making
decolonisation, and renaming of places 386–9
deconstruction, and architecture 289–90
'defensible space', and crime prevention 269
deliberative democracy 110, 162–3
democracy
  as 'a form of life' 113–15
  and ambiguity of 54–5
  and conflict 111
  and contingency of 59
  and deliberative 110
  and diversity 37, 115
  and exclusion 113
  and globalisation 34, 65–6
  and hegemony 34
    asymmetry and power 56–9, 65
    empty signifiers and undecidability 61–3
    incompleteness and renegotiation 59–61
    representation 63–5
  and liberalism 88
  and marginalisation 36
  and nationalism 75
  and negotiation 55
  and nihilism 113–14
  as only truly political society 61
  and plurality of social spaces 54
  and potentialities of contemporary 66
  and precondition for 58
  and public sphere
    lack of forms of identification 109

    weakening of 109–10
  and social movements 53
  and urban fear 232–3
  and viability of 53
Department of Justice (USA), and Anglo-American comparison 261–2
Derrida, J 247
development
  and post-colonial liberal condition 127
  and Regional Economic Strategies (RES) 144
devolution 80–1
  and United Kingdom 134–5
Dirlik, Arif 327
disbelonging 380
disorder 60
dispositions 336
  and affect 253
  and habitus 43–4, 252–3, 316
  and tacit knowledge 336
diversity, and democracy 37, 115
Doussa, Justice J von 362
doxa 340–1
durability, and habitus 37–40, 352, 400–2
Dynes, M 137

Ealing Broadway bomb 239
economic capital
  and definition of 24
  and international importance of 30
  and migrants 30–1
  and Newcastle City Council 31
  and regional development 30
Edelman, M 173
education, and habitus 11
Egan, Ted, and *The Drover's Boy* 357
elected representatives, local authority 29
  and planning decision-making 162, 164, 177
  corruption 168–9
  cultural backgrounds 173–5

effective 183–4
factions 172–3
favours 171–2
methodology 166
personal gain 169–70
persuasion 168
process/framework of 167–8
public posturing/vote-winning 175–6
receipt of gifts 170–1
recommendation/decision 'gap' 165–6, 183
social role taking 181–2
and planning officers 177–8, 181
  anticipation by 182
  damage limited by 179
  delegated authority 179–80
  information distorted/disclosed by 180–1
  warnings by 178
and resistance to 35
and symbolic capital 32, 176
Elias, Norbert 338
elitism, and liberalism 118
Emilia-Romagna region (Italy) 147–8
empathy theory 305
Enlightenment 86
  and conflictual consequences of 87–8
  and liberalism 86–7
  and relative social peace 88
  and utopianism of 87
Epstein, J C 270
equal opportunities, and Regional Economic Strategies (RES) 151–3
Esnault, David 320
ethnic minorities, and Regional Economic Strategies (RES) 152–3
exclusion
  and habitus 26
  and liberal democracy 113
  and nationalist practices of 223
explicit knowledge 337

factions, and planning decision-making 172–3
Falling Down (film), and urban fear 222–3
favours, and planning decision-making 171–2
fear, and the city 27–8
  and democracy 232–3
  and discourses of 219, 231
    counter-discourses 232
    potency of 231–2
  and *Falling Down* (film) 222–3
  and growth in literature on 221
  and the homely 221–2, 223
  and loss of imaginary of national space 223–4
  and management of 232
  and nationalist practices of exclusion 223
  and political economy of 230
    American urban crisis (1960s) 224–6
    fear of loss and change (Capetown) 228–9
    fear of the poor (Sao Paulo) 226–8
    fear of youth (Perth) 229–30
    mobilisation 231
  and public space 219, 232
  and solutions for 219–20
  and the stranger 221–2, 231
federalism 94–5
Feins, J D 270
feminism, and challenges to habitus 319
feudalism 71–2
fields
  and capital 24
  and definition of 22–3, 164, 286
  and habitus 47, 315–16
  and regions 155
  and structure of 316
Flyvbjerg, B
  and factions 172
  and habitus 12
Forester, John 163, 164, 166, 168, 177–8, 180–1, 182, 183

Fortier, Anne-Marie 302
Foucault, Michel 86, 89
  and governmentality 131, 141
  and the market 125
  and power 153
Fourny, Jean-François 14
Fox, J 334–5
Frankfurt, and Kabyle migrants 30, 31, 38, 329–30
  and anti-foreign feeling 326–7
  and children 326
  and disruption of habitus 325
  and disruption of place 328
  and local citizenship 328–9
  and transnational character of 327
  and women 323–4
Fraser, Mariam 308
Freedom Party (Austria) 329
Freud, Sigmund 237, 300
  and ghosts 249
  and grieving 252
  and identity 308

gated communities 227–8
gender identity
  and habitus 10, 319, 324
  as performatively produced 301
ghosts
  and affect 236
  and Australian first nations people 251
  and *Bringing out the Dead* 247–50
  and cities 236, 241–2, 252
    exorcising from 252
  and Freud 249
  and Irish Republican Army 238–40, 241
  and London's 239, 241
  and MI6 241
  and *Sixth Sense* (film) 243–7
Giddens, A 284
gifts, and planning decision-making 170–1
globalisation
  and Bourdieu 8
  and democracy 34, 65–6
  and Hirst 5
  and nation states 68–9, 79–82, 400
  and place attachment 381
  and politics 68
  and supra-national organisations 80
Gordon, Avery 235, 250, 251
Gordon, Colin 141
governance, and governmentality 143
government
  and governmentality 141
  and territoriality 133
  see also governmentality
Government Offices for the Regions (GOs, UK) 136–7
governmentality 131
  and definition of 132, 141
  and elements of
    action at a distance 142–3
    anti-naturalism 143
    government process 143
    identities and subjectivities 143
    knowledge 142
    objects of government 142
    political rationalities 142
    technical aspects 142
  and governance 143
  and increased use of concept 141
  and knowledge 132
  as methodological approach 132
  and Regional Economic Strategies (RES) 153
    action at a distance 149
    central government influence on 150–1
    cluster policy 149
    construction of regional economies 145–6
    development 144
    equal opportunities 151–3
    geographical knowledge 146–7
    knowledge acquisition 149, 150
    'new regionalism' 147–9
    performance before production 152

Index 417

regional development theory 147
  similarities in 151
  strategic thinking 144–5
 and space 153–4
Gow, Peter 334
Graham, Mary 375
Gramsci, Antonio 59
Greece, and city-states of 69–70
Greenhalgh, L 212
Grotius, Hugo 77
Guha, Ranajit 120

Habermas, J 112
 and deliberative democracy 162–3
habitus
 and Aboriginal people 360
 and acquired nature of 45
 and affect 236, 253
 and architecture 43, 285, 298
 and Bourdieu's concept of 6, 7–8
 and built environment 321, 398–400
  Kabyle houses 322–3
 and change in 37–40, 43, 45, 317, 338–40, 352, 395, 401–3
  breakdown of 320–1
  class mobility 318
  impact of city-living 319–20
  migration 318–19
  social challenges to 319
 and character 45
 as collective phenomenon 317
 and construction of 30–3
 and critiques of 402
 and definition of 21, 43, 164, 283, 298, 316, 336
 and dispositions 43–4, 252–3, 316
 and durability of 37–40, 352, 400–2
 and dynamic aspects of 13–14, 46–7, 401
 and embodiment of 284
 and fields 22–3, 47, 315–16
 and games 23
 and individual agency 14, 403–5
 and lifestyle 44–5
 and locus of 397–8

 at macro level 397–8
 and maintenance of 318
 at micro level 397, 398
 and oppression 33
 and place 26–9, 398–400
 and planning decision-making 164
 as principle of invention 46
 as product of history 21, 45, 338
 and reflexivity 405
 and regions 154
 and reproduction of 46, 338
 and scholarly work on 10–13
 and scholastic thinking 48–9
 and social interactions 23–4
 and social practice 284, 337
 and space 43, 398–400
 and structured improvisation 22
 and style 44
 as theory of groups 398
 and toleration 36
Habitus 2000: A Sense of Place 19
Haebich, Anna 358
Hage, Ghassan 220
 and *Falling Down* 222–3
 and national space 223–4
 and nationalist practices of exclusion 223
Hammersmith Bridge bomb 239
Hanseatic League 72, 73, 74
Harvey, David 145, 146, 153
Hawke, Hazel 361
Hayek, Friedrich 125, 126
Healey, Patsy 163
Hefner, R 347–8
Hegel, Georg Wilhelm 57
hegemony 56–8
 and asymmetry and power 56–9, 65
 and definition of 56
 and democracy 34
 and empty signifiers and undecidability 61–3
 and incompleteness and renegotiation 59–61
 and representation 63–5
Hillier, J 163, 285

and social movements 12
Hindess, Barry 4, 165
Hindmarsh Bridge, and conflict over 361–2
Hirst, Paul Q
  and activism of 3–4
  and associative democracy 4–5
  and death of 3
  and globalisation 5
  on war 90
  and writings of
    Pre-Capitalist Modes of Production 4
    War and Power in the 21st Century 5
Hogwood, Brian 135–6, 137
Holden, A 140
Hollier, D 292
Holy Roman Empire 74
  as international governance system 91–2
homo oeconomicus 44, 48
Howard, John 39
Howe, J, and habitus 12–13
human rights, and international treaties 84, 93
Hume, David 119
Hunter, T 169, 174

identification
  and lack of political 109–10
  with space 308
    mirrorings 303–7
    narrativisations 299–300
    performativity 301–3
immigration, and fear of the stranger 221
imperialism
  and liberalism 119–20
    colonial autocracy 120–2
    and post-colonial liberal condition 127–8
  see also colonialism
improvement, and liberal project of 127–8
improvisation, structured 22

individual agency, and habitus 14, 403–5
Indonesia, *see* Sa'dan Toraja people
Indonesian National Army (TNI) 341
inequality, and Bourdieu 5
Innes, Judith 163
insight 25
integration, and tolerant society 103
intellectual collective, and Bourdieu 9–10
interestedness 22
International Committee of Support for Algerian Intellectuals 6
international law, and control of 'non-civilised' 77
international order, the
  and antagonistic pluralism 95, 96
  and conditions for regime of toleration 100–1
    appeasement 102–3
    money 101
    separation 103–4
    sieges/stalemates 102
    truce seeking 101–2
  and confederal public powers 94–5
  and liberal pluralism 95, 96
  and nation states 77
  and New Medievalism 90–2
  and pluralisation of sovereignties 97
  and toleration 84, 85, 98–100
    as a 'regime' 99
  and totalitarianism 95
  and Westphalian System 92–4
International Parliament of Writers 6
interviews, and habitus 12
introjection 304, 306
invention, and habitus 46
Irish Republican Army (IRA)
  and fears of bombing campaign 239–40
  and ghosts of 238–40, 241
  and MI6 headquarters attack 238, 251
Iveson, K 230

Ivison, D 177

Jacobs, Jane 245, 269
Jameson, Fredric 299, 305–6
Japan, and habitus change 320
Jessop, Bob 142, 143
Johannesburg, and fear 219
Joyce, James 48
judiciary, and regulation of social relations 109
justice
  and the dead 250
  and liberal conception of 112
Juvenile Aid Group (Perth) 229–30

Kabyle 321
  and cultural capital 31
  and habitus
    gendered nature of 324
    world view 324–5
  and houses of 322–3
  and migration to Germany 30, 38, 323–4, 329–30
    anti-foreign feeling 326–7
    children 326
    disruption of habitus 325
    transnational character of 327
    women 323–4
Kant, Immanuel 98, 288
Keiller, Patrick 240
Kitchen, T 168, 175, 176
knowledge
  explicit 337
  and government 132, 142
  tacit 336, 405
Kosselleck, Reinhart 87–8
Kristeva, Julia 103, 221–2

Lahire, B, and habitus 14
landscape
  and meaning 334
  and social knowledge 334–5
  and topogeny 334–5
Langdon, C, and habitus 12–13
Lanzara, G, and habitus 12
Latour, Bruno 142

Lau, R W K, and habitus 11–12
Lee, F 174
Lefebvre, H 284, 320
Lefort, Claude 64
Liber 4
liberal democracy
  and critiques of 89
  and exclusion 113
liberal pluralism 95
liberalism
  and Absolutist State 86–7
  and art of separation 96–7
  and authoritarianism 118–19
    rationale for 128
  and autonomy 123–6
    authoritarianism 120–1
    categorisation of populations 126–7
    promotion of 126
  and challenges to 87, 94
  and colonial autocracy 120–2
  and democracy 88
  and development of liberal thinking 88
  and discussion and dialogue 89
  and elitism 118
  and imperialism 119–20
  and justice 112
  and liberty 118
  and the market 124–5, 128
  metropolitan 120
  and moralising 110
  and negotiation 89–90
  and organising principles of 89
  and peace 90
  and political homogeneity 90
  and politics 111
  and post-colonial condition 127–8
  and relative social peace 87, 88
  and state system 79
  and war 90
Liber-raisons d'agir 4
liberty, and liberalism 118
lifestyle, and habitus 44–5
local authorities, *see* city councils (UK); elected representatives,

local authority; Newcastle City Council
local citizenship, and migrants 328–9
Locke, John 121, 124
London
  and cosmopolitanism of 251–2
  and fears of IRA bombing campaign 239–40
  and ghosts of 239, 241
  and post-colonial Empire 251

MacAlpine, Alistair 172, 173
MacCormick, Neil 134–5
Machiavelli, Niccolo 69
Mahan, A T 77
manic capitalism 96
marginalisation, and liberal democracy 36, 113
market, the, and liberalism 124–5, 128
Marshall, T H 121
Marx, Karl 56–7
Massey, D 212
Mawson, J 133–4
Mayhew, P 269
McKellar, Dorothea 371
McNay, L, and habitus 10
medieval states 71–3
Meehan, Betty 366
Meerwald, A 174
memory, and spatial experiences 304–5, 306
Merleau-Ponty, Maurice 44, 284, 299
Merry, S 232
metaphor, and metonymy 59
methodological individualism 44
metonymy, and metaphor 59
Metz, Christian 303–4, 306
MI5 241
  and remit of 238
MI6
  and attack on 237, 251
    media reporting of 237
    'real' IRA 237
  and ghosts 241
  and headquarters of 240–1

migration
  and affinity environments 325
  and change in habitus 318–19
  and disruption of place 328
    local citizenship 328–9
  and economic capital 30–1
  and habitus change 38
  and integration 329
  and Sa'dan Toraja 346
  and social capital 31
  see also Kabyle
military alliances 84
Mill, John Stuart 121, 122, 125
  and imperialism 119
Miller, P 142
mimicry 303
Minson, Jeffrey 89, 181
mirrorings, and identification with space 301–3
miscognition 171
money, and conditions for regime of toleration 101
Mongol Empire 71
morality, and displacement of politics 110
Mouffe, C 163
multiculturalism, and tolerant society 103
Mulvaney, John 376
Mumford, Lewis 220, 221
Mutch, A, and habitus 11, 13–14

narration, the nation as 297
narrativisations, and identification with space 299–300
nation, as narration 297
nation states
  and borders of 76, 80, 94
  and characteristics of 76
    exclusion 74
    mutual recognition 74–5
  and devolution 80–1
  and globalisation 68–9, 79–82, 400
  and impact of 69
  and international economic order 78–9

Index   421

and international system 77
and liberal sovereignty 79
and nationalism 75
   democracy 75
and necessity for 81
and New Medievalism 91
and political homogeneity 75
and political nationalism 26
and politics 68
and territory 74–5, 77, 81–2
and war 75, 77
and Westphalian System 92–4
National Crime Victimisation
   Survey (USA) 265, 268
National Institute of Justice 259
nationalism
   and democracy 75
   and nation states 26, 75
negotiation
   and democracy 55
   and liberalism 89–90
   and peace 98
neo-liberalism
   and Bourdieu 8
   and poverty 190
   and strategic thinking 145
neo-Medievalism 90–2
Neostoicism 86, 89
networks, and social capital 287
New Labour, and cities 190–1
New Medievalism 90–2
'new regionalism', and Regional
   Economic Strategies (RES)
   147–9
New York City
   and 9/11 253–4
   and crime rates 266
   and fear 219
   and haunting of 253–4
Newcastle
   and community self-support 194
   and decline of 192
      in 1970s 195
      in 1980s 195–6
      in 1990s 196
   and economic and cultural change
      192, 199
   and expansion of service sector
      195–6
   and heartland neighbourhoods
      deprived area 196
      negative discrimination 197
      social tensions within 196
   and industrial past 194
   and out-migration 196, 197
   and post-war city development
      194–5
   and Quayside development 197
   and threats to viability of 197
   see also Newcastle City Council
Newcastle City Council 28–9
   and challenges facing 203
   and economic capital 31
   and economic development
      strategy (1998) 200
   and *Going for Growth: A Vision
      for Newcastle 2020* 200–4
      absence of citizens' perceptions
         204, 209
      aimed at external audience 208
      area master planning 202–3
      calculated risk of 208
      categorisation of areas 201–2
      community participation 201
      greater consultation 213
      political change 213–14
      protests against 191, 207, 209
      self-interest of 207–8
      shortcomings of 210–12
      social transformation 200–1,
         207, 208
      top-down paternalism 201, 209
      vocabulary of 203–4
   and growth strategy 191
   and habitus durability 39–40
   and image of city 198
   and Liberal Democrats 213–14
   and Local Strategic Partnership
      213
   and politics of 198–9
   and regional planning strategies
      199

and re-organisation of 199
and resistance to 35
as sectoral service delivery machine 198
and 'Thatcher' years 197–8 critical pragmatic entrepreneurialism 198
and *Unitary Development Plan* 202
and urban regeneration funding 210
and West End development 202–3
Masterplan for the West End 204–7
and West end Regeneration Strategy (1999) 206
see also Newcastle
Newcastle Initiative 197
Newman, Oscar 269
Next Steps agencies (UK) 137
Ngarrindjeri women, and Hindmarsh Bridge conflict 361–2
Nietzsche, Friedrich, and nihilism 113–14
nihilism 113–14
Noble, G, and habitus 10, 11, 14
Nooy-Palm, H 341
Northern Ireland, and peace process 239

Oc, T 272
Omagh bombing 240
One NorthEast 199
Opium Wars 79
oppression
  and architecture 34
  and class 34
  and colonialism 33–4
  and fall of regimes 60
  and habitus 33
organisation studies, and habitus 11
Ortega y Gasset, José 66
Osment, Haley Joel 243
Ostermann, A C, and habitus 10
Other, the 27–8
Ottoman Empire 71, 73, 91

as international governance system 92

Pagden, Anthony 119
Painter, J, and habitus 21
Paris, and fear 219
Park, Robert 220
  and prejudice 221
Parkindo (Indonesian Christian Party) 341
Pasquino, Pasquale 141
Passmore, John 376
Patriotta, G, and habitus 12
peace
  and liberalism 90
  and means of establishing 97–8
  and negotiation 98
  see also relative social peace
Peck, J 140
performativity
  and identification with space 301–3
  and modes of perception 307
Perry, P 169
persuasion, and planning decision-making 168
Perth, and fear of youth 229–30
Philadelphia, and *Sixth Sense* (film) 244–7
phronesis 25
Pitjatjantjara lands, and Aboriginal women 362–3
place
  and affect 236, 242–3
  and character of 328
  and decolonising names of 386–9
  and habitus 26–9, 398–400
  migrants, and disruption of 328
  local citizenship 328–9
  and politics of place-names 381–6
  as a project 327, 328
  and social life 133
  and space 299
  and spirituality of 376–8
  and topogeny 334–5
place-specific crime prevention 270

planning
  and crime 278–9
  and fear 219
    management of 222
  and habitus 12–13
  and quality of life 266
planning decision-making
  and effective 183–4
  and elected representatives 162, 164, 177
    corruption 168–9
    cultural backgrounds 173–5
    factions 172–3
    favours 171–2
    personal gain 169–70
    persuasion 168
    public posturing/vote-winning 175–6
    receipt of gifts 170–1
    social role taking 181–2
  and habitus 164
  and methodology 166
  and patterns of behaviour 164
  and planning officers 177–8, 181
    anticipation 182
    damage limitation 179
    delegated authority 179–80
    information distortion/disclosure 180–1
    warning elected representatives 178
  and planning theory 162–4
  and process/framework of 167–8
  and recommendation/decision 'gap' 165–6, 183
pluralism
  agonistic 115
  antagonistic 95, 96
  liberal 95, 96
Pocock, J G A 100
Polanyi, Karl 79
Polanyi, Michael 336, 405
police 28
  and crime data 259–60
political theory
  and displacement of politics by morality 110
  and Wittgensteinian approach to 111–12
politics
  and antagonism 110
  and aversion to 110
  and consensus 110–12
  and displacement by morality 110
  and globalisation 68
  and lack of forms of identification 109–10
  and liberalism 111
  and the nation state 68
  and New Medievalism 90–2
  and pre-modern bases of 69–73, 85
  and territory, in pre-modern period 69–73
Politics and Power 4
poor, the, and fear of (Sao Paulo) 226–8
poverty
  and crime 264–5, 278–9
  and neo-liberalism 190
power
  and capital 25
  and legitimation of 397–8
  see also symbolic power
procedural democracy 112
projection 305, 307
psychoanalysis
  and Bourdieu 14–15, 404
  and identification 303
public interest, and architecture 294
public space, and fear 219, 232

quality of life
  and crime 258, 266–8, 277
  and planners 266

race, and American urban crisis (1960s) 225
radical centre 53, 110
raison d'etat 86
rationality
  and action 44, 48
  and war 98

Read, Peter 372
  and Aboriginal concept of place 376
  and interview methodology of 378–9
  and non-indigenous relationship with land 373–8
Real IRA 237, 239, 251–2
Reay, D, and habitus 11
reciprocity, and receipt of gifts 170–1
reflexivity, and habitus 405
regional development
  and cultural capital 32
  and economic capital 30
  and habitus change 39
Regional Development Agencies Act (1998, UK) 138–9
Regional Development Agencies (UK) 30, 39, 400
  and central government guidance to 139
  and establishment of 137
  and genealogy of 135
  and governmentality 132
  and purposes of 138–9
  and regional chambers 139
  and Regional Economic Strategies (RES) 139–41, 153
    action at a distance 149
    central government influence on 140, 150–1
    cluster policy 149
    construction of regional economies 145–6
    development 144
    equal opportunities 151–3
    geographical knowledge 146–7
    knowledge acquisition 149, 150
    'new regionalism' 147–9
    North East region 148–9
    performance before production 152
    regional development theory 147
    similarities in 140, 151
    strategic thinking 144–5

Regional Economic Planning Boards (UK) 135
Regional Economic Planning Councils (UK) 136
Regional Economic Strategies (RES), *see* Regional Development Agencies (UK)
Regional Service for Clustering (UK) 149
regionalisation, and United Kingdom 135–6
regions
  and fields 155
  and habitus 154
Rein, M 182
relative social peace 83
  and Age of Absolutism 86
  and habitus of 36, 39
  and liberalism 87, 88
  and threats to 88
  and utopianism 87–8
religion
  conversion, and retention of indigenous myths 351
  and toleration 83, 93, 99–100
Renaissance, and political thought of 69
representative democracy 63–5
resistance
  and architecture 35–6
  and elected representatives 35
  and Newcastle City Council 35
  and terrorism 35
Richard Rogers Partnership 204
Robbins, Derek 298
Robson, B 140
Roelofs, H 172
Rogers, Richard 202
Roman Catholic Church, in medieval period 72
Roman Empire, and nature of state 70–1
Rose, Deborah Bird 377, 382
Rose, N 142
Rotella, Carlo 225
Ruddick, Philip 372

Saarinen, E 181, 183
Sa'dan Toraja people 27, 30–1
  and *Aluk to Dolo* (indigenous religion) 335
    benefits of decline of 349–50
    habitus generation 335
    literacisation of 349
    loss of adherents 341
    loss of knowledge of 347, 351
    official recognition of 340
    opposition to 347
    ritual life 342–6, 347, 351
  and characteristics of 340
  and Christianity 340
    associations with indigenous myths 350–1
    conversion to 341, 342, 346, 351
    influence of mission 341
  and community 348–9
  and cultural capital 31–2
  and habitus change 38, 347, 352
  and landscape 335, 351
    loss of meaning 349
  and migration 346
  and modernity 342
  and narrative recitation 335
Said, Edward 120, 123
San Francisco, and social movements in 53
Sandercock, Leonie 163, 212
Sao Paulo, and fear of the poor 226–8
Schatzki, Theodore 404
Schengen Agreement 76
Scheuer, J, and habitus 12
Schmitt, Carl 77, 89
scholastic thinking, and Bourdieu on 48–9
Schon, D 182
Schusterman, R 183
Schwartz, D, and interestedness 22
scientific research, and Bourdieu on 8–9
Scott, Allan 147
Scott, J 168
sea, the, and state system 77
Secret Intelligence Service, *see* MI6

separation
  and conditions for regime of toleration 103–4
  and liberalism 96–7
September 11 terrorist attack, and New York City 253–4
Shyamalan, M Night 243
sieges, and conditions for regime of toleration 102
Silicon Valley (USA) 147–8
Simmel, G 242
situational crime prevention 269
Sixth Sense (film) 243–7
  and cities 244–7
Smith, Adam 78, 124–5, 126
Smith, D M 262–3
social capital 286–7
  and architecture 287, 291–2
  and class 31
  and definition of 24
  and migrants 31
social movements
  and democracy 53
  and habitus 12
    challenges to 319
social practice, and habitus 284, 337
social space, and plurality of 54
socioanalysis, and Bourdieu 14, 15
South Africa, and fear of loss and change (Capetown) 228–9
sovereignty
  and Age of Absolutism 86
  and pluralities of 97
  and political homogeneity 90
  and Westphalian System 92–4
space
  and governmentality 153–4
  and habitus 43, 398–400
  and identification with
    mirrorings 303–7
    narrativisations 299–300
    performativity 301–3
  and loss of imaginary of national 223–4
  and place 299
  and social life 133

spirituality 33
  and the land 376–8
stalemates, and conditions for regime of toleration 102
state, the, *see* nation states
Stein, Gertrude 327
Stoker, G 211
Storper, Michael 147
stranger, the
  and ambivalence towards 222
  and the city 220–1
  and fear 221–2, 231
structuration 284
  and Bourdieu 6
style, and habitus 44
Sulawesi, *see* Sa'dan Toraja people
supra-national organisations, and globalisation 80
Swartz, D 288
Sweetman, P, and habitus 13
symbolic capital 24–5, 287–8
  and architecture 32–3, 288–9, 293
  and *avant garde* 289–90
  and colonialism 32
  and elected representatives 32, 176
  and terrorism 32–3
symbolic domination 287, 288
symbolic power 25, 395–6
  and architecture 399
systemacity, and habitus 44

tacit knowledge 336, 405
target hardening, and crime prevention 271–3
Taylor, C, and practical wisdom 25
Taylor, R 181, 183
tennis, and habitus 11
territory
  and government 133
  and governmentality 153–4
  and nation states 77, 81–2
    exclusion 74
    mutual recognition 74–5
  and political power, pre-modern 69–73
  and spatial tactics 299

terrorism
  and London's ghosts 239
  and resistance 35
  and symbolic capital 32–3
  see also Irish Republican Army (IRA)
Teutonic Knights 73
Theoretical Practice 4
Third Way 53, 110
Thrift, N 212
  and habitus 12
Tiesdell, S 272
time 337
Tocqueville, Alexis de, and imperialism 119
toleration
  and conditions for international regime of 100–1
    appeasement 102–3
    money 101
    separation 103–4
    sieges/stalemates 102
    truce seeking 101–2
  and definition of 84–5
  and habitus of 36, 39
  and the international order 84, 85, 98–100
  as a 'regime' 99
  and religion 83, 93, 99–100
topogeny 334–5
Toraja, *see* Sa'dan Toraja people
Tordesillas, Treaty of (1494) 77
totalitarianism 95
trade, and nation states 78–9
trade unions, and habitus 11–12
treaties, and human rights 84, 93
Tribute in Light, The (New York) 253
truces, and conditions for regime of toleration 101–2
Turner, Frederick 383–4
Tyne and Wear Urban Development Corporation 197, 198–9

uncanny, the 237
understanding 25

United Kingdom
  and centralisation 133–4
  and contested naming of 133
  and devolution 134–5
  and English political position 134–5
  and regionalisation 135–6
    English regions 136
    Government Offices for the Regions (GOs) 136–7
    Regional Development Agencies 137–9
  and territorial government 134
  see also crime; Regional Development Agencies (UK)
United States
  and urban crisis (1960s) 224–6
  see also crime
urban regeneration
  and building shared identities 212–13
  and democratic public realm 212
  and funding of 210
Urban Task Force 202, 204
urbanism
  and affect 28
  and institutionalisation of fear 27–8
utopianism
  and Enlightenment 87
  and relative social peace 87–8

Vischer, Robert 305

Wacquant, L 43, 317
  and capital 24
  and fields 22
Walker, D 137

Walzer, Michael 99
war
  and liberalism 90
  and states' use of 75, 77
  and types of 98
Warren, Mark 113
Watkins, M, and habitus 10, 11, 14
Weber, Max, and features of nation states 76
Wee, V 351
Weiss, G, and habitus 13
Welatje-Therre 360
Western Australia, *see* planning decision-making
Westphalia, Treaty of (1648) 74, 84
  and state system 92–4
White, Isobel 366
Widom, R 270
Wilkes, Richard 251
Willis, Bruce 243
Wilson, Harold 135
wisdom, practical 25
Wittgenstein, Ludwig 111–12
Wodiczko, Krzysztof 33
women
  and Kabyle migrants 323–4, 325
  see also Aboriginal women
Woodward, M 351
world government 97
Worpole, K 212

Young, Iris Marion 170–1

Zebua, S 351
zero tolerance, and crime 259
Zukin, Sharon 225, 232